Advanced Design Approaches to Emerging Software Systems:

Principles, Methodologies and Tools

Xiaodong Liu
Edinburgh Napier University, UK

Yang Li
British Telecom, UK

Senior Editorial Director:	Kristin Klinger
Director of Book Publications:	Julia Mosemann
Editorial Director:	Lindsay Johnston
Acquisitions Editor:	Erika Carter
Development Editor:	Michael Killian
Production Editor:	Sean Woznicki
Typesetters:	Natalie Pronio, Jennifer Romanchak, Milan Vracarich, Jr.
Print Coordinator:	Jamie Snavely
Cover Design:	Nick Newcomer

Published in the United States of America by
Information Science Reference (an imprint of IGI Global)
701 E. Chocolate Avenue
Hershey PA 17033
Tel: 717-533-8845
Fax: 717-533-8661
E-mail: cust@igi-global.com
Web site: http://www.igi-global.com

Library of Congress Cataloging-in-Publication Data

Advanced design approaches to emerging software systems : principles,
methodologies, and tools / Xiaodong Liu and Yang Li, editors.
      p. cm.
  Includes bibliographical references and index.
  Summary: "This book provides relevant theoretical frameworks and the latest
empirical research findings in the area, clarifying the present chaotic and
confusing literature of the current state of the art and knowledge in the
areas of the design and engineering of the many emerging software systems"--
Provided by publisher.
  ISBN 978-1-60960-735-7 (hardcover) -- ISBN 978-1-60960-736-4 (ebook) -- ISBN
978-1-60960-737-1 (print & perpetual access) 1. Systems software. 2.
Application software--Development. 3. Computer networks--Design and
construction. I. Liu, Xiaodong, 1966 Oct. 8- II. Li, Yang, 1973-
  QA76.76.S95A38 2012
  004.6--dc23
                         2011021481

British Cataloguing in Publication Data
A Cataloguing in Publication record for this book is available from the British Library.

Table of Contents

Section 1
Service-Based System

Chapter 1

Ville Alkkiomäki, Lappeenranta University of Technology, Finland
Kari Smolander, Lappeenranta University of Technology, Finland

Chapter 2

Eila Ovaska, VTT Technical Research Centre of Finland, Finland
Tullio Salmon Cinotti, Università di Bologna, Italy
Alessandra Toninelli, INRIA, France

Chapter 3

Shigeki Sugiyama, University of Gifu, Japan
Lowry Burgess, Carnegie Mellon University, USA

Chapter 4

Yong Zhang, Tsinghua University, China
Quansong Deng, Tsinghua University, China
Chunxiao Xing, Tsinghua University, China
Yigang Sun, National Library of China, China
Michael Whitney, University of North Carolina Charlotte, USA

Section 2
Pervasive Services and Internet of Things

Section 3
Clouds and Services

Detailed Table of Contents

Section 1
Service-Based System

Chapter 1

Ville Alkkiomäki, Lappeenranta University of Technology, Finland
Kari Smolander, Lappeenranta University of Technology, Finland

This chapter introduces QSE, the Qualitative Service Elicitation method. It applies qualitative research procedures in service elicitation. Service engineering practice lacks lightweight methods to identify service candidates in projects with tight schedules. QSE provides a systematic method to analyze requirement material in service-oriented systems development with a feasible effort. QSE uses the procedures of the grounded theory research method to elicit service candidates from business process descriptions and business use case descriptions. Chapter one describes the method with examples and a case study.

Chapter 2

Eila Ovaska, VTT Technical Research Centre of Finland, Finland
Tullio Salmon Cinotti, Università di Bologna, Italy
Alessandra Toninelli, INRIA, France

Smart spaces provide information about physical environments, shared with inherently dynamic applications. This chapter introduces a novel development approach with its focus on two key properties of smart space applications: the ability to interoperate and behave in a situation-sensitive manner. Sixteen principles are defined in order to guide the development of an interoperability platform for smart spaces and on how to create applications on top of it.

Chapter 3

Shigeki Sugiyama, University of Gifu, Japan
Lowry Burgess, Carnegie Mellon University, USA

When we look at the living creatures in the world, most of them have the communication methods in order to recognize within same species each other for protection, getting food, being multiplied, or seeing the world, etc. And they mostly use the five senses as the basic mechanisms for the communication among them in a quite natural way with a seamless manner without any difficult manipulation. These five senses in those behaviour look like being swirled around their bodies.

Chapter 4

With the boom of digital resources, there are urgent requirements to set up and manage Institutional Repositories (IRs) for companies and/or organizations. Cloud computing opens a new paradigm to build IRs by providing diverse services. The authors of chapter four apply cloud services in the building of IRs and present a new model, which is based on digital object model and Service Component Architecture, and consists of five service components, namely ID, metadata, content, log, and annotation service component.

Section 2

Pervasive Services and Internet of Things

Chapter 5

Service discovery is an essential task in pervasive computing environments. Simple and efficient service discovery enables heterogeneous and pervasive computing devices and services to be easier to use. In this chapter, we discuss the key issues and solutions for service discovery architecture and protocol design for pervasive computing environments.

The separation of concerns is a promising approach in the design of the context-aware adaptive processes (CAAPs) where the core logic is designed and implemented separately from the context handling and adaptation logics. In this respect, this chapter presents a conceptual framework for developing CAAPs and software infrastructure for efficient context management that together address the known software engineering challenges and facilitate the design and implementation tasks associated with such context-aware applications.

Steffen Ortmann, IHP Microelectronics, Germany
Michael Maaser, IHP Microelectronics, Germany
Peter Langendoerfer, IHP Microelectronics, Germany

Automatic event configuration is accomplished by using a flexible Event Specification Language (ESL) and Event Decision Trees (EDTs) for distributed detection and determination of real world phenomena. EDTs autonomously adapt to heterogeneous availability of sensing capabilities by pruning and subscription to other nodes for missing information. We present one of numerous simulated scenarios proving the robustness and energy efficiency with regard to the required network communications. From these, we learned how to deduce appropriate bounds for configuration of collaboration region and leasing time by asking for expected properties of the phenomena to be detected.

Jaemin Park, Convergence WIBRO BU, KT (Korea Telecom), Republic of Korea

This chapter presents the fundamental and security characteristics of UICC and current practices of UICC-based security services (e.g. banking, stock, network authentication, etc.) in pervasive FMC systems. Moreover, the author of this chapter proposes a novel UICC-based service security framework (USF), which implements the essential security functionalities used for FMC services, to provide the integrated security infrastructure and secure FMC services.

Youna Jung, University of Pittsburgh, USA
Minsoo Kim, University of Pittsburgh, USA

In this chapter, the authors' contribution is to organize previous work related to cooperation and then clearly present the position of community computing in comparison. In addition, they refine the proposed two models including all their intermediate models in the development process, such as CCM (Community Computing Model), CIM-PI (Platform Independent Community Computing Implementation Model), and CIM-PS (Platform Specific Community Computing Implementation Model).

Section 3
Clouds and Services

Chapter 10

Stamatia Bibi, Aristotle University of Thessaloniki, Greece
Dimitrios Katsaros, University of Thessaly, Greece
Panayiotis Bozanis, University of Thessaly, Greece

This chapter presents a study of the basic parameters for estimating the potential infrastructure and software costs deriving from building and deploying applications on cloud and on-premise assets. Estimated user demand and desired quality attributes related to an application are also addressed in this chapter as they are aspects of the decision problem that also influence the choice between cloud and in-house solutions.

Chapter 11

Vishnu S. Pendyala, Santa Clara University, USA
JoAnne Holliday, Santa Clara University, USA

This chapter explores the various aspects of Cloud Computing and makes predictions as to the future directions for research in this area. Some of the issues facing the paradigm shift that Cloud Computing represents are discussed and possible solutions presented.

Chapter 12

Luis M. Vaquero, Telefónica Investigación y Desarrollo, Spain
Luis Rodero-Merino, INRIA, France
Juan Cáceres, Telefónica Investigación y Desarrollo, Spain
Clovis Chapman, University College London, UK
Maik Lindner, SAP Research, UK
Fermín Galán, Telefónica Investigación y Desarrollo, Spain

Cloud computing has emerged as a paradigm to provide every networked resource as a service. The Cloud has also introduced a new way to control cloud services (mainly due to the illusion of infinite resources and its on-demand and pay-per-use nature). Here, we present this lifecycle and highlight recent research initiatives that serve as a support for appropriately engineering Cloud systems during the different stages of its lifecycle.

Chapter 13

Xiaoyu Yang, University of Southampton, UK

The idea of cloud computing aligns with new dimension emerging in service-oriented infrastructure where service provider does not own physical infrastructure but instead outsources to dedicated infrastructure providers. Cloud computing has now become a new computing paradigm as it can provide scalable IT infrastructure, QoS-assured services, and customizable computing environment.

Preface

Recently, the rapid and fundamental advances in computing technologies have been driving the role and scope of software systems to a new level. A number of new types of software systems are emerging, among which *service based systems, cloud computing, pervasive computing*, and *Internet of Things* are eminent examples. For these systems, availability of sound software engineering principles, methodology and tool support is mission-critical. However, traditional software engineering approaches are not fully appropriate for their development and evolution. The limitations of traditional methods in the context of these emerging software systems have led to many advances of software engineering as a specialist discipline, but research and development in this context is still immature and many open issues remain. There is an urgent need for research community and industry practitioners to develop comprehensive engineering principles, methodologies, and tool support for the entire software development lifecycle of these emerging software systems.

Service-Oriented Computing is a computing paradigm that exploits both web services and Service-Oriented Architecture (SOA) as fundamental elements for developing software systems. This paradigm changes the way software systems are designed, architected, delivered and consumed. The service-oriented paradigm is emerging as a new way to engineer systems that are composed of and exposed as services for use through standardized protocols.

Cloud Computing is rapidly emerging as the new computing paradigm of the coming decade. The idea of virtualizing not just hardware but software resources as well has attracted the attention of academicians as well as the industry. Cloud computing not only offers a viable solution to the problem of addressing scalability and availability concerns for large-scale applications but also displays the promise of sharing resources to reduce cost of ownership. The concept has evolved over the years starting from data centers to present day infrastructure virtualization.

Pervasive and ubiquitous computing are recently emerging paradigms that allow computer sciences and telecommunication techniques to converge towards ambient intelligence. Here we will focus on software engineering as a complete and rational production process. We are interested in theoretical foundations, methodologies, new programming paradigms, solid architectures and middleware, new technical solutions for the development of user interfaces, and new modalities of interaction.

The "Internet of Things" (IoT) has added a new dimension to the world of information and communication technologies: next to any-place connectivity for anyone, we will have connectivity to anything. "Things" are potentially all objects we encounter in our everyday lives. The IoT connects "Things" and devices to large databases and networks. "Things" carry embedded intelligence, using for example RFID (Radio Frequency IDentification) as identification system and sensor technologies to detect changes in their physical status and environment. Future success of the IoT depends not only on technical innovations in the underlying hardware (wireless sensors, nanotechnology, low power devices, RFIDs), but also on appropriate software methodologies, technologies, and tools in fields such as operating systems, middleware, and ubiquitous and pervasive computing technology.

This book of research aims to be the first book that systematically collects the above new approaches and resultant tools. The book will promote the acceptance and foster further developments of these new approaches and tools; it will meanwhile speed up the process of commercialization, i.e., pushing the approaches and tool to industry and market.

The book is helpful to clarify the present chaotic literature of the current state of art and knowledge in the areas of the design and engineering of those emerging software systems. The book will facilitate the exchange and evolution of the above software engineering advances among multiple disciplines, research, industry, and user communities. The book will systematically expand the knowledge of the readers with novel approaches and tools on the engineering of the four types of emerging software systems, their best application practice and future trends. It will trigger further ideas on research, development, and commercialization.

The book targets a spectrum of readers, including researchers, practitioners, educators and students and even part of the end users in software engineering, computing, networks and distributed systems, and information systems.

Xiaodong Liu
Edinburgh Napier University, UK

Yang Li
British Telecom, UK

Section 1
Service–Based System

Chapter 1
Service Elicitation Method Using Applied Qualitative Research Procedures

Ville Alkkiomäki
Lappeenranta University of Technology, Finland

Kari Smolander
Lappeenranta University of Technology, Finland

ABSTRACT

This chapter introduces QSE, the Qualitative Service Elicitation method. It applies qualitative research procedures in service elicitation. Service engineering practice lacks lightweight methods to identify service candidates in projects with tight schedules. QSE provides a systematic method to analyze require-ment material in service-oriented systems development with a feasible effort. QSE uses the procedures of the grounded theory research method to elicit service candidates from business process descriptions and business use case descriptions. The chapter describes the method with examples and a case study.

INTRODUCTION

For enterprises, the promise of service-oriented computing is to rapidly create low-cost applica-tions out of reusable and loosely coupled services (Cherbakov, Galambos, Harishankar, Kalyana, & Rackham, 2005). This promise is tempting, as the radical business process redesign projects are risky and expensive (Jarvenpaa & Stoddard,

1998; Sarker & Lee, 1999). Service-oriented com-puting can provide a way to make great changes in smaller portions by componentizing both the business and the IT and by incrementally build-ing on top of existing assets (Bieberstein, Bose, Fiammante, Jones, & Shah, 2006; Cherbakov et al., 2005). Transforming an enterprise into a service-oriented one is a complex task and the role of IT is no longer supportive, but has often a key role in the change. Alignment between the busi-ness and IT is the key towards a service-oriented

DOI: 10.4018/978-1-60960-735-7.ch001

enterprise, and the implementation of the services should be prioritized to support the incremental transformation of the enterprise. (Bieberstein et al., 2006; Cherbakov et al., 2005)

In this chapter, we propose Qualitative Service Elicitation, QSE, a new systematic method to be used in service elicitation. QSE provides practical means to prioritize and identify reusable service candidates in an enterprise context. The method is presented with an example of how to apply it in a sample project. The method is also tested in a real world project, and a case study of the project is provided.

THE CHALLENGE OF SERVICE ELICITATION

The service oriented approach differs fundamentally from the conventional development paradigms in the key concept of dynamically accessible services. The scope and performance of services are under constant development to support an increasing number of consumers. Components and objects do not provide this kind of run-time flexibility. Likewise, traditional requirement engineering practices do not support service composition nor do they encourage the identification of reusable services. (Papazoglou, Traverso, Dustdar, Leymann, & Kramer, 2006; Van Nuffel, 2007; Zimmermann, Schlimm, Waller, & Pestel, 2005)

Papazoglou et al. (2006) have listed the main challenges of the service-oriented engineering domain in their research roadmap. Novel approaches are required in service engineering to address the current challenges and to provide sound methods that allow enterprises to design and deploy services more efficiently while adapting to the changes matching the rate and pace of the business.

The QSE approach addresses some of the challenges identified by Papazoglou et al. (2006). For example, QSE supports the refinement of service compositions and links the compositions to service candidates identified in the projects. Similarly, QSE provides practical means to build an enterprise level service catalogue, which can be used in gap analysis. Additionally, the catalogue provides a ground for refining the right granularity of the services. The method itself does not provide automation in the analysis, but provides systematic procedures for the analysis, thus helping to reduce human errors. To enable systematic analysis, we have taken ingredients from research methodology. We believe service elicitation by nature much resembles qualitative research.

The identification of services has been studied for some time and various methods already exist, but they focus on specific areas and the elicitation of specific types of services. A survey by Ramollari et al. (2007) lists ten different methods with varying coverage of the SOA project life cycle. Arsanjani (2005) classifies the SOA approaches into six categories: business process driven, tool-based MDA, wrap legacy, componentized legacy, data driven and message driven approaches.

The existing approaches can be used to elicit certain types of services, but fail to provide a generic solution. SOMA combines features also from other disciplines, but it can be seen more as a collection of methods than a single method (Arsanjani et al., 2008). QSE borrows elements suitable for top-down analysis from several of the approaches above. QSE is a top-down analysis method, which starts from business process descriptions and digs down to the essentials of the service candidates with the help of business use cases. Elements from the existing process driven, data driven and message driven methods have been included in QSE.

QSE is meant only to analyze business processes, not to design them. Completely different approaches, such as The MIT Process Handbook (Walker, 2006), are needed for designing business processes.

Process Driven Services

Process driven SOA is a popular approach, and business processes can be seen as an ideal source for reusable services (Papazoglou et al., 2006; Van Nuffel, 2007). Various methods have been proposed to map and align services with business processes, but the field is somewhat dispersed with various engineering approaches and a vast number of different business process and workflow modeling languages.

The survey conducted by Papazoglou et al. (2004) identified two basic classes for complex web services: programmatic and interactive web services. Programmatic services encapsulate atomic business logic functionality to be used by other applications to build new applications. Interactive services include the logic for interacting with a user through the presentation service of a web application. The logic can contain the multi-step behavior of an interactive business process.

Patterns can be used to identify services in generic problem areas as long as they fit into the pre-defined scenarios. Different levels of patterns have been proposed in the area. For example Endrei at al. (2004) propose business patterns to be used to identify services in common business scenarios, while Zdyn et al. (2007) use more primitive software patterns to build processes out of building blocks.

SOMA (service-oriented modeling and architecture) is a software development method for SOA-based solutions containing a set of methods to support all phases of the SOA development (A. Arsanjani et al., 2008). SOMA provides several complementary methods to identify flows by analyzing business goals, business processes, as well as existing IT assets. However, details of the method have not been published.

Lo et al. (2008) propose a reference catalogue approach, which consists of two parts: a set of reference business models and a set of business service patterns. The needed business services are cataloged and used to identify services to be implemented.

There are also several methods using elements from product line engineering to manage the service specifications and production of new service variants based on analyzed needs. In these approaches, the services are seen as reusable application elements, which can be used to build new applications. (Adam & Doerr, 2008; Moon, Hong, & Yeom, 2008)

Overall, the methods above try to identify common process elements within the enterprise, some utilizing also familiar patterns from other enterprises to support the work.

Data Driven Services

The basic idea behind the data driven SOA or "Information as a Service" (IaaS) approach (Dan, Johnson, & Arsanjani, 2007) is to decouple the data and the business logic allowing systems to share the same data and data access logic. This approach has gained a great deal of interest lately, and also the market for IaaS tools is growing rapidly. Forrester predicts the market to exceed Enterprise Information Integration (EII), Enterprise Application Integration (EAI) and replication markets in size in the future (Forrester, 2008).

A survey by Papazgolou et al. (2004) lists three types of informational services: content services, information aggregation services and third-party information syndication services.

SOMA also provides several complementary methods to analyze information, a method called "domain decomposition" being the most interesting from our point of view (Arsanjani et al., 2008). In this method, the enterprise is first partitioned into functional areas, and then, business entities are identified within the areas. Different variations of the business entities are identified to ensure the reusability of the service design.

Data warehousing is another approach where data is gathered across the enterprise into a centralized database from where it can be read for business intelligent purposes. Having a unified view to the enterprise data can be very beneficial for the enterprise, and virtually all large enterprises are using this technique (Watson, Goodhue, & Wixom, 2002). For reporting needs, it is sufficient to have read-only access to the master data, making it possible to use a replica of the data instead of providing full master data functionalities (Walker).

Messaging Based Approach and Business-to-Business Communication

The message-driven approach to SOA focuses on the messages being transmitted between the systems (Arsanjani, 2005). This approach is well supported by many current BPM platforms, as they rely on messaging technologies to facilitate interactions between organizations running potentially heterogeneous systems (Sadiq, Orlowska, & Sadiq, 2005).

The message-based approach is popular in Business-to-Business (B2B) communication, where several standardization organizations are developing domain specific message standards. B2B communication consists of public and private processes and the connections between these two. Public processes can utilize B2B standards, which consist not only of the message format, but also of the process of how these messages can be used in inter-enterprise communication. (Bussler, 2001)

True B2B collaboration requires more sophisticated logic than a simple request-response approach provided by web services, and B2B communication is often based on a business agreement between the parties. Models for B2B communication typically require specified sequences of peer-to-peer message exchanges between the parties following stateful and long lasting business protocol used to orchestrate the underlying business process. These protocols define the messages as well as the behavior of the parties without revealing their internal implementation. (Bussler, 2001; Papazoglou & Dubray, 2004).

Messaging can also be used to implement private processes within an enterprise (Bussler, 2001; Sadiq et al., 2005). Services and web service technology can also be used to provide access to the existing messaging infrastructure by replacing the messaging adapters with web service wrappers (Harikumar, Lee, Hae Sool, Haeng-Kon, & Byeongdo, 2005).

QSE ANALYSIS

QSE is based on two principles. Firstly, it uses procedures from qualitative research to conceptualize and to categorize the service candidates. Secondly, it uses known characteristics of reusable services and the Zachman Framework (1987) as core categories for the analysis.

The grounded theory was originally introduced by Glaser and Strauss in 1967 and is now widely used in qualitative research (Robson, 2002; Strauss & Corbin, 1998). Grounded theory has been proposed to be used in the requirement engineering practice in earlier studies (Galal & Paul, 1999). The use of predefined core categories is against the principles of the original grounded theory, but is necessary to reuse the knowledge of known characteristics of enterprises and services. Therefore, QSE relies on the assumption that the enterprise fits into the Zachman Framework (1987) and that the reusable services in the enterprise have similar characteristics as identified in earlier research.

The QSE analysis consists of three phases:

- Conceptual analysis of the business process descriptions
- Conceptual analysis of the project business use cases
- Identification and prioritization of the service candidates using the outcomes of the analyses

Figure 1. Core categories for an enterprise in service elicitation

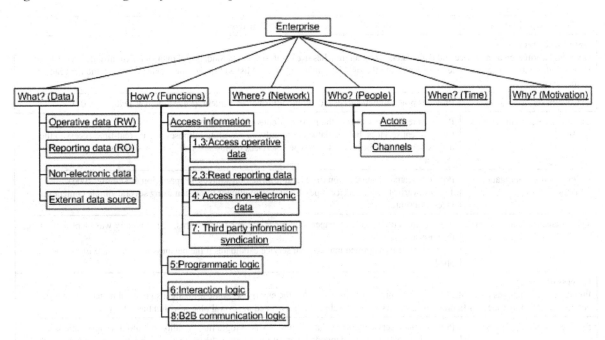

Core Categories

The Zachman Framework is used as a basis to discover all of the important aspects of an enterprise. John Zachman (1987) developed the framework in the 1980's and it "represents the logical structure for identifying and organizing the descriptive representations that are important in the management of the enterprises and to the development of systems".

The columns defined in the Zachman Framework (1987) act as core categories in QSE analysis. Relevant elements from the service elicitation point of view should fall into these categories. The core categories are further divided into sub-categories based on the service candidate type characteristics derived from the existing approaches discussed above. The predefined categories are merged in Figure 1, and the service candidate types and characteristics used are listed in Table 1.

QSE Process Phases

Development projects implement services, and the identification of the services is often based on the analysis for that particular project only. This does not enforce that the services created are reusable in following projects. To provide a wider context for the service candidates, QSE analysis (Figure 2) starts with a conceptual analysis of the business process descriptions, creating a skeleton for the service categories of the enterprise.

In the next phase, this skeleton is complemented with details from the project material describing the use cases being implemented in the actual project.

In the final phase, the service candidates are prioritized based on how often similar needs were identified at the business process level and how likely they are to be re-used later. Both conceptual analysis phases are conducted by applying the basic procedures of the grounded theory (Strauss & Corbin, 1998) to elicit the basic concepts of

Table 1. Service candidate types

Service candidate type	Characteristics
Data driven services Both the information as a service and data warehousing approaches use centralized data models and data stores to provide access to enterprise information. The key issues are identifying the right information to be published through the service interface and the granularity of the services.	
1) Content services (RW)	Provides programmatic access to simple information content. (Papazoglou & Dubray, 2004)
2) Reporting content services (RO)	Provides read-only access to the replica of enterprise data. (Walker) Like content services, but the data is used only for reporting purposes and no real-time access to the data is needed. Can be merged into type 1 services if the same data is needed elsewhere in an operative manner.
3) Information aggregation services	Provides seamless aggregation of several information sources. (Papazoglou & Dubray, 2004) This is a variant of the service types 1 and 2, providing information using several simple content services as a source.
4) Non-electronic master data.	Information stored solely on paper or in other non-electronic forms. This category was identified during the case study. (These can be transformed into content service candidates if the business processes are further developed.)
Process driven services Process driven methods try to identify common process elements within the enterprise, some utilizing also general patterns from other enterprises. The key aspect of finding reusable services is the shared logic needed in several places within the enterprise.	
5) Programmatic services	Programmatic services encapsulate atomic business logic functionality to build new applications. A service is an atomic and independent part of logic within the process, which returns a concrete result. (Papazoglou & Dubray, 2004)
6) Interactive services	Interactive services include stateful logic for interacting with a user through the presentation layer of an application. It can contain the multi-step behavior of an interactive business process. (Papazoglou & Dubray, 2004)
Message based communication Includes the logic needed in business conversations to bind public and private processes and messages together. This logic can be wrapped behind a service. (Bussler, 2001; Harikumar et al., 2005)	
7) Third-party information syndication	Information sources and services provided by an external party. (Papazoglou & Dubray, 2004)
8) Business-to-business communication services	The logic needed in complex electronic business-to-business conversations. Often based on a contract between the enterprises. The service can contain stateful communication logic with the business partner, possibly following a standard such as ebXML or RosettaNet. (Papazoglou & Dubray, 2004) Additionally, the service can act as a translator transforming the source data format to the target data format. (Harikumar et al., 2005)

an enterprise and to link them together at the conceptual level.

Conceptual Analysis Phases

Conceptual analysis uses the three coding phases of grounded analysis: open, axial and selective coding (Strauss & Corbin, 1998). Open coding is used to find the codes and their categories from the business data. During the axial coding, the identified categories are refined, differentiated and categories related to others are organized into sub-categories. Finally, the relations of the categories interesting from the service elicitation point of view are refined in the selective coding phase. Several iterations may be required to process the data and the phases should not be seen as distinguishable, but rather as different ways of handling the data than in grounded theory (Flick, 1998; Robson, 2002).

The purpose of the conceptual analysis is to find the essential business elements (categories)

Figure 2. Phases of the Qualitative Service Elicitation (QSE) method

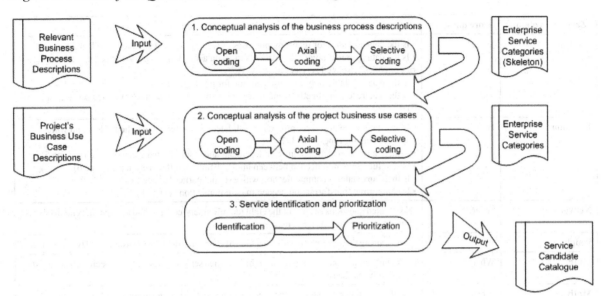

of the enterprise; especially the ones falling under the "Data", "Function" and "People" core categories. The categories under the core categories are identified and abstracted independently from each other, allowing the elements in each column to develop and saturate separately. The actual service candidates are identified from the codes under the numbered categories, and their granularity is dependent of the relations to other categories. For example, service candidates accessing data (content services) are identified from the codes under the "Function" core category, but their granularity is determined from their relations to the categories in the "Data" core category. In this case, also the level in hierarchy is important; if the relation is made to a category with sub-categories, the service candidate is an information aggregation service candidate instead of a content service candidate.

During the open coding, the raw data is divided into discrete parts and interpreted into codes or labels describing the parts of the data (Robson, 2002). This division depends on the raw material; parts can be parts of drawings in process descriptions, words or sentences in business use case descriptions, and so on. Each part is given a label or code describing for what the part stands. See Table 3 for an example.

To help thinking of the codes during the open coding, the seven questions of the Zachman Framework (1987) can be used repeatedly during the analysis as a catalyst (See Table 2). Codes can be seen as labels or names defining for what the part in question stands. The wording used in the material being analyzed can be used sometimes, but often the analyst needs to invent a descriptive name for a code. Categories are concepts, which can be used to group several codes together. For example both "toothbrush" and "toothpaste" can be grouped under the "dental care products" category, which can be seen as a sub-category for the "product" category.

Additional notes should be written down for each identified code to help divide the codes into categories. The questions in the note column of Table 2 are derived from the characteristics of the sub-categories defined in Table 1.

The purpose of the axial coding is to link together the findings of the open coding (Robson, 2002). In this phase, the codes are grouped into categories containing similar codes and categories

Table 2. Analysis core categories and catalyst questions for open coding

Zachman column	Core question	Detailed questions
Data	What?	• Is the data accessed for reporting purposes only? (Are related services type 1 or 2?) • Is the data aggregation of other data? Is the data actually a category containing other categories or codes? (Related services are type 3) • Is the data available only in non-electronic form? (Type 4) • Is the data received directly or indirectly from any external source? (Related services are type 7)
Function	How?	• Is any data being accessed, processed, validated, generated or searched? How and which data? (Details for types 1, 2, 3, 7) • Is there a logic, which is atomic, independent and resulting in a concrete result? (Type 5) • Is stateful interaction needed between human beings and the IT system? (Type 6) • Is there any stateful communication with external parties? (Type 8) • Is data format transformation needed in communication? (Type 8)
Network	Where?	(No detailed questions as none of the eight identified service types had any specific characteristics related to where the service is used.)
People	Who?	• Who is using the system and with what kind of channel or device? (Reusability of type 6 services)
Time	When?	(No detailed questions as none of the eight identified service types had any specific characteristics related to when the service is used.)
Motivation	Why?	• Why is the data processed in non-electronic form? (Is there need for type 1 or 2 services?)

into sub-categories. If different wording has been used for the same phenomenon during the open coding phase, then these codes should be merged, as well. Additionally any relationships between codes under the same categories should be identified. The questions in this phase are, for example:

- Are there any codes which mean the same thing and could be merged?
- Are there similar codes which could be grouped under a common category?
- Can any categories be seen as an aggregate of two or more categories?

In the last phase, selective coding is performed on the data identified in the previous phases. In this phase, the identified categories and codes are sorted into core categories based on the Zachman Framework and the sub-categories based on Table 1. The hierarchy of the categories is presented in Figure 1.

The use of partly pre-defined categories as a priori categories is against the inductive nature of the grounded theory research methodology. However, the recurring analysis of similar data, such as

in service elicitation, will probably benefit from a set of pre-defined categories. The pre-defined categories and their characteristics are needed to identify the service types known to be potentially reusable. Additional categories and sub-categories can be created inductively, if needed.

The actual service candidates are identified after the use case analysis and are generated from the codes under the "Function" core category with their relations to the codes and categories in the "Data" and "People" core categories.

Service candidate types 1, 2, 3 and 7 (Table 1) are identified from the codes under the "Access information" categories. The granularity of the candidate is determined with the relation to the codes and categories in the "Data" core category. The abstraction level is the one identified from the business process analysis, if available. Codes in the "Access non-electronic data" category can be transformed into content services if the business process itself is revised, as well.

Service candidate types 5 and 8 are identified from the codes under equivalent categories. If these codes have relations to other core categories, then these relations can be used to determine the

Table 3. Example business use case

Order Entry for ADSL Product (Relevant code sources marked with superscript)	Identified Codes
Goal and Triggers: The goal of the use case is to *get the customer and payment data checked and updated*[1], *verify the availability of the product in the delivery address*[2] and *to enter the sales order*[3] to the IT system *according to the customer's wishes*[4]. The use case is triggered when a customer calls the contact center and wishes to order an ADSL product.	**Why:** *flawless customer data*[1], *order validation*[2], *order entry*[3] *customer need clarification*[4],
Actors: Contact center agent (user)	**Who:** Contact center agent
Basic Course of Events: **The user opens the system using a web browser**[1] and selects the ADSL purchase function from the main menu. The user asks for the *installation address*[2] from **the customer**[3] and enters the address into the system. The system checks *the possibility to install*[4,5] the *ADSL line*[6] in the given address and returns *a list of possible speeds and add-ons*[7,5]. The user selects the ADSL add-ons one by one based on the customer's wishes and the system guides this selection by removing all incompatible add-ons after each addition[8]. The system shows *the price*[9,10] after the add-ons have been entered. If the customer agrees on the price, the customer is identified and the system user searches for existing customer data from the system with the *customer name*[11,12]. The user verifies the validity of the *customer's social security number (SSN), phone number and billing address*[11]. If the customer data is not found, the user adds a new customer into system with the data[13] queried from the customer. The system checks the validity of the given SSN[14] and stores the customer data[15]. The system conducts a *credit check*[16] for the customer using an external credit check agency[17]. The system shows if the credit check fails. In this case, all data is stored[15], but no *ADSL order*[18] is created. Instead, the customer is asked to come to the store and provide a *collateral deposit*[19]. If the credit check succeeds, the system creates an *ADSL order*[18,20] and creates a related *service order*[21] for a subcontractor[22]. The system returns to the main menu and informs the user of a successful sales order creation.	**Who: Contact center agent with browser**[1], **customer**[3] *What: installation address*[2], *availability*[4], *product*[6], *product configuration*[7], *product price*[9], *customer basic information*[11], *customer credit standing*[16], *sales order*[18], *collateral deposit*[19], *service order*[21] How: Get available product configurations with address[5], Guide configuration of ADSL product[8], get product configuration price[10], search for customer by name[12], create customer[13], validate customer SSN[14], update customer data[15], get customer credit standing[17] (external), create sales order[20], create service order[22] (external) Other codes: Communication with the customer, main menu

correct granularity. For example data transformation logic services should use the granularity of the data category, such as the service candidates under the "Access information" category.

Interaction logic candidates (Type 6) are identified from the codes under the equivalent category. These codes should have relations to the "People" core category, which can help to estimate the reusability. If the same interaction logic is needed with several different actors or the actors are using different channels to access the same logic, then these services are more likely to be reusable.

Candidate Identification and Prioritization Phase

The scope of a service can vary from a simple request to a complex system that can access and combine information from other sources. Enterprises can use simple services to accomplish a specific business task, while several smaller services can be combined to support more complex processes. The services should represent functionality that is meaningful from the business perspective. (Papazoglou & Dubray, 2004)

After the analysis, the codes from the analysis of the use cases are transformed into service

Figure 3. Order to Cash composite business process

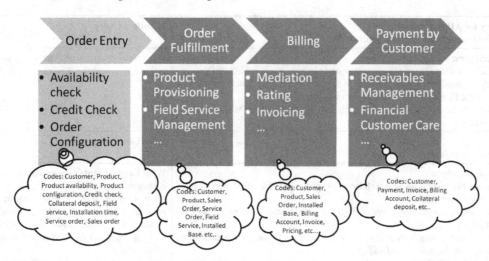

candidates. All of the codes under the "Function" core categories are service candidates and are given a descriptive name using the categories they represent and to which they are related.

With the help of the business process analysis, the service candidates can be prioritized based on how often they are mentioned in the business process descriptions. In our case study, we simply sorted the services into two classes: local and global service candidates. A service candidate is global if it belongs to any category identified from more than one business process and should be thus reusable in other projects, as well. Otherwise, the candidate is local and is not likely to be reused in other projects.

EXAMPLE

As an example, we use an imaginary "Order-to-Cash" composite business process and a project implementing an IT system to support the "Order Entry" business process in a contact center. The "Order Entry" process is merely one stage within the "Order-to-Cash" composite process, and thus, the use case analysis of the project will cover only this stage. However, the scope of the business process analysis can cover the whole

"Order-to-Cash" process, giving a more extensive view to the enterprise and providing a conceptual skeleton of the categories to be enhanced with the use case analysis.

The analysis of a typical "Order-to-Cash" composite business process reveals concepts such as customer, product, sales order, service order, field service, installed base, pricing, payment, billing account and so on. The example "Order-to-Cash" composite business process is outlined in Figure 3 and one of the processes is detailed in Figure 4. In our example, the conceptual analysis of the business processes produce the codes listed in Figure 3. Sources of the codes identified from the "Order Entry" process are underlined in Figure 4. The conceptual analysis of all business process descriptions provides the skeleton of the categories as presented in Figure 5 (The number of occurrences is provided in the brackets).

An example product in this project could be, for example, an ADSL connection, and thus, the business use case "Order Entry for ADSL Product" would be implemented in the project. The details of the example use case are presented in Table 3 with identified codes and categories. The codes and categories identified from the use case analysis are appended to the hierarchy as pre-

Figure 4. A detailed Order to Cash composite business process

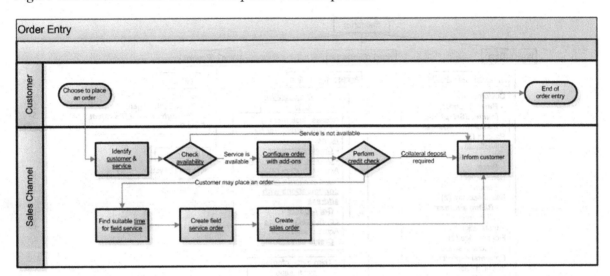

Figure 5. The category hierarchy after conceptual analysis

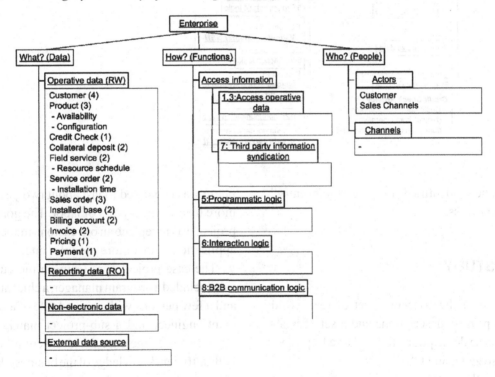

sented in Figure 6. These additions are in bold font.

The service candidates are underlined in Figure 6. In this analysis, most of the identified service candidates have relationships with a con-

cept identified from more than one business process, and therefore, they would be classified as "global" and reusable in other projects, as well. The only exception is "Get customer credit standing", which have a relationship with "Credit

Figure 6. The category hierarchy appended with categories and codes from the use case analysis

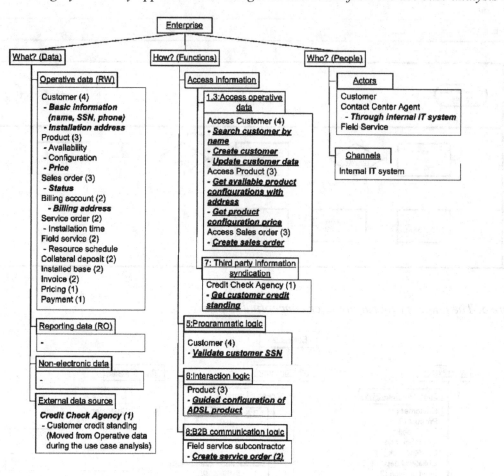

check" concept identified only from "Order entry" business process.

CASE STUDY

As a proof of the concept, a set of real world business process descriptions and a set of business use case descriptions from a large IT project were analyzed using QSE.

The implementation of this case project was outsourced to an external partner with a fixed price contract and thus the completeness of the requirements was essential. The scope of the contract was based on a requirements specification, use cases and a solution architecture. The implementation phase was estimated to last about two years with more than 15 man-years of labor. The goal of the project was to replace an old custom-made legacy application with a more modular one.

The case project core team on the customer side included a program manager, a chief architect and a few persons with a mixed role of a requirement engineer and a sub-project manager. The key persons of the case project were all experts with sufficient knowledge of the business domain. The core team was complemented with several temporal advisors especially for security, technology and legal issues.

The goal of the case study was to test how well QSE would uncover the service candidates in a real project and to compare the produced service

Figure 7. Top level categories of the case project (actual category names disguised)

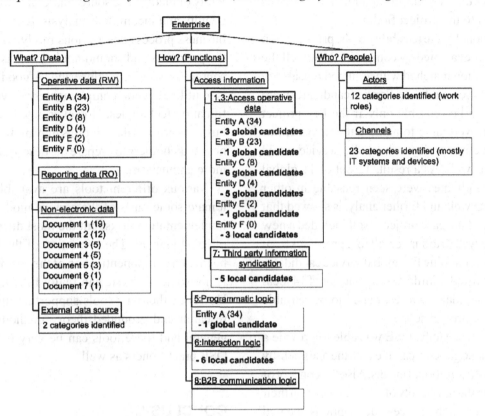

catalogue against the actual solution architecture made in the project with traditional methods by the experts. From the project point of view, this review acted as an additional verification for the solution architecture, and for the research, this comparison gave an opportunity to validate the outcome against similar analysis made by the experts.

The planned changes to the actual business processes were minor in the case project, as the main driver was technical renewal. Respectively, the needed interfaces and connections to the external systems were carefully identified by the project, as the existing solution provided a good basis for the project design. Similarly, the business process and use case descriptions were more or less up-to-date and solid, providing a good basis for QSE analysis.

A total of 47 business process descriptions were analyzed covering the main operative processes of one business line. The analyzed project scope included 16 business level use cases and the use case analysis resulted in 17 global and 14 local service candidates as shown in Figure 7. These service candidates were modeled using the Integration Use Case method (Alkkiomäki & Smolander, 2007), catalogued and compared to the solution architecture created by the project.

The comparison showed that QSE analysis was able to reveal all the services identified by the project with traditional methods. The scope and grouping of the service candidates were different compared to the project, but it was possible to map each elicited service candidate to the project design. On the other hand, the work made by the project was thorough and thus QSE analysis did not uncover any completely new services compared to the project findings.

Additionally, the feasibility of the prioritization model was evaluated by comparing how well the categorization matched with assumed reusability of each service candidate. Service candidates were assumed to be reusable only if the key project personnel were able to name either a system or another active project where the service could be used as well. As a result, 12 out of 17 global service candidates were seen reusable in other projects as well and further analysis showed that the scope of the case project itself included a new operative system to support all four processes from where the remaining five global service candidates were identified. Similarly only one out of 14 local service candidates was estimated to be reusable outside the project scope.

In this case study, QSE was able to provide a service catalogue comparable with the one made by experts with traditional means. Also the concept of estimating the reusability of services based on their occurrences in the process descriptions seemed to be promising in the case project. As a result, QSE seems to provide a promising way of doing service elicitation in early phases of the project, at least when used with high quality raw material.

FUTURE RESEARCH DIRECTIONS

The strength of QSE is its generic nature; it can be expanded with new service types with characteristics identified in other projects, it is technology neutral and the analyzed source material can be virtually in any human readable format. It would be also beneficial, if the laborious service engineering work could be done by less experienced analysts by following well-defined procedures. One of our future research directions will be to test how easily junior requirement engineers can adopt QSE.

Similarly to grounded theory, QSE depends purely on the material being analyzed. Thus,

faulty or incomplete source material will produce a faulty and incomplete analysis. In real life, the business process descriptions rarely cover all of the processes and should not be used as the only source for service engineering. A good practice is to utilize several complementary service identification techniques. However, intensive use of business process descriptions may motivate business stakeholders to prepare the descriptions with more enthusiasm.

Various different tools are available to automate some parts of the service modeling and implementation tasks, but the most difficult part remains manual. The elicitation of the business needs and componentization of the business itself is not something one can really fully automate. However, there are tools supporting qualitative research and grounded theory methodology in general and these tools can be very helpful for QSE practitioners as well.

CONCLUSION

In this chapter, we have introduced QSE, a method for Qualitative Service Elicitation that applies the qualitative research approach to service elicitation. The use of QSE in service-oriented systems development allows more consistent quality of analysis and enforces developers to concentrate on reusability aspects of services.

Based on the experiences from the case study, it is feasible to use QSE as a systematic and practical method for service elicitation with results comparable to similar analysis carried out by experts with traditional methods. The use of business process level concepts and vocabulary in the service candidates made it easy for requirement engineers to putting uses in place of usages for the service candidates outside the case project context. Also the idea of prioritization of services based on how often the related concepts appear in the business processes seemed to be promising, although it should be enhanced to take the relationships between categories better into account. Prioritization can help identifying the services with potential reusability outside of the project scope, giving the project a possibility to check the other business processes for potential new requirements for the services being implemented.

After all, even when the pace of change is getting faster in business, the basic concepts of business don't change quite as quickly allowing definition of somewhat stable service interfaces defining also boundaries between organizations. QSE provides means to design stable boundaries providing loose coupling between different parts of the enterprise, thus allowing these parts to be developed more or less independently. As a result, the additional agility can make a difference nowadays.

REFERENCES

Adam, S., & Doerr, J. (2008). *The role of service abstraction and service variability and its impact on requirement engineering for service-oriented systems*. Annual IEEE International Computer Software and Applications Conference.

Alkkiomäki, V., & Smolander, K. (2007). *Integration use cases – An applied UML technique for modeling functional requirements in service oriented architecture*. Paper presented at the Requirements Engineering: Foundation for Software Quality, 13th International Working Conference, REFSQ 2007, Trondheim, Norway.

Arsanjani, A. (2005). *Toward a pattern language for service-oriented architecture and integration, part 1: Build a service eco-system*. Retrieved January 19, 2010, from http://www.ibm.com/developerworks/webservices/library/ws-soa-soi/

Arsanjani, A., Ghosh, S., Allam, A., Abdollah, T., Ganapathy, S., & Holley, K. (2008). SOMA: A method for developing service-oriented solutions. *IBM Systems Journal, 47*(3), 377–396. doi:10.1147/sj.473.0377

Bieberstein, N., Bose, S., Fiammante, M., Jones, K., & Shah, R. (2006). *Service-oriented architecture compass: Business value, planning and enterprise roadmap*. Upper Saddle River, NJ: IBM Press.

Bussler, C. (2001). The role of B2B protocols in inter-enterprise process execution. In *Proceedings of the Second International Conference on Technologies for E-Services* (pp. 16-29). Berlin / Heidelberg, Germany: Springer.

Cherbakov, L., Galambos, G., Harishankar, R., Kalyana, S., & Rackham, G. (2005). Impact of service orientation at the business level. *IBM Systems Journal, 44*(4), 653–668. doi:10.1147/sj.444.0653

Dan, A., Johnson, R., & Arsanjani, A. (2007). *Information as a service: Modeling and realization*. Paper presented at the International Workshop on Systems Development in SOA Environments, Washington, DC.

Endrei, M., Ang, J., Arsanjani, A., Chua, S., Comte, P., & Krogdahl, P. (2004). *Patterns: Service-oriented architecture and Web services*. IBM Press.

Flick, U. (1998). *An introduction to qualitative research*. London, UK: Sage.

Galal, G. H., & Paul, R. J. (1999). A qualitative scenario approach to managing evolving requirements. *Requirements Engineering, 4*(2), 92–102. doi:10.1007/s007660050016

Harikumar, A. K., Lee, R., Hae Sool, Y., Haeng-Kon, K., & Byeongdo, K. (2005). *A model for application integration using Web services.* Paper presented at the Computer and Information Science, 2005. Fourth Annual ACIS International Conference.

Jarvenpaa, S. L., & Stoddard, D. B. (1998). Business process redesign: Radical and evolutionary change. *Journal of Business Research, 41*(1), 15–27. doi:10.1016/S0148-2963(97)00008-8

Lo, A., & Yu, E. (2008). From business models to service-oriented design: A reference catalog approach. In *Proceedings of the 26th International Conference on Conceptual Modeling - ER 2007* (Vol. 4801, pp. 87-101). Berlin / Heidelberg, Germany: Springer.

Moon, M., Hong, M., & Yeom, K. (2008). *Two-level variability analysis for business process with reusability and extensibility.* 32nd Annual IEEE International Computer Software and Applications, COMPSAC '08. Turku, Finland.

Noel Yuhanna, M. G. (2008). *The Forrester wave: Information-as-a-service Q1 2008.* Retrieved February 16, 2010, from http://www.forrester.com/rb/Research/wave%26trade%3B_information-as-a-service%2C_q1_2008/q/id/43199/t/2

Papazoglou, M. P., & Dubray, J.-J. (2004). *A survey of Web service technologies.* Retrieved February 16, 2010, from http://eprints.biblio.unitn.it/archive/00000586/

Papazoglou, M. P., Traverso, P., Dustdar, S., Leymann, F., & Kramer, B. J. (2006). Service-oriented computing: A research roadmap. In F. Cubera, B. J. Krämer & M. P. Papazoglou (Eds.), *Service oriented computing (SOC)* (vol. 05462). Internationales Begegnungs- und Forschungszentrum für Informatik (IBFI).

Ramollari, E., Dranidis, D., & Simons, A. J. H. (2007). *A survey of service oriented development methodologies.* Paper presented at the 2nd European Young Researchers Workshop on Service Oriented Computing, Leicester, UK.

Robson, C. (2002). *Real world research* (2nd ed.). Oxford, UK: Blackwell Publishing.

Sadiq, S., Orlowska, M., & Sadiq, W. (2005). *The role of messaging in collaborative business processes.* Paper presented at the IRMA International Conference, San Diego, USA.

Sarker, S., & Lee, A. S. (1999). IT-enabled organizational transformation: A case study of BPR failure at TELECO. *The Journal of Strategic Information Systems, 8*(1), 83–103. doi:10.1016/S0963-8687(99)00015-3

Strauss, A. L., & Corbin, J. M. (1998). *Basics of qualitative research: Techniques and procedures for developing grounded theory* (2nd ed.). Thousand Oaks, CA: Sage Publications Inc.

Van Nuffel, D. (2007). *Towards a service-oriented methodology: Business-driven guidelines for service identification.* In On the Move to Meaningful Internet Systems 2007: OTM 2007 Workshops (pp. 294-303).

Walker, D. M. (2006). *White paper - Overview architecture for enterprise data warehouses.* Retrieved February 16, 2010, from http://www.datamgmt.com/index.php?module=documents&JAS_DocumentManager_op=downloadFile&JAS_File_id=29

Watson, H. J., Goodhue, D. L., & Wixom, B. H. (2002). The benefits of data warehousing: Why some organizations realize exceptional payoffs. *Information & Management, 39*(6), 491–502. doi:10.1016/S0378-7206(01)00120-3

Zachman, J. A. (1987). A framework for Information Systems architecture. *IBM Systems Journal, 26*(3), 276–292. doi:10.1147/sj.263.0276

Zdun, U., Hentrich, C., & Dustdar, S. (2007). Modeling process-driven and service-oriented architectures using patterns and pattern primitives. [TWEB]. *ACM Transactions on the Web*, *1*(3), 14. doi:10.1145/1281480.1281484

Zimmermann, O., Schlimm, N., Waller, G., & Pestel, M. (2005). *Analysis and design techniques for service-oriented development and integration*. Paper presented at the INFORMATIK 2005 - Informatik LIVE! Bonn.

Chapter 2
The Design Principles and Practices of Interoperable Smart Spaces

Eila Ovaska
VTT Technical Research Centre of Finland, Finland

Tullio Salmon Cinotti
Università di Bologna, Italy

Alessandra Toninelli[1]
INRIA, France

ABSTRACT

Smart spaces provide information about physical environments, shared with inherently dynamic applications. This chapter introduces a novel development approach with its focus on two key properties of smart space applications: the ability to interoperate and behave in a situation-sensitive manner. Sixteen principles are defined in order to guide the development of an interoperability platform for smart spaces and on how to create applications on top of it. The interoperability platform deals with information and is agnostic with respect to ontologies, programming languages, service frameworks, and communication technologies. The interoperability platform also supports extensibility, evolvability and context based adaptation, which allows new applications to be added and to behave in a situation based manner. Agile application development is based on scenario specifications, implemented by the means of the ontology and model driven development. The approach has been applied to the development of smart personal spaces, smart indoor spaces, and smart city applications.

INTRODUCTION

Everyday life can be enriched by services that exploit pervasive computing environments, which are embedded into our surroundings. These computing environments rely heavily on sensors and sensor networks that produce a large amount of data to be analyzed and reacted to by users or/and devices (Hadim & Mohamed 2006). Since the number of these devices is increasing, the amount of information to be processed by people and devices is also rising. In order to handle the

DOI: 10.4018/978-1-60960-735-7.ch002

information overload, the environments are to be made to be smart.

The motivations for smart environments are quite well understood: to increase the visibility of opportunities, to support context understanding and ultimately to provide the correct information when and where it is required, even if not explicitly requested, with its content and format optimally adapted to the user situation and profile (Weiser 1993). Although smart spaces have been an interest of researchers and industrial professionals for years, there is hardly any easy working smart environment in practice. The main obstacle is the lack of the interoperability of devices and systems that provide the execution environment for ambient applications. Although the interoperability could be achieved at the device level by handling communication, connectivity and data with a set of standard protocols, selected for use in a situation based manner by using, e.g., the reflection pattern (Buschmann et al. 1996), there are still obstacles to handling the interoperability with higher system architecture levels, the service and information levels. Service interoperability concentrates on unambiguously describing service semantics, so that services can be searched and they can interact with each other (Kantarovitch & Niemelä 2008). Enhanced functionality is achieved through service discovery, matchmaking and the merged functionality of a selected set of services. Moreover, services enriched with semantic information on context and resources could provide the service that is the most suitable for the user's preferences and the situation at hand (Soylu et al. 2009). These enrichments however have costs; they make service centric systems more complex and error prone, and increase the need of computing resources.

Recently, two promising approaches for context-awareness have been proposed; a spatial application programming model (Meier, et al 2008) and an approach that is based on Model and Ontology Driven Development (Soylu et al. 2009). The spatial application programming model uses a small set of predefined types for composing information and context. The approach has some similarity with ours, but it relies on a specific programming model, not a model driven development approach that embodies a generic ontology used for information sharing. Soylu et al. (2009) link the model driven development with ontology engineering and aim to assist context-awareness in all phases of the application development life cycle, i.e. at design time and run-time. Their special focus is on the context-awareness of the digital world, where the use of abstract models is easier and efficient. However, the approach introduced is at a conceptual level and still requires long and short term research. Our goal, on the contrary, is to adopt the semantic web technologies to physical spaces and to make the existing entities of our environments both smart and adaptive.

Our approach facilitates interoperability at the information level and lets devices and systems use existing solutions for describing, managing and executing services to facilitate the functionality which is required from a smart space (Sofia 2010). Thus, ambience is based on information which is provided by sensors embedded into environments and existing services, running on heterogeneous devices and systems, for free use in smart space applications, which also share the semantics of information. Thus, smart space interoperability is based on information sharing and the adaptation to existing (legacy) devices and systems. We exploit ontology orientation to represent the semantics of information. This information is shared and mapped onto a graph that uses a triple (two nodes – subject and object - connected by a predicate) as an information elementary element. Native information from the legacy devices and services is captured by agents that translate it into the specified information format of the smart spaces. Thus, a legacy device may be controlled by the interoperability platform through an enhanced legacy application, which is able to access and subscribe to the smart space.

The objective of this chapter is to provide a practical way to develop intelligent applications for physical spaces, by exploiting existing hardware and software technologies and enhancing them for an integration environment. The aim is to encourage smart space managers to enhance spaces with added value services, by exploiting the information which is freely available in these spaces. So, the main goal is thus not to only support the integration of legacy systems and devices, but persuade smart space managers to innovate new services which are based on shared information. To this end, we elaborate the existing technologies that provide advances to transform to smart environments. Thereafter, we introduce our way of developing smart spaces and their intelligent applications. The approach has already provided positive signs of an improved and shared understanding, especially in terms of interoperability, adaptivity and advanced user experiences.

RELATED WORK AND BACKGROUND

This section first introduces the motivations and characteristics of smart spaces from four viewpoints: history, business, application fields and technology. Thereafter, the current research works concerned with interoperability, context-awareness and design methodologies are discussed.

Smart Spaces

Smart spaces are a milestone along the history of computer science, as they mark the convergence of two previously separate domains: Internet and Context-aware computing (Figure 1).

- Context-aware computing provides domain-specific assistance, optimized to the user situation.

Figure 1. Comparing the models of Context-aware computing (top left), Internet (top right) and Smart Space

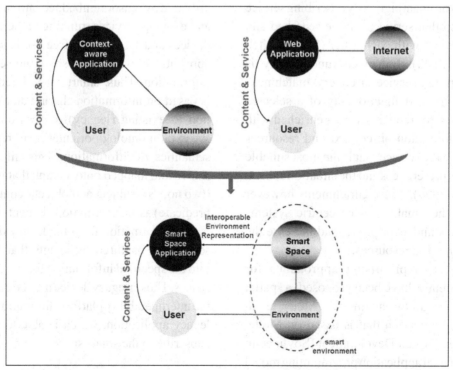

- The Internet provides multi-domain assistance, disregarding the user situation.
- Interoperable smart spaces provide multi-domain assistance, optimized to the user situation.

Context-aware computing is the proposed solution to deal with the overload of information, particularly when mobile. It intends to provide an answer to the need of getting the best possible content/service in the most suitable format with respect to the activity in which the user is currently engaged. Its principle is shown in Figure 1 (top left): users perceive their dynamically changing environment and situation with their senses. Devices sense the same through sensors and associated reasoning. Therefore, the user and the device share their perception of the environment, so that services can adapt to the situation, while the interaction and content exchange runs smoothly and is contextualized. The key questions are: How feasible and expensive is it to provide such context-awareness, and how feasible and expensive is it to build and maintain a set of contextualized data (and services) with their management system?

In fact, two of the greatest challenges, the same that were originally faced by context-aware applications, are the cost-effectiveness and the time-to-market. Applications are domain or/and application specific, as any application requires a different view of the environment. The collection of information from the environment is a difficult and expensive task, mainly due to the diversity of the technology used and to the uncertainty inherent in the sensing systems. Therefore, the development and deployment time is likely to be very long and the costs high. Thus, the collected information needs to be shared to become viable, but this is difficult as, with reference to Figure 1 top left, there are as many environments as there are applications.

On the one hand, the Internet is a flat ocean of shared, uncommitted and machine readable information, which is available to all users. No domain specific infrastructures, no niche market, no cost and time-to-market problems, thanks to the Internet technologies. The Internet is, however, largely unaware of the situation, location and environmental conditions of its users, and therefore, it can not filter out the information which is to be provided, based on the situation. On the other hand, due to its universal market size, it can afford huge investments and its technologies are progressing very fast. In this respect, the greatest challenge faced by the Internet in recent years was turning information representation from being machine readable to machine understandable (Berners-Lee et al. 2001), and the semantic web technologies went a long way in this direction (Lassila 2007). Bringing together the interoperability and the information centric, universal and multi-domain approach, enabled by the semantic web with the dynamicity, adaptability, and usability of context-aware applications, was the next step which smart spaces enabled.

Smart spaces (Sofia 2010) lead to an extremely simple and general approach to turn the information which is originated from the environment into a shared commodity. A smart space is a digital entity where the relevant real-world information (i.e. information about the environment and the objects therein located) is stored in an interoperable, machine understandable format, kept up to date and made available to unanticipated and authorized situation dependent applications. Therefore, the smart spaces may be considered to be the ultimate convergence between the Internet and context-aware computing. The beauty of smart spaces is their simplicity, their inherent being agnostics with respect to the information stored and their interoperability. The interoperability is based on a shared knowledge model, and governing the life cycle of this model is currently one of the most interesting and relevant challenges in the smart space research.

The vision behind smart spaces is that if all of the information about the surrounding environment is easily available, the variety of applications that can benefit is only limited by the imagination. The information can be collected by sensors which are embedded in devices and systems hidden in the environment, and the smart space technology may support their interoperability, as well as the abstraction of semantically rich information from the data collected from the environment. Emerging mobile devices already benefit through the addition of sensors to their set of traditional conventional resources. Sensors, such as cameras, compasses, gyroscopes, accelerometers, GPS, RF based devices and many others may provide inputs to the smart spaces. The smart spaces only take care of information interoperability, whilst connectivity, smart space and service discovery are orthogonal issues. Furthermore, as shown in Figure 1 (bottom), smart spaces envisage a clear separation between the data and applications. A solution introduced in (Lassila 2007) implements this concept with ontologies using the Resource Description Framework (RDF) mapped onto a common data model represented as a graph. An ontology is a shared knowledge standard or a knowledge model defining primitive concepts, relations, rules and their instances, which comprise topic knowledge (Zhou 2005). Ontology can be used for capturing, structuring, and enlarging explicit and tacit topic knowledge across people, organizations, and computer and software systems (Edgington et al. 2004). In smart spaces, ontologies can be used to describe the semantics of a space and the semantics of applications, services, data and the context where they are used. The standard set of Semantic Web languages (mainly, RDF and OWL) provided by the World Wide Web Consortium, represents the most widely adopted solution to implement ontologies.

A platform which is hosting a smart space may be very simple, as it may just require a service consisting of a repository for storing and managing graphs and a path query language for graphs with reasoning capabilities, where the reasoning role is to extract (deduct) information from the graph, which is not explicitly stated (Lassila 2008). This service is the core component of the interoperability platform considered in this chapter for our discussion on smart space design and it goes a long way in the direction of making smart space programming an easy task.

The Interoperability of Smart Spaces

From a technical viewpoint, interoperability is a property of computational units that makes them able to inter-operate. For smart spaces that rely on legacy systems and devices and their ability to work together to achieve a common goal, interoperability is a prerequisite that has to be fulfilled. That is only possible if the interacting units use the same interaction model at every abstraction level. Due to its objective, this interaction model is called an interoperability model.

The interoperability models proposed in literature are diverse; the levels of abstraction are different, and they differ in the methods applied to and the technical solutions used for achieving the interoperability. When comparing the maturity of five interoperability models, the following most significant potential, concerns and barriers were identified (Guédria et al. 2008):

- The use of standards creates potential (openness) and is addressed in every interoperability model. Thus, the use of standards provides advantages for open smart spaces.
- Data and service interoperability are the concerns of smart spaces. Data interoperability is addressed in LISI (Levels of Information System Interoperability) (C4ISR Interoperability Working Group 1998) and LCIM (Levels of Conceptual Interoperability Model) (Tolk & Muguira 2003). Only LISI concerns service interoperability.
- Conceptual and technological barriers were identified in two (LISI and LCIM)

of the five analysed interoperability models. Conceptual barriers were related to the syntactic and/or semantic differences of exchanged information. Technological barriers were related to the incompatibility of information technologies.

To summarize, none of the five interoperability models as such are suitable for our purposes. The interoperability models LISI and LCIM – the only ones that focus on data and/or service interoperability - have conceptual and technical barriers that hinder their adoption for the development of smart spaces.

The Connection, Communication, Consolidation, Collaboration Interoperability Framework (C4IF) (Peristeras & Tarabanis, 2006) exploits the concepts of language theories, such as the language form, syntax, meaning and the use of symbols and interpretations. C4IF separates the interoperability levels based on the communication type, focus and substance. The C4IF model is compared to the LCIM model in Table 1. As it can be seen, although the definitions of these interoperability models are different, they have many similarities in terms of focus, substance and communication type. When systems need to be integrated, the focus is on the network and connectivity. Thereafter, interoperability is considered on the levels of the data, the meaning of the data, the context and the meaning of the context. Modeling and implementation are the means for achieving interoperability on these levels, whereas abstraction and modeling are the means of handling interoperability on the level of behavior.

The main difference between the C4IF and LCIM models derives from their origins. C4IF, which has its origin in language theories, makes it easy to understand the four levels of interoperability. Thus, it is a valuable vehicle for communication. LCIM originates from intelligent systems, and it provides a more comprehensive understanding of the various aspects of data and

how to manage them. In summary, the strength of C4IF is in its simplicity and mappings to existing technologies. LCIM lacks concrete examples of existing common technologies that can be used for realizing the interoperability levels. The three upper levels (conceptual, dynamic and pragmatic) do not have a particular clear separation of concerns, nor proposals how to address them in the designs of interoperability. However, these two models were selected as they have the largest coverage on interoperability and they, together, provide all of the views of interoperability that smart spaces have to deal with.

Our design approach addresses the following types of interoperability, explained further in the next section:

- The meaning of data; an ability of the interoperability platform to understand data based on schemas derived from ontology; information is used as an object of integration; the usage of data is separated from the data.
- Context; an ability of the interoperability platform to understand a shared context specification.
- The meaning of context changes; an ability of the interoperability platform to understand context changes.
- Behavior; an ability of smart space applications to understand their scopes of the shared meaning of behaviors/actions which are required in a smart space in a situation at hand.

Context Awareness in Smart Spaces

The open issues of smart spaces relate to the need to i) minimize information communication/processing overheads and ii) adapt the behavior of smart applications to changing conditions in their operational environment. Since information overheads have an impact on performance, smart applications should avoid exchanging and

Table 1. A comparison of the C4IF and LCIM interoperability models

Focus	C4IF (Peristeras & Tarabanis 2006)	Enhanced LCIM (Tolk et al. 2006; 2008)
Behaviour	*Collaboration* interoperability focuses on the ability of actions/behaviors to act together, and uses a process as an object of integration. Technologies: Service ontologies, SOAs, Web Services, Semantic Web Service technologies.	*Conceptual* interoperability focuses on abstraction and modelling; it is targeted to the complete the shared understanding of the data model concepts, not only the concepts of a domain, but also those concepts which are not included in the data model. Thus, conceptual interoperability narrows the scope of the data model so that it is meaningful for its user(s) – the application agent(s). Technologies: Platform independent models, domain specific architectural frameworks.
Change of context	No separation of the context data from other data.	*Dynamic* interoperability deals with changes in the context data, the meanings of these changes and the inter-modal and intra-modal transformations that these changes require in a system. Technologies: Enhanced Meta-Object Facility, agent mediated decision support.
Context		*Pragmatic* interoperability deals with the context data specified as the internal state of the system and the specification of the particular system process that will employ the data. Technologies: Web Ontology language (OWL), Unified Modeling Language (UML), Model Driven Architecture (MDA).
The meaning of data	*Consolidation* interoperability focuses on the ability to understand data, uses information as an object of integration, and is out of usage. Technologies: Thesaurus, taxonomies, common vocabularies, RDF, Schemas, ontologies, Semantic Web technologies.	*Semantic interoperability* deals with the meaning of exchanged data to the data users, i.e. the meaning is shared. Technologies: eXtensible Markup Language (XML), namespaces, schemas.
Data	*Communication* interoperability provides the ability to exchange data, uses information as an object for integration, and is out of context. Technologies: Data formats, dictionary, Structural Query Language (SQL).	*Syntactic* interoperability defines the correct forms and the correct order of the exchanged data. Technologies: Simple Object Access Protocol (SOAP), XML tagging.
Network Connectivity	*Connection* interoperability provides the ability to exchange signals, uses a channel as an object of integration, and is out of content. Technologies: cable, infrared, Bluetooth.	*Technical* interoperability provides a technical connection to exchange digital signals, but the participating systems have to make an agreement on how to interpret these signals. TCP/IP, as an example technology.

reasoning about information that is potentially useless for them. Moreover, as smart environments are envisioned to be open, heterogeneous, and variable, it is crucial to ensure that the smart applications behave adaptively and efficiently in several deployment settings and runtime conditions. To enforce high-level adaptation strategies, it is also crucial to provide effective support for the monitoring of useful information, such as user movements, device status, resource availability and the Quality of Service, which will trigger application adaptations. Filtering and adaptation strategies should be expressed at a high level of abstraction by cleanly separating the application management from the application logic. This separation of concerns allows the complexity of application developments for pervasive environments to be reduced and enables rapid application prototyping, run-time configuration, and maintenance (Toninelli et al. 2009).

Context awareness represents an effective means to improve the scalability of smart spaces through the means of filtering and adaptation. The context-aware adaptation of applications basically requires the following three building blocks:

- a conceptual context representation model at a high level of abstraction, whose visibility could be properly propagated up to applications;
- a set of middleware services to effectively manage the context;
- appropriate specification models and services to define/enforce the context-dependent adaptation strategies for smart applications.

In the following, we will focus on models for representing the context and enforcing context-aware adaptation strategies, while leaving context management issues out of the scope of this section.

CONTEXT MODELS

Context has many definitions in literature. Dey & Abowd (1999) define context as follows: 'Context is any information that can be used to characterize the situation of an entity. An entity is a person, place, or object that is considered to be relevant to the interaction between the user and the application, including the user and applications themselves.' Understanding of the context information has heavily improved over the last ten years. Recently published journal articles indicate that knowledge on the specification, modeling and usage of context information might be mature enough for the realization of context aware smart space applications. Typically, context information has three dimensions; the physical, computational and user context (Bettini et al. 2009). In order to assist achieving interoperability on the levels that concern the context data and change of context (see Table 1), the context specification shall (Preuveneers & Berbers, 2008) i) have a comprehensive domain coverage and terminology; ii) be expressive and without semantic ambiguity; iii) be processed without complexity; and iv) be evolvable. The three types of context modeling and reasoning approaches analyzed in (Bettini et al. 2009) are an object-role based model, a spatial model and an ontology based model. The object-role based approach supports various stages of the software engineering process. Its weakness is a 'flat' information model, i.e. all of the context types are represented as atomic facts. The spatial context models are well suited for context-aware applications that are mainly location-based, like many mobile applications. The main consideration of the spatial context model is the choice of the underlying location model. Relational location models are easier to build up than geographic location models as they provide a simple means to map data and Global Positioning Systems (GPS) data. The drawback is the effort that the special context model takes to gather and keep the location data of the context information up to date. As an example of spatial context models, the spatial application programming model, introduced in (Meier, et al 2008), uses a small set of predefined types for composing information and context. The spatial programming model supports a topographical approach for modelling a space, i.e. the context of actors (e.g. sensors, devices, systems and users) is modelled as a geometric shape which is based on a sequence of coordinates. This enables actors to independently define and use potentially overlapping spatial context in a consistent manner, when the relationships between spatial objects are defined implicitly, i.e. as the positions of the spatial objects shape within the coordinate system. Moreover, the programming model defines a set of types for modelling data, i.e. the various roles that spatial objects and their context information may have within a space. In addition, the programming model supports context along the dimension of time, defined by a set of attributes. The approach is similar to ours, but relies on a specific programming model and not a common ontology of shared information.

Semantic-Based Context Modeling

Compared to other approaches, ontological models for context and context-aware adaptation strategies provide a clear advantage, both in the terms of heterogeneity and the interoperability of data, context and context changes. However, there is very little support for modeling temporal aspects in ontologies, and reasoning with ontologies based on Description Logics (e.g., OWL-DL) may pose serious performance issues. Semantic technologies have been applied to support the context-awareness in several emerging smart spaces and pervasive computing platforms, including (Chen et al. 2004, Wang et al. 2004) and many others. Most systems exploit semantic techniques to represent and reason context and adapt service/application behavior accordingly. Ontologies have also been developed for describing QoS, but a lack of completeness is common to all of the approaches; only one or a few qualities are considered, and the vocabulary or/and metrics are missing. Moreover, making tradeoffs between quality attributes and managing QoS at run-time are not supported. Concerning the contextual characteristics of services, several ontologies have been designed, some of which are more elaborate and others more succinct, depending on their scope. Most of the approaches address the vocabularies of pervasive computing. Typically, they include a set of vocabularies for describing people, agents, and places, as well as a set of properties and relationships that are associated with these basic concepts. However, rather little emphasis has been placed on temporal contextual information. Moreover, no attempts have been made to align the service and context ontologies.

Given the best variety of existing context ontologies, the following challenge is how to provide a suitable definition of the context for smart spaces. A major obstacle is that the set of context ontologies that have been proposed for pervasive computing environments has not been standardized nor widely accepted and systematically used.

The common approach is that SOUPA (Chen et al. 2005) is used as a starting point extended for the needs of the application field. Our first step towards a holistic view of context awareness in smart spaces has been introduced in (Toninelli et al. 2009; Pantsar-Syväniemi et al. 2010) by mapping the dimensions of context to the levels of the context defined in (Bettini et al. 2009). To avoid "yet another" definition of context based on the kind of information that it conveys, our approach is to shift the focus from the content to the purpose of the context. Instead of trying to describe all of the possible types of context data that might be of interest to the smart applications, we assume that any piece of data might be the context for a given application (and possibly not for other applications). Context is strongly application-specific: the same piece of information cannot be defined a priori as "the context" unless this notion refers to a specific smart application at a specific time. Thus, defining the context in smart spaces is more about how, why, and by whom the smart space-related information is used, rather than about what the information describes. Given that, we propose that "A context defines the limit of the information usage of a smart space application". The notion of "information usage" is intended to be as comprehensive as possible, and includes the retrieval, access, understanding, processing, production, and sharing of information by smart applications.

As a consequence of this approach, the context interoperability finally boils down to data interoperability, since the context itself is represented as information in the smart space. Therefore, the same semantic representation of data that ensures interoperability at the information level also supports the meaningful exchange of context across smart applications. This approach helps to understand how the context data is to be dealt with within the physical context, in order to achieve pragmatic interoperability (see Table 1). After that, the context data is enhanced with additional context data at the second level that is responsible for digital context management. This digital context data forms the basis for the dynamic behavior of smart spaces (i.e. dynamic interoperability, see Table 1); context monitoring, reasoning and adaptation are actors that make decisions based on enhanced context data. These actors work for a specific application or a group of applications, defined as a scope of the application context (i.e. collaboration interoperability in Table 1).

Context-Aware Adaptation

Depending on where and when an adaptation is implemented, context-aware adaptation can be achieved by the means of various software engineering techniques. At design time, the software adaptation relies on the use of metadata. At runtime, computational reflection and aspect-oriented programming serve well to structure and dynamically drive the adaptation process (Issarny et al. 2007). Design time adaptation exploits metadata for representing both context information (profiles) and the choices in application behavior at a high-level of abstraction (policies). Metadata specification exploits declarative languages to accommodate the users of various expertises, to simplify metadata reuse and modification, and to facilitate the analysis of potential conflicts and inconsistencies. Metadata runtime support is responsible for metadata distribution/updates and for adaptation policy activation/deactivation/enforcement, independently of application logic. In addition to the adoption of metadata, alternative approaches have been proposed for representing context and providing context-aware adaptation: reflective middleware and middleware based on dynamic aspect-oriented programming (AOP) paradigm. Reflection and AOP represent possible solutions to the issue of adapting application behavior based on context. While reflection is a programming principle that enhances software objects with the ability to inspect their own qualifying properties, AOP is a set of software engineering techniques, which allows the modeling of the middleware structure at a high level of abstraction, based on the assumption that the engineering of some "aspects" of a system cannot be hard-coded into the application logic at design time.

As proposed by Kapitsaki et al. (2009), AOP is an example of language-based approaches to context-aware application engineering (as opposed to model-driven approaches). Language based approaches, such as AOP and context-aware AOP, follow the separation of concerns: applications are developed with no explicit notion of the context, while the context is handled as a first-class entity of the programming language and separate constructs are used to inject context-related behavior into the adaptable skeleton. With respect to the simple AOP, context-aware AOP proceeds one step further: not only do the aspects define context-aware adaptation, but their run time execution is also driven by the context, i.e., a particular aspect may or may not be executed depending on the current context. Another approach to context-aware application engineering is the model-driven paradigm, discussed in the following section.

The Design Methodologies of Smart Spaces

Due to the fact that UML is the most widely accepted modeling language, model-driven approaches for smart space designs have also emerged. Typically, these approaches introduce a meta-model which is enriched with context related artifacts, in order to support context-aware service engineering. For example, the context-aware pervasive service creation framework (Achilleos et al. 2009) includes several artifacts that support smart space development; a context ontology, a context modeling language (i.e. a context metamodel) and a tool environment that assists in context-aware service creation. The tool environment supports i) context model definition and validation, ii) context model-to-model transformation and iii) context model-to-code generation. The transformation provides a mapping from the context metamodel to the target metamodel. The approach tackles the structural and static parts of smart space service creation, i.e. context categories, context sources, temporal constraints and contextual situation. However, the dynamic aspects of context-aware services are not supported. The ontology and the model driven development approach (Soylu et al. 2009) exploit the model abstractions of MDA and the commonly used modeling languages UML and OWL. The approach enhances the software engineering process with computing independent domain ontology for modeling platform independent applications and a context ontology for reasoning. The integrated process model of the approach is however very abstract and does not increase understanding about how the context ontology is to be specified, represented, and processed at design time and run time, and how the context ontology is to be transformed for the use of various architectural elements, i.e. applications, services and data, in run-time reasoning.

As stated above, the ontologies for defining quality attributes are rare and incomplete. In (Ovaska et al. 2010), the ontology orientation is used for defining quality attribute ontologies, especially for the defining of their metrics. On the one hand, the quality and model driven design methodology which is introduced exploits the ontology oriented design for specifying, representing and managing quality attribute specific knowledge by ontologies. On the other hand, architectural knowledge is specified, represented and managed as styles and patterns. Both of the types of models can evolve separately. The mapping is made by a tool chain that supports each development phase of the model and quality driven service engineering. Recently, the interest on using ontologies for describing and managing quality attributes has increased due to the growing awareness of the importance of quality characteristics in service oriented systems. Moreover, the quality aspects need to be managed not only at design time but also at run time. In (Kassab et al. 2009), an ontology for

non-functional requirements has been introduced with three views; an intramodel dependency view for describing the relations between the software entities, an intermodal dependency view for describing the structure of interdependent entities, and a measurement view for defining measurable requirements. These views are required for managing quality properties at run-time; the intermodal view defines what the quality property is and how to put it into realization, the intramodel dependencies are used for reasoning purposes; and metrics are used not only for defining quality goals, but also for measuring how these goals are achieved.

Agile Smart Space Development and Evolution

Despite the enriched set of software and service technologies and development methodologies which were introduced in the previous section, there are still some challenges and issues that the developers of smart spaces are encountering. To facilitate the agile development of smart spaces, we propose a novel methodology called Agile Smart Space Development and Evolution (ASSDE). To provide agility, ASSDE exploits some of the main properties of SCRUM (Scrum 2009):

1. It breaks the work down into manageable chunks, called scenarios, which can be implemented in a few weeks. Scenarios embody user centered design, which is another stone base of ASSDE.
2. It enables the project team to proceed systematically, even when a complete and stable design cannot be defined.
3. It allows large globally distributed teams to work like small teams by dividing work into pieces, proceeding in parallel but synchronizing continuously, stabilizing in increments, and continuously finding improvements through refinements and extensions.

Figure 2. Agile Smart Space Development and Evolution

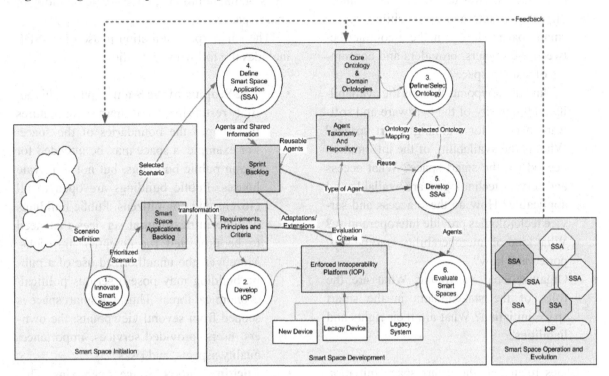

As depicted in Figure 2, ASSDE includes three main phases: Smart Space Initiation, Smart Space Development, and Smart Space Operation and Evolution. The Smart Space Initiation phase provides a backlog of smart space applications, described as scenarios. In the Smart Space Development phase, these scenarios are broken down into sprint(s) that describe an agent or a set of agents needed for an application. The application development exploits a set of predefined ontologies. In the Smart Space Operation phase, the smart space application (SSA) is tested which provides feedback to the earlier phases. The interoperability platform (IOP) is the key reusable component, on top of which applications are developed. These applications embody the ability to understand and process the defined scope of ontologies through the means of agents.

The phases of the ASSDE methodology are used as a framework for structuring this section into three phases. In each phase, first, the challenges and issues related to the phase are discussed

and explained. Second, concrete solutions which implement ASSDE are presented and exemplified based on our actual experience within Sofia (Sofia 2010). Third, open issues are briefly summarized for further discussions in the following section.

PHASE I: SMART SPACE INITIATION

Challenges and Issues

The challenges and issues of the smart space initiation phase relate to the specification of what a smart space is, why it is needed, what it should provide and how the space should be established. The challenges and issues include the following things:

• Business viewpoint: Can/must a smart space be profitable? What are the value creation model and the stakeholders' business models? How to estimate the business impact, markets and acceptability of the smart space? How to make a contract between the owners, providers and consumers of a smart space?

- Technical viewpoint: What is the availability and maturity of the hardware and software needed for realizing smart spaces? What is the availability of the information needed for the smart space? What access and service technologies are available and applicable? How do these access and service technologies provide interoperability? What kind of interoperability is to be supported and how?
- Organizational viewpoint: What are the roles of the stakeholders in the smart space initiation? What are their rights and liabilities?

Issues related to the smart space initiation phase concern: What interoperability levels must be supported and by which technologies? How to deal with the separation of concerns? What common technologies are applied? What space specific technologies are to be developed? Which domains and cross-domains are to be supported? What are the issues related to the interoperability level(s) to be supported, the legacy technologies to be adapted, and how is flexible and evolvable interoperability to be achieved?

Solutions and Recommendations

ASSDE deals with the above issues from the business and technical view point, by defining a set of analyses to be made before starting the smart space establishment. The organizational viewpoint is handled with a shared set of ontologies; i.e. we assume that technical, organizational and domain boundaries can be crossed by using shared 'standard' knowledge that is accepted by a set of industry sectors/fields as a foundation of

cross-domain ontology, i.e. the core ontology of smart spaces.

The smart space initiation phase of ASSDE includes the following activities:

- **The Scoping of the Smart Space**. This activity results in a set of smart space features that scopes the boundaries of the space. For example, a space may be intended for use in public buildings, but not in private houses. Public buildings are open to all citizens and non-citizens. Public buildings provide infrastructural services that need to be protected for potential intrusions. Moreover, the unauthorized use of a public building may pose a serious political/ economical threat. Thus, the smart space is scoped from several viewpoints: the owners, users, provided services, importance, quality aspects, and risks.
- **Eliciting Smart Space Scenarios**. This activity starts with a brainstorming session followed by team work for describing each scenario according to the template defined for that purpose. After each scenario has been described in detail, the scenario descriptions are presented to the group that participated in the initial brainstorming session. It is also checked that the identified scenarios cover the scope of the smart space. In so far as no new comment or idea has arisen, the scenario descriptions are labeled as completed and ready for impact analysis. Each scenario description defines the intent, stakeholders, the shared information and the actors involved in providing or/and consuming the information.
- **Impact Analysis.** The outcome of this activity is a report that explains the added value which is provided by the smart space, the stakeholders' interests and the expected market penetration enabled by the smart space and by the implementation of the associated scenario(s). The impact

analysis is made regularly; it is carried out the first time before making the decision on the smart space development. The analysis is started from the bottom up; starting from a single scenario and ending up with the whole smart space. If a smart space is expected to be profitable or not, depends on the purpose of the space. For example, personal spaces provide added value and experience for their users, and therefore, profitability is not a relevant question in that case. In smart cities that provide information services for a variety of users, profitability is a key issue to be assessed and calculated. In the later phases, impact analysis is performed after each promotion. Early promotions are used for estimating the acceptability of a smart space. Promotions are made for device developers, software developers, application developers at the national and international levels and for the joint European consortiums that work in different application fields or related technology areas. The results of these promotions are analyzed and used for estimating business impacts and market penetration. So far, these analyses are made case by case without any systematic approach, and thus, these analysis results do not provide any further understanding about the maturity of smart space ecosystems in general. Moreover, contract development is still at an immature level.

- **Risk Analysis.** Risk analysis covers the risks in business and technical issues. Business risks are related to the objective of the space, the role of the company in the space development and the partners involved in its development. Moreover, a return of investment is to be calculated considering the investments to be made for technology development, adaptation, skills development and the timeframe required for their development. The return

on investments is calculated so that it provides information for decision makers enabling them to estimate short term and long term requirements, limitations, and profits. Business and technical risks are represented as the costs and time required to pay them back.

- **Assets Analysis.** Concurrently to the risk analysis, the value of existing assets is analyzed in order to estimate what could be reused, such as, what assets need to be adapted and what kinds of new assets are to be developed. The focus of the assets analysis is on the functionality, quality, constraints and potential of existing assets in the context of the new smart space under consideration. Software assets may include architectural styles, middleware technologies, tools, languages and source code. Hardware assets might include devices, sensors, motes, networks, etc.

- **Prioritization and Selection.** This is the last activity of the smart space initiation phase. It results in a smart space applications backlog. This backlog consists of a set of prioritized scenarios, describing the smart space applications that are seen to have the highest potential, business impact and market penetration in a reasonable time frame. Prioritization defines in which order the scenarios are to be implemented and used for promoting the space.

In summary, the above mentioned smart space initiation activities tackle all of the technical challenges and issues, but there is lack of methods and supporting tools for analyzing business challenges and issues. Moreover, it is obvious that smart spaces will embody a rich set of roles for stakeholders that are not known yet. Therefore, there are still challenges and issues not solved: the roles of stakeholders in SS initiation and operation & evolution; and the rights and liabilities of the stakeholders representing those roles.

PHASE II: SMART SPACE DEVELOPMENT

Challenges and Issues

Smart spaces are fusions of different software, service and computer technologies. Therefore, there are several challenges and issues that relate to the underlying platform that provides the means for interoperation, i.e. an interoperability platform, IOP. The other part of the challenges and issues are related to the development of smart space applications that are executed on top of the IOP. The following challenges and issues were identified and explored:

- How to define the requirements for IOP?
- How to specify the main features of IOP architecture?
- How to apply model driven development to the IOP development?
- How to guarantee the interoperability of applications?
- How to design reusable building blocks and use them in SSA development?
- How to make sure that IOP is used correctly and effectively?
- How to guarantee that an SS provides the expected quality level?

Solutions and Recommendations

The development of IOP and SSAs is progressing concurrently. However, for the sake of clarity, the activities for specifying, designing and implementing IOP will be introduced first. Thereafter, we will explain how SSAs are developed on top of it. Thus, the understanding of IOP is a necessity in order to understand our model and ontology driven approach. In particular, based on the challenges and issues discussed above, this section will cover the following aspects: IOP development, ontology development, smart space application development and the evaluation of smart spaces.

IOP DEVELOPMENT

IOP Requirements

When the development of the IOP began, there was no full understanding of the interoperability models introduced in section 2. Thus, we studied the existing interoperability models and came to the conclusion of three interoperability levels; device level, service level and information level. The device level focuses on the connectivity, network and data as introduced in Table 1. The service level deals with the data, context, and the change of context (see Table 1). The information level is responsible for handling the meaning of data. Thus, the information level interoperability has a strong similarity with the consolidation interoperability of C4IF and the semantic interoperability of LCIM. The key point, and strength of our definition, is that we are only focusing on information interoperability and its realization in practice. We do not expect that all of the devices are fully interoperable on the device and service levels. The aim is that the device/system manufacturers and providers use their existing technologies and enhance their products with information interoperability in order to share a set of information with other device manufacturers and smart space owners/providers.

The IOP requirements were distilled from the scenarios defined for three smart spaces; personal spaces, smart indoor spaces and smart cities. In total, 56 scenarios with several sub-scenarios were analyzed and transformed to IOP requirements, classified into two categories; quality requirements and functional requirements. Quality requirements were related to the execution qualities: information security, availability, performance, reliability, adaptability, and usability; or evolution qualities like integrability and extensibility. The functional requirements of IOP concerned communication styles, evolvability, dynamic, proactive and context-awareness and heterogeneity of smart spaces. The requirements were defined on a tabular form with the following attributes: a significance for architecture/application/space and relations to the interoperability levels, related scenarios, existing enablers and required enablers.

Next, the specified requirements were carefully analyzed and prioritized. For ranking purposes, we used the same criteria as when ranking the scenarios: i) the maximum business impact, and ii) the fast and low-risk realization criteria. As a conclusion, the IOP requirements of high priority (16 quality requirements and 12 functional/non-functional requirements) were used as architectural drivers that guide the definition of the IOP principles to be followed while architecting the IOP. Evaluation criteria were also defined for IOP instances, based on these two sets of requirements.

IOP Principles

Prior to defining the IOP principles, several workshops were carried out in order to get a consensus on the focus of the IOP. As a conclusion of these discussions, the partners involved in the smart space development agreed on the main objective of IOP: to provide an infrastructure that assists users with added-value interoperable information about objects existing in the environment of the user. Therefore, the IOP reference model is to be defined at a high abstraction level and be simple and agnostic with respect to i) the use-cases, ii) information and iii) the physical environment (including legacy equipments). These were expected to enable the level of extensibility required to support multi-domain and cross-domain applications. Thus, IOP combines the information interoperability solution with existing service and physical level interoperability solutions. The interoperability is based on the common ontology models of information that may originate from heterogeneous legacy and embedded devices spread in the environment or may be produced by the aggregators of IOP information. IOP may be active and trigger external entities to react to relevant and selected environmental changes. Such

features should be met at a high quality level. Among the "qualities" considered to be relevant to assess the value of the IOP, the following items should be primarily addressed:

- business generated by the IOP based smart environments,
- the easiness to develop applications on top of IOP,
- models that describe interaction among users, their environment and their history
- the security and dependability of IOP based applications
- IOP performance, energy efficiency and scalability.

We claim that an IOP with significantly high scores on the above properties may originate a new market for applications that can interoperate independently from their business/vendor/manufacturer origin. This can introduce a radical change to the traditional application scenario, which is based on fixed business boundaries. The expected applications may be cross-domain, may adapt to the user situation, may spontaneously start when required and have the potential for significant market penetration and socio-economic impact. In order to define the architectural style of the IOP, sixteen principles were distilled, starting from the above vision, and summarized in Table 2.

IOP Enforcement

The IOP herewith is considered to be a simple, portable and open source implementation. It is called Smart-M3[2] and it takes the principles seriously. It consists of an interoperability component hosting the shared information space, seen as a service and accessed through a semantic protocol by engines interpreting the shared information space through an ontology; the shared information store is called SIB (Semantic Information Broker), the agents are named Knowledge Processors (KPs) and the semantic protocol, i.e. the interface between the

Table 2. The architectural style of IOP

IOP principle	Definition
Shared information	The IOP manages a shared information search domain called Smart Space (SS), accessible and understood by all the authorized applications. Information is about the objects existing in the environment or about the environment itself. The information is represented in a uniform and use-case independent way. Information interoperability and semantics are based on common ontologies that model information.
Simplicity	The IOP deals with information. The IOP information level is use-case agnostic.
Service	An SS is a service, offered by a service platform and intended for the sharing of interoperable SS information. Each application may interface to one or more SSs through a Smart Space Application Protocol. Use case specific functions may be performed at the service level before joining the SS.
Agnostics	The IOP is agnostic with respect to the adopted ontology, application programming language, service platform exposing the SS, communication layer and hosting device/system.
Extensibility	The IOP does not provide a-priori defined functionalities to manipulate information, in addition to inserting and removing the information for sharing. IOP functionality may be extended with domain ontologies and with information manipulation services. If these services become commonly usable, they are called "IOP extensions".
Evolvability	The IOP should support the addition of new applications. This principle envisages that the IOP provides the means to implement software that adapts to changes in SS without changing code. For example, if relevant sensor information is added to the SS, the SSA should benefit from it without changing any part of the application.
Context	Context management is an IOP extension, according to the extensibility principle. IOP should enable the aggregation of interoperable information into a higher level of context information, for the benefit of application usability and IOP performance. As the information returned by the IOP depends on the query and available information, the ontology is to define context semantics. Context may be managed and used both at the information level and service level.
Notification	Applications may subscribe to be alerted upon a context-change.
Usability	User interaction management may become an IOP extension, according to the extensibility principle. The user interaction model and the usability of SSAs should benefit from the context-dependence principle. The ontology defines the semantics of interaction events. The interaction between the users, their environment and SSA may be managed both at the information and service level,
Security and trust	Security, privacy and trust management is an IOP extension, handled both at the service level and information level. Appropriate ontologies define whether the IOP is required to respect privacy, enforce authentication and access control policies at finer granularity than SS itself, or if the shared information integrity, confidentiality and trust need to be provided.
Business model	The development tools and engineering phases of SSAs should be consistent with the IOP business models and mapped to the value chain(s) of the smart space stakeholders.
Legacy	Legacy devices and systems access and exchange information with the SS through a simple use-case independent protocol. Such exchanged information is modeled by Domain Ontologies. Legacy devices may provide information to the SS and subscribe to information from it.
Scalability	The IOP should scale with respect to the number of the users, devices, and resources available on each device, the amount of information stored in the SS, and the number of SSs.
Performance	Performance monitoring is an IOP extension. Performance of IOP realizations and SSAs should be evaluated at the development time and be measurable at run time. The criteria for run time performance monitoring should be defined through performance metrics ontology.
Reliability Availability	The reliability and availability of every IOP instance and of SSAs should be evaluated at development time and be measurable at run time.
Productivity	SSA development tools should support easy and fast agents and the application development with software reuse.

SIB and the KPs, is called Smart Space Access Protocol (SSAP). IOP can be taken into use either through standard TCP/IP sockets or by integrating it with some middleware technologies that support service oriented architecture. Examples of these kinds of middleware technologies are OSGi, NoTA, and Web Services. OSGi combines component and service oriented architecture applicable for client-server solutions, commonly used in indoor spaces. For example, Smart-M3-OSGi integration was applied to the smart maintenance of public buildings demonstrator (Manzaroli 2010). NoTA is a novel service architecture for networked embedded systems applied to a personal space demonstrator (Luukkala 2010). IOP based on Smart-M3 and Web Services are applied to a smart city pilot, still under development.

ONTOLOGY DEVELOPMENT

Smart space applications are based on three "abilities" that make them 'smart': i) an ability to understand the situation where the application is used and by whom, ii) an ability to interpret the semantics of shared information, and iii) an ability to tolerate uncertainty at development time and at run time. In particular, the first and the third point embody the concept of context-awareness, while the second relates to information interoperability. In this section, we will focus on the semantic modeling of data to achieve information interoperability. Thereafter, we will discuss how to develop context-aware smart space applications.

Several interoperability issues are raised by the heterogeneity of devices and software which are already in place in physical environments. To reduce development and deployment costs and to maximize the reuse of existing applications, our methodology tackles those interoperability challenges at the information level via the adoption of proper semantic technologies. The primary idea is to provide smart applications with highly interoperable and shared information spaces that maintain sensed data and information on currently available resources and services. The content of shared spaces is openly understandable and largely re-usable thanks to the exploitation of lightweight semantic technologies, first of all, Resource Description Framework[3] (RDF)-based ontologies to describe simple relationships between represented entities. The data model of RDF is generic and

well suited to modeling real-world phenomena, including entities, events, interactions and semantic connections in smart environments. Whenever greater expressivity is needed, simple RDF can be supplemented with OWL[4] constructs, constantly keeping attention at avoiding an unnecessary complexity in ontology definition. OWL provides further modeling primitives to describe properties and classes: among others, the relations between the classes, cardinality, equality, richer typing of properties and the characteristics of properties (e.g. symmetry), and enumerated classes.

Given the wide spectrum of targeted smart space applications, a crucial issue in ontology development is how to develop a set of suitable ontologies based on a common data model that can be specialized to each application field. This problem was not only a modeling issue, but also had strong performance implications since the loading of an oversized set of ontologies into a SIB or having it processed by a KP would affect both the efficiency and scalability of SSA. Therefore, we adopted a three-layered approach for the ontology development:

- a *foundational ontology layer* to provide the base concepts and relations needed for a real-world description model (e.g., the concepts of an event or person);
- a *core ontology* to provide the concepts and relations common to all SSAs (e.g., the concepts of a smart device or quality of information);
- a set of *domain ontologies*, specific to each application domain, to provide the concepts and relations describing targeted scenarios (e.g., the concepts of temperature and building in a home maintenance scenario).

Each layer is built on top of the previous one; in that way, the higher level exploits and extends the lower one. The DOLCE ontology (DOLCE 2010) was selected for the foundational ontology for its high level of abstraction and conciseness, as well as the deepness of its ontological analysis, which has been carried out by experts in the field. For the core ontology, some parts of two domain ontologies, SPICE Mobile Ontology (SPICE 2010) and CONON Ontology (Gu et al. 2004) were selected. The selected parts are i) the core concepts of SPICE and ii) the concepts and properties related to the quality of data from CONON.

Concurrently with the IOP principles, the domain ontologies were specified, starting from scenario analysis results and the information produced and consumed by the actors involved in the intended scenario. This information is crucial for the understanding of the requirements of the core and domain ontologies, although the previous developed ontologies helped in making selections and formulating the main concepts and properties of these ontologies.

The application development tools, expected to seamlessly integrate the ontology within the applications, were also developed concurrently with the core ontology. Moreover, several small domain ontologies, e.g. a common ontology for sensors were defined and applied in practice, in spite of the need to be mapped to the sensor concepts of the core ontology. This example depicts the ontology evolution in practice: while the core ontology evolves slowly, new ontologies emerge all the time, so that the evolution of ontologies needs to be tolerated and handled in one way or another. One way is that device manufacturers provide a mapping that maps the ontology that they have used to the SS core ontology. This mapping is taken into account during the application development process, as illustrated in Figure 2. Another way is that all of the application developers do the mapping by themselves, or there is a service in IOP that makes the mapping at run-time. The last option requires an IOP maintainer, who has special skills in ontology mapping algorithms and their automatic execution. Naturally, the SS owner is responsible for ontology evolution policies,

while the evolution enforcing is the responsibility of the SS manager.

SMART SPACE APPLICATION DEVELOPMENT

Supporting Context-Awareness

One driving force of smart spaces is their ability to enable applications that adapt to the dynamically changing situation of the smart environment. As defined in section 2, a context defines the limit of information understanding in a smart space. Thus, the context is relevant for the agents (i.e. KPs), applications and users. As KPs interact with the SIB, they manage interoperable information. The specific agent is exploited to provide context-aware adaptation based on QoS requirements. For instance, if a SSA finds out that a required quality level is not met, it inserts data about the current quality level into the SIB, which notifies the agent responsible for quality-driven adaptation. At a higher level of abstraction, it is possible to define the user context by deriving it from the context of agents which are interacting with that user in ongoing application sessions. In this case, the term "information usage" should be interpreted at the granularity and abstraction level suitable for SS end users, e.g., user profiles and preferences. Context awareness enables filtering mechanisms that enable scoping out of the "visibility" range for those SS data that are not considered to be of interest. We call such a visibility range the KP/user scope. The scope can be defined to be the output of the filtering process performed over the SS. For example, if a KPI can understand ontology A, but not ontologies B and C, its scope within the smart space will not include the SIBs (or the parts of them) whose data is expressed according to B and C. Therefore, KPs may have different visibility on the SS due to their current context. The scope of an SSA derives from merging the scopes of its composing KPs, and might possibly coincide with the user scope.

According to the IOP principle on "Context", context is provided by an IOP extension consisting of a set of cooperating KPs, which collectively provide the appropriate functionalities. The IOP itself already supports context storage, retrieval, and distribution; context is available to any SSA by querying information from SIBs. Therefore, the context extension provides the following functionalities: i) context specification, acquisition and monitoring, including data collection from context sources and ii) context pre-processing, aggregation, and/or reasoning, including context-based filtering. Based on this IOP extension, applications are able to make context-aware adaptations. For instance, context pre-processing KPs access SIBs to collect raw data and produce new information, such as context history and higher level context, to be inserted again in the SIBs. Similarly, context-aware filtering KPs act as intermediate entities between semantic repositories and application-specific KPs by dynamically determining the scope of an SSA. Moreover, the run-time quality management provides dedicated KPs that are in charge of specific quality attributes (e.g. security, reliability, and energy efficiency). They are capable of a context-dependent monitoring, reasoning and adaptation of SSAs, based on the measured quality and available resources/services in the SS. The implementation of context-aware features via dedicated KPs has a number of advantages:

- It keeps SIB very lightweight, can be implemented in a cost effective way and is also usable for context-independent applications.
- A simple and context-agnostic SIB clearly separates the application logic from the facilities, thus increasing the interoperability and reusability.
- Simple applications can be easily prototyped by working on a very simple reference model. This provides a real advantage

in the development of early demonstrators that encourage SS developers using the IOP and promotes its widespread exploitation, e.g., via low-cost and simple SS applications.

KP Development

When a KP is developed, the following rules should be kept in mind: KPs should i) not compromise the ontology consistency, ii) not violate any of the IOP principles, iii) address a single goal (a separation of concerns) and iv) be designed to be as reusable as possible. KP development is also strongly influenced by the adoption of RDF as a resource description solution. Developing KPs at the RDF graph level is similar to programming in the assembly language: it requires highly specific skills and the productivity is low due to the level of details that needs to be considered at the programming time. Therefore, KP developers need a more effective development approach that rises the level of abstraction, hides the graph level or/ and the code level, and also enables KP development by non-programmers. Therefore, we offer three ways to develop KPs: i) *"triple-based KP implementation"*, ii) *"triple-blind KP implementation"* and iii) *"model based implementation"*. The main difference between these three approaches is the visibility level of the knowledge base and the KP code.

With *triple-based implementation*, KPs access the SS through language dependent APIs called KPIs (Knowledge Processor Interfaces) which hide the protocol to access the smart space (i.e. the SSAP) and support basic graph manipulation functions, including insert, remove, update, graph traversal queries and subscribes; a single query may be matched to a sequence of steps in the graph. KPI libraries exist for Java, ANSI-C, C# and Python. The "triple-based" approach was adopted in the development of the early proof-of-concept applications. Since the direct manipulation of RDF triples is required, this approach became less manageable while the ontology size and the application logic complexity increased.

With the ***triple-blind implementation,*** KPs access the SS through methods offered by the ontology dependent convenience libraries generated off-line by an ontology processing tool. Convenience libraries map ontology classes into language classes, hiding the RDF graph from the programmer. Built on top of the KPIs, a convenience library is required for each programming language. The "triple-blind" development approach is expected to become the preferred approach of KP programmers. However, this approach requires the availability of SSA development tools.

The ***model based approach*** supports the development of entire SSAs, each consisting of a set of KPs. This approach is suitable for end-users and those developers that do not have a deep knowledge of ontology manipulation. The model based KP development relies on a graphical tool called SmartModeller (Katasonov & Palviainen 2010), which allows modeling of the KP logic by using existing reusable building blocks stored in a KP repository. Actions, which are not available, need to be coded manually, and once tested, they can be stored in the repository for further reuse. The tool follows the metamodel that is consistent with the IOP principles and exploits its own software ontology for producing the logic part of the source code for KPs. Currently, a code generator has been implemented for Java and Python, but other languages may be supported in the future. Generated KPs can also be tested by the SmartModeller.

In all of the KP development methods, the repository of reusable KPs is considered to be the main instrument to meet the IOP productivity principle. In order to properly manage such a repository, the following incremental steps should be taken: i) the definition of a KP taxonomy, ii) the definition of a KP ontology, used not only at development time but also at run time, and iii) turning KPs into services, with the aim of making these services discoverable at run time, by matching the user context to the service ontology. In this chapter, only the first step, i.e. the definition of a KP taxonomy, is considered.

KP Taxonomy

The purpose of the KP taxonomy is to facilitate a smooth growth of SSAs and to maximize KP reuse by assisting the developer in searching for an applicable KP from the KP repository and storing new ones therein. Different classifications of KPs are possible, based on the adopted criteria. In the following, we will present two classifications, based on (i) the reusability level of KPs and (ii) the role of KPs in the smart space.

With respect to their reusability level, the KPs are classified into the following four classes:

1. *Application specific* or *Domain specific* KPs that represent a specific domain (e.g. personal space) or application area (e.g., health monitoring applications).
2. *Adaptable* KPs that can be adapted to instantiate new domain specific KPs.
3. *Common* KPs that can be used as such or configured by parameters for multiple domains. The parameters could be set at design time or at run time. Common KPs may become integration elements between domains, used in cross-domain applications.
4. *Core* KPs that impact the IOP architecture at the service level, extending the initial version of the IOP.

A KP usually originates as an application-specific KP, later promoted through the entire KP category-chain, through a generalization process. At the time of writing, although several KPs were still in their early stage of development, they were expected to become building blocks of IOP extensions, introduced as "Common" or "Core" KPs. This is the case, for example, for all the KPs that support context-awareness, dispatch transport independent messages and manage

Figure 3. A fragment of adaptable KPs taxonomy

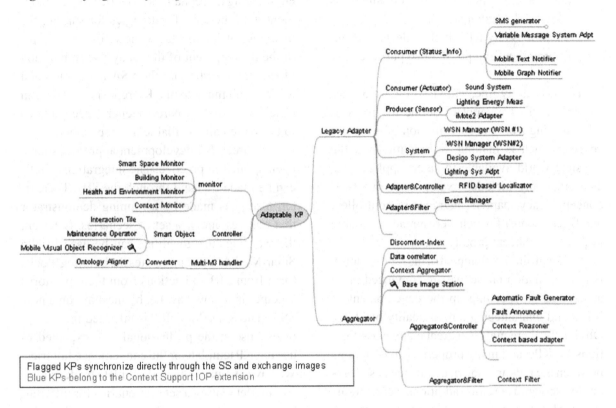

interaction devices, smart objects and semantic connections in smart environments. Figure 3 represents a fragment of an *Adaptable KP*'s taxonomy arranged as a tree. Some of the tree leaves may be *Application-Specific KPs,* which will be turned into *"Adaptable KPs"* as soon as a new KP is implemented, starting from one of them. For example, the flagged KPs in Figure 3 are the identified candidates of *Common KPs.* As the number of KPs is expected to grow very quickly, the KP taxonomy is becoming large and needs tool support.

With respect to their role in the smart space, five KP role classes were defined as follows:

- *Adapter* is any KP that interacts with the SS and entities which are external to the SS itself. Adapters are called *legacy adapters* if the external entity handled by the KP already existed before the SS, e.g., sensors,

actuators, message dispatchers and wireless sensor networks.

- *Aggregator* is any KP that interacts with one or more SS(s) and with no other entity. Aggregators enrich SS with information produced by processing information originating from the SS itself. Reasoning and prediction KPs are examples of aggregators.

- *Controller* is any KP that dynamically updates semantic connections in the SS. Any KP that is involved in the digitalization of the physical world is a potential controller KP as it may need to update semantic connections in real time.

- *Filter* is any KP that processes and filters data before storing it to the SS. It may collect data from an external system (*Filter&Adapter*) or process data which is already stored in the SS (e.g.

the context filter/reasoner, classified as *"Filter"* & *"Aggregator"*).

- *Monitor* is any KP which collects relevant information for a pre-defined purpose.

The taxonomy tree, shown in Figure 3, represents our first attempt to define the roles of KPs, starting from the core mission of the smart spaces, which is making "information" in the physical world available to smart applications. The taxonomy includes examples of proof-of-concept legacy adapters, aggregators, controllers and filters, some of which were already available as proof-of-concept prototypes.

Although the development of the KP taxonomy is in its initiation phase, we are convinced of its advantages in speeding up the development of SSAs and guaranteeing a high quality of SSAs. Obviously, there may be a great many classifications for KPs, and many properties and relations between the KPs are hidden by the tree based taxonomy shown. Therefore, additional descriptions (and tooling) are required when a KP ontology is revised from this KP taxonomy. This is considered to be a challenging and promising opportunity, as a KP ontology would be extremely useful both at design time and at run time for searching for the most suitable KP.

THE INTEGRATION AND TESTING OF SMART SPACE APPLICATIONS

When the KPs required for an SSA are identified and defined, their implementation can be deployed to the concurrent distributed teams, which proceed according to the productivity principle, searching first the repository for existing KPs to be reused. The KP may be specified by using an appropriate KP template (in a tabular form) or the SmartModeller tool (Katasonov & Palviainen 2010). The KP template was useful in the early phase when no KPs had been implemented yet. The SmartModeller assists in adopting ontology driven software

engineering that enhances model driven development with the use of ontologies for sharing the meanings of domain, tasks and software concepts in the development of the ready-to-use building blocks for speeding up the SSA integration and testing with the help of a KP repository. Thus, an efficient use of the SmartModeller expects actions to be written and available in a repository.

All three SSA development approaches have been applied in practice. The integration of KPs can be made by hand through the SIB. Thereafter, testing is made by a running demonstrator that realizes one or a set of scenarios. Later on, the working functionalities can be used by the SmartModeller that integrates the building blocks (data from SIB and actions from the repository) together in a new way, i.e. by mashing up a new SSA. The SmartModeller is intended for the use of end-users; the professionals are expected to use the KP template or the convenience libraries. We have evaluated the KP template by designing and implementing a set of scenarios for different kinds of smart spaces. The convenience libraries are still under testing. The SmartModeller has been tested in a laboratory setting by professionals and improved based on the evaluation results. So far, a set of end-users (not experienced with the IOP nor SS development tools) have begun an exercise with the SmartModeller. These evaluation results will be used towards the further improvement of the tool.

THE EVALUATION OF SMART SPACES

In smart space evaluation, the ASSDE approach focuses both on the instantiated IOP and the developed SSAs. As the SSA is intended to be used in a smart environment, it cannot be evaluated without the IOP. Thus, the evaluation is performed as a combined effort of the IOP developers and application developers. As IOP is already working and the applications are made by end-users, the

Table 3. Mandatory criteria for functional IOP evaluation

Principle	Criteria
Shared information	IOP provides the functionality required for information interoperability and service interoperability
Simplicity	The service interoperability level provides constructs for handling the building blocks of the information interoperability level
Agnostics	IOP is agnostic to used software technologies including ontologies, programming languages service technologies, and legacy.
Extensibility	Space is extensible; information is extensible and knowledge interpretations are extensible. IOP supports run-time information mash-up. A qualitative evaluation method is used for extensibility evaluation.
Notification	A set of detection and notification mechanisms are provided for context sensing, activating specific functionality and alarming for upcoming events, i.e. the reactive and proactive actions activated by changes, data or events should be possible.
Security and Trust	IOP produces information with relevant indicators of its source and the quality of its source.
Evolvability	IOP provides an evolvable information sharing environment, i.e. devices and services can be changed without having an effect on applications.
Context	IOP provides a mechanism for searching and adapting information which is relevant for the requestor's purposes, if the information exists in SS and is available for the requestor.

evaluation and testing is the duty of the application developers. However, the testing is to be made as easy as possible if not automatic.

The evaluation criteria for IOP have been derived from the IOP requirements. These criteria are classified into two categories; i) criteria for functional evaluation; and ii) criteria for design time and run-time quality evaluation. The mandatory functional criteria are listed in Table 3. Optional functional criteria concern the IOP extensions, which are not required in every IOP instance.

The quality criteria, defined in Table 4, concentrates on the capabilities that should be covered by designs and implementations and should be evaluated at development time and/or run time. In smart spaces, these quality criteria are taken into account in the designs of the interoperability platform and the applications which are developed on top of it. At design time, qualities can be evaluated through simulation or by using the quality attribute specific prediction methods as described in (Ovaska et al. 2010). Simulation and prediction are used only for some parts of smart spaces, and not for evaluating the whole smart space, since, due to the dynamics of an SS, it is not possible to simulate all of the possible states. Thus, the quality evaluation has two parts: i) Simulation and prediction methods are applied to a specific purpose and part of IOP, e.g. the performance of SIB deployment, and ii) run-time quality monitoring and visualization is used to evaluate the fulfillment of the quality criteria at run-time. As security, performance and dependability are execution qualities, they are evaluated from a running smart space. The metrics to be used during the development time and at the execution time are different, and therefore, various measuring techniques are required. The criteria for execution time evaluation are defined by a set of ontologies, each of which focuses on one specific quality attribute. So far, we have defined a security metrics ontology. The development of reliability and performance metrics ontologies are under work. All of these require extensive experimentation and validation before leveraging them among the SSA developers.

Although a systematic evaluation of the defined quality characteristics is still under development, the following concurrent development activities are ongoing: First, a design time evaluation

Table 4. Mandatory and optional criteria for IOP quality evaluation

Quality	Mandatory criteria	Optional criteria
Security	The identity of users and devices has to be authenticated. There are various authentication levels to be supported.	The separation of personal information from other information is to be supported.
	Access to SS is controlled through appropriate countermeasures for users/devices/services. No access without authentication is provided.	The actions of users and devices are to be accounted and available for non-repudiability purposes.
	Unauthorized access to smart spaces is prevented.	The identification and ignoring of harmful content are to be supported.
	Information integrity is to be proved during transmissions between information sources and sinks.	The security auditing mechanism of IOP supports various security levels.
Performance and Dependability	Records on available resources are to be kept. SS should be able to continue its operation without losses of resources/failures produced by disasters.	Real-time notification and information delivery.
	Scalable: the number of resources, information providers and consumers should scale up to the numbers that are compatible with application and deployment scenarios.	Reliable information delivery.
	The autonomic adaptation of a smart space. Various types of adaptation are to be supported; resources, services, information, the quality of information/services/resources.	

method is developed in order to identify the bottlenecks of smart spaces and to guarantee that the IOP is scalable for a diversity of spaces; second, intelligent monitoring and reasoning mechanisms are developed for querying and interpreting measured quality attributes at run time. These have both passed the early verification and validation phase in a laboratory setting and are now under feasibility testing by a set of cross-domain scenarios selected for the next evaluation step.

PHASE III: SMART SPACE OPERATION AND EVOLUTION

Challenges and Issues

Although the smart spaces, developed for various domains, are still in their initiation phases, we can identify some challenges and issues that have arisen or will arise when smart spaces are in operation for a longer period of time. We categorize these things into two classes:

- Issues on how to gain an understanding about the operation of the space: i) the dynamic nature of a smart space, i.e. what is changing and how often, ii) how well the smart space is working, and iii) how the users experience the smart space.
- Challenges that arise from i) the variety of the domains that the space is crossing, and ii) the various timeframes of evolving domains, ontologies and technologies used in the smart space.

In order to tackle these issues and challenges, a set of supporting facilities are to be provided. First, the dynamisms of the space shall be illustrated to its stakeholders from different viewpoints. The space owner is mostly interested in how the space users experience the space. A service/information provider is interested in how well the space is working and how many potential users are visiting the space. Maintenance and smart space developers would like to see how the space behaves under normal and stress operations. Thus, all of these issues should be tackled by the facilities that help the stakeholders gain the maximum benefit of the space.

The main challenge of a cross-domain interoperability platform is how to solve the problems which are encountered due to changes that will happen in spatial and timing spaces. Due to this, the smart space is only 'smart' if it is able to handle these changes in a way that makes the smart space attractive for its application providers and end-users.

Solutions and Recommendations

In order to improve the understanding of the stakeholders, i.e. application/information providers, smart space providers, maintenance providers and the owners, we have developed and tested a set of facilities, implemented as KPs and a tool that is connected to the smart space for monitoring data, events, quality, structure and the behavior of the smart space according to the interests of the respective stakeholders. The tool is able to record and visualize what is happening in a space and how perfectly it works. However, it doesn't record how individual space users behave, what their interests are, and how they experience the smart space. Although we don't expect these kinds of special KPs to bring any technical problems, there is a privacy issue that has to be considered: the recording of habits, desires and experienced quality has to be made anonymously. So far, demonstrators are used for validating the capabilities of a smart space. However, field tests will also be carried out when the cross-domain pilots are refined and ready for the use of real end-users.

Ontology driven software engineering that enhances the model driven engineering is one step forward in seeking a comprehensive solution for managing the evolution of cross-domain architectures, due to the facts that i) abstraction helps the understanding and sharing of knowledge among developer teams; ii) aggregation by a means of shared information makes it easy to develop partial solutions and integrate them via a smart space; and

iii) the inherent dynamism of smart spaces makes it possible to tolerate changes that happen all the time in the spatial and timing dimensions. The stack of the defined ontologies (i.e. foundational, core, domain, application) helps in the separation of concerns. Moreover, the separation of concerns is also made while retrieving a view of the core ontology for the specific purpose of an application under development. In this case, the separation of concerns is supported by the SmartModeller tool. Aggregation is understood to be an activity that retrieves information from a smart space, enhances it and provides the results for the use of the smart space entities. A set of mechanisms have been defined and implemented for handling the dynamism of smart spaces; the adaptable KPs developed for monitoring, reasoning and adapting quality, context and behavior of a smart space are assets that facilitate the managing of the changes in the spatial and timing spaces.

As a conclusion, although many of the supporting software services are still under development and need to be validated in field tests, most of the challenges and issues related to the operation and maintenance of smart spaces have already been identified or/and partly solved. However, it still remains open how to collect feedback from smart space end-users and how to communicate it back to the smart space developers and owners.

FUTURE RESEARCH DIRECTIONS

The development of smart spaces has, at least, two main trends: the focus of smart space development is on i) combining the physical, digital and user contexts in order to provide enriched experiences for the smart space users; or/and ii) constructing smart spaces that are able to self-monitor, self-reason, self-configure, and self-organize their capabilities and resources based on trade-offs analysis made at run-time. The 'context-awareness' trend aims at an increased added value of end user applications. The 'autonomic smart spaces' trend aims at a higher added value for all stakeholders with decreased (development and) operation costs. The origins and terminology of these trends are different and, therefore, their fusion is a complex task to be made in order to achieve viable solutions for smart spaces and their applications.

Due to the dynamic nature of smart spaces, it is crucial that the development methodology supports the attaining of this dynamism at design time and run time. This dynamism needs to be supported by:

- Agile methods that have proved to embody an ability to support dynamic work allocation among development teams and still provide results of high quality.
- Ontology and model driven software engineering methodology that helps in managing design knowledge on different abstraction levels, the separation of concerns, and binding times. These three properties, i.e. abstraction, separation and binding, are the core elements of dynamic systems.
- Evolution support that requires new lightweight solutions for ontology mapping, ontology retrieval, model transformation and reasoning, and learning algorithms for adding intelligence into smart space applications.

Therefore, the following research items require an extensive attention within the smart space communities:

- Specifying a minimal standard context ontology that covers all the dimensions of context and is applicable to all the types of smart spaces.
- Encouraging the fusion of ontology orientation and model driven engineering by developing tool environments for the different stakeholders, i.e. owners, service providers/consumers, developers, opera-

tion staff, and (end-user) application developers. These tools shall tolerate the evolution of smart spaces and software/service engineering technologies.

- Providing viable techniques/methods for collecting end-user experiences, analyzing the collected information and representing the analysis results in a convenient form for all of the stakeholders in order to get their future improvements incorporated into the smart space evolution cycle.

CONCLUSION

The ASSDE approach exploits ontology orientation for realizing interoperability and context-awareness in smart space application development and evolution. The approach follows a set of principles defined for the development of the interoperability platform and the applications executed on top of it. The key drivers of the approach are: i) interoperability provided on the information level; ii) shared information represented in a uniform and application independent way; iii) a flexible platform that can be used with any programming language, service platform and ontology; iv) a platform that can be enhanced with new ontology and required functionality; and v) a platform that provides adaptive services and supports context-aware applications. Besides these technical drivers, there are also non-technical ones; the smart space application engineering should be consistent with the IOP business models and it should be mapped to the value chain(s) of the smart space stakeholders. This is to ensure that the platform provides support for all of the stakeholders involved in the smart space development. Moreover, legacy devices and systems should be able to exchange information through smart spaces by using domain ontologies. This guarantees that the legacy can be exploited in the initiation and evolution of smart spaces. In practice, this feature was tested several times when scenarios of the personal space, indoor space and smart city were implemented in order to test the idea behind the approach and the technical solutions developed, i.e. the ontologies, platform and development tools.

REFERENCES

C4ISR Interoperability Working Group. (1998). *Levels of Information Systems interoperability (LISI)*. Technical report, US Department of Defence, Washington, DC.

Achilleos, A., Yang, K., & Georgalas, N. (2010). Context modelling and a context-aware framework for pervasive service creation: A model-driven approach. *Pervasive and Mobile Computing, 6*, 281–296. doi:10.1016/j.pmcj.2009.07.014

Berners-Lee, T., Hendler, J., & Lassila, O. (2001). The Semantic Web. *Scientific American, 284*(5), 34–43. doi:10.1038/scientificamerican0501-34

Bettini, C., Brdiczka, O., Henricksen, K., Indulska, J., Niclas, D., Ranganathan, A., & Riboni, D. (2010). A survey of context modelling and reasoning techniques. *Pervasive and Mobile Computing, 6*, 161–180. doi:10.1016/j.pmcj.2009.06.002

Buschmann, F., Meunier, R., Rohnert, H., Sommerlad, P., & Stal, M. (1996). *Pattern-oriented software architecture: A system of patterns*. West Sussex, UK: John Wiley & Sons Ltd.

Chen, H., Finin, T., & Joshi, A. (2005). *The SOUPA ontology for pervasive computing. Whitestein Series in Software Agent Technologies*. Springer.

Chen, H., Finin, T., Joshi, A., Kagal, L., Perich, F., & Chakraborty, D. (2004). Intelligent agents meet the Semantic Web in smart spaces. *IEEE Internet Computing, 8*(6), 69–79. doi:10.1109/MIC.2004.66

Dey, A. K., & Abowd, G. D. (1999). *Towards a better understanding of context and context-awareness*. (Technical Report GIT-GVU-99-22), Georgia Institute of Technology, College of Computing.

DOLCE. (2010). *Laboratory for applied ontology*. Retrieved March 8, 2010, from http://www.loa-cnr.it/

Edgington, T., Choi, B., Henson, K., Raghu, T., & Vinze, A. (2004). Adopting ontology to facilitate knowledge sharing. *Communications of the ACM, 47*(11), 85–90. doi:10.1145/1029496.1029499

Franchi, A., Di Stefano, L., & Salmon Cinotti, T. (2010). *Mobile visual search using smart-M3*. In IEEE Symposium on Computers and Communications, (pp. 1065-1070).

Gu, T., Wang, X. H., Pung, H. K., & Zhang, D. Q. (2004). *An ontology-based context model in intelligent environments*. In Communication Networks and Distributed Systems Modeling and Simulation Conference, San Diego, CA, USA.

Guédria, W., Naudet, Y., & Chen, D. (2008). Interoperability maturity models – Survey and comparison. In R. Meersman, Z. Tari, & P. Herrero (Eds.), *OTM 2008 Workshop, LNCS 5333*, (pp. 273-282), Berlin / Heidelberg, Germany Springer-Verlag.

Hadim, S., & Mohamed, N. (2006). *Middleware for wireless sensor networks: A survey*. In the 1st International Conference on Communication System Software and Middleware, (pp. 1-7).

Issarny, V., Caporuscio, M., & Georgantas, N. (2007). *A perspective on the future of middleware-based software engineering*. In Future of Software Engineering, (pp. 244-258).

Kantorovitch, J., & Niemelä, E. (2008). Service description ontologies. In Khosrow-Pour, M. (Ed.), *Encyclopedia of Information Science and Technology* (2nd ed., *Vol. VII*, pp. 3445–3451). Hershey, PA: Information Science Reference. doi:10.4018/978-1-60566-026-4.ch547

Kapitsaki, G., Prezerakos, G., Tselikas, N., & Venieris, I. (2009). Context-aware service engineering: A survey. *Journal of Systems and Software, 82*, 1885–1297. doi:10.1016/j.jss.2009.02.026

Kassab, M., Ormandjieva, O., & Daneva, M. (2009). *An ontology based approach to non-functional requirements conceptualization*. In the 4th International Conference on Software Engineering Advances, (pp. 299- 307), IEEE Computer Science.

Katasonov, A., & Palviainen, M. (2010). *Towards ontology-driven development of applications for smart environments*. In International Workshop on the Web of Things, IEEE Intl. Conf. on Pervasive Computing and Communications, (pp. 696-701).

Lassila, O. (2007). *Programming Semantic Web applications: A synthesis of knowledge representation and semi-structured data*. PhD thesis, Helsinki University of Technology, November, 2007.

Lassila, O. (2008). *Semantic Web programming using PIGLET – Programmer's guide to the PIGLET Semantic Web toolkit*. Nokia Research Center 2008.

Luukkala, V., Binnema, D.-J., Börzsei, M., Corongiu, A., & Hyttinen, P. (2010). *Experiences in implementing a cross-domain use case by combining semantic and service level platforms*. In IEEE Symposium on Computers and Communications, (pp. 1071-1076).

Manzaroli, D., Roffia, L., Salmon Cinotti, T., Azzoni, P., Ovaska, E., Nannini, C., & Matarozzi, S. (2010). *Smart-M3 and OSGi: The interoperability platform*. In IEEE Symposium on Computers and Communications, (pp. 1053-1058).

Meier, R., Harrington, A., Beckmann, K., & Cahill, V. (2009). A framework for incremental construction of real global smart space applications. *Pervasive and Mobile Computing, 5*, 350–368. doi:10.1016/j.pmcj.2008.11.001

Ovaska, E., Evesti, A., Henttonen, K., Palviainen, M., & Aho, P. (2010). Knowledge based quality-driven architecture design and evaluation. *Information and Software Technology, 52*(6), 577–601. doi:10.1016/j.infsof.2009.11.008

Pantsar-Syväniemi, S., Simula, K., & Ovaska, E. (2010). *Context-awareness in smart spaces*. In IEEE Symposium on Computers and Communications, (pp. 1023-1028).

Peristeras, V., & Tarabanis, K. (2006). The connection, communication, consolidation, collaboration interoperability framework (C4IF) for Information Systems interoperability. *IBIS – Interoperability in Business Information Systems, 1*(1), 61-72.

Preuveneers, D., & Berbers, Y. (2008). Internet of things: A context-awareness perspective. In Yan, L. (Eds.), *The Internet of things: From RFID to the next generation pervasive networked systems* (pp. 287–307). CRC Press. doi:10.1201/9781420052824.ch13

Scrum. (2009). *What is Scrum?* Retrieved March 8, 2010, from http://www.scrumalliance.org/learn_about_scrum

Sofia.(2010). *Smart objects for intelligent applications*. Retrieved March 8, 2010, from http://www.sofia-project.eu/

Soylu, A., De Causmaecker, P., & Desmet, P. (2009). Context and adaptivity in pervasive computing environments: Links with software engineering and ontological engineering. *Journal of Software, 4*(9), 992–1013. doi:10.4304/jsw.4.9.992-1013

SPICE. (2010). *Spice mobile ontology*. Retrieved March 8, 2010, from http://ontology.ist-spice.org/index.html

Tolk, A., Diallo, S. Y., Turnitsa, C. D., & Winters, L. S. (2006). Composable M&S Web services for netcentric applications. *Journal for Defense Modeling and Simulation, 3*(1), 27–44. doi:10.1177/875647930600300104

Tolk, A., & Muguira, J. A. (2003). The levels of conceptual interoperability model. In *Proceedings of the Simulation Interoperability Workshop*, (p. 10).

Tolk, A., Turnitsa, C., & Diallo, S. (2008). Implied ontological representation within the levels of conceptual interoperability model. [IOP Press.]. *Intelligent Decision Technologies, 2*, 3–19.

Toninelli, A., Pantsar-Syväniemi, S., Bellavista, P., & Ovaska, E. (2009). *Supporting context awareness in smart environments: A scalable approach to information interoperability*. In International Workshop on Middleware for Pervasive Mobile and Embedded Computing, Article No: 5, ACM, IFIP, USENIX.

Wang, X., Dong, J. S., Chin, C., Hettiarachchi, R. S., & Dhang, Z. (2004). Semantic space: An infrastructure for smart spaces. *IEEE Pervasive Computing / IEEE Computer Society [and] IEEE Communications Society, 3*(3), 32–39. doi:10.1109/MPRV.2004.1321026

Weiser, M. (1993). Some computer science issues in ubiquitous computing. *Communications of the ACM, 36*(7), 75–85. doi:10.1145/159544.159617

Zhou, J. (2005). *Knowledge dichotomy and semantic knowledge management*. In 1st IFIP WG 12.5 Working Conference on Industrial Applications of Semantic Web, Jyväskylä, Finland.

KEY TERMS AND DEFINITIONS

Knowledge Processor (KP): An agent that processes information and inserts/removes and/or consumes content from SIB, according to ontology.

Knowledge Processor Interface (KPI): A set of functionality in smart objects that enables the access and use of information semantics in applications. KPI consists of SSAP, definitions of information semantics and optional functions related to information security, reliability, etc.

Semantic Information Broker (SIB): An information world entity for storing, sharing and governing the information of one smart space as RDF triples.

Smart Environment: An entity of the physical world that is dynamically scalable and extensible to meet new use cases by applying a shared and evolving understanding of information. At least one smart space is associated to a smart environment with two or more knowledge processors.

Smart Object: A device applicable to interact within a smart environment.

Smart Space: A named search extent of shared information. A logical entity composed by a set of SIBs.

Smart Space Access Protocol (SSAP): A service level protocol used by KPs when accessing SIB.

Smart Space Application (SSA): A set of KPs that uses one or more smart spaces as resources to perform a desired functionality visible to an end-user as an enhanced application.

ENDNOTES

[1] Previously affiliated to and still collaborating with Alma Mater Studiorum, Univesità di Bologna, Italy
[2] http://sourceforge.net/projects/smart-m3/
[3] http://www.w3.org/TR/rdf-concepts
[4] http://www.w3.org/standards/techs/owl#w3c_all

Chapter 3
Principle for Engineering Service Based System by Swirl Computing

Shigeki Sugiyama
University of Gifu, Japan

Lowry Burgess
Carnegie Mellon University, USA

ABSTRACT

When we look at the living creatures in the world, most of them have the communication methods in order to recognize within same species each other for protection, getting food, being multiplied, or seeing the world, et cetera. And they mostly use the five senses as the basic mechanisms for the communication among them in a quite natural way with a seamless manner without any difficult manipulation. These five senses in those behaviour look like being swirled around their bodies.

Today, we have "an external communication method among us beyond the five senses" by using Information Technologies (IT); TV, telephone, cellular phone, laptop computer, the Internetworking, software (SaaS, VPN, SAP, SOA, Cloud, etc.), etc. But they are costly and need cutting edged high skills and technologies for the usages. And what is more, they are not yet intellectually and technologically matured for the usages compared with the five senses.

Under these circumstances, if we have a system "swirled" around us (Burgess 2008) like the five senses in a relation to networking for communications with other entities (a system, a facility, knowledge, data, etc.) which will be neither necessary to be conscious about the related facilities nor the high level of the technological manipulations, this environment will give us convenient services and also will give us important knowledge of extended entities in many aspects.

So in this chapter, the main theme is to discuss and to introduce "The Principle for Engineering Based Service System by Swirl Computing" in Service Science.

DOI: 10.4018/978-1-60960-735-7.ch003

INTRODUCTION

Pre-historically speaking, all that we were doing was to eat fruits, nuts, insects, animals, buds, and leaves that were naturally raised on the earth. That is to say, these eras were nothing to do with a creative knowledge for mankind (vague in creativity). Historically speaking, we started the civilization by the engineering (tooling) for Hunting and Cultivation within a movable area, and then by the engineering of Farming in a living area (vicinity of mankind), and then by the engineering of Motorization, and then now by the engineering of the Information Technology with a networking and communication at a place around us (not necessarily to move). And then, we will be facing to an engineering of "Knowledge of Science with extended entities", which is mostly concerned with knowledge (brain itself).

So by considering the history of the engineering, we may say that the way of engineering development in the history of the civilization is coming from "vague" to "environment around a movable area", and then to "vicinity of mankind", and then onto "mankind itself", and then into "the center of mankind; knowledge (brain)".

If we look at this phenomenon from another aspect -physically speaking-, the direction of the civilization is from the outside world into the center of mankind. On the other hand -relatively speaking, a mental matter involved in mankind is expanding from "Ourselves" to "Every Dimension in space of the world (Expansion of Ourselves)".

In chronological order, we may have the following schematic expression about the trend of the civilization contents in terms of engineering.

- Hunting and Collecting (**Collection with Simple Tools; Awakening of Culture**)
- Farming (**Creation with Technology**)
- Motorizing (**Creation of Artificial Power**)
- Informing (**Creation by Science**)
- Knowing (**Pure Creation of Knowledge by Science**)

During the eras of "Hunting and Collecting" and "Farming", an individual had little power to do anything. And during the era of "Motorizing", an individual was able to have relatively big power for "Hunting and Collecting", "Farming", Production, and Transportation by using an artificial power. Now, as we are at the age of "Informing", an individual is not individual any more if one uses Information Technologies for relations and connections with others. Because the principal matter of "Informing" is intangible and the entity itself of an intangible matter is invisible. So it might be easier to handle it if we will have a transparent facility by an ideal environment of IT around us. So in this framework, we may be able to be individually independent on our own thoughts and activities in societies. Under this situation, the way of life may depend on individual "thoughts and activities". What is more, we are likely to think that we can do anything what we want to without interruption by or about others. On this stage, the most important thing to get is "free and freely accessible atmosphere into any environment surrounded us".

But this environment is not always easy to get even though we have some methods and the facilities to access into surroundings in the world. Because the present technologies and the theories cannot assist us in an ideal manner (technologically less maturity). And also necessary facilities of infrastructure are quite expensive and need time for constructions. So it will not allow us easily to accomplish these environments at the time when we want to. In another words, if it is possible, it will offer an ultimate service for us.

Here, it will mention about definitions of "Service" and "Service Science" in engineering.

- "Service" is to benefit another or others tangibly or intangibly by an activity or an action."
- "Service Science" is a method or a thought for Service that is created or invented newly by means of Science.

BACKGROUND

Generally speaking, we have now a system for service in order to get a request done almost in all categories in various aspects like book, food, entertainment, sport, house, opportunity hunting, travel, music, culture, study, education, training, management, control, production, marketing, transformation, etc. by means of IT facilities, a networking, and a communication. As we know well, we are able to appreciate those services especially through the Internetworking and other IT facilities. In the case of "book" matter, book purchase, reading, searching, writing, publishing, and book data storage can be done through the Internetworking quite easily, for example. And the same kind of services can be seen almost all in other fields. And this direction for service will be going further on in the future.

The mechanisms that are used for these services are mainly realized by computer and the Internetworking with data storage, data retrieval, and processing techniques. So the numbers of the key technological mechanisms that are used are not many, which mean that the complexity of these services is not deep and wide in terms of the technologies and the methods. Of course, if we think about a security of these services, the issues are a bit different and complicated.

If these services are described by an abstract expression, these matters will be provided by simply "Demand or Search" through "the Processes" as shown in Table 1 (Sugiyama 2008).

Systematically speaking, this kind of system can be made by using a tree structure of system that will be able to offer a demanded (requiring) matter by step-by-step method. The reason for this is that an active new change in system is not considered in this situation. That is to say, a new factor in the system does not come up for an available use. If it does, another new system should be made for this purpose. And so we can say that these processes are rigid and static, so that only the matters related with the processes are retrieving data and reuse them for getting output.

Here we will see the service systems more in detail that have been explained in the above by giving some examples. And also some subjects that are existed in the systems will be mentioned briefly too.

1. **Business Plan Service System:** This Service offers a business plan for users as it is desired in a required field, and this Service may give a necessary advice at each process if it is necessary. But the contents of business plans cannot be changed instantly and easily.

2. **Market Research Service System with GPS:** This Service offers a market research in a target category and for a targeted purpose by using GPS, for example. But the basic analysis and synthesis methods cannot be changed easily.

3. **Engineering Training/Education Service System:** This Service offers training and education in terms of business category as they are required by using the Internetworking or database. But those method and contents cannot be improved quickly at the moment when they are required (Larson 2009).

4. **Sales Service System:** This Service offers DM by DTP and Email Service as it is wanted

Table 1.

Demand and Search	→	Processing; Database, Matter, etc.	→	Output; Thing, Information, Data, etc.
(Requiring)		(Search, Retrieve, Production, etc.)		(Thing, Goods, Plan, Management, Data, Information, Knowledge, etc.)

with a quick service by using the Data. But the method cannot be changed quickly and instantly.

5. **Necessary Information Retrieval Service System:** This Service offers necessary information by customer's involvement of making the database, for example. But if some kind of new processes are required, the system structure must be improved as well, which is not easy matter to do.

6. **Strategy Planning Service System**: This Service offers a support for making a business strategy plan by using database. But if the strategy is needed to change, it might be suggested to make a new system according to a new strategy. Because it should be studied from the first stage about the strategy and then it needs to reconstruct the whole system again. And so it needs lots of time and money again.

7. **Publishing and Information Service System:** This Service offers any service in Publishing and Information by IT. But if other functions are required to add into the system, it cannot be done easily and instantly.

8. **Production Service by CAD/CAM system:** This Service offers a total production support from design to production. But it is very difficult to change the system even though it is quickly required because the system should be made from the first stage in the system flow with new processing methods and data (Sugiyama et al. 2007).

9. **E-Learning Service System:** This Service offers a learning opportunity for any one at any place and any time (Larson 2009). But it needs time to change the system when it is required.

10. **Home Security Service System:** This Service offers a present situation of Home by sight, which mean whether or not "TV is on ?", "Air condition is off ?", "Nobody there ?", or "is there anybody ?", etc. But if the

Figure 1. Conventional System Image

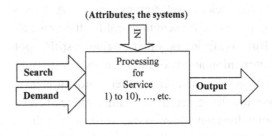

system is required to add another function, it must need time and more money. etc.

As shown in the above, we have lots of service systems by using this basic "Demand and Search" method. The above Service Systems will be also described schematically as shown in Figure 1.

At this point, we have to make clear that these Service Systems will offer necessary processes and outputs with step-by-step manipulations when they are required under the conditions that "Computer Systems with IT and Communication Technologies" are available in an ideal manner.

MAIN FOCUS OF THE CHAPTER

Principle for Engineering Service Based System by Swirl Computing

We firstly think about the development of Information and Communication Technology (ICT). After the internetworking and the related technologies have been come up to our daily life originally from the initiators' institutes in US, and then from major universities in US, and then from major universities in the world, and then from the major institutes of related companies in the world, we are able to enjoy communicating with anyone and anything at any time in the world once when we have the necessary systems and the facilities. And after having passed these times, they have been able to be applied to various categories of fields, like entertainment, selling goods, education, medicine, welfare, stock market, commercial, etc. And then we come to the present moment for the usages.

But it is afraid to say that we cannot still forget about manipulations of the necessary matters in ICT at any instance. In another words, it is now possible to have a ubiquitous atmosphere of communications anywhere in the world only if there are the necessary facilities equipped with around vicinity of us and only if we have the skills of the necessary manipulations of the facilities that are equipped with.

In order to get rid of the above difficulties for usages, here will study a principle of "Swirl Computing".

The Swirl Computing consists of three categories, the first is "Principle", and the second is "Swirl Oriented Architecture: (SOA)", and then the third is "System Structure by Mathematical Expression".

Principle

This section discusses on two environments which are important for establishing the Swirl Computing.

As it is mentioned in the above section, it is possible for us to have a complete ubiquitous atmosphere if we have time and money with ICT skills and manipulations. But it is usually hard to accomplish it for each requirement at the instance that is required when we are apart from Laptop at an office or in a laboratory, for example. What is more, the most difficult part to accomplish is to make a desired computer system change to the required environment which will suit with for establishing our purpose at every moment when it is required (Lifton et al. 2002). Because we have to use different data, strategy, plan, and scheme, etc. when we have a problem or a different requirement (target) at each time or at each place, for example. So it is very important to have the following environment.

A. Flexible Computer Environment (FCE): Flexible Computer Environment (FCE) has a mechanism that a system, a plan, a scheme, a strategy, a function, data, an analysis, a method, etc. can be transformed into the desired forms by using the idea of "Grid".

And also, it can be said that we can do one more thing if we have our hands free or if we have an additional hand. The same thing can be said when we think about the Swirl Computing (Burgess 2008). That is to say, we can do one more thing if a manipulation of the computer system environment by the third hand (just by thinking about, for example) will be able to be done. So it is very important to have the following environment.

B. Swirl Manipulation Environment (SME): Swirl Manipulation Environment (SME) has a mechanism that "thinking" can be transformed into a kind of activity (of a behavior) for manipulations of system. So SME will behave just like the third hand.

Here talks about the principle by considering the above two important environments.

Principle of Swirl Computing

"The principle of the Swirl Computing" is "a mechanism that is able to communicate with another at any place at any time within Flexible Computer Environment (FCE) and Swirl Manipulation Environment (SME) without burden of the usages, which will seamlessly and naturally offer a required service".

By using this principle, for example, we can get necessary information and connection with people at a meeting without difficulty and time-consuming manipulation of ICT facilities. And also, wherever we go with kids, for example, we would be able to get important information of the atmosphere at the place where we want to go. At home, for example, we would be able to get a

Figure 2. Principle of the Swirl Computing

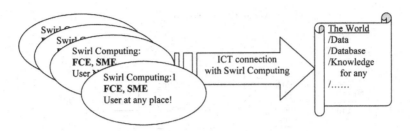

necessary assistance through the Swirl Computing even for people who are not experts in ICT technologies and facilities.

So, this idea is just like "a complete transparency" through an environment in order to get communicated with anyone or with anything or with any matter that is tangible or intangible which will be far away or near to or at a virtual space. This should be done without bothering any facilities near or on a body or without difficult manipulations of those. And these things should be done smoothly and naturally without any knowledge.

This way of doing with these methods will be simply illustrated schematically in Figure 2.

Swirl Oriented Architecture: SOA

This section studies and introduces "Swirl Oriented Architecture".

In the Swirl Computing, just like the five senses of the living creatures in this world, it is important to be able to communicate with others (including man-made entities) without any difficult activities on computer. For doing this, firstly, detection or a sensing of human what he/she wants to do is very important matter ("Swirl Manipulation En-

vironment: SME"), and then extracting requests of human through a sensor is also very important matter. And then, through the extracted data by being desired, the Swirl Computing will do computing for the service by giving the information, or by opening the communication channel, or by controlling the facility of system in the laboratory, or by watching, or by managing, etc. These activities will be done by choosing the most appropriate and suited system from the knowledge of database that is stored in the system (Sugiyama 2008). And when it is necessary to change the environment of the present system that is chosen for usage, "Flexible Computer Environment: FCE" will be used for making the necessary changes.

So the Swirl Oriented Architecture (SOA) will have "Flexibility" in system by adding the mechanisms (the environments of SME and FCE), which will make a system useful and applicable to any requirement.

If the Swirl Computing with Swirl Oriented Architecture (SOA) is simply described by using an abstract expression, this will be done by "SME" through "Swirl Computing with FCE" as shown in Table 2.

Table 2.

Anywhere in Search with SME	→	Take System with FCE	→	Swirl Computing	→	Output
(By thinking about)		(Take Plan, Data, etc.)		(Everything swirled)		

Figure 3. Schematic View of Swirl Oriented Architecture

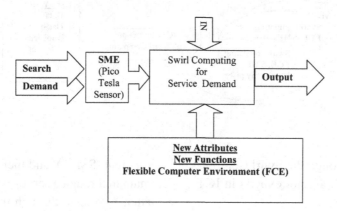

And also this service system is schematically described as shown in Figure 3.

The differences between the conventional service system and the swirl computing are the followings.

1. In the conventional systems, the systems offer necessary information within limitations in forms, methods, and networking. On the other hand, the Swirl Computing will give the simplest use of the system in the atmosphere (computer, system, etc.) as "Service" in the flexible manner.

2. In the conventional systems, information in need will be offered by the technical manipulation. On the other hand, the Swirl Computing will give the necessary information with the simplest method as "Service" with SME.

3. In the conventional systems, lots of human interaction will be necessary for getting the desired information. On the other hand, the Swirl Computing will give the necessary environment for getting a necessary and important information, etc. as "Service" with FCE.

Here will touch upon the general functions of the Swirl Computing and will show some system functions concerned with including the categories: "SERVICE", "MAKE CHANGE", "KNOWLEDGE", and "INTEGRATION". Through this stream, we may understand the processes that will be taken for getting Service.

General Function 1: "SERVICE"
  [Everything in Service Science]
    /Enter into the system from here.
  [System in Service Oriented Architecture]
    /Look into the system whether or not there is the one that just wanted.
  [Desired in First, and Proper Offering Next]
    /If there is the one that just suits to the requirement, then go and get into the system. And go to the General Function 3.
    /If there is not the one that just suits to the requirement, then go into the General Function 2.

General Function 2: "MAKE CHANGE"
  [Simple and Easy for Customer to Use]
    /Go into the system to find the most appropriate one in order to make the necessary changes of the system.
  [Required Atmosphere]

/There are some methods to make the necessary changes in order to suit the requirement.

General Function 3: "KNOWLEDGE"
[ANALYSYS and SYNTHESIS]
/Knowledge Base, AI, Statistics, SWOT, TRIZ, Transformation, etc. will be used for the necessary changes of the system that is used now.

General Function 4: "INTEGRATION"
[Swirl Computing]
/It may be said that this method of system is a kind of Cloud for accomplishing a targeted purpose. But it is not true to say that the Swirl Computing is the whole Cloud. So the Swirl Computing can be understood as "Directional Cloud", that is to say, the usages are limited within a filed for accomplishments of the purposes. And this will work under Cloud Computing.
[Cloud Computing]
/Not only for desired things done, but also there might be other usages in the Internetworking. In this sense, the Cloud Computing is the top of all hierarchically, which may consist of many kinds of Swirl Computing.

The Functions mentioned above can be performed under the idea of "Grid to Mediator" operation, which is not a direct processing method but it is a stage processing method as described below.

1. "SERVICE"; (Grid 1)
   ◦ The first stage is "Grid" in "SERVICE for MAKE CHANGE";
   ◦ The content is explained more in detail. We can require any thing as Service to the system with SME by choosing a necessary term in a related category. And we will get the most appropriate Information, or System, or Plan, or Production, or Matter, etc. (Sugiyama et al. 2007.

Sugiyama 2008). And we will see the content of it whether it is the one that is just wanted or not. If it is so, it will be used for getting the required matter. If it is not, there needs some amendments and changes for Data, Function, Scheme, Management, etc. as described in the following second stage.

2. "MAKE CHANGE"; (Grid 2)
   ◦ The second stage is "Grid" in "MAKE CHANGE for KNOWLEDGE";
   ◦ If the system that was chosen in "Service" is appropriate enough to offer the desired thing, the system is to use as it is. But if the system chosen is not appropriate enough, then the system environment should be changed as it should be. And in this way, the system will choose the necessary functions, data, and etc. in order to transform them into the appropriate forms and data for the system.

3. "KNOWLEDGE"; (Grid 3)
   ◦ The third stage is "Grid" in "KNOWLEDGE for INTEGRATION";
   ◦ At this stage, we have the necessary matters that should be transformed, so each matter is going to be transformed to an appropriate form by using the mediator of Grid. This mediator will be a function, or an analysis method, or a theory, or a thought, or just data. So at this stage, all the matters that are needed to be transformed will be changed into the desired forms for the system (Sugiyama 2009). And those transformed matters will be prepared for the integration into the system at the next stage.

4. "INTEGRATION"; (Grid 4)
   ◦ The fourth stage is "Grid" in "INTEGRATION for OUTPUT";

Figure 4. Grid for Interchange in Processes

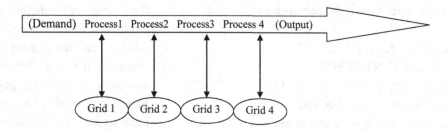

○ The fourth stage is to integrate all changes into "Swirl Computing" or is to make the system accessible to "Cloud Computing" (Sugiyama 2010).

The "Grid" is discussed further on. "Grid" is a method to change "Data", "Method", "Target", "Knowledge", etc. into new required forms of them which will suit for a newly required environment. A method to change (mediator) will be like "SWOT", "Data Analysis", "Histogram Analysis", "ABC Analysis", "Segment Analysis", "Distribution Analysis", "Ranking Analysis", "RFM Analysis", "TRIZ", "Game Theory", "Three Sigma Analysis", "Knowledge", "Transformation", "Market Research", "Management", etc.

Functionally speaking, "Grid" consists of three categories about attributes as described below.

1. Category 1; {**OLD**; Old Data, System, Plan, Function, etc.}
2. Category 2; {**TRANSFRM**; Function, Method, Technique, Analysis, Theory, etc.}
3. Category 3; {**UPDATED**; New Data, System, Plan, Function, etc.}

So in short, "Grid with Mediator" works as "a method" or "a function" or "a mechanism" or "a technique" or "an index" or "data change" or "a thought" or "theory" which are able to change a target matter to the required form through the three categories of the processes; Category 1, Category 2, and Category 3.

And these processes will be able to be done just by a simple manipulation with **SME** and **FCE**.

The above explanation about **SOA** in terms of "Grid with Mediator" will be simply shown schematically in Figure 4.

Mathematical Expression

This section studies on mathematical expressions of the Swirl Computing.

As the "demand and requirement" are considered as "Service", so the general expression of "demand and search (requirement)" is expressed by "Service". And "Service" is offered by the method of "Swirl Computing; Swirl", and so it is defined as [AISE].

So we have the following expression.

[Demand and Requirement] = [Service]
= Swirl (Demand and Requirement)
= Swirl (Demand and Requirement: [AISE])

As it has been mentioned, "the Swirl Computing" consists of three categories. The first one is "Knowledge Base" for established systems, like "CAD/CAM", "process control", "production control", "company management", "plans and schemes", "DM", "market research", "target control", etc. And the second one is "Make Change", like "data transformation", "process change in plan", "target change in market", etc. The third one is "Update Knowledge base". That is to say, [AISE] consists of three parts including itself. The first part is the static part ([SAISE]) like

"Knowledge Base or Business Plan or etc.", and the second part is the dynamic part ([DAISE]) like "Data Transformation or Knowledge Transformation, etc.", the third part is [AISE] itself.

So, we have the following equation.

$$[AISE] = [SAISE] + [DAISE] \qquad (1)$$

[SAISE] consists of [Isaise] and [Gsaise], and [DAISE] consists of [Idaise] and [Gdaise]. And those are expressed as shown below.

$$[SAISE] = [Isaise] [Gsaise] \qquad (2)$$

$$[DAISE] = [Idaise] [Gdaise] \qquad (3)$$

[Isaise] consists of [System] with [Function] and [Data]. And each content is rewritten by [Ssaise], [Fsaise], and [Dsaise]. So we have the following equations.

$$[Isaise] = [System] + [Function] + [Data] = [Ssaise] + [Fsaise] + [Dsaise] \qquad (4)$$

[Gsaise] is {the Grid of the static}. And it consists of {Change in the elements of [Fsaise] and [Dsaise]}. So we have the following equation.

$$[Gsaise] = \{Grid \ of \ the \ static; \ Changes \ in \ the \ elements \ of \ [Fsaise] \ and \ [Dsaise]\} \qquad (5)$$

[Idaise] consists of [Function], [Connection], and [Data]. And each content is rewritten by [Fdaise], [Cdaise], and [Ddaise]. So we have the following equations.

$$[Idaise] = [Function] + [Connection] + [Data] = [Fdaise] + [Cdaise] + [Ddaise] \qquad (6)$$

[Gdaise] is {the Grid of the dynamics}. And it consists of {Transformation in the contents of [Fdaise], [Cdaise], and [Ddaise]}. So we have the following equation.

$$[Gdaise] = \{Grid \ of \ the \ dynamics; \ Transformation \ in \ the \ contents \ of \ [Fsaise], \ [Cdaise], \ and \ [Ddaise]\} \qquad (7)$$

And as for [Ssaise], [Fsaise], [Dsaise], [Fdaise], [Cdaise], and [Ddaise], each one may have each own functions and elements. And when a [System] is defined, all the [Ssaise], [Fsaise], [Dsaise], [Fdaise], [Cdaise], and [Ddaise] may be decided relationally as shown below.

$$[Ssaise] = [Ssaise; \ Xss, \ Yss, \ Zss] \qquad (8)$$

$$[Fsaise] = [Fsaise; \ Xsf, \ Ysf, \ Zsf] \qquad (9)$$

$$[Dsaise] = [Dsaise; \ Xsd, \ Ysd, \ Zsd] \qquad (10)$$

$$[Fdaise] = [Fdaise; \ Xdf, \ Ydf, \ Zdf] \qquad (11)$$

$$[Cdaise] = [Cdaise; \ Xdc, \ Ydc, \ Zdc] \qquad (12)$$

$$[Ddaise] = [Ddaise; \ Xdd, \ Ydd, \ Zdd] \qquad (13)$$

By using the equations in the above, it has been shown that it is possible to express the Swirl Computing mathematically. Of course, these are the generally expressed forms, that is to say, the all elements should be dependent on each system by system in each case and that those elements should be optimized in someway when those are decided.

Swirl Sensor

There are many kinds of sensors (ex. BMI and BCI) for interfacing between human and computer in order to offer a direct communication by using Micro Intelligent sensors (Santhanam et al. 2006).

There are some ideas about to use "human" as a sensor itself for communication with others. It will be possible to realize this idea because we may have emissions of an electro-magnetic wave out of our body when we (will) move some part of our body or when we are thinking about. Those movements and thinking will be closely related with our actions by body and brain. And there should be some relations among those actions and the brain. So that -theoretically speaking-, it should be possible to understand the meanings of those actions by sensing the electro-magnetic emissions out of our body.

Now it is possible to sense an electro-magnetic emission from muscles' movement when they (will) move. And they can be used for empowering muscles' movements more, for example. For another application, it is used for a robot control in a simple way by sensing a brain's activity with a head mount electro-magnetic sensor.

In terms of a brain activity sensor, it is still hard to sense activities especially at the parts deep inside brain, which might be related with fingers' movements, for example. And also, we now have to have those sensors stuck on for covering a brain when we want to sense, which will lose our freedom in actions.

We have now Nano-Tesla (NT) electro-magnetic sensor but this will not be able to give a clear image of human electro-magnetic wave change. So we need further fine sensor, which is Pico-Tesla (PT) electro-magnetic wave sensor in order to sense all of our body from the surface to inside. In the mean time, we can say that we can put the PT electro-magnetic wave sensor on glasses or on buttons of the clothes that will detect the PT electro-magnetic wave differences about our body and brain. This kind of sensor will be positioned at important places, like glasses and hat (for sensing sides and top of brain), sleeves (for sensing hands), buttons (for sensing a heart, etc.), and trouser (for sensing legs) in order to sense key positions of human behaviours. That is to say, this kind of sensor will be used for detecting our behaviour or thinking (SME).

Through this mechanism (SME), we can access into a cellular phone in pocket or to an available access point which is able to go further into the Internetworking that is stationary or in movement of a satellite. Once this atmosphere will have been established, we can enjoy the Swirl Computing just thinking about a matter what we want to do.

FUTURE RESEARCH DIRECTIONS

It has been shown that the Swirl Computing will be able to be realized by the ideas of [Principle], [SOA], [Mathematical Expression], and [Swirl Sensor] which will give free and seamless atmosphere for communication and retrieving knowledge just like thinking about a matter, but there are still some subjects that will be waiting for being improved and solved.

So, this section will touch upon each subject for future research direction.

1. **SOA** will be realized by using various technologies of today. But SME is not yet available in a market. However, there are slightly similar ones for simple manipulation purposes like robot movement for toys, home electronic facility control, and cursor control of computer. Of course, it would be possible to realize it technologically by using fMRI, for example. But it is not the one that we want to use. Because it is too expensive to buy and is too big to carry. We need the SME that will not be even recognized by us, which means that it should be very small and light. It might be possible to make it physically by using the present technologies except the signals processing method. The difficulties are existed in using many sensors for detecting of many places of the targeted parts. So the positions of the sensors will be the issues and also the signals processing method (ex. multi-modal processing) will be the issues too. And one more important subject is concerned with costless.

2. **Mathematical Expression** has been given generally, but it should be more exact in descriptions and it needs to correspond with a real world. However, these are not the

major problem at all, because those would be decided when a real usage is on the view. The most difficult and important problem is to find expression about an accessing point system mechanisms and the environment. If the access point (person) has an established connecting point in the Internetworking, it should be all right. But if not, the access point will be a cellular phone brought by personally. In this case, the system mechanism will be clear but the environment that is to know will be very difficult to see and understand.

3. **Swirl Sensor** has a subject to study and a matter to improve in mechanism and processing. It should detect PT electro-magnetic wave change (Aichi Steel Corporation 2009). So that it might be necessary to know whether it needs to study a brand new method for detection, or it would be just a matter of amplification mechanism. And there are many parts for detection and so the PT electro-magnetic waves may have lots of noise in the environment. And also the positions for the sensor would be another subject to study. So noise exclusion and an extraction of each differentiate wave for a particular targeted point are the issues to study too.

CONCLUSION

We will be in the era which will make anything possible individually. This could happen because of the development of ICT and the Internetworking technology. But when we talk about the usability of the technologies, the methods, and the theories, those are far from easiness technologically and monetary. So through this chapter, the concept and the mechanisms of "The Engineering Service Based System by Swirl Computing" in Service Science have been discussed and studied in order to resolve some of the problems facing. And some

of the issues related with the Swirl Computing are mentioned too for further discussions and studies.

As the conclusion, the following results have been given about a principle, a method, a mechanism, and a system in terms of "the Swirl Computing".

1. The idea of "Service and Service Science" has been introduced by looking at the brand new idea of "The Swirl Computing".
2. The whole structure and mechanisms of the Swirl Computing is explained by introducing the ideas of SOA and the mathematical expressions.
3. It is shown that the ideas of SME and FCE are the main environments and mechanisms of the Swirl Computing. And also the idea of "Grid" has been introduced in order to update Old data, function, mechanism, thought, system, etc. into new ones.
4. A method of free, seamless, and ubiquitous communication method by using the idea of "the Swirl Computing" has been introduced.
5. For implementing the Swirl Computing, the following functions are introduced; "Principle", "Swirl Oriented Architecture: (SOA)", "System Structure by Mathematical Expression", and "Grid".
6. It will be shown that the Swirl Computing will give us seamlessly and naturally convenient services in order to get knowledge from extended entities without bothering complicated manipulations and reconstruction of system.
7. It will be shown that the possibility of sixth sense; "the Swirl Computing", may be introduced.
8. Some of the issues related with SOA, the mathematical expressions, and the swirl sensors are introduced too for further discussions and studies.

REFERENCES

Aichi Steel Corporation. (2009). MI sensor. In *The general catalogue*.

Burgess, L. (2008). *Swirl. Notes on Swirl*. CMU.

Larson, R. (2009). Education: Our most important service sector. *The Service Science, 1*(4), i–iii.

Lifton, J., Seetharam, D., Broxton, M., & Paradiso, J. (2002). *Pushpin computing system overview: A platform for distributed, embedded, ubiquitous sensor networks*. London, UK: Springer-Verlag.

Santhanam, G., Ryu, S., Yu, B., Afshar, A., & Shenoy, K. (2006). A high-performance brain–computer interface. *Nature, 442*(13). doi:.doi:10.1038/nature04968

Sugiyama, S. (2008). Fundamental behaviour in communication method. In *Proceedings of IEEE/INFORMS International Conference on Service Operations and Logistics, and Informatics*. Beijing, China.

Sugiyama, S. (2008). Ubiquitous framework in service science. In *Proceedings of The 2008 Logic and Science of Service (The New Wealth and Wellbeing of Nations)*, Hawaii, US.

Sugiyama, S. (2009). Feature extraction in system. In *Proceedings of INFORMS International Conference on Service Science*. Hong Kong, China.

Sugiyama, S. (2010). Business plan oriented service in service science. In *Proceedings of INFORMS Service Science Conference*. Taipei, Taiwan.

Sugiyama, S., & Tharumarajah, A. (2007). Fundamental behavior of holonic system. *The International Journal of Services Operations and Informatics, 2*(4). INDERSCIENCE.

KEY TERMS AND DEFINITIONS

AISE: Absorbing Incarnation System Entity; {Basic Data, Knowledge, System, Processing, Production, Management, etc.}. This is shown by using the examples in the "BACK GROUND" section of this chapter.

Cdaise: Connection for DAISE.

DAISE: Dynamic AISE.

Ddaise: Data for DAISE.

Dsaise: Data for SAISE.

Fdaise: Function for DAISE. X, Y, Z: any functions, any elements, any attributes.

SAISE: Static AISE.

Fsaise: Function for SAISE.

Gdaise: Grid for DAISE.

Gsaise: Grid for SAISE.

Idaise: Input for DAISE.

Isaise: Input for SAISE.

Ssaise: System for SAISE.

Chapter 4
A Service Component Model and Implementation for Institutional Repositories

Yong Zhang
Tsinghua University, China

Quansong Deng
Tsinghua University, China

Chunxiao Xing
Tsinghua University, China

Yigang Sun
National Library of China, China

Michael Whitney
University of North Carolina Charlotte, USA

ABSTRACT

With the boom of digital resources, there are urgent requirements to set up and manage Institutional Repositories (IRs) for companies and/or organizations. Cloud computing opens a new paradigm to build IRs by providing diverse services. We apply cloud services in the building of IRs and present a new model, which is based on digital object model and service component architecture, and consists of five service components, namely ID, metadata, content, log, and annotation service component. The five components are implemented by five corresponding clouds. These clouds provide two kinds of services: Web service and mashup service. We develop a framework and a code generation tool to generate an IR that can be used to manage the digital resources by invoking the five cloud services. Our approach is applied to the digital library on the history of water conservancy in China of Tsinghua University Library to demonstrate its feasibility.

DOI: 10.4018/978-1-60960-735-7.ch004

1. INTRODUCTION

As institutions and organizations strive to meet the needs of a technologically savvy society, they are confronted with the problem of managing a massive amount of digital resources. If they are to meet societal needs, they must incorporate a digital resource management system that is capable of affording individuals an opportunity to access their digital resources in a readily available and useful manner. In response, many have started to use an Institutional Repository (IR) which is an online system for digitally collecting, preserving, and disseminating intellectual output (Smith 2002) (Institutional Repository 2010). Although IR originates from academic fields, more and more organizations are setting up their own IRs that extend the original academic elements such as institutionally defined, scholarly content, cumulative and perpetual, interoperability and open access (Johnson 2002).

Meanwhile, Cloud Computing has been booming for several years. It is an extension of Grid Computing which emphasizes the on-demand usage of computing powers. In comparison, Cloud Computing focuses on higher-level services or well-designed services. More so, Clouds are defined as a large pool of easily usable and accessible virtualized resources (such as hardware, development platforms and/or services) (Vaquero et al. 2009). These resources can be dynamically configured to adapt to variable load (scale), leading to optimum resource utilization. This pool of resources is typically utilized on a pay-per-use model in which guarantees are offered by the Infrastructure Provider by means of customized SLAs.

Overall, Cloud Computing has three advantages that can help us manage digital resources. First of all, it is a pay-per-use utility model that decreases the cost of setting up, operating and upgrading an Institutional Repository. Secondly, it is scalable to deal with the massive digital resources that are continuously growing. Thirdly,

it provides flexible services to be integrated with existing applications.

In addition, there exist many legacy digital resource management systems that require integration with the emerging systems. The current software usually provides Web Services to be invoked from the old systems. However, to integrate these Web Services, it is necessary to modify the codes and re-compile which can be very cumbersome. So as to improve upon this practice, we offer Mashup services as a means to support this integration. This is because Mashup Service can be integrated at a higher level, which reduces the workload to some extent. It serves as a straightforward way to create new Web applications by combining existing Web resources utilizing data and Web APIs (Benslimane et al. 2008).

The software that we have developed is the Digital Resource Management System Version 2.0 (DRMS2.0), which is an upgrade of the DRMS1.0 which was a stand-alone system that provided the management of digital resources from ingestion, storage, index to services. For DRMS2.0, we design it as a middleware between application layer and network layer, which includes five clouds, a digital resource management container and an assistant tool. The five clouds provide three kinds of services: SaaS, Mashup Services and Web services. The SaaS services include management of digital object identifiers and digital content. Mashup service consists of Web APIs to be integrated in the user interface of a Web application. Web services provide the programmable interface to operate the digital resources. The digital resource management container called MenuFrame provides the Web interfaces, role-user management, privilege management, and supports central authentication. The assistant tool helps the user create an Institutional Repository for the customized digital resources, or just an empty framework for common use. The five clouds themselves are also created by this tool.

In traditional digital resource management systems, the content of the digital resource is normally static after it is ingested. But from our point of view, we regard that the value of a digital resource to not only be decided by the author, but also enhanced by its users. For example, on Flickr.com, a picture is annotated with social tags which are relevant keywords associated with or assigned to a piece of information (e.g., a Web page), describing the item and enabling keyword-based classification (Chirita et al. 2007). The tags are more precise to describe the content of the photo and provide an up-to-date taxonomy (Hunter et al. 2008) (Marlow et al. 2006). While emergent semantics of social tagging are used to help evaluate similarity measures (Markines et al. 2009), we emphasize the participation of users and support them by importing social annotations such as tags, scores and comments.

Our overall goal is to both enrich the value of the digital resources with user-generated-content and also help users find required digital resources. To achieve the second target, we have to find what they want, this is, the users' interests. The interests of the users can be expressed in two ways: explicit and implicit expressions. The explicit expressions are provided by the users (i.e., keywords list) while the implicit expressions are the records of the users' actions such as click-streams, and previously used resources. In addition, annotations help discover the users' interests by calculating the similarities between digital resources and between users (Sen et al. 2009) (Aurnhammer et al. 2006) (Song et al. 2008).

This paper is organized into eight sections. The second section discusses the related work. A Digital Resource Service Component model is depicted in section 3. Section 4 describes the architecture supporting DRSC model. The design and implementation of the clouds are given in section 5. In section 6, the tool and process of building an IR are described in details. And section 7 comes the system requirements and installation. The last sections are the future work and conclusion.

2. RELATED WORKS

There are many well-known platforms and programs available to help institutions build their own repositories, such as DSpace[1], Fedora Commons[2] and EPrints[3] to name a few. However, they have to maintain the whole systems on the basis of these platforms and programs which is not what we call cloud services. To the best of our knowledge, there are only two Institutional Repository projects trying to bring in the advantages that cloud services provide: Fedorazon[4] and DuraCloud[5].

Fedorazon is an out-of-the-box version of the Fedora Commons repository software that comes preconfigured for installation in the Cloud. It regards that a Cloud Repository is Fedora Commons Repository plus Amazon Web Services (i.e., Fedora + Amazon = Fedoarzon). The Aim of project Fedorazon is to enhance the content of repositories throughout the UK's HE and FE sector by providing solutions for the scalability of repositories as they grow in size and complexity. As a rapid innovation project, it looks to remove the "hardware" barriers involved in launching and maintaining a repository. It accomplishes this by enabling the use of Fedora Commons repository software on-top-of Amazon's virtual servers (EC2 & S3). By pre-configuring these servers, any HE/FE institution can "rent" Amazon server space and launch their own secure Fedora repository without having to pre-configure a local server within their institution. In short, institutions can launch their repository service on the same day they decide to have one, and without hiring a "hardware" expert.

To pursue a common mission, Fedora Commons and the DSpace Foundation merged into DuraSpace. DuraSpace is committed to serving the creators and stewards of scholarly, scientific, and cultural heritage by providing technologies and services that help to ensure that digital content is accessible over the long term. Accordingly, the DuraSpace technology portfolio inherently addresses the issue of durability of digital content. DuraCloud is a hosted service and open technology developed by DuraSpace that makes it easy for organizations and end users to use cloud services. DuraCloud leverages existing cloud infrastructure to enable durability and access to digital content. DuraCloud particularly focuses on providing preservation support services and access services for academic libraries, academic research centers, and other cultural heritage organizations. The service builds on the pure storage from expert storage providers by overlaying the access functionality and preservation support tools that are essential to ensuring long-term access and durability. DuraCloud offers cloud storage across multiple commercial and non-commercial providers, as well as compute services that are keys to unlocking the value of digital content stored in the cloud. DuraCloud provides services that enable digital preservation, data access, transformation, and data sharing. Customers are offered "elastic capacity" coupled with a "pay as you go" approach. DuraCloud is appropriate for individuals, single institutions, or for multiple organizations that want to use cross-institutional infrastructure. DuraCloud has been in a pilot phase since the beginning of fall 2009 and will be released as a service of the DuraSpace not-for-profit organization in the fall of 2010.

Through the surveying of the two aforementioned projects, we are able to compare our work (A service component model and implementation for institutional repositories) with theirs. In actuality, the two projects share some commonality with our work: all try to bring in the advantages that cloud services provide such as flexibility, scalability, elasticity and a pay-per-use model that are inherent in cloud. Nevertheless, these three works have different emphases.

With regard to Fedorazon, its objectives are fairly clear. It is a preconfigured instance of Fedora repository installed on rentable servers from Amazon so as to host the computing stack (EC2) and the storage components (S3). In this case, In Fedorazon, cloud means virtual server services as provided by Amazon. As for DuraCloud, their idea is more similar to ours than Fedorazon's. DuraCloud is a mediator between institutional or end-user applications and a variety of 3rd party cloud services. The purpose of the service is to provide a trusted intermediary that offers different levels of service aimed at making digital content durable and usable (DuraCloud Overview 2009). In this case, in DuraCloud, cloud menas not only Amazon but also other 3rd party cloud storage and computing services, yet DuraCloud still needs to store some information needed to mediate storage and retrieval of content with 3rd party storage providers. In comparison, our work (A service component model and implementation for institutional repositories) lies on more cloud services than the envisioned DuraCloud project (as it begins at fall of 2009 and still in its process) because the middleware we designed does not have to locally store the content of one resource, and it even does not need to store its metadata and other extra information. By doing so, it will bring convenience to an institution while they set up their own repository.

Next, we'll describe the digital resource service component model we designed in detail, which targets to support cloud services easily and enhance the efficiency of managing digital resources.

3. SERVICE COMPONENT MODEL OF DIGITAL RESOURCES

To manage a digital resources effectively, it is necessary to define a model to identify the related information and categorize the functions. Fedora regards that a digital object is composed of: identifier, object properties, data-streams that represents MIME-typed content items and disseminators that associate external services with the object for the purpose of providing extensible views of the object or of its data stream content (Lagoze et al. 2006). There are three kinds of digital objects in Fedora: data objects, Behavior Definition Objects, and Behavior Mechanism Object (Smith 2002).

Figure 1. SCA component

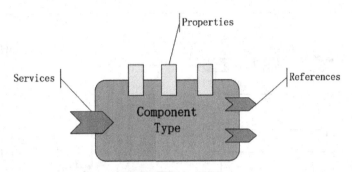

In comparison, DSpace emphasizes more on the organization structure of an institution. The way data is organized in DSpace is intended to reflect the structure of the organization using the DSpace system. Each DSpace site is divided into communities, which can be further divided into sub-communities reflecting the typical university structure of college, department, research center, or laboratory. Communities contain collections, which are groupings of related content. A collection may appear in more than one community. Each collection is composed of items, which are the basic archival elements of the archive. Each item is owned by one collection. Items are further subdivided into named bundles of bit streams.

Unfortunately, these two models cannot be directly used in Clouds. Therefore, we designed our model (DRSC model) with the concept of supporting Cloud Computing Services. The combination of Cloud Computing and SCA can give the applications maximum flexibility. If the cloud services are implemented using SCA, it is easy to hide the affect on the applications when change occurs. Based on SCA, we design the DRSC model to represent the properties, services and references of a digital resource.

As for the DRSC model, it is an extension of the traditional digital object model. For a normal Institutional Repository, an object identifier can be generated as an auto-incremental number or some other pre-defined number. For the digital identifiers in clouds, they should have the unique-

ness property whenever and wherever they are generated. Appropriately, we choose a Universally Unique Identifier (UUID) as the identifier because a UUID is 128 bits long, and can guarantee uniqueness across space and time. UUID is originally used in the Apollo Network Computing System and later in the Open Software Foundation's (OSF) Distributed Computing Environment (DCE), and then in Microsoft Windows platforms.

As shown in Figure 1, an SCA component consists of services, references and properties. The component provides services to other components, which are defined in terms of a business interface. It references to services provided by other components, which are also defined in terms of a business interface. The properties configure the component behavior.

The service component is recognized through its services by outside. We define a DRSC object as the composition of five atomic services (Figure 2): ID, Metadata, Content, Log and Annotation which will be explained in the following sections.

3.1. Five Atomic Components

3.1.1. Identifier (ID) Component

This is a component with properties of a unique identifier, registration information and the pointers to other services for the same digital resource and is generated as a UUID. The registration information includes agency, registration date/time and

Figure 2. DRSC object

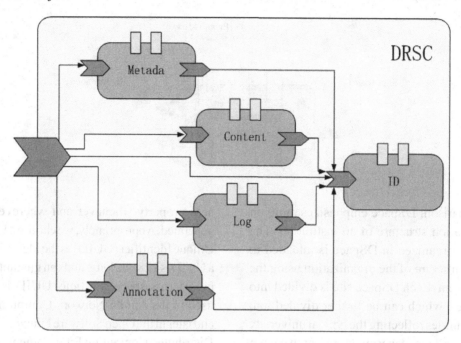

approver. It may include Dublin Core metadata that can be used to support simple queries. The pointers refer to the locations of metadata components, content components, log components and annotation components. In addition, the relationship between the ID component and other component is 1:N. Also, the services provided include registration, search and locating.

3.1.2. Metadata Component

This component not only includes the information of the DRSC object itself, but also the relationships with other DRSC objects. Its private properties include the general Dublin Core metadata and other specific metadata. The relationships with other digital object are expressed as binary tuples such as (ID2, parent) that means the current DRSC object is the parent of the DRSC objet with ID2. Metadata component may also include the redundant information such as the location of the DRSC content component. There are two service groups: data manipulation and data access.

3.1.3. Content Component

This is a component with the properties of multiple versions of resource content. The properties of separate version include creation date, format, and creator/modifier. The services include the upload and the download services of the resource content. For the upload process, if it is a new resource, a component is created; but for an existing resource, the version and other information such as the modification have to be stored separately to keep the whole history of the digital resource. This component supports the whole lifecycle of the content of a DRSC object.

3.1.4. Log Component

This is a component with the properties of operator, operation type, operation text and operation result. There are two kinds of logs: one is the access log that doesn't change the metadata and content of the DRSC object and the other records the operations that modify the metadata or content of the DRSC object. Access log is a record of the access history that can be used to analyze the patterns and preference of the users. Operation log is used to track the modification of the DRSC objects for auditing and recovering. There are two kinds of services provided: log recording service and log analysis service.

3.1.5. Annotation Component

This is a component with properties of score, tags, comments and usage-status. As discussed in section 1, the annotation information is different from the metadata in several ways. The first difference is that metadata is given by the experts, but annotations are given by users who might not have the expertise knowledge. Secondly, metadata is chosen from a controlled word list, while annotation is freely given as the user wishes. Thirdly, the quality of metadata can be guaranteed while the qualities of the annotation vary a lot. However, the advantage of annotations is that they are evolving with time so that they can reflect the current understanding of the DRSC object, while the metadata is normally fixed after it is created. There is much research on how to create a dynamic taxonomy from tags, if you're interested, see (Hunter et al. 2008) (Marlow et al. 2006) for example.

The scores can be used to calculate the quality of a DRSC object, and help the ranking of the search results. Comments are free text description of the user's opinion or notes, which can be processed by text mining or combined with tags by extracting the keywords from them. Usage-status is optional according to the content type of the DRSC object, which helps the users to manage their learning or studying processes. Usage-status can also be used to help the calculation of the tightness between user and resource. These annotations can also be used in collaborative filtering for recommendation. We use a tuple with six elements to represent the annotations for a DRSC object given by a user: <user, resource, score, tags, comments, usage-status>. From the annotations,

we can calculate the similarities between the users or between the resources.

3.2. The Composition of a DRSC Object

The above five components constitute one DRSC object as shown in Figure 2. Importantly, these service components do not need to exist in one computer, but rather be distributed over the Internet. However, the behavior of a DRSC object is configured by its properties, such as the links to the corresponding components. To add, SCA supports multiple interfaces through one implementation, which results in the flexibility to the applications of a DRSC object. What this means is that the component applications can be implemented in different languages, such as Java, C++ and COBOL etc. according to the corresponding specifications that can be downloaded from OSOA's web site (SCA Specification 2009).

The four components: Metadata, Content, Annotation and Log are all based on the ID component. The ID component consists of the pointers to the other four components. When the stored information of one resource in the four components changes, they will notify ID component to update the registration. The high flexibility of a DRSC object is that it can be automatically integrated with different transportation protocols such as Web Service, MQ, HTML, REST and so on.

This service component model of digital resources has the advantages as follows: it simplifies the development, composition and distribution process in assembling a solution of digital resource management; it improves the portability, reusability and flexibility in managing the digital resources; and it also reliefs the burden of the organizations by hiding the details of the backside technology from them.

For one kind of digital resource, there are two steps to create a DRSC object for it. The first step is to refine and classify its properties and functions into the five components and the second step is

Figure 3. Relationships between the components

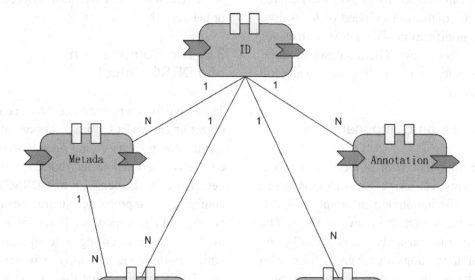

to create a management system. In the first step, the metadata is to be extracted from the digital resource first and foremost (this includes the Dublin Core metadata and other specific metadata). As for the content, there are some extra information added such as the format type, file size, created date, version etc. Besides the original format, one has to know the kinds of format that can be supported in the future. When the required format is confirmed, the original resource is converted into that format. The format conversion function can be added to the content component manually if an automatic conversion module does not exist. The annotation to a digital resource may not be corresponding to a record in the Metadata component. The relationships between them are shown in Figure 3. The relationships between ID component and other four components are 1:N. And the relationship between Metadata component and Content component is 1:N. However, at some time, to improve the efficiency of the applications, the content can be retrieved directly without accessing the ID component.

After analyzing the properties and functions of a digital resource, the next step is to create a management system for it. There are several methods for the administrator to create the system. One method is to create it through the use of our assistant tool that can generate the source code and distribution package, given the analysis of the digital resource from the above sections. Once complete, it is possible to set up a standalone system to manage the digital resources as described in section 6.

A second method to create a management system is to use the atomic components available on the Internet. Again, our assistant tool can also help users generate the corresponding source code and distribution packages. within comparison to the first method, the set-up and operation cost of the second method is much less. The administrator only needs to install a small system without any locally stored data.

The third method is to create the digital resource component directly on the Web. The administrator inputs the specific information

Figure 4. Comparison of the three methods of DRSC object creation

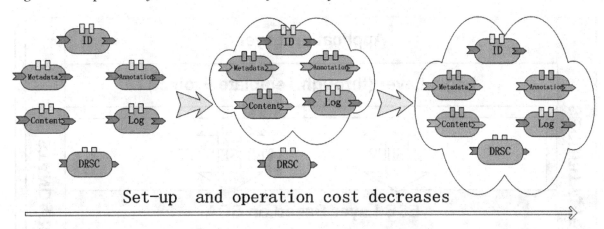

Set-up and operation cost decreases

of the digital resource. Once complete, a SaaS interface is provided for the user to manage the digital resources. In all, these three methods are from local installation to remote service, from complex to easy (Figure 4).

After a DRSC object is created, there are two kinds of user groups: end users and developers. If end users only need the basic functions of add, delete, update and search, they can use the Web interfaces provided. However, it is typical that end users require more functions and/or different user interfaces. If this is the case, the developers can utilize the programmable interfaces provided by the DRSC object to build new functions and user interfaces. Furthermore, not only can the DRSC object be used in a new digital resource management system, but it can also be invoked from the existing software systems to support the new digital resource.

As apparent, the second and third methods to create a DRSC object utilize web resources. Obviously, this causes a security concern in relation to the distribution of the DRSC object. However, while the security problem is not solved by the components themselves, it is resolved through appropriate management at the system level and the data level that will be explained in Section 5.

To continue, the assistant tool is implemented in Java. However, the DRSC model is only a specification that is an application of SCA in the digital resource management field. Importantly, other programming languages and tools can also be used to create the components.

In this section, we present a digital resource service component model which is different from the traditional digital objects. This model is based on SCA specifications. A DRSC object is composed of five atomic components: ID, Metadata, Content, Log and Annotation. The composition of a DRSC object is flexible by adopting different Internet transportation protocols. The processes to analyze and create a DRSC object are given. We also discuss the usage of a DRSC object. In the next section, we will focus on the system architecture.

4. ARCHITECTURE SUPPORTING DIGITAL RESOURCE SERVICE

Our architecture includes the function modules, the invoke relationships, and the transportation methods of messages. The architecture describes how an IR manages digital resources based on DRSC model (Figure 5).

To further describe Figure 5, an institutional repository is composed of five layers (Network Infrastructure Layer, Cloud Layer, ESB Layer

Figure 5. The IR architecture based on DRSC model

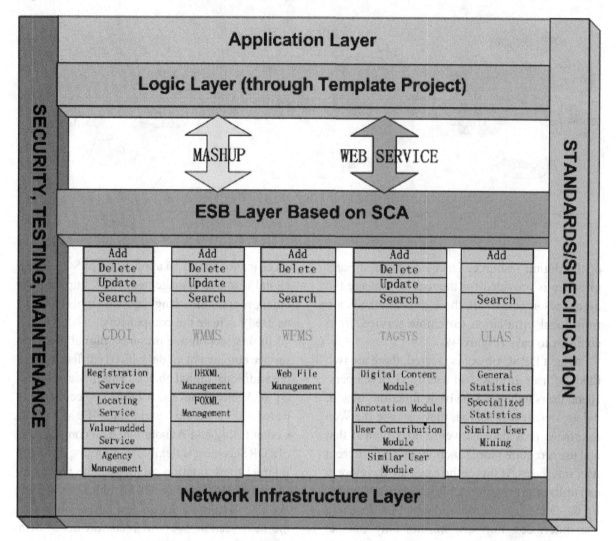

based on SCA, Logic Layer and Application Layer) which are based on the five clouds. The two supportive columns in Figure 5 are Standards/Specification and Security, Testing and Maintenance.

The fundamental layer needed for a successful institutional repository is the Network Infrastructure Layer. This is because all of the methods discussed above must rely on a stable and fast network. Otherwise, it is impossible to build an Institutional Repository in the cloud environment.

Above the Network Infrastructure layer, there is the cloud layer which consist of the five clouds

that correspond to the five DRSC components. The CDOI (Chinese Data Object Identifier System) implements the ID service component by providing the basic Add, Delete, Update and Search functions and further functions such as Registration, Locating, Value-added and Agency Management services. The Metadata service component is running in WMMS (WeST Matadata Management System) that stores the metadata in XML database. The content of a digital resource is managed by WFMS (Web File Management System) and the Annotations and Logs are separately maintained by TAGSYS (TAG SYStem) and

ULAS (User Log Analysis System). Not only can these five clouds be installed on one web server, but also distributed on separate cross-boundaries web servers. The interfaces (invoking addresses) used for the services of the components in these systems are configured in the configuration file of the Institutional Repository. The configurable interfaces make it easy to upgrade and deal with failure circumstances. We provide two kinds of interfaces here: Web Service interface and Mashup Service interface. Because our implementation is based on ESB (Enterprise Service Bus), which is a message broker supporting many transportation protocols, we can get more interfaces by modifying the definitions of the endpoints. If there is an interface that is not included in the ESB package, the framework is provided so as to implement one.

The ESB layer, which connects the clouds with the logic layer, plays a critical role in the Institutional Repository. This layer is a virtual layer, as it exists on the servers of the five clouds. The most important advantage of ESB is to provide many interfaces with different transportation protocols. There are many ESB implementations, such as Mule, ServiceMix, JBoss ESB and other commercial software. In our implementation, we choose Mule, which is an open-source lightweight enterprise service bus and integration platform that allows one to easily connect applications together. It can be embedded into other applications easily such as Spring, Tomcat, and so on. For our work, we embeded mule in the Tomcat server and invoked Spring functions. It also provides JUnit test packages that make the development of services more testable so as to guarantee the quality of the code.

The ESB layer connects the clouds with the logic layers through two kinds of services: Web Service and Mashup Service. Web services today are frequently utilized as Application Programming Interfaces (API) or web APIs that can be accessed over a network, such as the Internet, and executed on a remote system hosting the requested services. A Mashup is a web page or application that combines data or functionality from two or more external sources to create a new service. Our five clouds provide these two kinds of services to build an Institutional Repository. These services can be classified into two groups: management services and access services. The services these two groups provide compose the DRSC services.

The logic layer deals with the business logic of the digital resources management. Through the code automatic generation tool named Template (as described later) the program with the basic business logic is generated. Our framework provides the support to the central authentication of applications, which is implemented by using the LDAP server ApacheDS and CAS (a single sign-on protocol for the web). By using a central authentication, the Institutional repository can be integrated into the current applications without the need to replicate user information over several databases. Furthermore, the logic layer also supports a workflow that is very useful to set up the specific business logic within the institution. The workflow function is provided by integrating OSWorkflow into the logic layer. By modifying the configuration file, the application can support different business logics without modifying the source code. In addition, the user registration process in the logic layer is implemented by using OSWorkflow, which consists of two steps: (1) User can freely register through the submission of personal information; (2) the administrator can view the list of the new registers, verify the registration, then approve or reject the registration. If needed, this process can also be hardcoded, but in doing so, it will lose flexibility.

The application layer provides the user interface to the end users. It receives the requests from the users, calls the logic layer to accomplish corresponding functions, then renders the returned results. There are two kinds of interfaces: an interface for the normal user and an interface for the administrator. The general user interface requires a high quality UI experience while a plain interface is more acceptable for the administrator interface. With this in mind, our framework can provide the basic administration interface to manage the digital resources including add, delete, update and search functions. Other administration functions and interfaces have to be customized to be implemented.

Ajax (shorthand for asynchronous JavaScript and XML) is a group of interrelated web development techniques used on the client-side to create interactive web applications. With Ajax, web applications can retrieve data from the server asynchronously in the background without interfering with the display and behavior of the existing page. In our framework, we import two common libraries to support Ajax: Prototype and JQuery.

In this architecture, standards are very important for the interoperability. In consideration, we follow the OSOA standards during the building and maintenance of our DRSC model. Based on these standards, we provide the specification of digital resources, which are used to describe the atomic service components and the composition rules. For each service component, we give out the specification of the properties, service interfaces and references. From these standards and specifications, the DRSC model can be implemented in different languages and environments and still easily communicate with each other.

Besides the support of standards and specifications, we also consider the security, testing and maintenance in the architecture. Our framework provides two kinds of security methods: role-based authentication and encryption-based content security. In the system, users are assigned one or more predefined roles. These roles then determine the user's privileges, the information they can view and access, and items they are able to change. We provide an interface for the administrator to define different roles. To enable the authentication, we add a filter so as to invoke the Struts actions. Therefore, every request is checked according to the privilege list. On the web pages, fine-grained access control is applied for the display of the page content. In addition, we also afford administrators

with the ability to drag and drop privileges from one role in order to create a new role.

Users may worry about the security of the content host server because if the host server is attacked, the content on the server may be accessed by some unauthorized person. The encryption-based method solves this problem by encrypting the content as it is uploaded to the clouds. Even if the attacker obtains the content, they should not be able to decrypt the content. After the content is downloaded from the server, using the key stored locally, the content is decrypted automatically. For specific content, one can choose whether to encrypt it or not. Currently, we only support the encryption using Winzipaes from Apache.

In order to build and deploy the application, we use Apache Ant. Apache Ant is a software tool used to automate the software build processes. More so, it uses XML to describe the build process and its dependencies. Ant also includes a task JUnit, which is a simple, open source framework to write and run repeatable tests. Therefore, the framework supports test-driven programming. Based on JUnit, Mule ESB extends JUnit test case in order to test the services without embedding them into a J2EE container. This set of automatic testing tools support a smoking test that can keep the software usable and qualified for release.

After the release of an Institutional Repository, we continue to maintain it by correcting coding errors, improving the performance and extending the functions of the software. We have a specification of maintenance which defines the detailed processes, such as how to release the patches, and how to add a new function. Releasing an Institutional Repository is only the first step of its lifecycle, as the continuous support is very important. We investigated how to set up a wiki to help maintenance.

After the institutional repository runs, there may be a large amount of legacy data that needs to be imported into the new system. Thusly, we provide a tool that generates the code needed to import the legacy data into the new system from

Figure 6. The architecture of cloud supporting DRSC model

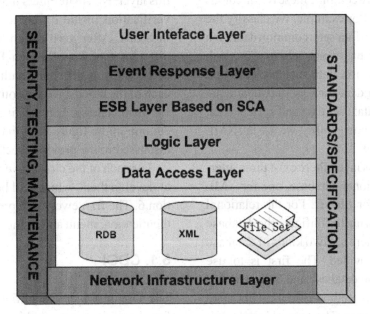

a text file. The format of the text file corresponds to the properties of the five atomic DRSC components. The data in the text file is imported to the clouds by invoking the web services of the DRSC object.

In short, this architecture provides users with the flexibility needed to build an institutional repository. Users can set up the component services on local servers or just use available cloud services on the Internet. That is the advantage of the SCA model: you can call a service through different protocols. The clouds are the key components to build an institutional repository. Of course, the availability and quality of the cloud services will affect the application very much. We will introduce the architecture and functions of them below.

5. DESIGN AND IMPLEMENTATION OF THE CLOUDS

The Clouds can be distributed across the Internet and provide the functions of accessing and manipulating the data. Similar to the architecture of the Institutional Repositories built on the clouds,

the structures of the clouds themselves are also based on SCA. As shown in Figure 6, there are seven layers: network infrastructure layer, data layer (including Relational Database - RDB, XML database and file sets), data access layer, logic layer, ESB layer based on SCA, event response layer and user interface layer.

To further describe Figure 6, the network infrastructure layer provides the basic communications. There are three kinds of data storage mechanisms. The first is the relational database which is used to store the common and fixed structured information such as login name, password and Dublin Core metadata, as the change of the RDB structure will bring too much modification for the application. The second storage mechanism is the XML database which is used to store the changeable data such as the specific metadata of a digital resource that are semi-structured, as the schema of an XML file is easy to be extended. The third storage mechanism is the file set which is used to store unstructured data such as image, audio and video resources.

In the design of a DRSC object, these three kinds of data have to be clearly classified. For some special data, we combine these two methods of RDB and XML. For example, we classify the user's properties into four sets: common data such as login name and password, admin data such as ID card number, user data such as email and gender, and system data such as statistical data. As for the admin data, user data and system data, in order to keep the extensibility, we use the XML format to store them.

In the data access layer, there exist three interfaces: one for relational database, one for XML database and one for file set. For the relational database, we use Spring to configure the database connection pool. There are two kinds of database access methods provided. The first is to use JDBC to connect the database and SQL to query the data. The second method is to use Hibernate to package the database. The second interface is Hibernate which makes it seem as if a database contains plain Java objects. For the XML database, we use XQuery that is a language from the W3C designed to query and format XML data. And for the file set, we use SOAP/http to upload and download files.

Above the data access layer is the logic layer. In this layer, we implement the business logic of the cloud functions using different data from the data layer through corresponding access methods provided by the data access layer. Above the logic layer is the ESB layer which is based on SCA. By using ESB, the business logics of the cloud functions can be implemented in different interfaces. The detail functions of each cloud will be introduced in the later sections.

The event response layer is between the user interface layer and the ESB layer. We provide two basic interfaces to interact with the users in the user interface layer: one is the common Web interface which is used while the cloud is running as a standalone system, and the other is Web service interface which is used while the cloud is running as a remote service on the Internet. When the user sends a request to our cloud through the user interface, the event response layer is invoked. In this layer, we create filters that perform privilege verification inside different actions as defined in Struts. After verification, this layer invokes different functions through ESB and responds accordingly as different results are returned. For each of the clouds, we give out the specifications for them. The security, testing and maintenance column in the figure is similar to the techniques discussed in the previous section.

For each of the clouds, we use our framework to develop them, which will be described in section 6. The framework can provide the basic authentication, menu and frameset-based interface.

5.1. CDOI

The Digital Object Identifier (DOI) System is for identifying content objects in the digital environment, just like DNS for domain names. DOI names are assigned to any entity for use on digital networks. They are used to provide up-to-date information, including where they can be found on the Internet. Information about a digital object may change over time, including where to find it, but its DOI name will not change. However, there exist several problems of using DOI:

- Naming rule: the length of DOI name is of variable length and can reach 128 bytes, which is not efficient for computer system to store and process.
- Name generation: it requires human intervention, which is impossible to deal with considering the massive user-generated content based on Web2.0.
- Integration: DOI cannot support the integration of the digital resources distributed on different repositories because these repositories may have the same digital object identifier for different resources. For example, they probably use the internal ID such as an auto-incremental number to name a digital resource, which may cause the problem of ID conflict.

To solve these problems, we have selected UUID as the unique ID in the CDOI cloud. In CDOI, we adopt two UUIDs to replace the DOI name. The first UUID is the organization/person identifier name; the second UUID is the internal identifier name. The overall length of a CDOI name is 64 bytes. The advantages of using UUID are: UUID can be generated automatically by many programs while guaranteeing the uniqueness; the length of the CDOI name is fixed, which is good for storage and index; it is easy to be automatically processed, which can be used to name the massive user-generated content from Web2.0 applications; and it is easy to be distributed on many servers, which provides CDOI with high scalability.

The services that this cloud provided are register, delete, update an ID, and resolve ID to the real location of the resource or the metadata of the resource. Besides the direct services, we also provide the service of agency management.

5.2. WMMS

WMMS is used to manage the metadata of the digital resources. The properties of it can be classified into two parts: the basic part and the extension part. The basic part includes the basic metadata of the digital resource, for which we use Dublin Core set to present it. However, for a digital resource, there are many different properties belonging to the extension part and it is difficult to maintain these properties in a fixed column relational database. As for a digital resource, its properties may change as it evolves. In regards to data storage, we chose BerkleyDB which is a high performance open source XML database. It is implemented in C/C++, we use JNI to call it and XPath/XQurey to query the database.

The services it provides are creating a new XML document (similar to a table in RDB), querying on the documents, and deleting a document. Each document is included in a single file. For a new type of digital resource, we use a file to store the data. In regards to the size of the single

file, BerkelyDB can support up to 4TB. As for the query on multiple documents, BerkelyDB provides functions to open them all for complex query.

The schema of a digital resource can be generated from the tool automatically. Once complete, the database can verify the data formats according to this schema file. To speed up the query, the indexes are built. We plan to support dynamic index creation according to the statistical analysis of the query history at the next stage.

Because CDOI and WMMS both include the Dublin Core information, there exist the possibility for data inconsistencies to occur. We solve this problem by providing a special mark in WMMS called "cdoiReference" that points to the ID entry in CDOI.

For the query result, we provide two formats to return to the user: one is XML, and the other is JSON which uses two-dimensional array to package the whole result. This was chosen because JSON decreases the size of the result, thus increases the efficiency of transportation.

5.3. WFMS

Generally, every website provides its own uploading and downloading modules so that users can share resources. However, the resources uploaded to websites' servers are often lack of unified and professional management. What's more, when the amount of users using the uploading and downloading modules increases, it will bring a high pressure on the website's server in terms of bandwidth. WFMS is used to solve these problems. It provides a unified interface for multiple websites to upload, download and manage resources professionally, and decreases the developing costs and bandwidth pressure as well.

As a service container, WFMS provides two kinds of services. One is to use WFMS as a SaaS service. Users can apply for Web storage and use it on the Internet directly. The other is to utilize it in the applications which can be used in two ways. One is to use it as a Web Service provider, from this interface, the program can call the services provided to upload and download digital resources. The other way is to use it as a Mashup service. The application can embed it in the web page directly and manage the digital content.

In this cloud, we use UUID as the identifier of a file. Because of the uniqueness, the application program can generate the UUID itself without creating a duplication problem. UUID makes the application of the Mashup service to upload file asynchronously. That is, the application can save the digital resource immediately without waiting for the resource ID returned from WFMS. Therefore, the performance of the application can be improved. The uniqueness of UUID also enables the distributed deployment of WFMS servers, which will be implemented at the next stage.

Although the digital contents are in the format of files, for the security reason, these files cannot be accessed directly. Rather, the files must be downloaded for which there are two methods.. One is to include the whole file in the response of the request. The other is to copy the file into a temporary directory with a random name and provide a link. In conjunction, there is a routine to clean the temporary files periodically. Overall, the first method is appropriate for the seldomy downloaded files that consume a lot of memory. The second method is appropriate for parallel download processes, which can decrease the workload a lot.

5.4. ULAS

The logs are very important to track the users' behaviors and system changes. There are several disadvantages to keep the logs locally. Writing the logs to local disk requires file IOs, which will decrease the performance of the system significantly. Secondly, if the local disk is crashed, the logs may be corrupted at the same time. Therefore, it will bring difficulties to re-construct the system data.

We use ActiveMQ to transfer the logs to the ULAS cloud. Because ActiveMQ can keep the logs locally, and send them to ULAS when the system is in low workload, the performance of the system can be improved. By keeping the logs on the remote server, concern for the security of the data might be relieved. In addition, keeping the logs on several ULAS clouds is also supported.

Corresponding to the Log Component in section 3.1.4, there are two kinds of logs supported in the ULAS. ULAS can analyze the two kinds of logs and present the results in a chart. Additionally, ULAS supply the service of adding logs through ActiveMQ. It also provides SaaS service. Therefore, a user can also upload log files to the system, and then ULAS can help analyze the log files and give visualized charts.

5.5. TAGSYS

As the common information retrieval technology cannot meet the requirement of queries with different backgrounds and intents, personalized services appear to provide different services to different users. Personalization can improve the service quality and access efficiency, thus to pull more visitors. More so, a personalized annotation system is used to collect annotations of a user, predicate users' preferences and recommend resources according to users' current preferences and taste (Sen et al. 2009).

TAGSYS is a personalized resource annotation, management and recommendation system based on tags, score, comments and usage status. It provides the support to the process of resource utilization. In the traditional digital resource management systems, the value of a digital resource will not change. With the help of TAGSYS, the users' feedback can enrich the semantics of the digital resources and help with other users' learning processes. The dynamic generation of tags can help to generate the up-to-date taxonomy. By analyzing the annotations of the users, TAGSYS can recommend related digital resource to users.

The services provided by TAGSYS include the management of annotations and recommendation of resources. TAGSYS provides the interfaces for other systems to store their annotation information, and recommends resources based on the annotations or other information such as the tags from Wikipedia. For example, a user can annotate the resource when he visits applications integrated with TAGSYS services. These systems are loosely coupled with TAGSYS, and only need to provide a data structure including system id, user id and resource id. Then they can get the services of feedback and recommendation from TAGSYS, such as finding similar users.

In this section, we introduce the five atomic clouds supporting an Institutional Repository. In the next section, we will introduce our tools to help with the building of an Institutional Repository.

6. TOOL AND PROCESS OF BUILDING AN IR

We provide a tool called Template to help the creation of an Institutional Repository. It is based on our SCA framework named MenuFrame, and the current version is 6.0 (shorthand as Menu6). This framework consists of the following modules: role management, user management, central-authentication, workflow, component library and user interface. The target of the framework is to decrease the effort of setting up an application. Developers can focus on their own specific requirements without spending too much time on routinely tedious work. This framework supplies the application with two kinds of interfaces: GUI interface and service interface. The GUI interface is a frameset based Web pages. The customization of menus and privileges is provided. The service interface can be set up easily because Mule ESB is embedded.

Based on this framework, we provide two methods to create new applications. The first method is to create a common Web-based application. The application is generated with role, user, menu and privilege management. Users can

configure the frameset based user interface, and add new functions as required. The document of how to add a new function is provided. The construction of a common web application is done by using ant script. In the build file, users can configure the basic information of the application such as application name, description, running port, database user name and password etc. After the application is created, a simple ant command can run it.

The most valuable function of Template is that it supports the creation of an Institutional Repository based on the DRSC model.

As depicted in figure 7, the process to create an Institutional Repository includes three components: digital resource descriptions, Menu6 framework and a set of template files. The digital resource descriptions include the metadata, the functions, and the constraints. The descriptions are defined in an XML file. Template receives the descriptions and uses ant to invoke Freemaker templates to create the related Java files, JSP files and configuration files such as Struts, Spring and Hibernate configuration files, which are in the Menu6 framework. The generated IR core is built and running on Tomcat. It calls the services provided by the five clouds. It also has a Web interface contained in Menu6 framework and provides the functions of adding, deleting, updating and querying. If you want to extend the functions of the basic Institutional Repository, you can follow our instructions similar to the first method.

During the process, the key step is to give out the descriptions of the digital resources. Writing XML files by hand often brings some unexpected errors, thus we provide an interface to input the metadata and other information. For the moment, we only provide the function to generate the codes for one kind of digital resource. If there is more than one kind of digital resource, the codes have to be generated separately, and merged together manually. In the future, we will support multiple kinds of digital resources. And we will provide

Figure 7. Process to create an Institutional Repository

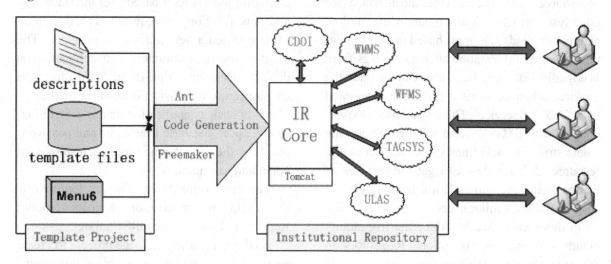

SaaS service to allow users to input the metadata and generate a Web application for them automatically to manage these kinds of digital resources.

This tool has already been used in the Digital Library on the History of Water Conservancy in China of Tsinghua University Library, which is used to manage the books, images and some other digital resources of water conservancy. We only generate the codes for basic management, because the front-end interfaces are too various, which is difficult to create templates for. For the digital library, it requires a customized interface. Tsinghua University Library provides the Web interfaces in HTML format; and we integrate them into the digital library.

7. REQUIREMENTS AND INSTALLATION

In order to function, the clouds and assistant tool in DRMS2.0 require Java Server Tomcat, MySQL database, BerkelyDB and Mule ESB. The program is deployed with an Apache Ant Script that runs cross-platforms to simplify the process of installation. DRMS2.0 can be easily configured and put into production very fast. This characteristic

is crucial because the system will be most useful at institutions with relatively weak technical support and urgent requirements. Finally, DRMS2.0 is free of charge under an academic and research use license and the technical details of installation are handled easily.

8. CONCLUSION AND FUTURE WORK

This paper presents a new middleware based on cloud services to set up an Institutional Repository. Clouds are defined to be a large pool of easily usable and accessible virtualized resources. These resources can be dynamically re-configured to adjust to a variable load, allowing also for optimum resource utilization. It is not economic to set up an Institutional Repository for an organization itself. Based on SCA, we designed a model for managing digital resources named DRSC model, which regards a digital resource as a composite of five atomic service components, i.e. ID, metadata, content, annotation and log service component. These components provide two kinds of services: Web service and Mashup service. In order to support the DRSC model, we design and implement five corresponding atomic clouds. These clouds are implemented by using ESB, which support different transportation protocols. The applications can invoke these services directly. Among these clouds, TAGSYS supports the involvement of users so that it can help the users find required digital resources. We also provide an assistant tool to help users set up a new Institutional Repository. Based on the description of one kind of digital resource, a basic Institution Repository can be created fast and easily. We use the Digital Library on the History of Water Conservancy in China of Tsinghua University Library as an example to demonstrate the feasibility of our approach.

However, there are also many works to be done to enrich the functions and improve the performance of our clouds. The first job we need to do is the version control and provenance management of digital resources. The second is to improve the Template tool: we plan to develop Web interface for the creation of an Institutional Repository for multiple kinds of digital resources, and we also plan to provide a SaaS way that allows Web users to manage their own digital resources more conveniently. We believe that the digital resource management systems built on Cloud Services will become the next generation Institutional Repositories.

REFERENCES

Aurnhammer, M., Hanappe, P., & Steels, L. (2006). *Integrating collaborative tagging and emergent semantics for image retrieval*. WWW Collaborative Web Tagging Workshop, 2006.

Benslimane, D., Dustdar, S., & Sheth, A. P. (2008). Services mashups: The new generation of Web applications. *IEEE Internet Computing, 12*(5), 13–15. doi:10.1109/MIC.2008.110

Chirita, P., Costache, S., Handschuh, S., & Nejdl, W. (2007). *PTAG: Large scale automatic generation of personalized annotation TAGs for the Web*. WWW 2007.

DuraSpace Organization. (2009). *DuraCloud overview 2009*.

Hunter, J., Khan, I., & Gerber, A. (2008). *Harvana: Harvesting community tags to enrich collection metadata*. Joint Conference on Digital Libraries 2008, (pp. 147-156).

Johnson, R. K. (2002, November). Institutional repositories: Partnering with faculty to enhance scholarly communication. *D-Lib Magazine, 8*(11).

Lagoze, C., Payette, S., Shin, E., & Wilper, C. (2006). Fedora: An architecture for complex objects and their relationships. *International Journal on Digital Libraries, 6*(2), 124–138. doi:10.1007/s00799-005-0130-3

Markines, B., Cattuto, C., Menczer, F., Benz, D., Hotho, A., & Stumme, G. (2009). Evaluating similarity measures for emergent semantics of social tagging. *WWW, 2009*, 641–650. doi:10.1145/1526709.1526796

Marlow, C., Naaman, M., Boyd, D., & Davis, M. (2006). HT06, tagging paper, taxonomy, Flickr, academic article, ToRead. *Proceedings of the Seventeenth Conference on Hypertext and Hypermedia*, 2006, (pp. 31-40).

SCA. (2009). *Specification*, final version 1.0. Retrieved from http://www.osoa.org/display/Main/Service+Component+Architecture+Specifications

Sen, S., Vig, J., & Riedl, J. (2009). Tagommenders: Connecting users to items through tags. *WWW, 2009*, 671–680. doi:10.1145/1526709.1526800

Smith, M. (2002). DSpace: An institutional repository from the MIT libraries and Hewlett Packard laboratories. *ECDL, 2002*, 213–226.

Song, Y., Zhuang, Z. M., Li, H. J., Zhao, Q. K., Li, J., Lee, W., & Giles, C. L. (2008). Real-time automatic tag recommendation. *SIGIR, 2008*, 515–522. doi:10.1145/1390334.1390423

Vaquero, L. M., Rodero-Merino, L., Caceres, J., & Lindner, M. (2009). A break in the clouds: Towards a cloud definition. *ACM SIGCOMM Computer Communication Review*, *39*(1), 50–55. doi:10.1145/1496091.1496100

Wikipedia. (2010). *Institutional repository*. Retrieved from http://en.wikipedia.org/wiki/Institutional_repository

ADDITIONAL READING

ACM. (2009). Cloud Computing: An Overview. [Distributed Computing, DEPARTMENT: CTO roundtable distributed computing.]. *Queue*, *7*(5), 2009.

Alkhatib, G. I. (2005). Web Service Standards Road Map. *IEEE Proceedings of the International Conference on Next Generation Web services Practices (NWeSP'05)*, 2005:4-5.

Arms, W. Y. (1995). Key Concepts in the Architecture of the Digital Library. *D-Lib Magazine*, (July): 1995.

Bamman D. & Crane G. (2008). Building a dynamic lexicon from a digital library. *JCDL 2008*.

Beyer D., Chakrabarti A., & Henzinger T. A. (2005). Web service interfaces. *WWW 2005*.

Buchanan G., Bainbridge D., Don K. J., & Witten I. H. (2005). A new framework for building digital library collections. *JCDL 2005*.

IBM Corp. Connecting enterprise applications to websphere enterprise service bus. IBM Corp. PO Box 10659 Riverton, NJ USA.

Ferris, C., & Farrell, J. (2003). What are Web Service? *Communications of the ACM*, *46*(6), 31. doi:10.1145/777313.777335

Halvey M. & Keane M. T. (2007). An Assessment of Tag Presentation Techniques. *WWW 2007*.

Hazelhurst, S. (2008). Scientific computing using virtual high-performance computing: a case study using the Amazon Elastic Computing Cloud. *Proceedings of the 2008 annual research conference of the South African Institute of Computer Scientists and Information Technologists on IT research in developing countries: riding the wave of technology*, pp.94-103, 2008.

Khoo M. (2006). Evaluating the national science digital library. *JCDL 2006*.

Lenk, A., Klems, M., Nimis, J., Tai, S., & Sandholm, T. (2009). What's inside the Cloud? An architectural map of the Cloud landscape. *Proceedings of the 2009 ICSE Workshop on Software Engineering Challenges of Cloud Computing*.

Meinl, T., & Blau, B. (2009). Web service derivatives. *WWW*, *2009*, 271–280. doi:10.1145/1526709.1526746

Moreno-Vozmediano, R., Montero, R. S., & Llorente, I. M. (2009). Elastic management of cluster-based services in the cloud. *International Conference on Autonomic Computing Proceedings of the 1st workshop on Automated control for datacenters and clouds Barcelona*, Spain SESSION: Across environments Pages 19-24.

Murray, P. (2009). Enterprise grade cloud computing. *European Conference on Computer Systems Proceedings of the Third Workshop on Dependable Distributed Data Management Nuremberg*, Germany Pages 1-1.

Qi, N. Z., Kudo, M., Myllymaki, J., & Pirahesh, H. (2005). A function-based access control model for XML databases. *CIKM*, *2005*, 115–122.

Roşu, M. (2007). A-SOAP: Adaptive SOAP Message Processing and Compression. *IEEE International Conference on Web Services (ICWS 2007)*, 200-207.

Schilit B. N. & Kolak O. (2008). Exploring a digital library through key ideas. *JCDL 2008*.

Sefton, P., & Dickinson, D. (2010). An Architecture for a Distributed Digital Library. *JCDL, 2010*, 389.

Sen, S., Lam, S. K. T., Rashid, A. M., Cosley, D., Frankowski, D., & Osterhouse, J. (2006). Tagging, communities, vocabulary, evolution. *CSCW, 2006*, 181–190. doi:10.1145/1180875.1180904

Sigurbjornsson, B., & Zwol, R. V. (2008). Flickr tag recommendation based on collective knowledge. *WWW, 2008*, 327–336. doi:10.1145/1367497.1367542

Weingroff M. & Bhushman S. (2005). Tools for managing collaboration, communication, and website content development in a distributed digital library community. *JCDL 2005*.

Xu Y. & Papakonstantinou Y. (2005). Efficient keyword search for smallest LCAs in XML databases. *SigMod 2005*.

Xu, Z. C., Fu, Y., Mao, J. C., & Su, D. F. (2006). Towards the semantic web: Collaborative tag suggestions. *WWW Collaborative Web Tagging Workshop, 2006*, p8.

Zhou, D., Bian, J., Zheng, S. Y., Zha, H. Y., & Giles, C. L. (2008). Exploring social annotations for information retrieval. *WWW, 2008*, 715–724. doi:10.1145/1367497.1367594

KEY TERMS AND DEFINITIONS

Cloud Computing: Internet-based computing, whereby shared resources, software, and information are provided to computers and other devices on demand, like the electricity grid.

DOI: Digital Object Identifier, A character string used to uniquely identify an electronic document or other object.

Fedora: A modular architecture built on the principle that interoperability and extensibility is best achieved by the integration of data, interfaces, and mechanisms (i.e., executable programs) as clearly defined modules.

Institutional Repositories: An online locus for collecting, preserving, and disseminating, in digital form, the intellectual output of an institution, particularly a research institution.

Mashup: In Web development, a mashup is a Web page or application that uses and combines data, presentation or functionality from two or more sources to create new services.

Middleware: Computer software that connects software components or some people and their applications.

SCA: Service Component Architecture, a set of specifications which describe a model for building applications and systems using a Service-Oriented Architecture.

Web Service: Application programming interface (API) or Web API that is accessed via Hypertext Transfer Protocol (HTTP) and executed on a remote system hosting the requested service.

ENDNOTES

[1] http://www.dspace.org
[2] http://www.fedora-commons.org
[3] http://www.eprints.org
[4] http://www.ukoln.ac.uk/repositories/digirep/index/Fedorazon
[5] http://duraspace.org

Section 2
Pervasive Services and Internet of Things

Chapter 5
Service Discovery Architecture and Protocol Design for Pervasive Computing

Feng Zhu
University of Alabama in Huntsville, USA

Wei Zhu
Intergraph Co, USA

Matt W. Mutka
Michigan State University, USA

Lionel M. Ni
Hong Kong University of Science and Technology, China

ABSTRACT

Service discovery is an essential task in pervasive computing environments. Simple and efficient service discovery enables heterogeneous and pervasive computing devices and services to be easier to use. In this chapter, we discuss the key issues and solutions for service discovery architecture and protocol design for pervasive computing environments. Service design addresses the static and dynamic properties of services. Directory design focuses on scalability, topology, and infrastructure issues. Service integration uses services as building blocks to achieve complex services. Cross-layer design optimizes the performance of the protocols for ad hoc and sensor networks by integrating service discovery processes into lower layers of the network protocols. Security and privacy design protects the information, communication, devices, and services. We also point out the future research issues.

DOI: 10.4018/978-1-60960-735-7.ch005

INTRODUCTION

In pervasive computing environments, people are surrounded by a variety of computing devices. Those devices communicate with each other and provide network services and information without people's active attention (Weiser, 1991). Presently, PCs, smartphones, MP3 players, and laptops surround us. In the near future, additional networked computers, ranging from sensors, RFID tags to extremely dynamic and heterogeneous devices will provide a variety of services. It becomes overwhelming to manage these devices, configure different kinds of applications, and dynamically find the available computing services in such pervasive computing environments.

Service discovery protocols enable computers to be easier to use. They facilitate interaction between computers, with an aim to approach zero administration overhead and therefore free users from tedious and redundant administrative and configuration work. Therefore, service discovery research is critical to the success of pervasive computing (Kindberg & Fox, 2002).

The objective of this chapter is to discuss the key design issues and solutions for service discovery protocols in pervasive computing environments. In the last 15 years, many service discovery protocols were designed by industry, academia, and international standards development organizations. The protocols emphasize on aspects of the service discovery. We analyze the design of the major components, their interactions, service selection, performance optimization, and security and privacy issues.

BACKGROUND

Before we present representative service discovery protocols, we describe three general models. The models focus on the functionalities of computing devices or software in the service discovery

processes and the basic steps that each device or software component is taken.

Service Discovery Models

There are three service discovery models. A trivial service discovery model is one in which a *client* (computing device) knows a *service* (network service) in advance, or the client has already cached the service's information, so that the client does a local lookup before contacting the service. The second model is the client-service model as shown in Figure 1 (a). The model performs best in simple environments such as home environments. Clients inquire about all services. If a service matches the client's enquiry, it replies back. Then, the client communicates with and accesses the service. To support thousands of computing services, such as the services in public environments, we may optionally use *directories* to store all the service information. This third model is call client-service-directory model. A client queries a directory for service information and then contacts services. We discuss the different perspectives of the clients, services, and directories.

Client View

In most cases, a client is a program that runs on behalf of a user and interacts with the user. It usually takes the following steps.

- A client queries directories for services. A client either browses services or looks for a specific service.
- Alternatively, without going through directories, a client directly queries all the services. All the services that meet the query requirement reply back to the client.
- Then the client program or the user selects a service to use.
- Finally, the client uses the service.

Figure 1. Interactions among the components in service discovery models. (a) Interactions in the client-service model. (b) Interactions in the client-service-directory model

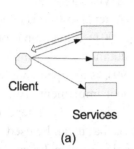

(a)

(b)

With service discovery software installed, the client does not need to configure service settings. If a device driver is needed to access a service, the driver will be installed just-in-time before the service accesses. Therefore, users will be released from the burden of installing software on all client devices.

Service View

A service has a name, a list of attributes, and user privileges. For instance, a printer says it provides printing service and it is able to provide color printing at 720 by 720 dpi. It might only allow people in the marketing department to use it. When the device needs to use other services, the device becomes a client. Services work as follows.

- A service announces its information to clients or directories. For example, every ten minutes a temperature sensor announces its information to let clients or directories know its existence.
- Alternatively, a service answers directory solicitation or client queries.
- A service authenticates and authorizes the user when a client asks for service.
- Finally, the client is granted service access and uses the service through the service's interface.

Directory View

With directories available, a client queries twice, the first time asking directories and the second time contacting the service(s). Without directories, a client looks for services directly.

- On hearing a service announcement, directories first check privileges of the service; and then service information will be updated or recorded in the directories.
- Alternatively, directories may ask what services are available instead of waiting for the service to be announced.
- When receiving a query from a client, directories authenticate, authorize, and reply to the client.

Service Discovery Protocols

Research activities in service discovery have been very active in academia, industry and international standards development organizations. Here, we list a few representative protocols in each of the communities.

Academia. IBM Research's DEAPspace (Nidd, 2001) is a service discovery protocol for single-hop ad hoc environments. Each node that runs the DEAPspace algorithm caches service information. Then, it broadcasts on the wireless channel the cached service information and its own service information to one-hop neighbors. All nodes acquire their knowledge from other nodes, and thus service lookup is done by searching local cache. Intentional Naming System (INS) (Adjie-Winoto, Schwartz, Balakrishnan, & Lilley, 1999) from MIT is a new naming system to name and discover different services. The innovative characteristic of INS is late binding, which enables service and service location mapping just before the service access. A following project, INS/Twine (Balazinska, Balakrishnan, & Karger, 2002), hashes and stores service attributes in mesh structure directories. It uses peer-to-peer technology to look up services. Peer-to-peer technology allows INS/Twine to be able to scale up to millions of services. But on the other hand, service lookups may have to go through several directories and thus have additional latency. Researchers at UC Berkeley proposed SSDS (Czerwinski, Zhao, Hodes, Joseph, & Katz, 1999). SSDS focuses more on security and scalability issues. Privacy and security are enabled by public key and symmetric key encryption. Different hierarchical directory structures are considered to support scalability.

Industry. Sun Microsystems' Jini is based on Java technology (Sun Microsystems, 2001). Java technology makes Jini platform independent of the underlying operating systems and hardware, but all the clients, services, and directories need Java runtime environments directly or indirectly. Microsoft Corporation ships operating systems with UPnP (Miller, Nixon, Tai, & Wood, 2001). UPnP targets unmanaged networking environments, such as home environments. UPnP uses XML format to store service information and communicate among services and clients. Thus, UPnP is platform and programming language independent and device-oriented. Rendezvous at Apple Computer's is a DNS-based service discovery protocol (Cheshire, 2002). The ubiquity of DNS servers might facilitate the Zero Configuration networking (Zeroconf) prototocol to be adopted (Apple Computer Inc, 2003).

Organizations. Bluetooth, from the Bluetooth Special Interest Group (SIG), is now widely used. It allows nearby devices to discover and communicate with each other at low power consumption (Bluetooth SIG, 2001). Salutation protocol, proposed by the Salutation Consortium (Salutation Consortium, 1999), is an open source protocol. Salutation protocol implements two interfaces, one of which is designed to be independent to the transport layer, so that it can be used on various transport protocols. Service Location Protocol (SLP) is posted by IETF in enterprise environments (Guttman, Perkins, Veizades, & Day, 1999). SLP defines a way to locate a service, but it leaves the interaction between clients and services after service discovery to the application developers.

AN ANALYSIS OF ARCHITECTURE AND PROTOCOL DESIGNS

Much active service discovery research has been occurring as we discussed in the last section. Targeted at different environments, these service discovery protocols have different design criteria and choices.

Issues, Controversies, Problems

Service discovery protocols provide desired functionalities, yet they face great challenges. First, unlike traditional network services, the services and devices are highly dynamic. New devices and services may be added without users' knowledge. Sensors, services, network connections may not be available all the time. Second, the pervasive computing environments are extremely heterogeneous. Different types of operating systems, network topologies, network protocols and devices, owned and administrated by different people or organizations.

Most service discovery protocols are designed as application layer protocols. Thus, many heterogeneous issues are handled by underlying network protocols and become transparent to the service discovery protocols. Our discussion first focuses on design issues and solutions at the application layer protocols. Towards the end of the chapter, we discuss a set of service discovery protocols that choose to use cross-layer design to integrate service discovery protocol with lower network layers for performance reasons. Cross-layer design violates the network design principle and trades clean design for performance improvements.

Often, software functionality is the first priority, whereas security and privacy are the second priority. Such software design and development practice is the case for service discovery protocols. Once devices run service discovery protocols and communicate over wireless networks, they may easily be found and accessed by any other devices without the devices owners' knowledge. For instance, a person may walk by a house and discover and control devices in the house. Security and privacy remain to be a serious challenge.

Figure 2 shows the main components for the service discovery architecture and protocol design. The following sections analyze various design choices made by service discovery protocols and point out remaining issues.

Service Designs

We describe a service as some computing resource used by users, user programs, or other services. For example, printing services, location based information, and wireless network connections are services.

Service Naming. A service has a name. Suppose Bob uses a printer. Printing is the name of the service. Nevertheless, the problem is when Bob looks for a printing service, a printer calls itself a print service. Then Bob is unable to find the printer. Most protocols solve this problem by defining a service naming standard, which avoids the naming conflict (Kindberg & Fox, 2002). Bluetooth maps service names to 128-bit numbers.

Defining services in SLP should follow a service template (Guttman, Perkins, & Kempf, 1999).

It is likely that many service discovery protocols co-exist. When a mobile client moves from one service discovery domain to another service discovery domain, the mobile client needs to understand different service protocols and use different vocabularies, for example saying print service at one time and printing service at another time.

The other problem is how to support new services. Although it is easy to add a new service name to a service protocol standard, it is difficult for users and client programs to know it automatically. Very likely, users need to browse for service names and then learn the new terms.

Service Attributes. A service usually has many attributes. To avoid conflicts, service attributes also have standard naming conventions as service names. A client's request is matched against services' attributes. When a client supplies more precise query requirements, fewer services will be selected. As a result, less network traffic is generated and fewer services are involved. If a query is too strict, no services may be matched and then the client needs to query again with fewer constraints. In addition to search functionality, most service discovery protocols provide wild card searches, which let clients examine all the available services.

Service Invocation. After discovering the service, a client invokes the service through a service interface. Some protocols such as the Bluetooth Service Discovery Protocol leave the service interface for applications to define. Some protocols base on Remote Procedure Call (PRC). Salutation is such an example. Some protocols use downloadable code. For example, Jini uses downloadable Java code. Other service protocols only transfer data. UPnP achieves service invocation based on eXtensible Markup Language (XML), Simple Object Access Protocol (SOAP), and Hyper Text Transform Protocol (HTTP).

Service invocations in Jini and UPnP need TCP/IP protocols, HTTP servers, or Java Virtual

Figure 2. Main components and classification of service discovery architecture and protocol design. Rectangles show the main architecture and design components. Rounded rectangles show the classifications of the component design

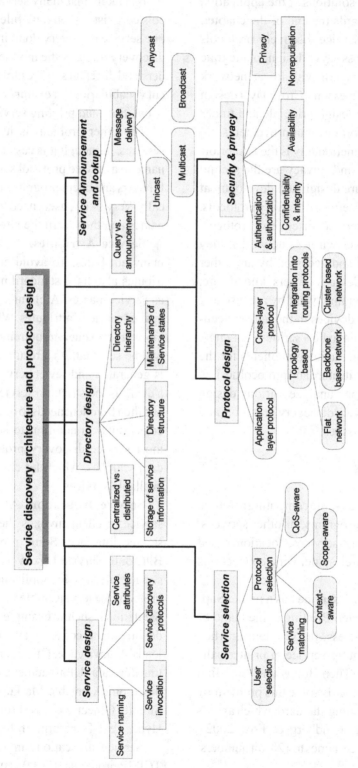

Machines (JVMs), which may not suitable for very resource limited devices. Special design considerations are needed for those wireless devices that have limited network bandwidth and power.

Service Status Inquiry. A client may be interested in services' events or status changes. One way of knowing about them is by polling the service. Another way, known as service event notification, is by registering with the service and the service will notify clients who have shown interest. Most protocols implement service event notifications. If events are generated very frequently or a service status changes very fast, it is better to use service polling.

It is even better to have agents do event filtering and aggregation. Jini provides several such methods. Services send events to agents and let agents make sure all the events are delivered to clients; an agent may act as a sink for events, which will be filtered, aggregated, and then sent to clients; or an agent may also resemble a mailbox to filter events over time. Although clients and services benefit from event filtering and aggregation, some resources (computers in networks) need to provide the functions and handle the events.

Directory Designs

Directories cache service information and answer clients' lookup requests. Thus, the overhead of handling unrelated requests for services and the communication between clients and unrelated services are removed. More importantly, this facilitates large-scale service discovery. Directory architectures, service information cache strategies, and hierarchies are different depending on the environments.

Centralized vs. Distributed Directories. A centralized directory stores all the services' information in a central location. The directory is likely to be a bottleneck and the single point of failure, which causes the whole system's failure. In large service discovery domains, it is inefficient to go through a centralized directory all the time.

Many service discovery protocols use distributed directories, which store services' information within their own domains. Service information is distributed among directories. A directory failure only affects part of the system. With less information in each directory, service lookup within a directory is more efficient. On the other hand, a service lookup may go through several directories. In contrast, a service lookup in a centralized directory only goes to one directory with less network communication overhead and latency.

Storage of Service Information. For each service, the service information may be a single copy, multiple copies, or fully replicated in directories. Many protocols have a single copy of services in its domain. A directory failure will affect the domain for which it is responsible. In Jini and SLP service discovery environments, multiple directories may coexist. Therefore, multiple copies of service information may exist. It is more reliable with multiple copies of service information in several directories, but the greater the number of directories, the greater the overhead. INS implements fully replicated copies within a sub domain. The advantage of fully replicated directories is that a service search only goes to the directory to which a client is attached. Multiple copies or fully replicated copies of service information should be consistent in directories. Otherwise, querying different directories may result in different service information and may cause problems.

Directory Structure. In a flat directory structure, directories maintain peer-to-peer relationships and are equally important. In one type of flat directory structure, directories connect to each other and exchange information. In INS, for instance, directories have a mesh structure and exchange information with other directories, so that all service information is available locally and the service search is very efficient. These information exchanges generate much communication traffic, and therefore it is not scalable. INS/Twine based on peer-to-peer technology is much more scalable because service information is not replicated.

While in a hierarchical directory structure, directories have parent and child relationships. Domain Name System (DNS) is an example of a hierarchical directory structure. Searching through the directory hierarchy is necessary. For example, a service discovery protocol is based on widely available DNS servers to do service discovery (Cheshire, 2002). Many other service discovery protocols also use tree-like hierarchical structures to provide scalable solutions. Nevertheless, it is difficult to make directories both scalable and efficient.

Service State in Directories. Most service discovery protocols choose to use soft states. In a service announcement, the life span of the service is specified. Before the service expires, it should announce itself again to renew the service. Or, the service will not be valid after the life span. In the mean time, expired service entries will be wiped off from the directories periodically. In case a service is down, that service will not be available after its lifespan and clients will not use it. Therefore, directories are free from monitoring service states. Soft state service management mechanism greatly simplifies the system design. On the other hand, regular service announcements require more network bandwidth, and put extra load on the directories.

On the contrary, directories may maintain service status as hard state. In this case, the directories keep the service status until it is told to change the service status information. Using hard state directories, few service announcements and housekeeping jobs are required. But the disadvantage is the difficulty to guarantee all service information is up to date in hard state directories. Services may go down without notifying directories or out of date service status results from network communication error.

Directory Hierarchies. A single hierarchy directory has a tree structure, while a multiple hierarchy structure could be a forest or many trees sharing a set of leaf directories. Multiple hierarchies index service information on different keys. Like a database index, service information search based on a key may greatly speed up the search. Extra computing resources are obvious overhead for multiple hierarchy directories.

Service Announcement and Lookup

Service announcement and lookup are the key parts of service discovery protocols. Query and announcement are the two basic mechanisms for clients, services, and directories to exchange information. Four different communication techniques are used in service discovery protocols: unicast, anycast, multicast, and broadcast. Based on the OSI reference model, these four communication techniques may be at the data link layer (media access control sub-layer), at the network layer, or at the application layer.

Query vs. Announcement. The two methods for clients to learn which services are available are query and announcement, also known as active and passive or pull and push. As announcements go to all the clients or directories, interested clients or directories do not need to ask separately for the same service. Nevertheless, clients or directories have to handle all the announcements, regardless of whether they are interested. When asking actively, a client or a directory will receive an immediate response. While listening to service announcements, a client or a directory may wait up to the interval of service announcement.

Unicast. Unicast is widely used in many service discovery protocols. When a client knows a directory's network address in advance, it will send a unicast message to the directory. If a client knows a service provider's address, it will contact the service provider directly. Furthermore, if a service's address is known to a directory or vice versa, service announcements and queries between a directory and a service are also using unicast.

Anycast. A set of similar services all may meet a client's request. The service request sent to one of the set of services is known as anycast. For instance, INS uses overlay network anycast, so its anycast is at the application layer. In INS, a client's request goes to a directory. After searching that directory, INS routes the request to a service based on the application-defined service weight. Thus, a client request goes to a service with the best service weight.

Multicast. The drawback of unicast is that the network address needs to be configured or known ahead of time. On the contrary, in many situations, the addresses are unknown. A solution is that clients, service, and directories use multicast addresses for announcements and queries. For example, SLP uses TCP/IP network layer multicast addresses. It is simpler for mobile clients and will be automatically compatible when new services or directories are added later, because global multicast addresses are used. Nevertheless, there are very limited globally multicast addresses at the network layer. Moreover, multicast is not allowed on some routers even though the routers have multicast capabilities. Using multicast also introduces more communication overhead compared to unicast, since more nodes are involved in the communication.

Broadcast. Sometimes broadcast is used in service discovery protocols. For example, Bluetooth Service Discovery Protocol uses broadcast to find other services. In Bluetooth, as other communication techniques are based on broadcast, it is simpler to use broadcast directly. Another example is that Salutation can utilize broadcast if underlying protocols support broadcast. Regardless, data link layer broadcast is usually limited to its subnet.

Using unicast usually saves much communication traffic; using anycast simplifies client side processing; using multicast saves administrative overhead; and using broadcast is sometimes more efficient.

Service Selection

While many similar services are available to a client, which service should the client use? It is challenging to find services for users efficiently and accurately.

User vs. Protocol Selection. Service discovery protocols may select services for a user. In INS, for example, the protocol decides which service a client should use. For most service discovery protocols, client programs or users choose from a matched list of services. The advantage of protocol selection is that it simplifies client programs or little user involvement is needed. On the other hand, protocol selection may not select the proper service that a user wants. Predefined selection criteria may not apply to all cases. Alternatively, too much user involvement causes inconvenience. It may be tedious for a user to examine many services and compare them. A balance between protocol selection and user selection is preferred.

Service Matching. Some service discovery protocols match one of the services for a client. In Matchmaking, a classified advertisement matchmaking framework, client requests are matched to services and one of the matched services is selected for a user (Raman, Livny, & Solomon, 1998). In INS, the service discovery protocol matches the best service based on application defined metrics. Most protocols match all the services and let the user choose.

Context-awareness. Context information is useful in selecting services. For example, when Bob drives on the highway, his cell phone uses a Bluetooth connection to find his earphone. While he wants to access his email, his cell phone uses a 3G connection. In the above two scenarios, selections of the connections for the cell phone are based on context information. Either intelligence should be built in his cell phone or user involvement is necessary for better service discoveries. So far, only a few projects use location information as a kind of context information to help service selection.

Scope-awareness. To support a large amount of services, defining and grouping services in scopes facilitates service search. Location-awareness is a key feature in pervasive computing (Weiser, 1991) and location information is helpful in many service discovery cases. Location information may be integrated with service discovery protocols. For example, a project at MIT (Chakraborty, 2000) integrates Cricket into INS to provide location dependent service discovery. Another example is Jini, in which location information is an optional attribute for services. Moreover, administrative domains are another kind of scope, which is supported by many protocols. Often, in enterprise environments, services are arranged in administrative domains. These geographical location information and administrative domain information may be set as attributes of services.

Much research has proposed locating objects in a wide area. Some of them use a single directory hierarchy, and others use multiple directory hierarchies. No matter if there is a single hierarchy or multiple hierarchies, the difficult problem is to express the service information at different levels of the hierarchies. First, what services need to be listed in upper level directories? Second, what service information to store in lower level directories and what service information to store in higher level directories? To avoid being a bottleneck, upper level hierarchy directories should be concise. Filtering and aggregating service information is necessary when building the upper level hierarchies. Third, updating service information in the upper level hierarchies may overwhelm the directories, when many services update information at the same time. Service status changes and mobile services moving all cause the directories to be busy updating. In SSDS, service information in non-leaf level directories is created by using Bloom filters to achieve high compression ratio. Nevertheless, the directories need to be built again and again over time, since the algorithm is not able to remove stale services. Another example of locating mobile objects in a

wide area is Globe (Steen, Hauck, Homburg, & Tanenbaum, 1998).

QoS-awareness. Providing users with better services and balancing services usage are nice features for service discovery protocols. For better service matching, service requests may be directed to less loaded services or better resource price ratio services.

Service attributes are defined to match client requests more precisely. Nevertheless, most protocols only support static attributes. Sometimes, dynamic information about the current status of a service should be taken into consideration, for instance the current load of a service. Much more communication traffic may be generated and directories may be more busy handling announcements. To reduce the directory's update and network overhead, services may wait for clients to query.

At the service side, sharing the loads and balancing them on different services is also preferred. Few protocols define application metrics-based load balancing. A good example is INS. Applications define their metrics and service lookups are based on the metrics.

Cross-Layer Optimization

Most service discovery protocols are designed as application layer protocols. These protocols enable clients and services that run on different hardware, software platforms, and network protocols stacks to interoperate with each other. Nevertheless, these protocols may not be efficient for dynamic and resource constrained environments such as ad hoc networks. An active service discovery research area is to explore the cross-layer design to optimize the performance of service discovery protocols and adopt design approaches used in wireless sensor networks and ad hoc networks.

Topology based. Ad hoc or sensor networks may form three types of topologies: *flat* networks, *backbone* based networks and *cluster* based networks. In flat works, all nodes perform the same role. DEAPspace targets at one hop ad hoc network (Nidd, 2001). Nodes take turns to broadcast their service information together with the information about other services that they have learned from the broadcast messages. To disseminate service advertisements beyond a simple hop and to reduce the overhead of flooding the networks, a mechanism, called Service*, selectively chooses some neighbors as brokers to forward the service information (Nedos, Singh, & Clarke, 2005). If a backbone is established in a wireless sensor network or an ad hoc network, service information and requests may be distributed and forwarded to the backbone nodes. Thus, the service information is accessible to all nodes and a node can search the whole network for services(Kozat & Tassiulas, 2004). In cluster based networks, nodes that form clusters may exchange their service information within a cluster as in Allia (Ratsimor, Chakraborty, Joshi, & Finin, 2002)and let cluster heads store and forward service information as in Service Ring (Klein, Konig-Ries, & Obreiter, 2003). Cluster heads (known as Service Access Points in Service Ring,) further form other level of hierarchy to exchange information among the cluster heads.

Integration into routing protocols. Service discovery protocols may be tightly integrated with routing protocols. Instead of sending service discovery messages separately, the messages may be embedded into routing protocols such as DSR or AODV (Garcia-Macias & Torres, 2005; Varshavsky, Reid, & Lara, 2005). Simulations results have shown that integrated service discovery protocols always outperform application layer service discovery protocols in ad hoc networks (Varshavsky, et al., 2005). It is especially beneficial when it is necessary to rediscover or reselect services.

Security and Privacy

We discuss security in the following aspects: user authentication, authorization, confidentiality,

integrity, non-repudiation, availability, and user privacy for service discovery protocols. Although there is much research related to service discovery, a few protocols have security and privacy functionalities.

User Authentication and Service Authorization. Protecting services from unauthorized use is essential. For example, one does not want a home theater service to be accessible by anyone. The problem is that it is difficult for each service even in home environments to maintain its users and an access control list (Ellison, 2002). Authentication and authorization in home environments may as complex as enterprise environments. As users interact with many different service providers in various environments, they may have many credentials to interact with the service providers. Authentication becomes more tedious and less usable. PrudentExposure encodes all credential information of a user into a network packet and discovers the appropriate credential information for authentication and authorization purposes (Zhu, Mutka, & Ni, 2006). The credential information exchanged between a client and a service is in a code word format, such that only legitimate service providers recognize the code words. The approach is limited to the case the users and service providers know each other and share secrets. Splendor project targets public environments, where users and service providers may not be familiar with each other (Zhu, Mutka, & Ni, 2003). Users/clients, services, and directories exchange their public key certificates to verify their identities. Authentication is less feasible in ad hoc environments unless other methods such as side channels are used for clients and services to verify each other (Zhu, Mutka, & Ni, 2005). It is even worse for some devices with very limited processing and communication capability to do authentication and authorization.

Confidentiality and Integrity. Confidentiality and integrity in service discovery are primarily communication security. Communication between service discovery components needs to be safe.

Malicious users may listen to communication channels or even actively attack systems. These requirements are translated to use of message encryption and message authentication code. Several service discovery protocols including SSDS and PrudentExposure use cryptographic approaches to encrypt and digitally sign the discovery messages, announcements, and other communication messages (Czerwinski, et al., 1999; Zhu, et al., 2003, 2005).

Availability, Non-repudiation, and User Privacy. Services and directories may be targets of attackers. Making services and directories available against attack is similar to other network applications. We are not aware of any existing service discovery protocols that explicitly address the availability issues.

User privacy is always a concern. We want to use services easily but keep our information private. A progressive and secure service discovery protocol exposes users' query information and service providers' service information over multiple rounds (Zhu, Zhu, Mutka, & Ni, 2007). In each round, several bits of the information in an encrypted form are exchanged. If the client and the service provider find the matches in the request and reply, they continue interacting with each other. Otherwise, the interaction is stopped and not further information is exchanged. The approach is also limited to users and service providers who are familiar with each other.

Deploying security in service discovery protocols means more administrative overhead. Proper permissions need to be set for services and users. With thousands of services and hundreds of users in an enterprise, groups or roles need to be created and privileges need to be assigned. In dynamic environments, daily administrative tasks may be overwhelming. Even if service discovery protocols try to make service usage easier, overwhelming security administrative tasks may offset some advantages.

Service Integration

Services provide different functionalities. Taking services as building blocks, service integration can build complex and very powerful services. Service integration is also known as service composition.

Simple Service Integration vs. Complex Service Integration. Simple service integration chains services together. One service's output is another service's input. Ninja Paths is an example of simple service integration (Gribble et al., 2001). To get a composite service, a path is created. Along that path, services are dynamically selected and connected.

Complex service integration may provide more complicated services. Two complex service integration methods are discussed in (Mennie & Pagurek, 2000). One way is to create a service interface to interact with multiple services. Another way is to compose services and build a stand-alone service. Those integrated services may be used as service components to build other services.

Static vs. Dynamic Service Integration. Static service integration integrates services before a client uses the services. If one of the services fails, service integration needs to start over again. Dynamic service integration may replace failed services or add in more services if necessary without starting over the service integration processes. Dynamic service integration is more difficult to implement than static service integration since every service component of the dynamic service is being monitored and should be replaced immediately in case of failure.

Fault Tolerance and Failure Recovery. In dynamic and distributed environments, fault tolerance and failure recovery for service integration are two difficult issues. In the Ninja Architecture, services are monitored and paths are dynamically changed to guarantee optimal services (Gribble, et al., 2001). Another example is a service integration architecture based on software hot-swapping technology proposed by Mennie and Pagurek (Mennie & Pagurek, 2000). Dabrowski, et al.

modeled and analyzed different failure recovery strategies in (Dabrowski, Mills, & Elder, 2002). Jini and UPnP were the two protocols that they tested. Performance responsiveness, effectiveness and efficiency were explored in that work.

FUTURE RESEARCH DIRECTIONS

Dynamic, heterogeneous, secure, and private properties remain the major challenges for service discovery protocols in pervasive computing environments. Although there are many service discovery protocols proposed, no protocol addresses all the issues and empowers users to access network services and information without administrative overhead. The main research issues need the efforts from academia, industry, and international standards development organizations.

- First, secure and private service discovery in unfamiliar environments is perhaps the most challenging issue. In addition, pervasive computing environments may not be easily separated by network firewalls as traditional enterprise or home environments.
- Second, it is unlikely that a single protocol will outperform all other protocols in heterogeneous computing environments. Different network topologies, protocol stacks, hardware, and other constraints pose the crucial challenges. Researchers need to explore appropriate approaches to balance specific and high performance solutions and general solutions.
- Third, interoperability among different service discovery protocols is important. Without it, users will not be able to discover and access all available services. Moreover, additional strategies and algorithms are needed to select the proper service discovery protocols for different computing environments.

CONCLUSION

Service discovery is a critical component for pervasive computing environments. We discussed the elements of service discovery protocols and their design issues. Classifications of the service discovery protocols were given. Different protocol designs were compared. Much research is still needed to empower users to easily access network information and services with desired feature in the dynamic and heterogeneous pervasive computing environments.

REFERENCES

Adjie-Winoto, W., Schwartz, E., Balakrishnan, H., & Lilley, J. (1999, December). *The design and implementation of an intentional naming system.* Paper presented at the 17th ACM Symposium on Operating Systems Principles (SOSP '99), Kiawah Island, SC.

Apple Computer Inc. (2003). Rendezvous website Retrieved May, 2003, from http://developer.apple.com/ macosx/rendezvous/

Balazinska, M., Balakrishnan, H., & Karger, D. (2002, August). *INS/Twine: A scalable peer-to-peer architecture for intentional resource discovery.* Paper presented at the Pervasive 2002 - International Conference on Pervasive Computing, Zurich, Switzerland.

Bluetooth, S. I. G. (2001). *Specification of the Bluetooth system -- Core* (version 1.1). Retrieved from http://www.bluetooth.org/docs /Bluetooth_V11_Core_22Feb01.pdf

Chakraborty, A. (2000). *A distributed architecture for mobile, location-dependent applications.* Master's thesis, Massachusetts Institute of Technology, Cambridge, MA.

Cheshire, S. (2002). *Discovering named instances of abstract services using DNS: Apple Computer.*

Czerwinski, S., Zhao, B. Y., Hodes, T., Joseph, A., & Katz, R. (1999). *An architecture for a secure service discovery service.* Paper presented at the Fifth Annual International Conference on Mobile Computing and Networks (MobiCom '99), Seattle, WA.

Dabrowski, C., Mills, K., & Elder, J. (2002, July 2002). *Understanding consistency maintenance in service discovery architectures during communication failure.* Paper presented at the 4th International Workshop on Active Middleware Services, Edinburgh, UK.

Ellison, C. (2002). Home network security. *Intel Technology Journal, 6*(4), 37–48.

Garcia-Macias, J. A., & Torres, D. A. (2005). *Service discovery in mobile ad-hoc networks: Better at the network layer?* Paper presented at the 2005 International Conference on Parallel Processing Workshops (ICPPW'05).

Gribble, S. D., Welsh, M., Behren, R. v., Brewer, E. A., Culler, D., Borisov, N., et al. (2001). The ninja architecture for robust Internet-scale systems and services. *IEEE Computer Networks, 35*(4).

Guttman, E., Perkins, C., & Kempf, J. (1999). *Service templates and service: Schemes: Sun Microsystems.*

Guttman, E., Perkins, C., Veizades, J., & Day, M. (1999). *Service location protocol,* version 2.

Kindberg, T., & Fox, A. (2002). System software for ubiquitous computing. *IEEE Pervasive Computing / IEEE Computer Society [and] IEEE Communications Society,* (January-March): 70–81. doi:10.1109/MPRV.2002.993146

Klein, M., Konig-Ries, B., & Obreiter, P. (2003). *Service rings – A semantic overlay for service discovery in ad hoc networks.* Paper presented at the 14th International Workshop on Database and Expert Systems Applications (DEXA'03).

Kozat, U. C., & Tassiulas, L. (2004). Service discovery in mobile ad hoc networks: An overall perspective on architectural choices and network layer support issues. *Ad Hoc Networks, 2*(1), 23–44. doi:10.1016/S1570-8705(03)00044-1

Mennie, D., & Pagurek, B. (2000, June 12, 2000). *An architecture to support dynamic composition of service components.* Paper presented at the 5th International Workshop on Component-Oriented Programming, WCOP 2000, Cannes, France.

Miller, B. A., Nixon, T., Tai, C., & Wood, M. D. (2001). Home networking with universal plug and play. *IEEE Communications Magazine,* (December): 104–109. doi:10.1109/35.968819

Nedos, A., Singh, K., & Clarke, S. (2005). *Service*: *Distributed service advertisement for multiservice, multi-hop MANET environments.* Paper presented at the 7th IFIP International Conference on Mobile and Wirelss Communication Networks Marrakech, Morocco.

Nidd, M. (2001). Service discovery in DEAPspace. *IEEE Personal Communications,* (August), 39-45.

Raman, R., Livny, M., & Solomon, M. (1998, July 28-31). *Matchmaking: Distributed resource management for high throughput computing.* Paper presented at the Seventh IEEE International Symposium on High Performance Distributed Computing, Chicago, IL.

Ratsimor, O., Chakraborty, D., Joshi, A., & Finin, T. (2002). *Allia: Alliance-based service discovery for ad-hoc environments.* Paper presented at the 2nd International Workshop on Mobile Commerce Atlanta, Georgia, USA.

Salutation Consortium. (1999). *Salutation architecture specification* (Version 2.0c).

Steen, M. v., Hauck, F. J., Homburg, P., & Tanenbaum, A. S. (1998). Locating objects in wide-area systems. *IEEE Communications Magazine*, (January): 104–109. doi:10.1109/35.649334

Sun Microsystems. (2001). *Jini™ technology core platform specification* (version 1.2). Sun Microsystem. Retrieved from http://wwws.sun.com/ software/jini/specs/

Varshavsky, A., Reid, B., & Lara, E. d. (2005). *A cross-layer approach to service discovery and selection in MANETs*. Paper presented at the 2nd International Conference on Mobile Ad-Hoc and Sensor Systems (MASS), Washington, DC.

Weiser, M. (1991). The computer for the 21st century. *Scientific American*, *265*(3), 66–75. doi:10.1038/scientificamerican0991-94

Zhu, F., Mutka, M., & Ni, L. (2003, March 23-26, 2003). *Splendor: A secure, private, and location-aware service discovery protocol supporting mobile services*. Paper presented at the 1st IEEE Annual Conference on Pervasive Computing and Communications, Fort Worth, Texas.

Zhu, F., Mutka, M., & Ni, L. (2005). Facilitating secure ad hoc service discovery in public environments. *Journal of Systems and Software*, *76*(1), 45–54. doi:10.1016/j.jss.2004.07.014

Zhu, F., Mutka, M., & Ni, L. (2006). A private, secure and user-centric information exposure model for service discovery protocols. *IEEE Transactions on Mobile Computing*, *5*(4), 418–429. doi:10.1109/TMC.2006.1599409

Zhu, F., Zhu, W., Mutka, M., & Ni, L. (2007). Private and secure service discovery via progressive and probabilistic exposure. *IEEE Transactions on Parallel and Distributed Systems*, *18*(11), 1565–1577. doi:10.1109/TPDS.2007.1075

ADDITIONAL READING

Adjie-Winoto, W. (2000). *A Self-Configuring Resolver Architecture for Resource Discovery and Routing in Device Networks. Engineering in Electrical Engineering and Computer Science.* Cambridge, MA: Massachusetts Institute of Technology.

Adjie-Winoto, W., Schwartz, E., Balakrishnan, H., & Lilley, J. (1999). *The design and implementation of an intentional naming system.* Paper presented at the 17th ACM Symposium on Operating Systems Principles (SOSP '99), Kiawah Island, SC.

Avancha, S., Joshi, A., et al. (2002). "Enhanced Service Discovery in Bluetooth." IEEE Computer 35(Issue 6): 96-99. Apple Computer Inc. (2003). Rendezvous Web Site Retrieved May, 2003, from http://developer.apple.com/ macosx/rendezvous/

Balazinska, M., Balakrishnan, H., & Karger, D. (2002). INS/Twine: A Scalable Peer-to-Peer Architecture for Intentional Resource Discovery. Paper presented at the Pervasive 2002 - International Conference on Pervasive Computing, Zurich, Switzerland.

Bettstetter, C., & Renner, C. (2000). A Comparison of Service Discovery Protocols and Implementation of the Service Location Protocol. Proc. 6th EUNICE Open European Summer School: Innovative Internet Applications (EUNICE'00), Twente, Netherlands.

Bluetooth, S. I. G. (2001). Specification of the Bluetooth System -- Core (Version 1.1 ed.). Retrieved from http://www.bluetooth.org/ docs/ Bluetooth_V11 _Core_22Feb01.pdf.

Bluetooth SIG (2004). Specification of the Bluetooth System.

Castro, P., Greenstein, B., et al. (2001). Locating Application Data Across Service Discovery Domains. ACM SIGMOBILE MOBICOM 2001, 7th Annual Int. Conf. Mobile Computing and Networking, Rome, Italy

Chakraborty, D., & Joshi, A. (2006). Toward Distributed Service Discovery in Pervasive Computing Environments. *IEEE Transactions on Mobile Computing, 5*(2), 97–112. doi:10.1109/TMC.2006.26

Chakraborty, D., Perich, F., et al. (2001). DReggie: Semantic Service Discovery for M-Commerce Applications. Workshop on Reliable and Secure Applications in Mobile Environment, 20th Symposium on Reliable Distributed Systems, New Orleans, USA.

Chen, H., Chakraborty, D., et al. (2000). Service Discovery in the Future Electronic Market. Proceedings of the Knowledge Based Electronic Markets AAAI 2000, Austin, TX.

Chen, H., A. Joshi, et al. (2001). "Dynamic Service Discovery for Mobile Computing: Intelligent Agents Meet Jini in the Aether." Baltzer Science Journal on Cluster Computing 4(Issue 4).

Cheshire, S. (2002). Discovering Named Instances of Abstract Services using DNS: Apple Computer.

Cheshire, S., & Krochmal, M. (2004). *DNS-Based Service Discovery*. Apple Computer.

Czerwinski, S., Zhao, B. Y., Hodes, T., Joseph, A., & Katz, R. (1999). An Architecture for a Secure Service Discovery Service. Paper presented at the Fifth Annual International Conference on Mobile Computing and Networks (MobiCom '99), Seattle, WA.

Dabrowski, C., & Mills, K. (2001). Analyzing Properties and Behavior of Service Discovery Protocols using an Architecture-based Approach. Working Conference on Complex and Dynamic Systems Architecture.

Dabrowski, C., Mills, K., & Elder, J. (2002). Understanding Consistency Maintenance in Service Discovery Architectures during Communication Failure. Paper presented at the Proceedings of the 4th International Workshop on Active Middleware Services, Edinburgh, UK.

Dipanjan Chakraborty, A. J. Yelena Yesha, Tim Finin (2002). GSD: A Novel Group-based Service Discovery Protocol for MANETS. 4th IEEE Conference on Mobile and Wireless Communications Networks.

Friday, A., & Davies, N. (2001). *Supporting Service Discovery, Querying and Interaction in Ubiquitous Computing Environments. Second ACM international workshop on Data engineering for wireless and mobile access 2001*. California, United States: Santa Barbara.

Garcia-Macias, J. A., & Torres, D. A. (2005). Service Discovery in Mobile Ad-Hoc Networks: Better at the Network Layer? Paper presented at the 2005 International Conference on Parallel Processing Workshops (ICPPW'05).

Goland, Y. Y., Cai, T., et al. (1999). Simple Service Discovery Protocol 1.0, Microsoft Co. http://www.upnp.org/download /draft_cai_ssdp_v1_03.txt.

Gribble, S. D., Welsh, M., Behren, R. v., Brewer, E. A., Culler, D., Borisov, N., et al. (2001). The Ninja Architecture for Robust Internet-Scale Systems and Services. IEEE Computer Networks, 35(Issue 4).

Guttman, E., Perkins, C., & Kempf, J. (1999). Service Templates and Service: Schemes: Sun Microsystems.

Guttman, E., Perkins, C., Veizades, J., & Day, M. (1999). Service Location Protocol, Version 2.

Helal, S. (2002). Standards for Service Discovery and Delivery. *IEEE Pervasive Computing / IEEE Computer Society [and] IEEE Communications Society, 1*(3), 95–100. doi:10.1109/MPRV.2002.1037728

Helal, S., Desai, N., et al. (2003). Konark – A Service Discovery and Delivery Protocol for Ad-Hoc Networks. third IEEE Conference on Wireless Communication Networks WCNC, New Orleans.

Hodes, T., & Czerwinski, S. (2002). An Architecture for Secure Wide-Area Service Discovery. *ACM Wireless Networks Journal*, *8*(Issue 2/3), 213–230. doi:10.1023/A:1013772027164

Kagal, L., & Korolev, V. (2001). *A Highly Adaptable Infrastructure for Service Discovery and Management in Ubiquitous Computing*. Dept. of Computer Science and Electrical Engineering, University of Maryland, Baltimore County.

Klein, M., Konig-Ries, B., & Obreiter, P. (2003). Service Rings – A Semantic Overlay for Service Discovery in Ad hoc Networks. Paper presented at the 14th International Workshop on Database and Expert Systems Applications (DEXA'03).

Kozat, U. C., & Tassiulas, L. (2003). Network Layer Support for Service Discovery in Mobile Ad Hoc Networks. 22nd Annual Joint Conference of the IEEE Computer and Communications San Francisco.

Kozat, U. C., & Tassiulas, L. (2004). Service discovery in mobile ad hoc networks: an overall perspective on architectural choices and network layer support issues. *Ad Hoc Networks*, *2*(1), 23–44. doi:10.1016/S1570-8705(03)00044-1

Lee, C., & Helal, S. (2002). Protocols for Service Discovery in Dynamic and Mobile Networks. *International Journal of Computer Research*, *11*(1), 1–12.

Lee, C., & Helal, S. (2002). *A Multi-tier Ubiquitous Service Discovery Protocol for Mobile Clients*. Gainesville: University of Florida.

MacBeth, A. (2001). *An Autoconfiguring Server-based Service Discovery System*. Department of Computer Science & Engineering, University of Washington.

McGrath, R. E. (2000). *Discovery and Its Discontents: Discovery Protocols for Ubiquitous Computing*. Urbana, Champaign: National Center for Supercomputing Applications, University of Illinois.

Mennie, D., & Pagurek, B. (2000, June 12, 2000). An Architecture to Support Dynamic Composition of Service Components. Paper presented at the 5th International Workshop on Component-Oriented Programming, WCOP 2000, Cannes, France.

Miller, B. (1999). Mapping Salutation Architecture APIs to Bluetooth Service Discovery Layer, Bluetooth SIG. http://www.salutation.org/ whitepaper/ BtoothMapping.PDF.

Miller, B. A., Nixon, T., Tai, C., & Wood, M. D. (2001). Home Networking with Universal Plug and Play. *IEEE Communications Magazine*, (December): 104–109. doi:10.1109/35.968819

Nedos, A., Singh, K., & Clarke, S. (2005). Service*: Distributed Service Advertisement for Multi-Service, Multi-Hop MANET Environments. Paper presented at the 7th IFIP International Conference on Mobile and Wirelss Communication Networks Marrakech, Morocco.

Nidd, M. (2000). Timeliness of Service Discovery in DEAPspace. Proceedings of the 2000 International Workshops on Parallel Processing (ICPP'00 - Workshops).

Nidd, M. (2001). Service Discovery in DEAPspace. IEEE Personal Communications(August), 39-45.

Preuß, S. (2002). JESA Service Discovery Protocol Effcient Service Discovery in Ad-Hoc Networks. Second International IFIP-TC6 Networking Conference: Networking 2002, Pisa, Italy, Springer-Verlag.

Preuß, S. and C. H. Cap (2000). Overview of Spontaneous Networking - Evolving Concepts and Technologies. Rostocker Informatik-Berichte, Fachbereich Informatik der Universit{\"a}t Rostock. 24: 113-123.

Ratsimor, O., Chakraborty, D., Joshi, A., & Finin, T. (2002). Allia: alliance-based service discovery for ad-hoc environments. Paper presented at the Proceedings of the 2nd international workshop on Mobile commerce Atlanta, Georgia, USA.

Ratsimor, O., Korolev, V., et al. (2001). Agents-2Go: An Infrastructure for Location-Dependent Service Discovery in The Mobile Electronic Commerce Environment. First ACM Mobile Commerce Workshop, Rome.

Richard, G. G. III. (2000). Service Advertisement and Discovery: Enabling Universal Device Cooperation. *IEEE Internet Computing*, (September-October): 18–26. doi:10.1109/4236.877482

Salutation Consortium. (1999). Salutation Architecture Specification (Version 2.0c ed.).

Sun Microsystems. (2001). Jini™Technology Core Platform Specification (Version 1.2 ed.): Sun Microsystem. Retrieved from http://wwws.sun.com/ software/jini/specs/.

Varshavsky, A., Reid, B., & Lara, E. d. (2005). A Cross-Layer Approach to Service Discovery and Selection in MANETs. Paper presented at the 2nd International Conference on Mobile Ad-Hoc and Sensor Systems (MASS), Washington, DC.

Ververidis, C., & Polyzos, G. (2008). Service Discovery for Mobile Ad Hoc Networks: a Survey of Issues and Techniques. *IEEE Communications Surveys*, *10*(3), 30–45. doi:10.1109/COMST.2008.4625803

Zhu, F., Mutka, M., et al. (2004). PrudentExposure: A Private and User-centric Service Discovery Protocol. 2nd IEEE Annual Conference on Pervasive Computing and Communications, Orlando, Florida, IEEE Computer Society Press.

Zhu, F., & Mutka, M. (2005). Service Discovery in Pervasive Computing Environments. *IEEE Pervasive Computing / IEEE Computer Society [and] IEEE Communications Society*, *4*(4), 81–90. doi:10.1109/MPRV.2005.87

Zhu, F., Mutka, M., & Ni, L. (2003, March 23-26, 2003). Splendor: A Secure, Private, and Location-aware Service Discovery Protocol Supporting Mobile Services. Paper presented at the 1st IEEE Annual Conference on Pervasive Computing and Communications, Fort Worth, Texas.

Zhu, F., Mutka, M., & Ni, L. (2005). Facilitating secure ad hoc service discovery in public environments. *Journal of Systems and Software*, *76*(1), 45–54. doi:10.1016/j.jss.2004.07.014

Zhu, F., Mutka, M., & Ni, L. (2006). A Private, Secure and User-centric Information Exposure Model for Service Discovery Protocols. *IEEE Transactions on Mobile Computing*, *5*(4), 418–429. doi:10.1109/TMC.2006.1599409

Zhu, F., Zhu, W., et al. (2005). Expose or Not? A Progressive Exposure Approach for Service Discovery in Pervasive Computing Environments. 3rd IEEE Annual Conference on Pervasive Computing and Communications, Kauai island, Hawaii.

Zhu, F., Zhu, W., Mutka, M., & Ni, L. (2007). Private and Secure Service Discovery via Progressive and Probabilistic Exposure. *IEEE Transactions on Parallel and Distributed Systems*, *18*(11), 1565–1577. doi:10.1109/TPDS.2007.1075

KEY TERMS AND DEFINITIONS

Application Layer Service Discovery: Usually, service discovery protocols are implemented at the application layer. Thus, they are independent of the underlying media, lower layer network protocols, and operating systems.

Cross-Layer Optimization: Cross-layer optimization is sometimes used in service discovery protocols for wireless ad hoc networks. The service discovery mechanisms are integrated with routing protocols to reduce the overhead.

Service Announcement: Service announcement is a basic mechanism for services to inform clients, peer services, and directories their up to date information. Services usually have life spans and will be invalid after the life span. Services use the service announcements to notify interested parties that they are available.

Service Attribute: Service attributes are the properties of services. For example, printing speed, resolution, and paper sizes are the attributes of a printer. Unlike the traditional services that are identified by their names, IP addresses, and port numbers, service attributes are used to identify services in service discovery protocols.

Service Discovery: Service discovery is a type of network protocols. The protocols reduce the administrative overhead and automate configuration and setup to use service. Via a set of service discovery mechanisms, clients and services exchange service information, properly configure, and install necessary drivers before service usage.

Service Integration: Service integration enables complex services that are built from individual services. Often, a service's output is used as the input of another service. Service integration is also known as service composition.

Service Lookup: Service lookup mechanisms facilitate the matching from a client's request to an existing service or services.

Chapter 6
A Software Engineering Framework for Context–Aware Service–Based Processes in Pervasive Environments

Zakwan Jaroucheh
Edinburgh Napier University, UK

Xiaodong Liu
Edinburgh Napier University, UK

Sally Smith
Edinburgh Napier University, UK

ABSTRACT

Context-awareness is considered to be the cornerstone technique for developing pervasive computing applications that are flexible, adaptable, and capable of acting autonomously on behalf of the user. However, context-awareness introduces various software engineering challenges. The separation of concerns is a promising approach in the design of the context-aware adaptive processes (CAAPs) where the core logic is designed and implemented separately from the context handling and adaptation logics. In this respect, this chapter presents a conceptual framework for developing CAAPs and software infrastructure for efficient context management that together address the known software engineering challenges and facilitate the design and implementation tasks associated with such context-aware applications.

INTRODUCTION

Context-awareness refers to the capability of an application or a service being aware of its physical environment or situation (e.g. context) and to respond proactively and intelligently based on

this awareness (Baldauf et al. 2007). It is widely acknowledged that, compared to desktop applications, pervasive environments introduce a new wave of software engineering challenges.

Firstly, in such highly dynamic environments the ultimate objective is to amplify human activi-

DOI: 10.4018/978-1-60960-735-7.ch006

ties and demanding minimal attention from the user. Context-aware applications aims to meet these objectives or requirements by adapting to a subset of the current context considered relevant to the task at hand such as the user location, time, and user activity. In this chapter we focus on developing context-aware service-based processes applications. In addition, we define the context-aware process adaptation as *the action that modifies the process in a way that causes process behavior to evolve according to the evolution of business and users' requirements, and the context considered relevant to that process*. To this end, process modeling must be flexible enough to deal with constant changes – both at the business level (e.g. evolving business rules) and the technical level (e.g. contextual information and platform upgrades). The flexibility could be provided or addressed by incorporating variabilities into a system (Koning et al. 2009). Therefore, the notion of an *evolution fragment* and *evolution primitive* that capture the process variability in a logical way are introduced.

Secondly, in order to have the transition of the context-aware applications out of the laboratory to the marketplace, there is a need for a software engineering framework that simplifies the design and implementation of context-aware software. To this end, the approach proposed in this chapter could apply an adaptation to processes modeled or developed without any adaptation possibility in mind and independently of specific usage contexts. In addition, it supports the viewpoint of context-aware adaptation as a crosscutting concern with respect to the core "business logic" of the process. In this way, the design of the process core can be decoupled from the design of the adaptation logic which significantly eases the process design and rapid prototyping.

Thirdly, to ease the development of such applications it is necessary to decouple the application from context acquisition and representation, and

at the same time provide universal models and mechanisms to manage context. Thus, generic and dynamically manageable context models are of interest since they can be reused by different applications and ease context sharing between systems (Chen et al. 2004). Therefore, in this chapter, we present a context management infrastructure based on a flexible product line based context model which significantly enhances reusability of context information by providing context variability constructs to satisfy different application needs.

The rest of the chapter is organized as follows: In "Context Management Framework," the context management infrastructure is described. It this section the conceptual model for context management is introduced as well as the rationale behind it; then we describe how to model the context information considering the application requirement perspective. For this purpose we leverage ideas from software product line techniques. In "A Model-Driven Framework for Managing Context-Aware Adaptive Service-Based Processes," a MDD-based (Model-Driven Development) framework called *Apto* (Latin word for Adapt) is introduced. We show how to capture the variability in the service-based process in a logical form by introducing the notion of context fragments and context primitives. The proposed approach contributes to a solution to automatically generating a customized process based on the context. Another feature is that Apto supplies a set of automated tools for generating and deploying executable process definitions e.g. WS-BPEL (OASIS, 2007) which in turn significantly reduces the development cost. In "Case Study," we illustrate the proposed frameworks by giving a simple example of Conference Event Advisor process. The related work and concluding remarks ends the chapter.

CONTEXT MANAGEMENT FRAMEWORK

Context-Aware Systems

Context-aware applications are those that consider the current situation of their users in order to provide services and information tailored to their needs. An important topic when dealing with context-aware systems is how to model, manage, and manipulate the context information. To ease context representation, context sharing and semantic interoperability between heterogeneous systems, a formal and generic context model is needed (Gu et al. 2005). In this work, we are interested in developing a context-aware application development methodology (Software Engineering perspective); and in particular we are focusing on context modeling (Knowledge Engineering perspective).

In the literature, there are many definitions for context. Definitions given by earlier works agree on the key idea that contexts describe situations. For example (Dey 2001) confirmed this by defining context as: "Any information that can be used to characterize the situation of an entity. An entity is a person, a place, or a physical or computational object that is considered relevant to the interaction between a user and an application, including the user and application themselves." This work is based on two other definitions of context. The first states that in using open-ended phrases such "any information" and "characterize" the context becomes so broad that it covers everything (Winograd 2001). Winograd indicated also that "something is context because of the way it is used in interpretation, not due to its inherent properties. The voltage on the power lines is a context if there is some action by the user and/or computer whose interpretation is dependent on it, but otherwise is just part of the environment." In this work, we adopt his definition of context: "context depends on the interpretation of the operations involved on an entity at a particular time

and space rather than the inherent characteristics of the entity itself."

The second indicates that "context is always related to a focus and that, at a given focus, the context is the aggregation of three types of knowledge: Contextual Knowledge (CK), External Knowledge (EK) and Proceduralized Context (PC)" (Viera et al. 2008). They argue that context should always be considered related to a focus, which is a step in a task execution, in a problem solving or in a decision making process. Moreover, the context evolves dynamically according to the focus, which enables a context-aware system to separate relevant from not relevant knowledge in order to determine the context.

Figure 1 illustrates the proposed working definition of the context (Jaroucheh et al. Feb 2010). The term context primitive (for short, we will refer to it as CP) refers to a piece of contextual knowledge such as entity, entity attribute, relationship between two entities, their constraints, or inference rules –used to define context situations and infer new knowledge– that can be used to define the context. We consider that the context knowledge is composed of a set of small pieces. Given a focus, a relevant subset of these pieces, namely context primitives, will be used to generate the current context. Thus, the generated context is in alignment with the requirement of current task.

The Variability in Context Information

Several middlewares and ontology-based models for describing context information have been developed in order to support context-aware applications. However, the context variability, which refers to the possibility to infer or interpret different context information from different perspectives, has been neglected in the existing context modeling approaches.

In order of the context management infrastructure to serve different types of applications, it should provide context-specific programming

Figure 1. The proposed context working definition

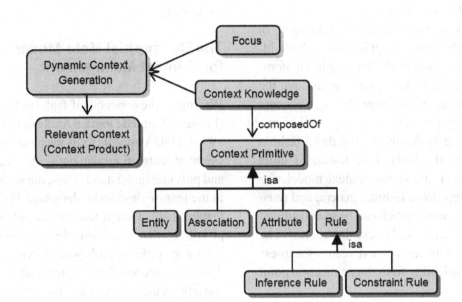

abstraction or constructs that model the context variability. Indeed, different context knowledge could be extracted from the context repository by focusing on different views of the context information. For example, in the smart meeting room, a seat may be equipped with light and temperature sensors to reason about its occupation. The seat could be either free or occupied. Two occupation variants may be identified: occupied by object and occupied by a person. These variants represent two facets to the same fact. Another example of context variability is the context information classification. For instance, the room temperature could be classified as low, moderate and high according to some specified temperature ranges; but these ranges could be different if the room type is a sitting room or a sauna. To the author's best knowledge, the existing approaches do not provide application developers with software constructs through which a view-based customization of the context knowledge could be expressed.

As one of the successful research directions in software engineering, software product line research could contribute to the context modeling.

Commonality and variability management techniques from software product line can be applied to handle context variabilities for customization and adaptation (See "Context as a Dynamic Product Line"). Therefore, in this chapter we explore the synergy between feature modeling and context modeling. On the other hand, feature modeling is a key concept in product line engineering. Thus, the feature model of the system context will be considered as a composition of segmented context features models; each of which models a part of the whole context. Based on the context feature model, specific context −member of a product line− can be constructed by composing features from context information.

In this section we focus on dealing with context variability from the application requirement perspective. The proposed approach does not model the context information itself by using feature model as the feature models are less powerful than ontologies, and are more appropriate for expressing a subset of what ontologies can express (Czarnecki et al. 2006). Instead, the aim is to represent the context information from the requirement perspective. The rationale behind this approach is as follows.

Firstly, in terms of modeling philosophy, in ontology modeling a concept is described by adding its details and implicitly defining in a bottom-up fashion the scope of the concept through the details. Whereas, in feature modeling, a concept is described by first setting its scope and hierarchically adding its details in a top-down fashion (Czarnecki et al. 2006). This feature is quite interesting as it allows the context modeler to devise, in a top-down fashion, generic and reusable context features which can be shared among all applications that need to use this context. The relationships between context features express the context variability from the application point of view.

Secondly, according to the context working definition previously presented in "Context-Aware Systems," we consider that the context knowledge is composed of a set of small contextual knowledge pieces namely context primitives which include context entities, attributes, associations, and rules. Each context feature corresponds to a specific set of context primitives. The focus is a concept representing the point of view the application is interested in looking at the current context. Each focus corresponds to a specific set of context features. Given a focus, a relevant subset of these pieces will be used to generate a per-application customized contextual knowledge. Obviously, considering only the relevant context primitives will improve the reasoning performance and reduce response time which is a vital issue in a pervasive environment.

Thirdly, as developers usually do not have full understanding of the context internal semantic, "promoting" the context information using the feature model will enable the contextual knowledge visibility from different views in a top-down fashion. Another advantage is that these context features might be shared between applications which significantly enhances the reusability of context information and reduces application complexity.

The Conceptual Meta-Model for Context Management

We import the concepts of features from FODA (Feature Oriented Domain Analysis) (Kang et al. 1990). FODA appeals to us because features are essential abstractions that both context consumer and provider understand. Thus, the main concept in the feature description language FODA is the feature itself. Here a feature is a set of context primitives that is relevant to some stakeholder from a specific "focus" point of view. Figure 2 depicts the proposed conceptual metamodel. The concepts of the conceptual metamodel were identified and grouped into two different sections: the context related concepts (white), and the context features concepts (shaded).

The main construct for representing context knowledge is the *ContextPrimitive* which represents the base context constructs (primitives) mentioned above: entity classes, entity attributes, entity associations, and rules. Two types of rules could be identified: (i) Consistency rules provide a mechanism for context consistency by specifying conditions that must be held in the context information. For example, a consistency rule could specify that if the person is cooking, she must be in the kitchen. (ii) Inference rules used to generate new context information after reasoning on the existing one. For example, an inference rule could conclude that a person is sleeping if the light is off and the time is night. Further modeling constructs are axioms that add additional facts about the entities and attributes. These are: specialization and equivalence relationships that may be specified between two entity classes, two attribute classes, or two association classes.

Figure 2. The conceptual meta-model

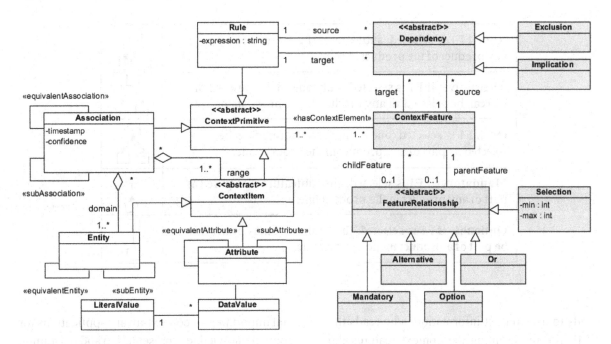

Context as a Dynamic Product Line

According to (Northrop 2002), a software product line (SPL) is a set of software-intensive systems sharing a common, managed set of features that satisfy specific needs of a particular market or mission, and that are developed from a common set of core assets in a prescribed way. Feature modeling is a domain modeling technique, which has generated a lot of interest in the software product line (SPL) community. Modeling product family as a hierarchy of features their similarities, differences and relationships among them, feature models can be used for modeling common and variable requirements of products in a SPL, scoping SPLs, and product configuration and derivation.

Commonly there are five types of relations possible in a feature model (Wang et al. 2007) (See Table 1). Additional constraints between features may exist that describe how features interact with each other e.g. requires and excludes constraints.

In order to identify which of the context information is eligible for being modeled as a

feature, we have adopted a simplified criteria composed of the three steps shown below, followed by the correspondent modeling decisions:

- Identify the context information required by the application adaptation e.g. user location. This should be represented by a generic feature in the feature model.
- Identify the context model transformations or interpretations of the currently available context information in order to be shared by all application instances e.g. room-, floor-, and building-resolution user location information. These interpretations should be represented by different feature variants.
- Regrouping the different identified context features into a logical hierarchy of features in a top-down manner that could be reused by different applications.

The context feature model will be published in a public registry. When an application developer

Table 1. Feature Type Relations

And: if F1 is selected, subfeatures (F2,F3) must be part of any product of the product line	
Alternative: if F1 is selected, only one subfeature (F2 or F3) can be selected in any product in the product line.	
Or: if F1 is selected, one or more subfeatures can be selected as part of any product in the product line.	
Mandatory: if F1 is selected, the subfeature is required as part of any product in the product line.	
Optional: if F1 is selected, the subfeature may or may not be part of a product in the product line.	

needs to use context information, s/he reads the XML file representing the context features the context manager is able to deliver to understand the context semantics. Then s/he is able to configure the feature model and use the context management infrastructure services to get the necessary context information.

On the other hand, ontologies are a very promising instrument for modeling contextual information due to their high and formal expressiveness and the possibilities for applying ontology reasoning techniques. Thus, we focus on context management employing ontologies as the underlying technology. Several successful efforts have been developed in order to support context-aware applications through ontology-based middlewares and models for describing context information. Common to most of the existing approaches the usage of ontologies (e.g. using OWL) to describe the concepts and properties defining context information in the relevant domain: context types correspond to classes defined in the ontology. RDF is implicitly used as the common, standard language to express classes and individuals (i.e. context types and their instances). Obviously the reasoning capabilities of the ontology are of cru-

cial importance to context-aware applications for context knowledge representation and reasoning.

Although a feature model can represent context commonalities and variabilities in a very concise taxonomic form, features in a feature model are merely symbols. Mapping features to the context ontology gives them semantics. In the following section we describe the proposed approach of mapping the feature model to the ontology context model.

Annotated Context Model

An overview of the proposed approach is shown in Figure 3. A context model family is represented by the context feature model and the ontology-based context model (OCM). The elements of OCM namely the context primitives may be annotated using existence conditions (ECs) and meta-statements (MSs). These annotations are defined in terms of features and feature attributes from the feature model, and can be evaluated with respect to a feature configuration. An EC attached to a context primitive indicates whether the primitive should exist in or should be removed from a context product. MS is mainly used to modify or

Figure 3. Overview of the proposed approach

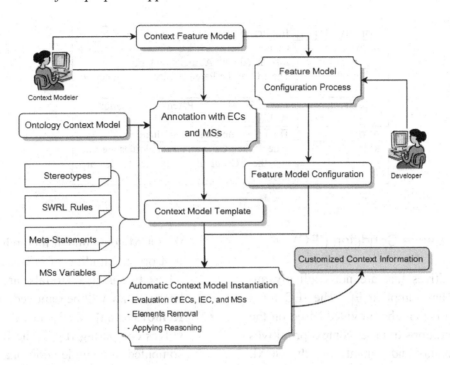

compute the attributes of context model element. This is important for managing context variants as we will see in the case study in "A Model-Driven Framework for Managing Context-Aware Adaptive Service-Based Processes."

An instance of a context model family, which we call context product (CP), can be specified by creating a feature configuration based on the context feature model. Based on the feature configuration, the corresponding context product is generated automatically. The generation process, which is model-to-model transformation, involves evaluating the ECs and MSs with respect to the feature configuration, removing context primitives whose ECs evaluate to false and, possibly doing additional processing such as removing related context primitives.

Obviously, a particularly interesting form of ECs is a Boolean expression over a set of variables each of which corresponds to a feature from the feature model. Given a feature configuration, the value of a feature variable is true if and only if the corresponding feature is included in the feature configuration. In our prototype implementation we use either Boolean expressions in Disjunctive Normal Form (DNF), or more general XPath expressions which can access feature attributes and use other XPath operations, as long as the XPath expression evaluates to a Boolean value. The EC is represented by one or more stereotypes. For example, the stereotype «!f1&&f2||f3» in DNF denotes the Boolean expression $\overline{f_1} \cdot \left(f_2 + f_3\right)$. Once created, the stereotype is available for annotating context primitives.

On the other hand, the ECs should be interpreted with respect to the OCM containment hierarchy. In other words, if a context primitive container is removed all the contained context primitives are removed. For example, if entity x is a sub-entity of the entity y, removing y requires removing x as well.

Table 2. IEC for different context primitives

Primitive Type	Implicit Existence Condition
Association	Conjunction of the EC of the two Entities associated with Association type.
SubEntity	The EC of the Parent Entity is evaluated to true.
SubAssociation	The EC of the Parent Association is evaluated to true.
Attribute	The EC of the Entity is evaluated to true.
Rule	True iff the ECs of all required rules are true and the ECs of all its excluded rules are false.

Implicit Existence Condition (IEC)

Context primitives that are not explicitly annotated will have implicit EC. The IEC for a context primitive can be provided based on the existence conditions of other context primitives and on the syntax and semantics of the OCM. For example, according to the ontology syntax, an object property requires a class at each of its ends. Thus, a reasonable choice of IEC for an object property would be the conjunction of the ECs of both classes. This way, removing any of the classes will also lead to the removal of the object property. IECs reduce the necessary annotation effort of the user.

Table 2 shows our choice of IECs for the context primitives. An IEC for a given primitive is assumed based on its type.

Context Information Generation

A context information generation process involves computing MSs and ECs, and removing elements whose ECs are false. The complete context product instantiation algorithm can be summarized as follows:

- **Evaluation of MSs and explicit ECs:** The evaluation is done while traversing the OCM containment hierarchy in depth-first order. Children of context primitives whose ECs evaluate to false are not visited because they will be removed.

- **Removal Analysis:** Removal analysis involves computing IECs. The IECs can be computed in a single additional pass after evaluating explicit ECs. In addition, in this step all the individuals and statements whose subjects are included in the elements to be removed are also marked to be removed. For example, if the Room entity is known to be removed, all its individuals and all triples whose subject is of type Room should be marked to be removed.

- **Primitive Removal:** In this step, primitives whose ECs are false are removed.

- **Applying Reasoning:** In order to interpret the remaining context information from the perspective specified by the context feature configuration, it is necessary to apply the corresponding remaining rules. The result of the reasoner will be the context product.

In the implemented prototype we use rule-based inference reasoners. Different rule-based systems provide different logical inference support for context reasoning. To reason about ontologies, a description logic reasoner, namely Pellet is applied. We use the Semantic Web Rule Language (SWRL) on top of OWL for interpreting context using domain specific rules and producing new facts. However, the approach could be extended to use other reasoner types.

Discussion

The proposed approach can be seen from two perspectives: (i) identifying context features and giving them semantics by mapping context feature models to OCM; and (ii) using feature models to provide a representation of variability in context models. This has several advantages.

Firstly, from the context modeler usability perspective, the proposed approach is intuitive; it allows her to think about the context information from different perspectives and use the feature model available tools. Indeed, it is possible to think about the context information from different point of views and design different feature models. For example, the context modeler may choose to split the context feature model into more than one sub feature models each of which may be designed to look at the context from a different view point.

Secondly, context feature model allows the context modeler to devise context-specific features that can be shared among all applications that need to use this context. Moreover, retrieving context information using general-purpose query mechanisms remains possible by devising a special context feature. Thirdly, unlike the reasoning on a one monolithic context information, the proposed approach gives the possibility to provide the context information on arbitrary levels of abstraction thanks to the arbitrary composition of context primitives e.g. inference rules. Fourthly, the use of context-specific features may improve the overall performance of the system, since it might decrease the number of network interactions between an application and the context provider.

A MODEL-DRIVEN FRAMEWORK FOR MANAGING CONTEXT-AWARE ADAPTIVE SERVICE-BASED PROCESSES

Many different solutions have been proposed by researchers to the problem of context-aware adaptation during process development and provision. Indeed, process design and modeling must be flexible enough to deal with constant changes. The flexibility could be provided or addressed by incorporating variabilities into a system (Koning et al. 2009). Most of the approaches tackle process adaptation on the process instance or definition level by explicitly specifying some form of variation points. To date, a variety of different adaptation approaches have been proposed for capturing variabilities (e.g. Mietzner and Leymann 2008). Common to all these approaches is that they capture the process variant as a monolithic structure containing variation points to differentiate between process family members. By making appropriate choices to resolve the variation points, either at design time or at runtime, a single process variant could be constructed. The problem is that, for example, each task in the process is modeled as a variation point in and of itself, each governed by its own clause to determine inclusion or exclusion. This is in contradiction with how the developer or architect logically views the process variant i.e. in terms of the features that determine the difference between process variants in each usage context. Moreover, managing and understanding the process variants becomes more difficult when the number of variabilities and their relationships increase.

Motivated by these problems and directives in mind, we propose an MDD-based framework called *Apto* that introduces the evolution fragment and evolution primitive constructs to capture the variability in a more logical and independent form.

Figure 4. The conceptual model for context-aware adaptation

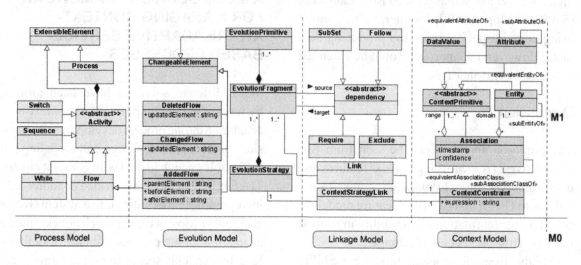

A Conceptual Model for Context-Aware Adaptation

Apto adopts MDD methodology whose primary objectives are: portability, interoperability and reusability. The proposed conceptual model is structured in four main sections that address, respectively, the modeling of the service-based process, context, evolution, and linkage between evolution and context models (see Figure 4).

Basic Process Model

In *Apto* we denote the original process as a basic process. This can be either an existing process model or a newly created one. The basic process could be defined for the most frequently executed variant of a process family, but this is not a requirement. We use a UML process definition model. For illustration purposes, Figure 4 depicts some of the main meta-classes representing the key elements of BPEL process model, and their relationships.

Context Model

As in previous work (Jaroucheh et al. Feb 2010) the main construct for representing context knowl-

edge is the *ContextPrimitive* which represents the base context constructs (primitives): entity classes, entity attributes and entities associations.

- **Entity class:** represents a group of entities (e.g. users, places, devices, etc) sharing some properties.
- **Attribute class:** represents an entity's attributes e.g. preference, position, temperature, etc.
- **Association class:** represents a relationship between one entity and either another entity or an attribute.

Further optional modeling constructs are additional facts about the entities and attributes. These are: specialization and equivalence relationships that may be specified between two entity classes, two attribute classes, or two association classes. In addition, we introduce the context-dependent constraint concept which allows us to specify conditions that must hold to introduce some kind of context-aware adaptation by specifying the evolution fragments that should be applied to the process as described in the next sections.

Figure 5. Generating evolution metamodel

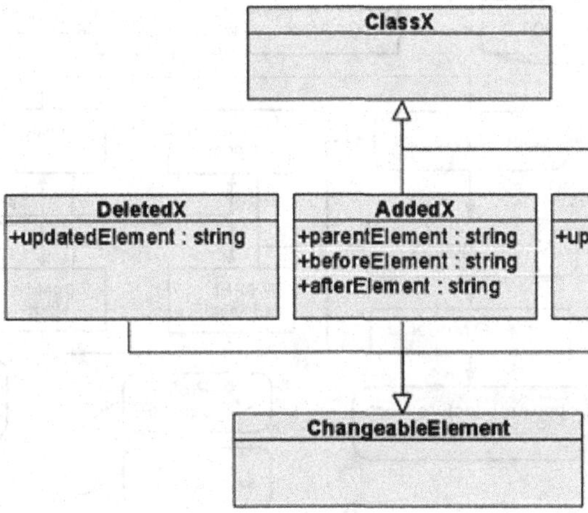

Evolution Model

The adaptation in a process usually involves adding, dropping and replacing tasks in the process. In this respect, and in order to achieve deep change ability, we propose to add for each class X in the BPEL metamodel three classes: AddedX, DeletedX, and ChangedX describing the difference between the basic process model and the respective variant model (See Figure 5). Other change types can be mapped to variations and combinations of these ones. For instance, moving an activity is achieved by dropping the activity and inserting it at a later position of the process.

The evolution metamodel (Figure 4) consists of an EvolutionStrategy class that contains one or more EvolutionFragments. The EvolutionFragment in turn consolidates related Evolution Primitives (a set of elements of type ChangeableElement) into a single conceptual variation. Our approach promotes evolution fragments (EFs) to be first-class entities consisting of closely-related additions, deletions and changes performed on the basic process model.

The evolution metamodel could be automatically generated from the BPEL model. One possible approach is presented in a previous work

(Jaroucheh et al. July 2010). Figure 4 shows only one example of the three generated classes from the Flow class (AddedFlow, DeletedFlow and ChangedFlow).

Linkage Model

Because in the MDD world everything should be a model, the mapping between the context constraints and the EFs will be represented by the linkage model. This mapping will be used as information for driving the model transformation. Moreover, the linkage model is used to represent the dependencies between the EFs which we prefer to keep it separate from the evolution model itself. Dependencies are used to describe relations between EFs in order to constrain their use. The relations supported in *Apto* are as follows: dependency (*Require*), compatibility (*Exclude*), execution order constraint (*Follow*), and hierarchy (*SubSet*). *Require* arises when elements introduced by one EF depends on elements introduced by another. The *Exclude* relationship dictates which EFs are incompatible with each another, based on conceptual design knowledge of the architect. *SubSet* denotes composition relationship which means that when choosing the child EF the par-

Figure 6. Apto architecture

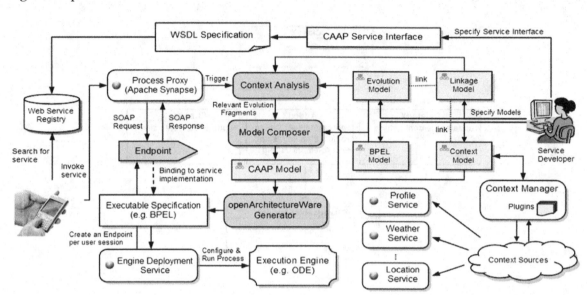

ent EF must be applied first. As one EF might insert an activity whose attributes are changed by a second one, the execution order of these EFs becomes crucial. Therefore, the *Follow* relationship enables the order in which EFs are applied to the basic process to be specified.

Apto **Architecture**

The selection of a process variant in a particular context should be done automatically. Therefore the process context in which this selection takes place has to be considered. To this end, the basic process model, the defined EFs, the context and the linkage models are used to configure the models of the different variants. A single process variant is created by applying a number of EFs and their related evolution primitives to the basic process.

As a proof-of-concept we implemented a Java application prototype for the process variant generation. The Eclipse Modeling Framework (EMF) was used to model the aforementioned models. Having specified these models, the *Apto* framework is able to deliver CAAP on a basis of user request as follows (See Figure 6). The user

request for the process service is intercepted by the Process Proxy service which in turn triggers the Context Analysis module. The Context Analysis module evaluates all context constraints of the context model. Using the constraints elements evaluated to "true" and the linkage model we are able to determine the relevant EFs and the order in which they should be applied to the basic process model. We consider that the context model is acquired from the context-management infrastructure described in "Context Management Framework."

These relevant EFs are used by the Model Composer module which supports context-aware process configuration; i.e., it allows for the configuration of a process variant by applying only those EFs relevant in the process context. The result is the CAAP Model. This model is automatically transformed, using a set of transformation rules, to generate the executable specification of the target platform. At this time, the proxy service creates a new virtual end point which will be bound to the resulting deployed process. Then it invokes the service deployment of the corresponding execution engine to deploy the gener-

Figure 7. Overview of the frameworks architecture

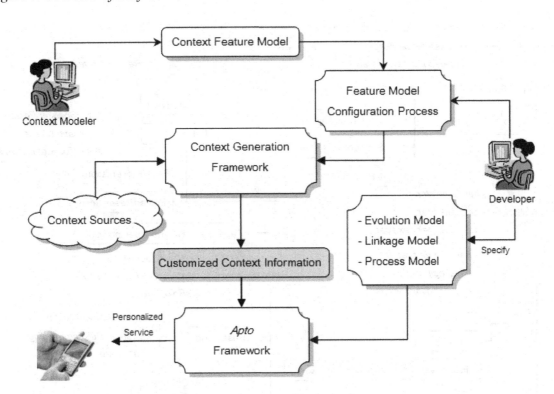

ated process. The client request is then transferred to the new end point; and the client will be provided with a personalized process that takes into account her context and preferences. In Apto, we use the model-to-code transformation that takes as input the CAAP model and generates code in an executable language (e.g. BPEL). For more details the reader is referred to a previous paper (Jaroucheh et al. July 2010).

Finally, run-time support for context-aware adaptive processes, as well as for related tasks such as management of context, is provided by a software infrastructure. Figure 7 shows an overview of the architecture of this infrastructure we have developed as proof-of-concept.

CASE STUDY

In order to demonstrate the concepts and modeling capabilities of the proposed frameworks,

this section describes a case study of different applications supporting a conference event. The key feature of the approach is the ability to support variable ontology reasoning in a distributed dynamic environment. This means that properties about a particular person, place and activity can be described by distributed heterogeneous context sources, and the contexts of these individual entities can be dynamically inferred through classification. In addition, different applications register their interest in the context information they need by specifying the relevant context features i.e. by configuring the context feature model. Given the relevant context information the proposed framework will be able to generate an application process in response to the change of the context information.

In pervasive computing environments e.g. conference campus, sensors are often used to detect the presence of people in rooms and buildings. For example, Bluetooth sensors can detect

Figure 8. A snippet of the used ontology

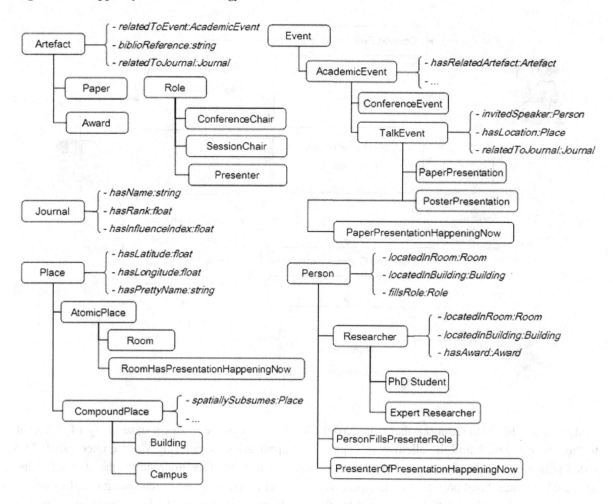

the proximity presence of the Bluetooth-enabled personal devices and conclude the presence of the device owners. We use some concepts of the SO4PC ontology (Man et al. 2005) for expressing context information associated with persons, time, and spaces; and another ontology for describing the research related concepts. Figure 8 shows a snippet of the classes and properties used in the ontology.

Figure 9 (a) shows an example of a context feature model that represents different features that could be shared among different applications. For example, if the Location feature has been selected, then two mutually-exclusive options are available; either as a room resolution; or as a

building resolution. In either case, different concepts, properties, attributes and rules should be considered. In a similar manner, the Role feature regroups two features: the static role (e.g. a Reviewer, OrganisingCommitteeMember, etc) or the current role played during the conference (e.g. Presenter, SessionChair, etc). Figure 9 (b) shows one possible context feature configuration.

Each feature may have several attributes. For example, in Figure 10 that shows a part of the feature model configuration XML file, the HavingJournalPublications feature has two attributes: value which indicates the selection of the feature or not, and minimumJournalRank. This feature allows the retrieval of researchers who have been

Figure 9. Example of context feature model

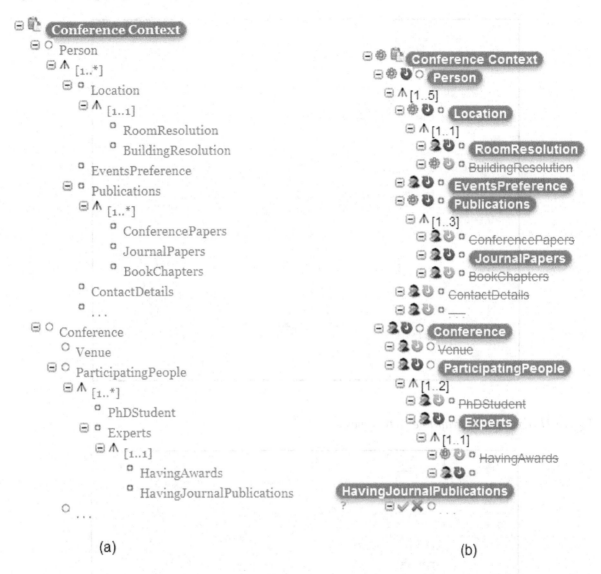

(a)   (b)

published in journals whose rank is superior to the attribute minimumJournalRank value. As previously mentioned, in order to link the context feature model to the context primitives, we use stereotypes to annotate ontology elements as well as the SWRL rules. Figure 11 shows a snippet of the XML files containing the available stereotypes to use for annotation. Each stereotype expression is expressed, as described above, in terms of the features' values of the context feature model.

Figure 12 shows a sample of the annotated ontology elements. We use the Label property to specify the correspondent stereotypes of each element. On the other hand, as mentioned above, MSs can be expressed using XPath. As an example, the MS represented in Figure 13, uses the SPQRL Update expression to update the datatype property minimumJournalRank of the entity FMConfiguration by a value retrieved from the variable $minimumJournalRankVariable whose value is determined by the XPath expression of

Figure 10. Feature model configuration

```xml
<configuration model="Context Feature Model">
  <feature id="Person">
     <value>1</value>
  </feature>
  <feature id="Location">
     <value>1</value>
  </feature>
  <feature id="RoomResolution">
     <value>1</value>
  </feature>
  <feature id="BuildingResolution">
     <value>0</value>
  </feature>
  <feature id="EventsPreference">
     <value>1</value>
  </feature>
  <feature id="Experts">
     <value>1</value>
  </feature>
  <feature id="HavingAwards">
     <value>0</value>
  </feature>
  <feature id="HavingJournalPublications">
    <minimumJournalRank>350</minimumJournalRank>
     <value>1</value>
  </feature>
     ...
</configuration>
```

Figure 11. Example of available stereotypes

```xml
<stereotypes>
<stereotype name="Person" expression="$ConferenceContext"/>
<stereotype name="RoomResolution" expression="$RoomResolution
|| $BuildingResolution"></stereotype>
<stereotype name="BuildingResolution"
expression="$BuildingResolution"></stereotype>
<stereotype name="Paper" expression="$ConferencePapers ||
$JournalPapers || $Experts"></stereotype>
<stereotype name="ConferencePaper"
expression="$ConferencePapers"></stereotype>
<stereotype name="Conference" expression="$Conference"/>
<stereotype name="JournalPaper" expression="$JournalPapers"/>
<stereotype name="Location" expression="$Location ||
$Venue"></stereotype>
<stereotype name="Publications" expression="$Experts ||
$Publications"></stereotype>
<stereotype name="Experts" expression="$Experts">
<stereotype name="ExpertHavingAwards"
expression="$HavingAwards"/>
<stereotype name="ExpertHavingJournalPublications"
expression="$HavingJournalPublications"></stereotype>
...
</stereotypes>
```

Figure 12. Example of annotated ontology

```
<owl:Class rdf:ID="CompoundPlace">
  <rdfs:subClassOf rdf:resource="#Place"/>
  <rdfs:label>BuildingResolution</rdfs:label>
</owl:Class>
<owl:Class rdf:ID="Building">
  <rdfs:subClassOf rdf:resource="#CompoundPlace"/>
  <rdfs:label>BuildingResolution</rdfs:label>
</owl:Class>
<owl:Class rdf:ID="Room">
  <rdfs:subClassOf rdf:resource="#AtomicPlace"/>
  <rdfs:label>RoomResolution</rdfs:label>
</owl:Class>
<owl:Class rdf:ID="MeetingRoom">
  <rdfs:subClassOf rdf:resource="#Room"/>
  <rdfs:label>RoomResolution</rdfs:label>
</owl:Class>
<owl:Class rdf:ID="Journal">
  <rdfs:subClassOf
rdf:resource="http://www.w3.org/2002/07/owl#Thing"/>
  <rdfs:label>ExpertHavingJournalPublications</rdfs:label>
</owl:Class>
...
<owl:ObjectProperty rdf:ID="relatedToJournal">
  <rdfs:domain rdf:resource="#Artefact"/>
  <rdfs:range rdf:resource="#Journal"/>
  <rdfs:label>ExpertHavingJournalPublications</rdfs:label>
</owl:ObjectProperty>
...
```

Figure 13. Example of meta-statement

```
<metastatements>
 <metastatement name="MS1">
  <expression>
     PREFIX cxt:&lt;http://www.napier.ac.uk/candel#&gt;
     PREFIX xsd:&lt;http://www.w3.org/2001/XMLSchema#&gt;
     DELETE
        { cxt:FMConfiguration cxt:minimumJournalRank "100.0"
         ^^xsd:float }
     INSERT
        { cxt:FMConfiguration cxt:minimumJournalRank
                "$minimumJournalRankVariable"^^xsd:float }
  </expression>
  <stereotype>ExpertHavingJournalPublications</stereotype>
 </metastatement>
...
```

the variable minimumJournalRankVariable in Figure 14.

Figure 15 shows a sample set of annotated SWRL rules. For example, Rule1 is used to reason about the paper presentations that are currently taking place. To determine if the researcher is an expert we have two options: by choosing the HavingAwards or HavingJournalPublications features. The Rule4 corresponds to the former option. The Rule2 and Rule3 correspond to the latter option and are used to determine if the researcher has been published in journals having a specified minimum rank and minimum influence index respectively. Rule5, Rule6 and Rule7 are

Figure 14. Example of meta-statement variable

```
<metastatementsVariables>
<metastatementVariable name="minimumJournalRankVariable"
expression="//feature[@id='HavingJournalPublications']/minimumJou
rnalRank"></metastatementVariable>
...
</metastatementsVariables>
```

Figure 15. Example of annotated SWRL rules

```
<swrlrules>
 <swrlrule name="Rule1">
   <expression> PaperPresentation(?p) ^
hasStartDateTime(?p, ?s) ^ hasEndDateTime(?p, ?e) ^
swrlb:currentDateTime(?c) ^ swrlb:beforeTime(?s, ?c) ^
swrlb:beforeTime(?c, ?e) ->
PaperPresentationHappeningNow(?p) </expression>
   <stereotype>CurrentRole</stereotype>
 </swrlrule>
 <swrlrule name="Rule2">
   <expression>Researcher(?r) ^ authorOf(?r, ?p) ^
relatedToJournal(?p, ?j) ^ hasRank(?j, ?rank) ^
FMConf(?conf) ^ minimumJournalRank(?conf, ?minRank) ^
swrlb:greaterThan(?rank, ?minRank) -> ExpertResearcher(?r)
   </expression>
   <stereotype>ExpertHavingJournalPublications</stereotype>
 </swrlrule>
 <swrlrule name="Rule3">
   <expression>Researcher(?r) ^ authorOf(?r, ?p) ^
relatedToJournal(?p, ?j) ^ hasInfluenceIndex(?j, ?II) ^
FMConf(?conf) ^ minimumInfluenceIndex(?conf, ?minII) ^
swrlb:greaterThan(?II, ?minII) ->
ExpertResearcher(?r)</expression>
   <stereotype>ExpertHavingJournalPublications</stereotype>
 </swrlrule>
 <swrlrule name="Rule4">
   <expression>Researcher(?r) ^ authorOf(?r, ?p) ^
hasAward(?p, ?award) ^ FMConf(?conf) ^ topAwardName(?conf,
?award) -> ExpertResearcher(?r)</expression>
   <stereotype>ExpertHavingAwards</stereotype>
 </swrlrule>
...
</swrlrules>
```

among the rules used to reason about the person location in building resolution. The stereotype of the rule is specified by the stereotype element.

Figure 16 shows an example of the retrieved context information after sending the feature model configuration (of Figure 9 (b)) to the implemented middleware prototype.

On the other hand, and from the application perspective we can imagine different scenarios of using different subset of the available context information by different applications according to their needs. For instance, different applications could be imagined to serve the conference attendees. We introduce a simple case study, namely, the Event Advisor application. This ap-

Figure 16. The retrieved context information

```
...
<ExpertResearcher rdf:ID="Alice">
    <rdf:type rdf:resource="#Researcher"/>
    <authorOf>
      <Paper rdf:ID="SecondPaper">
        <relatedToJournal>
          <Journal rdf:ID="Journal4">
            <hasRank
rdf:datatype="http://www.w3.org/2001/XMLSchema#float"
>462.0</hasRank>
            <hasInfluenceIndex
rdf:datatype="http://www.w3.org/2001/XMLSchema#float"
>2.78</hasInfluenceIndex>
            <hasName
rdf:datatype="http://www.w3.org/2001/XMLSchema#string"
>ACM TRANSACTIONS ON COMPUTER SYSTEMS</hasName>
          </Journal>
        </relatedToJournal>
        <biblioReference
rdf:datatype="http://www.w3.org/2001/XMLSchema#string">Product
Line based Context Management </biblioReference>
      </Paper>
    </authorOf>
    <authorOf rdf:resource="#FirstPaper"/>
    <locatedInRoom rdf:resource="#C35"/>
    <clientType
rdf:datatype="http://www.w3.org/2001/XMLSchema#string">
ResearchOriented</clientType>
</ExpertResearcher>
...
```

plication provides the conference attendee (the user) with a personalized suggestion for a conference event (e.g. paper, workshop, or poster presentation, etc) according to the user preferences and context. We consider a generic service application that users can access through a wireless connection using their own portable devices. The application displays a GUI through which users may use the application services for displaying information about conference events.

Figure 17 depicts a part of the static structure of this application. This application could be enhanced by automatically filling in the ClientType parameter, using for this purpose information provided by the context infrastructure. Being a research-oriented customer means that she is not interested in getting suggestions for the industrial demos. Therefore there is a need to change the process structure so that the activity that invokes the IndustrialDemo is deleted.

Figure 18 shows a simple example of the context model that contains two entities: Alice and Bob. The association elements assign the attributes to the entities so that Alice has an attribute ClientType whose value is ResearchOriented whereas Bob's ClientType is IndustrialOriented. The context constraint named UserIsResearchOriented is an example of the constraints having parameterized expression. It contains a variable named $UserName whose value is extracted either from the customer request information or from any other data source. In either case the above-mentioned proxy service is responsible for assigning the variable value.

Figure 19 shows a sample of the evolution fragments ef1 that regroups different evolution primitives that should be applied when the customer type is research oriented. The linkage model (Figure 20) contains one link element that links between the context constraint named Use-

Figure 17. Event advisor process

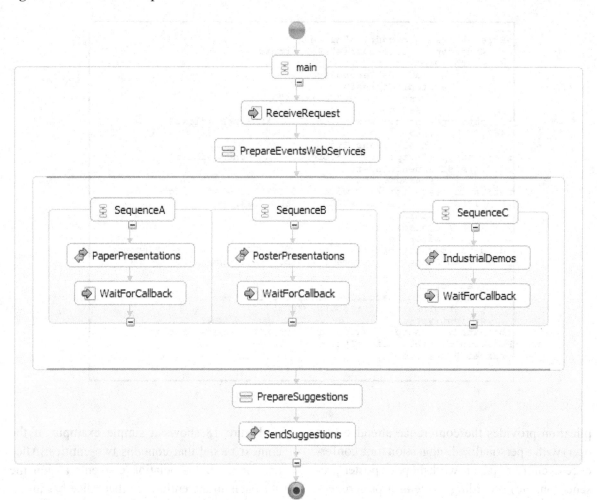

rIsResearchOriented and the CF named cf1. Finally, the developed prototype will generate the customized process which contains only the suggestions for paper and poster presentation events.

RELATED WORK

(Henricksen and Indulska 2004) presented conceptual models and a supporting software infrastructure capable of facilitating a variety of software engineering tasks involved in the development of context-aware software. The aim is to simplify the design and implementation of context-aware software by introducing context modeling approaches that describe context at two different levels of granularity, a preference abstraction, and a pair of complementary programming models, namely trigger and branching models. In addition, they developed the situation abstraction as a way to define high-level contexts in terms of the fact abstraction of CML. These situations can be combined to enable complex situations to be easily formed incrementally by the programmer. However, in the proposed approach, and thanks to the inherent power of software product line in modeling the context variability, the context features are more expressive; also the programmer

Figure 18. The context model

```
...
<Researcher rdf:ID="Alice">
    <locatedInRoom rdf:resource="#C33"/>
    <authorOf rdf:resource="#FirstPaper"/>
    <authorOf rdf:resource="#SecondPaper"/>
    <clientType
rdf:datatype="http://www.w3.org/2001/XMLSchema#string">
ResearchOriented
    </clientType>
</Researcher>

<Researcher rdf:ID="Bob">
  <authorOf rdf:resource="#FirstPaper"/>
  <clientType
rdf:datatype="http://www.w3.org/2001/XMLSchema#string">
IndustrialOriented
    </clientType>
</Researcher>

<Constraint rdf:ID="UserIsResearchOriented">
  <expression
rdf:datatype="http://www.w3.org/2001/XMLSchema#string">
    <Person rdf:ID="$UserName">
      <clientType
rdf:datatype="http://www.w3.org/2001/XMLSchema#string">
ResearchOriented
        </clientType>
    </Person>
  </expression>
</Constraint>
...
```

Figure 19. The evolution model

```
<es:EvolutionStrategy  xmi:version="2.0"  xmlns:xmi="http://www.omg.org/XMI"
xmlns:xsi="http://www.w3.org/2001/XMLSchema-instance"
xmlns:es="http://napier.ac.uk/es">
<EvolutionFragments name="ef1">
 <children xsi:type="cs:DeletedSequence" updatedElement="SequenceC"/>
 <children xsi:type="cs:DeletedCopy" updatedElement="DemosSuggestion"/>
 <children xsi:type="cs:ChangedCopy" updatedElement="SuggestionResponse">
  <to variable="..." part="suggestionsData"/><from literal="..."/>
 </children>
</EvolutionFragments>
</es:EvolutionStrategy>
```

Figure 20. The linkage model

```
<linkage:LinkageModel xmi:version="2.0"
xmlns:xmi="http://www.omg.org/XMI"
xmlns:linkage="http://napier.ac.uk/linkage">
  <links name="l1" contextConstraintName="UserIsResearchOriented"
changeFragmentName="ef1"/>
</linkage:LinkageModel>
```

is alleviated from defining the context features as it is the role of the context modeler to define the context feature model that could serve as much applications as possible. In addition, unlike their approach, using the proposed context modeling approach we can describe context at arbitrary different levels of granularity which is necessary to serve different applications' needs.

Similar to our work, (Sheng et al. 2009) presented ContextServ, a platform for simplifying the development of context-aware Web services, which adopts model-driven development where context-aware Web services are specified using ContextUML, a UML based modeling language. ContextServ offers a set of automated tools for generating and deploying executable implementations of context-aware Web services. However, *Apto* approach takes a step further. Typically, according the separation of concern principle, the application developer has to focus on the core application business logic and then define separately the customization and business rules, and weave them to the core application. *Apto* separates the system modeling into four separate models; and it is able to generate according to the acquired context information the customized version of the process. Moreover, context-aware Web services should continue to work even in the absence of context information. Unlike their approach which is tightly dependent on context, *Apto* adopt the basic process logic idea which will be generated in absence of context.

(Grassi and Sindico 2007) presented a model-driven and aspect-oriented approach to deal with context-aware adaptation in the design process of an application. Similar to our approach, they consider the adaptation as a crosscutting concern with respect to the core application logic; and their approach facilitates the plugging of different adaptation strategies within the same basic application, tailoring it for different contexts. However, as they leverage the idea of aspect weaving, their approach may not be flexible enough to accommodate the deletion or changing of application

tasks; which means that the approach could only be used to accommodate adding different tasks according to different contexts.

(Muller et al. 2004) propose "AgentWork", an interesting approach for workflow adaptation to customize the hospital cancer treatment workflow to suit each patient's medical profile by adding and deleting tasks in the running workflow instance according to the predefined extended ECA rules. The adaptation in this approach provides dynamic and automatic workflow adaptations and suggests and implements a predictive adaptation strategy. Apto, on the other hand, takes another approach so that adaptation can be applied to processes modeled and developed without an adaptation possibility in mind and independently of specific usage contexts.

VxBPEL (Koning et al 2009) is an adaptation language that is able to capture variability in processes developed in the BPEL language. VxBPEL provides the possibility to capture variation points, variants and realization relations between these variation points. Defining this variability information allows capture of a family of processes within one process definition and switching between these family members at run-time. Unlike Apto, VxBPEL works on the code level and the variants are mixed with the process business logic which may add complexity to the process developer task. Further, unlike the generative approach of Apto, VxBPEL is specific to the BPEL language.

Another interesting work that is similar to our work is the Provop approach (Reichert et al. 2009), which provides a flexible solution for managing process variants following an operational approach to configure the process variant out of a basic process. This is achieved by applying a set of well-defined change operations to it. However, Apto deviates from Provop in that it uses the MDD approach and defines the evolution fragments as evolution model elements not as change operations.

FUTURE RESEARCH DIRECTIONS

Future work includes extending the proposed context management framework to the distributed context management architecture. Therefore, for the purpose of interoperability, we need a formal common semantics for context feature models managed by different context servers.

In addition, in order to achieve the possibility of making deep changes we intend in our future work to extend the *Apto* idea to regroup different process views' models. Indeed, as the number of services or processes involved in a process grows, the complexity of developing and maintaining these processes also increases. One of the successful approaches to managing this complexity is to represent the process by different architectural views. Examples of these views are collaboration view, information view, orchestration view etc. The idea is to give the developer the possibility of applying the necessary evolution fragments in each view and then the automated tool verifies the integrity of the changes and generates the adapted process variant artifacts accordingly. This involves tackling the correct combination of evolution fragments when creating a variant. Sophisticated techniques are needed to prevent errors (e.g., deadlocks) or other consistency problems.

CONCLUSION

Change is the only constant in the software/service development world due to the evolution in business or user context and requirements. Therefore, there is a need to customize processes by generating a process variant that corresponds to the change in the business and user requirements. We have presented an approach for supporting context-aware applications based on a flexible product line based context model. The proposed approach to model the context information allows the context modeler to specify the context information in a high-level and logical way that regroups context variabilities; and provides application developers with context-specific programming constructs to express their needs from context information. The result is a more intuitive way to represent context and improve overall systems performance.

On the other hand, we have described the *Apto* model-driven approach for managing and generating process variants. One of the advantages of using MDD is that the context management and adaptation logic are included in models rather than directly implemented in code. Based on logically-viewed well-defined evolution fragments and evolution primitive constructs; on the ability to group evolution fragments in reusable components; and on the ability to regroup these components in a constrained way, necessary adjustments of the basic process can be correctly and easily realized when creating or configuring a process variant. We have adopted the viewpoint that this kind of adaptation can often be considered as a crosscutting concern with respect to the core application logic. Hence, one of our main goals has been the decoupling of the design and implementation of the adaptation logic from the design and implementation of the main process logic. Finally, Apto allows for the dynamic configuration of process variants based on the given process context.

REFERENCES

Baldauf, M., Dustdar, S., & Rosenberg, F. (2007). A survey on context-aware systems. *International Journal Ad Hoc and Ubiquitous Computing, 2*(4).

Chen, H., Finin, T., & Joshi, A. (2004). An ontology for context-aware pervasive computing environments. *The Knowledge Engineering Review, 18*(3), 197–207. doi:10.1017/S0269888904000025

Czarnecki, K., Hwan, C., & Kalleberg, K. T. (2006). Feature models are views on ontologies. In *Proceedings of the 10th International on Software Product Line Conference* (vol. 1). IEEE Computer Society.

Dey, A. K. (2001). Understanding and using context. *Personal and Ubiquitous Computing, 5*(1), 4–7. doi:10.1007/s007790170019

Grassi, V., & Sindico, A. (2007). *Towards model driven design of service-based context-aware applications.* International Workshop on Engineering of Software Services for Pervasive Environments in conjunction with the 6th ESEC/FSE joint meeting - ESSPE '07, (pp. 69-74). New York, NY: ACM Press.

Gu, T., Pung, H., & Zhang, D. Q. (2005). A service-oriented middleware for building context-aware services. *Journal of Network and Computer Applications, 28*(1), 1–18. doi:10.1016/j.jnca.2004.06.002

Henricksen, K., & Indulska, J. (2004). A software engineering framework for context-aware pervasive computing. In S. Das & M. Kumar, *Proceedings of the Second Annual Conference on Pervasive Computing and Communications* (pp. 77-86). Los Alamitos, CA: The IEEE Computer Society.

Jaroucheh, Z., Liu, X., & Smith, S. (February 2010). CANDEL: Product line based dynamic context management for pervasive applications. In *International Conference on Complex, Intelligent and Software Intensive Systems (ARES/CISIS 2010)* (pp. 209-216). Krakow, Poland: IEEE Computer Society.

Jaroucheh, Z., Liu, X., & Smith, S. (July 2010). *Apto: A MDD-based generic framework for context-aware deeply adaptive service-based processes.* In 8th IEEE International Conference on Web Services (ICWS2010). Florida: IEEE Computer Society.

Kang, K., Cohen, S., Hess, J., Novak, W., & Peterson, A. (1990). *Feature-oriented domain analysis (FODA) feasibility study.* Pittsburgh, PA: Carnegie Mellon University Software Engineering Institute.

Koning, M., Sun, C., Sinnema, M., & Avgeriou, P. (2009). VxBPEL: Supporting variability for Web services in BPEL. *Information and Software Technology, 51*(2), 258–269. doi:10.1016/j.infsof.2007.12.002

Man, J., Yang, A., & Sun, X. (2005). Shared ontology for pervasive computing. *Lecture Notes in Computer Science, 3818,* 64–78. doi:10.1007/11596370_7

Mietzner, R., & Leymann, F. (2008). *Generation of BPEL customization processes for SaaS applications from variability descriptors.* 2008 IEEE International Conference on Services Computing, (pp. 359-366).

Muller, R., Greiner, U., & Rahm, E. (2004). AW: A workflow system supporting rule-based workflow adaptation. *Data & Knowledge Engineering, 51*(2), 223–256. doi:10.1016/j.datak.2004.03.010

Northrop, L. (2002). SEI's software product line tenets. *IEEE Software, 19*(4), 32–40. doi:10.1109/MS.2002.1020285

Reichert, M., Rechtenbach, S., Hallerbach, A., & Bauer, T. (2009). *Extending a business process modeling tool with process configuration facilities: The Provop Demonstrator.* In BPM'09 Demonstration Track, Business Process Management Conference (vol. 1). Ulm, Germany.

Sheng, Q. Z., Pohlenz, S., Yu, J., Wong, H. S., Ngu, A. H., Maamar, Z., et al. (2009). *ContextServ: A platform for rapid and flexible development of context-aware Web services.* 2009 IEEE 31st International Conference on Software Engineering (pp. 619-622).

Viera, V., Brézillon, P., Salgado, A. C., & Tedesco, P. (2008). A context-oriented model for domain-independent context management. *Revue d'Intelligence Artificielle, 22*(5), 609–627. doi:10.3166/ria.22.609-627

Wang, H. H., Li, Y. F., Sun, J., Zhang, H., & Pan, J. (2007). Verifying feature models using OWL. In *Web Semantics: Science, Services and Agents on the World Wide Web, 5*(5), 117-129.

Winograd, T. (2001). Architectures for context. *Human-Computer Interaction, 16*(2), 401–419. doi:10.1207/S15327051HCI16234_18

Chapter 7
High Level Definition of Event-Based Applications for Pervasive Systems

Steffen Ortmann
IHP Microelectronics, Germany

Michael Maaser
IHP Microelectronics, Germany

Peter Langendoerfer
IHP Microelectronics, Germany

ABSTRACT

Within pervasive intelligent environments, Wireless Sensor Networks (WSNs) will surround and serve us at any place and any time. A proper usability is considered essential for WSNs supporting real life applications. With this chapter, we aim at ease of use for specifying new applications that have to autonomously cope with expected and unexpected heterogeneity, sudden failures, and energy efficiency. Starting with general design criteria for applications in WSNs, we created a user-centric design flow for pervasive applications. The design flow provides very high abstraction and user guidance to refrain the user from implementation-, deployment- and hardware-details including heterogeneity of the available sensor nodes. Automatic event configuration is accomplished by using a flexible Event Specification Language (ESL) and Event Decision Trees (EDTs) for distributed detection and determination of real world phenomena. EDTs autonomously adapt to heterogeneous availability of sensing capabilities by pruning and subscription to other nodes for missing information. We present one of numerous simulated scenarios proving the robustness and energy efficiency with regard to the required network communications. From these, we learned how to deduce appropriate bounds for configuration of collaboration region and leasing time by asking for expected properties of the phenomena to be detected.

DOI: 10.4018/978-1-60960-735-7.ch007

INTRODUCTION

Pervasive computing significantly increases the human-computer interaction as well as the environment-computer interaction and enables a direct interplay between the real world and the information technology. The vision of pervasive intelligent environments surrounding and serving us at any place and any time will become reality in the near future. Computing devices will be embedded in everyday objects allowing information technology to fade into the background and become nearly invisible to their users. Wireless Sensor Networks (WSNs) are one of the first real world examples enabling pervasive computing. Envisioned to be distributed like "Smart Dust", these networks support a broad range of applications and may become the perfect service and surveillance tool. Based on their capability to identify physical phenomena, sensor networks can be applied for environmental and structural control, context-awareness for personal services, military applications or pervasive healthcare, to mention a few (Mainwaring, Culler, Polastre, Szewczyk, & Anderson, 2002; Werner-Allen, Johnson, Ruiz, Lees, & Welsh, 2005; Akyildiz, Su, Sankarasubramaniam, & Cayirci, 2002; Aboelaze & Aloul, 2005). To summarize, ambient assisting technology based on WSNs will amazingly increase our quality of life.

Despite of the emerging advantages and potential applications, there are still a lot of challenges and problems to solve before WSNs can be used as consumer technology. WSNs are expected to be deployed with high density in large areas where hundreds or thousands of nodes are used. Due to the pervasiveness of envisioned systems, those are caught in a crossfire of external and internal influences. Sudden changes in operational conditions, varying deployment and hazardous environments adversely affect the reliability of applications. The configuration of a pervasive system is yet hard for

experts, which usually customize WSNs manually to application and deployment requirements. It is an obvious fact that most approaches for WSNs hardly consider or even disregard the configuration complexity of a WSN. However, a proper usability is considered essential for WSNs supporting real life applications. Making the programming and deployment of a WSN accessible for non-experts could become the most important issue in order to gain broad consumer acceptance of WSNs.

Pervasive systems are expected to consist of various devices providing different capabilities, hardware and software. Approaches aiming at ease of use for specifying new applications have to autonomously cope with expected and unexpected heterogeneity, fault tolerance and energy efficiency. Provision of means that enable non-professional users to make use of the WSN is required to make them widely accepted. These users are usually short on experience of programming languages and sensor networks. They cannot be asked for applying programming languages or data-base abstractions for WSN configuration. These users require a straightforward method for task definition and sensor node configuration without the need to know about hard- or software or node deployment of the WSN under configuration. Further, the algorithms used for configuration of the sensor nodes must be robust enough to autonomously overcome sudden failures during runtime, such as unavailability of sensing features or of collaborating nodes. Nevertheless, all necessary internal configuration and adaptation processes have to be completely hidden from the user.

This chapter introduces general design criteria for application design in WSNs. Based on these design criteria, this chapter motivates a significant change from a WSN-centric to user-centric design flow of pervasive applications. Instead of customizing applications to the conditions of the deployed WSN, which is the WSN-centric design, the design flow of application programming is here tailored to user needs. In such a user-centric design flow, the user only needs to describe the physical phenomenon to be sensed without regard to WSN properties. The major goal is to allow users to define applications by a generally valid description of the "things" to be sensed (phenomenon), as it is exemplified in Figure 1. All further steps required for configuration and adaption of these applications to a certain WSN remain fully transparent to the user. The sensor nodes autonomously configure to a generally defined task description given by the user. Therefore the user can specify a physical phenomenon via a GUI by defining the required sensing features, the spatial and temporal resolution and the actions to be triggered. Based on that, an event specification generator expresses a description of the phenomenon to be detected in an intuitive XML-dialect. This event specification is automatically adapted to the requirements of the target platform. Finally, a minimized deployable event specification is disseminated within the sensor network. The sensor nodes autonomously configure to the received event specification.

BACKGROUND

Traditional sensor network applications report all sensor readings to a global sink either continuously or if certain conditions are met. Sinks are usually special nodes that provide more resources and make the final decision about sensed phenomena based on received readings. Such data gathering applications exchange extensive amounts of data, cause much traffic and consume much energy. Hence, they reduce lifetime, throughput and responsiveness of the network. Thus, only certain changes in sensor readings, called events, shall be transmitted. Events provide a suitable abstraction of real world phenomena, whose physical properties can be measured by sensors (Romer & Mattern, 2004). Events typically describe a number of measurement related constraints, e.g., thresholds of sensor readings. Sensors fire an event if current measurements indicate the exceedance of these thresholds. Fired events usually trigger further actions, such as the activation of alarms or the recording of detailed data for further analysis.

Figure 1. User-centric application design allows abstraction of the task definition process from WSN-related properties and internal configuration processes. The user merely specifies the phenomenon to be sensed, which is then autonomously configured to the desired target sensor platform.

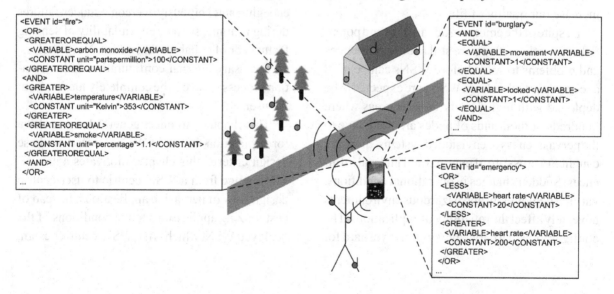

There are primitive and complex events. Primitive events describe the exceedance of one configured threshold by a single sensed value. Many applications demand detection of simultaneous occurrence of several primitive events. This is particularly true if identification of complex real-world phenomena is required. A combination of several primitive events is a complex event. For example, the occurrence of an event *fire* should be denoted as a combination of the primitive events

(temperature > 50°C) AND (smoke > 1.1%)

instead of using the primitive events only. Complex events based on different sensing capabilities indicating the same phenomenon, here temperature and smoke, gain a higher false alarm immunity and enhance the reliability of event detection (Shih, Wang, Yang, & Chang, 2006).

An ease of use for event configuration in a WSN by non-professional users requires provision of two major configuration means, i.e., a high level abstraction for description of events to be detected and a robust method for autonomous configuration and detection of defined events. The following introduces and compares available approaches for such configuration means.

High Abstraction for Sensor Network Configuration

Available higher abstractions for sensor network programming and configuration mainly base upon programming languages or database-like querying. In case of WSN, configuration is perceived as setting of detection parameters, e.g., thresholds, and linking of those. A configuration allows concluding whether actual sensor readings match the defined settings or not. One of the most famous approaches using database abstractions for collection and fusion of sensor readings is TinyDB (Madden, Franklin, Hellerstein, & Hong, 2005). TinyDB extends SQL to support in-network data queries on sensor nodes using the operating system

TinyOS (Levis, Madden, Gay, Polastre, Szewczyk, Whitehouse, Woo, Hill, Welsh, Brewer, & Culler, 2005). Very similar to that is the COUGAR project (Yao & Gehrke, 2002), which also supports data queries in a SQL-like dialect. Both approaches provide a good abstraction layer to specify data collection in database-query style but still work on the node level and hence, require detailed knowledge about the WSN to be configured. Based on TinyDB, the Tiny Application Sensor Kit (TASK) (Buonadonna, Gay, Hellerstein, Hong, & Madden, 2005) is most closely related to the aims of this chapter. It is a kit for configuring low data rate environmental monitoring applications while remaining "self-explanatory, easy to configure and easy to maintain". In addition to TinyDB, TASK provides a complete application background from field tools over gateways and internet connectivity up to support of external tools for proper sensor data preparation and network monitoring. Further, it supports inferior power management and considers fault tolerant performance in case of node crashes.

All approaches reduce the configuration complexity to a certain amount by transparent high programming abstraction. Among the available high-level abstractions TASK is a valuable step towards a user-centric method for WSN configuration. It provides users with a lot of tools on top of improving event detection only. However, all approaches are still unsuitable for non-professional deployment of WSNs. Besides the unfeasibility of letting non-professional users apply database abstractions, these approaches carry some WSN-related drawbacks along. They make use of a centralized topology with at least one coordinating node continuously collecting and evaluating raw sensor readings. Hence, these approaches transport huge amounts of data, consume much energy and reduce the responsiveness and throughput of the network. Further, analyzing collected data at central nodes inherently creates a Single Point of Failure (SPoF).

High-level programming languages are of prominent use for definition of WSN applications. There exist a couple of projects trying to adapt widely used high-level programming languages like Java (Simon, Cifuentes, Cleal, Daniels, & White, 2006; Brouwers, Corke, & Langendoen, 2008) to sensor nodes. Of course, this enables a rapid development of new WSN applications by professionals but consequently requires programming skills in distributed system design. The macro programming language STOP (Wada, Boonma, & Suzuki, 2007) is a scripting language explicitly designed for data collection in WSNs. It allows to create data queries from a global viewpoint without considering details of single nodes. Based on migrating agents, which collect required data according to a given script, STOP provides a more comfortable data collection. Nevertheless, the usage of general languages requires a complex run-time environment and Virtual Machines (VMs) on every node. Further, VMs are usually adapted to certain sensor platform only and do not support application design across several platforms.

Finally, these approaches still require to make use of scripting or programming languages, which is not feasible for non-scientific deployment. A straightforward sensor configuration providing a proper usability of WSNs for non-scientific deployment is still missing. A configuration concept that aims at ease of use for sensor configuration must be tailored to the user and self-configure to defined tasks. Thus, the user only needs to describe the phenomenon to be sensed without taking care of WSN properties and deployment conditions.

Autonomous Collaborative Event Detection

An ease of use for WSN configuration starts with a straightforward definition process but must also provide reliable and robust execution of defined tasks during runtime. Robust application is already a challenge for homogeneous systems, but gets even harder if heterogeneous systems using miscellaneous sensor nodes need to be configured to the same task. Hence, sensor nodes may not provide all sensing capabilities needed for local detection of the phenomenon to be sensed. In that case, sensor nodes must collaborate and share their sensing capabilities to continue with event detection. For reliable application it is a necessity to enable sensor nodes to autonomously deal with different conditions as being expected in pervasive systems, i.e., heterogeneous distributed sensing capabilities, missing resources, node mobility, varying network topology, failed sensors or sensing units etc. The following discusses some previously presented mechanisms of collaborative event detection.

Vu et al. (Vu, Beyah, & Li, 2007) introduced a composite event detection scheme for sensor networks composed of different nodes with varying sensing capabilities. They split complex event detection among different nodes into sets of so called atomic events, which are similar to primitive events (threshold values). Atomic events are merged by special gateway nodes to determine final results. The gateway nodes however build SPoFs. This approach provides configurable levels of fault tolerance by selecting an appropriate k for k-watching sets of sensors while considering the energy consumption and the event notification time but requires an expensive setup phase. Phani Kumar et al. (Phani Kumar, Reddy V, & Janakiram, 2005) present a similar collaboration scheme. They create event-based trees for complex events containing all assigned sensor nodes. These nodes collaborate using a content-based publish/subscribe communication model, where child nodes publish readings of interest to parent nodes. The root node of the event tree obtains all sensor readings and decides about the monitored event. Again, this root node is a SPoF and introduces vulnerability to the system.

Krishnamachari et al. (Krishnamachari, & Iyengar, 2003; Krishnamachari, & Iyengar, 2004) introduced a self-organizing algorithm that provides a distributed fault tolerant approach for regional event extraction in sensor networks. All nodes with readings of interest in a given vicinity, i.e., the region of event, are formed into a cluster where the node with the lowest id-number becomes the cluster head. The cluster head collects all readings and performs a majority decision. Since their approach is based on binary event detection where all nodes signal a "Yes" or "No" instead of sending their measurements, the cluster head simply counts all statements. If more than 50 percent of the participating nodes state a positive event, the cluster head forwards this event to the central sink in the network. Beside performance issues, they do not take care on energy resources because large event regions produce much overhead for communication.

Krasniewski et al. proposed TIBFIT (Krasniewski, Varadharajan, Rabeler, Bagchi, & Hu, 2005), a protocol able to cope with arbitrary data faults and malicious nodes. It shall enable reliable and fault tolerant data gathering by assigning trust values to the sensor nodes. These values confirm the plausibility of correct measurements or state a lack of credibility for single nodes. The head node of a cluster collects the readings and trust values of all nodes and decides whether an event has occurred or not. Due to the decision of the head node, the trust values of all correct reporting nodes increase whereas the other values decrease respectively. To make sure the trust values are correct, at least two shadow head nodes monitor all activities and results of the decision process in background and take corrective action if necessary. TIBFIT achieves a good fault tolerant performance even if more than 50 percent of the sensor measurements are faulty, provided that the initial monitoring phase is long enough to establish the trust values. Additionally, this protocol is able to cope with malicious nodes, which can only temporary influence the decision process because their confidence values decrease with every faulty report. This is only true if the number of malicious nodes is less than the number of correct reporting nodes. Unfortunately, required overhead was not measured or calculated. However, the algorithms used for collecting and distributing sensor readings and trust values allow assumption of an enormous overhead, especially for the usage of shadow head nodes. Hence, the efficiency of the provided fault tolerant performance strongly depends on the application it is used for.

Kamiya et al. (Kamiya, Mineno, Ishikawa, Osano, & Mizuno, 2008) applied a P2P network of sensor gateways to maintain event detection across several heterogeneous sensor networks. Each sensor gateway accesses and manages a certain sensor network. To define event detection in one or more maintained sensor networks, the sensor gateways provide an XML event description parser that splits complex events into required atomic ones and registers these at the corresponding sensor gateways. The underlying sensor networks continuously report their raw sensor readings to the gateway nodes, which finally evaluate the atomic and respective complex events. Even here the sensor gateways constitute a SPoF. Just like all other discussed approaches relying on gateway or centralized nodes, this is again very inefficient with regard to energy consumption and network load. Due to the fact that atomic events are not forwarded to the actually measuring sensor nodes for evaluation, all sensor readings need to be sent to the gateway nodes even in case of no event is triggered. By that the energy consumption is far from optimal. Nevertheless, autonomous management of sensor networks based on an event description parser is a promising approach to reduce the complexity of node and network configuration. Unfortunately, the XML descriptions used at the parser are not presented making it impossible to draw conclusions about their applicability.

The Context Dependent Event Detection (CoDED) platform (Schwiderski-Grosche, 2008) presents an architecture for context-dependent event detection in sensor networks. In order to save energy resources, events are monitored in certain monitoring context only. The context description is defined by a propositional logic, which evaluates to true as long as a specified context is given. Combinations of primitive events may form global complex events that may even be distributed. Those are observed by a composite event detection engine. That engine seems to adapt automatically to current network situations but the general question of how composite events are distributed and processed on several devices is left open. Unfortunately, the author does not provide implementation details.

Criteria for Reliable Autonomous Execution of Event-Based Applications

User-centric application design of course requires a process of automatic WSN configuration to support reliable applications in WSNs. In order to enable an appropriate comparison of existing approaches and to set the objectives of user-centric application design, this section introduces design criteria for development of reliable event-based applications. A suitable approach for reliable event detection in WSNs must consider the following design criteria:

Robustness: Sensor nodes and its applications must continue event detection even if the context changes, sensors fail or nodes move. The sensor nodes need to (re-)adapt their on-node as well as in-network processing for automatic resource-oriented event configuration. This regards both, on-node adjustments in case of missing or failed sensing facilities and adaptation of distributed detection if connections to collaborating nodes are interrupted due to failed or moved nodes.

Autonomy: In addition to the autonomous nature of sensor nodes, every node in the network must be enabled to perform all necessary tasks for event detection. A fully decentralized approach avoiding assignment of superior devices such as super nodes (Cardei, Yang, & Wu, 2008), event gateways (Vu, Beyah, & Li, 2007) or fusion centers

(Wang, Han, Varshney, & Chen, 2005) prevents from having potential SPoFs.

Transparency: Dealing with heterogeneous nodes and network structures, sudden changes in the environment or failures during collaboration etc., consequently requires continuous adaptation and device configuration. These processes must be hidden to remain fully transparent to the user. Especially pervasive WSNs are expected to make use of various sensors with similar or complementary capabilities. An automatic hard- and software abstraction can cover such heterogeneity.

Energy efficiency: Small devices, like wireless sensor nodes, usually are subject to strict energy constraints, e.g., by battery packs providing limited power only. Transmission is the most power-hungry operational mode of WSNs consuming orders of magnitudes more energy than local processing. Since collaboration simultaneously requires communication between sensor nodes, it significantly increases the energy consumption and hence, decreases the maximum reachable node lifetime. To cope with that, enhancing the cost-efficiency of collaboration by reducing the number of transmissions and the amount of exchanged data is of primary concern. In addition, all parameters regarding sensing intervals, duty and sleep cycles, adaptation rate etc., should ideally be configurable to best customize the energy consumption to application requirements.

Convenience: To gain a broad consumer acceptance of WSNs, it is required to provide means that enable the non-professional users to make use of a WSN. These non-professionals are usually short on experience of programming languages and sensor networks, Therefore a straightforward method to define tasks and configure sensor nodes without requiring knowledge about hard- or software or node deployment is in demand. Convenient design of WSN applications not only requires the task definition part to provide a high abstraction level. It additionally implies to support fully automatic WSN configuration regarding the aforementioned criteria.

Assessment of Related Work

For comparison, presented event detection schemes are evaluated against the introduced criteria in Table 1. First of all, there exists no approach that addresses and fulfils all criteria. Krishnamachari and Krasniewski provide the best robustness and even enable to autonomously cope with malicious nodes but increase the required overhead by at least a factor of three. Because detection reliability is a prerequisite, all approaches allow for adaptation to changing conditions but usually focus on certain changes only, e.g., faults, malicious nodes, unavailable resources, environmental changes, connectivity etc. Except for CoDED, which unfortunately was not implemented so far, all approaches carelessly neglect the autonomy required in a sensor network. Fully distributed concepts not depending on special nodes are in great demand, which by design enables all nodes to fulfill every task required for event detection in prevention of SPoFs.

To summarize, robustness and transparency are best provided, whereas energy efficiency, autonomy and convenience are marginally taken into account or are even completely missing. There exists no approach that associates all introduced criteria. As shown in existing work, providing high robustness is possible indeed but partially results in a significantly increased stress of resources. All approaches poorly perform with particular regard to energy consumption and cost-efficiency for collaboration. There is no doubt that a robust application requires an overhead but the efficiency of an application significantly depends on a proper balance between the application requirements and the implementation. Further, most approaches shift final decisions to centralized nodes and are vulnerable if these nodes are faulty or fail completely. The existence of backup nodes, which can substitute the task of these centralized nodes if necessary, enhances the robustness against node failures but significantly increases the effort. However, only a fully decentralized approach will provide a proper autonomy for the sensor nodes.

It is quite obvious that fulfilling all criteria up to a level of 100 percent is almost impossible but existing approaches usually tackle only a subset of those. The event detection concept presented here is inspired by some ideas of the discussed approaches and combines these in a new suitable event detection scheme tackling all design criteria. This chapter introduces a novel concept for autonomous sensor network configuration considering all mentioned criteria. Based on the description of the phenomenon to be recognized, the respective event detection is autonomously

Table 1. Comparison of discussed event detection schemes in consideration of the introduced design criteria. There exists no approach that addresses and fulfils all criteria. Best provided is robustness and transparency, whereas energy efficiency, autonomy and convenience are marginally taken into account or are even completely missing.

	Robustness	Autonomy	Transparency	Energy efficiency	Convenience
Vu	(+)	(-)	(0)	(0)	(?)
Phani Kumar	(+)	(-)	(+)	(--)	(?)
Krishnamachari	(+)	(-)	(+)	(--)	(-)
Krasniewski	(++)	(0)	(0)	(--)	(?)
Kamiya	(0)	(--)	(+)	(--)	(0)
Schwiderski	(?)	(+)	(0)	(-)	(-)
Validation: (++) very good; (+) good; (0) regular; (-) bad; (--) very bad; (?) not mentioned					

configured and observed, even if it requires organizing collaboration between nodes to deliver the results.

USER-CENTRIC DESIGN FLOW OF PERVASIVE APPLICATIONS

A user-centric design flow decouples the processes of task definition and respective WSN configuration. Such design flow allows users to fully abstract from WSN-related properties. It simplifies the task definition process to a level that is even suitable for non-professionals. Therefore, this chapter introduces an intuitive XML-styled Event Specification Language (ESL). ESL allows purely defining the physical phenomenon to be sensed without regard to any properties of the WSN used. It features hardware independent description elements to define complex phenomena and enhances these by tailor-made application constraints. Hence, the user remains enabled to define task for the WSN, but simultaneously the user does not require programming skills or knowledge of the actual WSN under configuration anymore. In addition, the ESL, derived from XML, provides ideal properties to be implemented and used by Web services. This offers great potential to realize remote configuration concepts for pervasive technology via the Internet. To hide necessary XML-styled descriptions from the user, an interactive Graphical User Interface (GUI) supports the user in application design and automatically generates the respective XML description of the application.

Based on that XML description, a novel fully decentralized mechanism to autonomously set up distributed event detection, called Event Decision Tree (EDT), and a cost efficient means to maintain such EDT, are presented. EDTs are efficiently constructed on every sensor node using a tiny Generating Finite State Machine (GFSM) requiring eight states only. The EDT is a software construct reflecting the XML-tree structure of the

ESL-defined phenomenon description. By that, it implements a sensor node configuration that directly processes and evaluates sensor readings from the sensors attached to the nodes. It further enables every node to self-divide event queries according to its own resources and self-adapt to the assigned tasks. Simultaneously, the established EDTs provide the interface for efficient collaboration using a lease-based publish/subscribe approach.

To appropriately distinguish the abstractions presented to and described by the user and the hard- and software constructs, we name and define the following entities.

*A **phenomenon** is a physical condition that can be measured by sensors. It is not required that a single sensor can detect or measure that phenomenon on its own. This is an abstraction known real life users.*

*An **event** is a software construct announcing a detected phenomenon or that a sensor measurement meets certain condition. The mere exceeding of a threshold by the sensor reading is named a **primitive event**. The combination of primitive events by logical expressions is named a **complex event**.*

*An **event specification** is the description of the phenomenon to be sensed including all application constraints. It is defined in an XML dialect namely the **Event Specification Language (ESL)**.*

*A **binary event specification** is the compact representation form of the user defined event specification. It is adjusted to hardware specifics and sensing features of the sensor nodes in the WSN. Binary event descriptions are disseminated in the WSN for direct configuration of sensor nodes.*

*An **Event Decision Tree (EDT)** is the on-node representation of the event specification.*

A **collaboration region** *is the vicinity of each node, in which neighboring nodes are permitted to share their sensing features for collaborative event detection. This collaboration region depends on the expected expansion of the phenomenon and the average distance of the deployed sensor nodes.*

Design Flow

Before presenting technical details of every configuration step, this section overviews the work-

flow of the WSN-configuration concept based on ESL and EDTs. Figure 2 depicts a graphical representation of this workflow. The uncoupled task definition process allows the user to define the "things-in-mind" to be sensed independently from the WSN. Therein, the user merely describes a phenomenon and adds some phenomenon-related parameters such as identifiers and update rates.

Having finished the description process, the user device automatically expresses these "things-in-mind" in ESL, resulting in the **event specifica-**

Figure 2. Graphical representation of the user-centric workflow for WSN-configuration based on the ESL and EDTs. The uncoupled task definition process allows the user to define the "things" to be sensed independently from the WSN, which is automatically configured to each designed task.

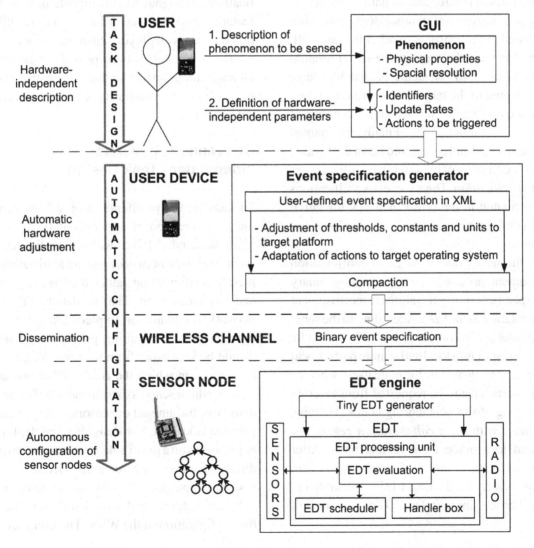

tion. The event specification is the machine-processable form of the user's description. It contains the involved sensing features as well as phenomenon related constraints concerning the spatial and temporal expansion, detection intervals and associated handlers that are triggered by upon event. Here it shall be emphasized that an appropriate event specification is sufficient for successful configuration of the sensor network. Every processing and transformation step based on the event specification and its derivations is automatically done by the event configuration system.

It is quite obvious, that general event specifications cannot be uniformly transferred to different sensor nodes of heterogeneous hardware. Hence, event specifications are preprocessed before being distributed in the sensor network. First, an XML parser generates the respective tree representation. Various XML elements of that tree have to be adapted to the targeted sensor system, i.e., conversion of values for sensing, renaming of identifiers and functions etc. Finally, the adapted tree is converted and compacted into a deployable event specification of minimal size, called *binary event specification*. Binary event specifications are distributed in the sensor network for initial event configuration as well as for updates and deletions.

On the sensor nodes, the event configuration environment processes every incoming binary event specification to generate the respective event representation as an ***EDT***. According to the sensing features and resources provided by the node, the EDT is split into local and remote parts. Local parts can be evaluated by the node itself, whereas remote parts have to be requested from external sources, e.g., from neighboring nodes. Thereby, only those within the *collaboration region* are regarded to provide these remote parts. After further adaptations and configurations of event related constraints, the final EDT is integrated to the EDT processing unit. The EDT processing unit

- autonomously collects required sensor readings,
- frequently evaluates the EDT with respect to the configured detection interval,
- manages necessary collaboration with other nodes and
- triggers associated handlers in case of positive event evaluation.

The EDT processing unit is enabled to administrate and process several EDTs simultaneously, too. This is a prerequisite to ensure proper flexibility by allowing the sensor nodes to execute several tasks concurrently. An integrated update mechanism enables to replace binary event specifications analogous to code update means. This feature allows easy reconfiguration or recalibration of already deployed sensor networks.

The following sections provide insights into all configuration steps in the user-centric design by applying an illustrative example aiming at detecting fires.

Convenient Hardware-Independent Task Design

To increase the proliferation of WSNs, convenience in creation of applications on WSNs is highly demanded. It is considered that the deployment of sensor networks and its applications is merely configuration rather than programming and implementation. That is, details on sensor network hardware or implementation issues, especially those requiring programming skills, should be kept away from the user. We consider a scenario, in which the configuration assistant knows, which sensors exist in the WSN. Also the density or the amount of sensors or sensor nodes per area is known. For designing and deploying applications on a priori unknown sensor networks discovery means are required. Given that the assistant application knows the key data of the WSN, it supports and guides the user through the configuration of the WSN. The user may just start with an idea of the phenomenon that shall be detected by the WSN. Obviously, the user has to know the properties of the phenomenon to be able to model it. This knowledge about properties may be even very high level, e.g., "a fire is hot and produces smoke". An experts system or WSN configuration assistant will be able to guide the user with questions as simple as possible. Such assistant is drafted in Figure 3. It will request the properties of the phenomenon and based on that, the boundaries of respective physical measurements, which are typical for the phenomenon in mind. Without knowing, the user already specified primitive events. In case multiple measurements jointly describe the phenomenon, mutually or alternatively, the user can be supported in combination and arrangement of these measurements. It is easier for users with no programming or mathematical background to understand the semantics of words like: together, mutually, alternatively or sequentially, than to understand logical operations and relations. Since the assistant uses those simpler words in its questions, complex descriptions of phenomena can be created by ingenuous users. The intelligence to transform a together into an AND or even a mutually into "this AND NOT that, OR NOT this AND that" is embedded in the assistant and concealed from the user. By just these few questions the user is guided to formally describe a phenomenon.

A complete event specification requires constraints that have to be defined by users as well.

Those constraints are, for instance, sampling intervals and regions of collaboration. Also these can be derived from the answers to more intuitive questions, e.g., "After what time the phenomenon has to be detected latest?" or "How long have batteries to last?". Without explicitly known to the user, the EDT provides robustness through collaboration of neighboring sensor nodes with heterogeneous sensing capabilities. The distance or relative area in which neighboring nodes shall collaborate is a constraint that has to be set in the event specification. As we learned from our simulations and measurements, the appropriate size of the collaboration region can be derived from the expected expansion of the phenomenon and the average distance of deployed sensor nodes. The minimum size of the collaboration region should be the mean distance between neighboring sensor nodes, which is determined by the density of the sensor network, and transmission technology. The maximum size of the collaboration region is the estimated size of the phenomenon. Both constraints applied to these parameters result in an appropriate region size. These parameters can be queried from the user with simplified questions, e.g., "What is the estimated diameter of the phenomenon expected?" or "How large is the area in which the WSN is deployed?" and "How many sensor nodes the WSN consists of?". Despite a circular region will likely be sufficient for most phenomena, different shapes can also be considered.

Figure 3. Guided derivation of machine processable event specification from vague human ideas.

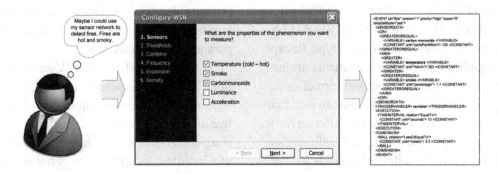

With getting answers to appropriate questions, such experts system is able to derive a complete event specification, describing a real world phenomenon and detection constraints. While the assistant produces the event specification in the ESL, users do not have to get in contact with programming languages. The output can then be automatically processed and the user has not further to be involved, compare Figure 2. Since a number of phenomena are interesting to a number of WSN users, the assistant may also provide the user with phenomenon patterns to choose from. Using such patterns, various WSN applications may be deployed in a one-click manner. We also consider that the assistant can be implemented as an online tool, enabling it to learn phenomena descriptions from the community and hence evolve. Such wide use of an expert system will also enable to refine and improve the questions catalogue that is presented to users.

Automatic Generation of Event Specifications

The first step in automatic WSN-configuration is to convert the user-defined phenomenon and its parameters created with the assistant into a processable form. The ESL provides means to easily combine several sensing capabilities and respective primitive events to complex ones within the <SENSORDATA> element. Primitive events can be defined as the sensor reading matching an exact value or through single-bounded intervals the sensor reading falls into. This equality or the intervals are described using the following relational elements: <EQUAL>, <LESS>, <GREATER>, <LESSOREQUAL>, <GREATEROREQUAL>. The result of a relation is of Boolean type. Except for the equality relation these elements are not commutative and hence, require correct order of assigned subelements. It is quite obvious that *(temperature < 10)* is semantically different from *(10 < temperature)*, for example. Configuration of primitive events is setting thresholds for cer-

tain sensor readings using relational elements. Therefore, relational elements define respective binary relations between two elements. These are variables, constants and/or algebraic operations defined on top of these.

A variable identifies a sensing capability and is defined by the <VARIABLE> element. The value of a variable is given at run-time by sensor readings. In contrast to that, the <CONSTANT> element defines a constant value, which is used as threshold. Constants usually require to set an additional measuring unit. The unit attribute allows for assigning different units to constants, e.g., time and distance units like *seconds*, *minutes*, *meters* etc. In certain cases constants may not require a unit, for example if a pure quantity is in demand. Such a constant is specified without the unit attribute. Conversion of specified constants with respect to the hard- and software used on the sensor nodes, e.g., converting *seconds* to *milliseconds* if necessary, is task of the language interpreter and is not of concern for the user. That allows for a straightforward definition process, in which the user practicably applies the units that personally suit best.

Variables and constants apply numerical values. To support a broad usability as well as to enable conversion of values, the ESL enables to define binary algebraic operations using variables, constants or results of further algebraic operations as parameters. Consequently, functions result in numerical values. The ESL provides the following operations: <SUM>, <DIFFERENCE>, <PRODUCT>, <QUOTIENT>, <MODULO>. Of course, differences, quotients or modulo operations are also not commutative. Just as mentioned at relational elements, here the order of applied parameters is crucial, too.

By design, the ESL also allows to define relations between two sensor readings, constants or algebraic operations of equal type. Since this is feasible for variables and operations, e.g., for comparing inside and outside temperature readings of a building, its application is rather useless for two constants. The result of a relation between two constants is of constant Boolean type, too. In that case, the event specification is redesigned and the Boolean result of such relation is directly inserted instead.

To support definition of complex phenomena, configured thresholds can be composed by logic operations. Logic operations are also specified by XML tags, namely: <AND>, <OR>, <NOT>. Similar to relational elements, the elements <AND> and <OR> define a respective logic operation between two relational or two logic elements or a mix of both. Since both operations are commutative, the order of the linked elements is irrelevant. The <NOT> element specifies an unary operation and can only be used on top of one relational or logic element. As known from Boolean algebra, it inverses the Boolean result of the underlying element. Of course, it is also possible to link several logic operations together. Logic elements further allow to define 2-bounded intervals for certain sensing capability by combining several primitive events. For example, measuring a temperature between 20 and 25 results in a combination of two primitive events, exemplified in Listing 1.

To simplify matters only three logic elements are available, but these are sufficient to define every possible logic combination. Supporting more language elements may slightly increase the usability for end-users but even implies to implement more complex interpretation means on the sensor nodes. This would require using more processing and memory resources. For this reason and to keep the language quite simple, the integration of further logic elements like NAND or NOR, is omitted. This is vitally important for implementing a language interpreter on sensor nodes, which provide scarce resources only. Since the event specification is created by support of a user assistant, a respective mapping of the required logical operation into the available logic elements can be achieved automatically. Further, the commutative algebraic and logic operations might even have more than two operands. The expressiveness of XML even allows for specification of such multi-nary operations. But with regard to aspects of simplicity and minimization of the binary event specification, we limit to binary operations.

Definition of Hardware-Independent Parameters

A complete event specification consists of three mandatory and one optional element represented by respective tags. As already introduced, the <SENSORDATA> element defines the required sensing capabilities for primitive or complex

Listing 1. Example specification of a phenomenon as complex event, which detects temperature between 20 and 25 centigrade.

```
<AND>
    <GREATER>
        <VARIABLE> temperature </VARIABLE>
        <CONSTANT unit="centigrade">20</CONSTANT>
    </GREATER>
    <LESS>
        <VARIABLE> temperature </VARIABLE>
        <CONSTANT unit="centigrade">25</CONSTANT>
    </LESS>
</AND>
```

events. Having specified the phenomenon in ESL, the event specification associates the phenomenon with customizable application constraints. Configurable execution intervals and appropriate event handlers have to be assigned. Further, a region defining the spatial expansion of the phenomenon can be optionally defined. Each event specification contains an <EXECUTION> element that states the frequency of event detection or measurement data gathering. Appropriate processes, which are triggered upon positive event evaluation, are listed in the <CONSEQUENCE> element. To improve the event specification complexity, the optional <DIMENSION> element enables to fine tune the event observation behavior by defining the expansion of the collaboration region. The collaboration region is configured around the node, e.g., as a circle, ball, square, cube or number of hops. It contains all devices, allowed to participate in collaborative event detection.

For configuring several events simultaneously, attributes are embedded in the <EVENT> element. The id assigns a globally unique identifier to event specifications. It enables to associate requests and updates to a particular event specification. The version number identifies different versions of the same event specification. It reduces maintenance and online reprogramming complexity. Incoming event specifications with higher version numbers substitute all older versions of the targeted event specification, which are deleted to save memory. For removal of event specifications from a network, an empty event specification containing the event identifier only is used. The priority attribute optionally assigns a priority level to the event specification to support multi-event evaluation. Consider a sensor network gathering temperature readings for climate control that is used in parallel to detect forest fires. In such a setting the detection of forest fire would have the higher priority because it is a safety-critical event. Currently, the ESL provides three priority levels, which are *high*, *normal* and *low*, whereas *normal* is the default value if not explicitly specified.

To overcome the problems of varying context, fluctuating environment and node mobility, sensor networks must frequently self-adapt to the current situation. Especially if nodes collaborate with each other, these connections may suddenly be disturbed or not available any longer. Prevention of such changes is hard or even impossible. To handle those situations, sensor nodes must provide means to renew or establish collaboration with other sensor nodes in their vicinity. This again requires a processing and communication overhead. To customize the adaptiveness and efficiency of the communication scheme used for collaboration between neighboring nodes, the lease and reliableMode attributes are specified. The lease defines the frequency of adapting collaborative relations between neighboring nodes. It specifies the time-lag between two adaptation phases as a multiplier of the regular event detection frequency stated in <EXECUTION>. Short lease intervals (small lease factor) provide a high adaptation rate whereas long lease intervals can significantly reduce the number of messages and the energy consumption. For example, highly fluctuating WSNs should apply short lease factors to cope with changing topology and moving nodes. In contrast to that, WSNs with static deployment may use long lease factors to reduce the number of required collaboration messages. The reliableMode attribute permits to choose between a higher reliability in data exchange or reduced energy consumption. It introduces retransmissions on the application level in case of message loss. Enabling the reliableMode instructs to explicitly acknowledge every data exchange that is associated to a certain event. The reliable mode consequently requires a communication overhead but enhances the reliability of the application. Thus, safety-critical events should make use of the reliable mode, whereas simple data collecting scenarios could omit the required overhead in favor of less energy consumption. It is quite obvious that configuration of both parameters strongly depends on the application as well as the application context. Detailed descriptions and configurations of these elements are presented in later Sections introducing publish/subscribe and leasing time.

Of course, proper adjustment of both parameters requires skills in distributed computing or experience in WSN configuration. Hence, the user assistant shall be able to customize these parameters automatically based on experience data or available patterns. In addition, the assistant should provide an expert mode, which allows users to manually customize each parameter.

Addition of Execution Constraints and Associated Handlers

Next, the temporal expansion of the phenomenon is to be configured. Real-world phenomena are usually subject to different temporal expansion, which must be considered for event specification as well. For example, the acoustic wave of an explosion can only be detected within a few milliseconds and hence, requires a short sensing interval. The frequency of event evaluation and coupled collaboration processes consequently affects the energy consumption of the sensor nodes. Energy consumption is an essential and very critical issue when designing WSN-based applications. Sensor nodes provide different modes of operation that result in significantly different amounts of energy consumption. Active modes like data processing or data transmission are draining the energy resources much more than passive modes such as sleeping. Thus, active periods must be kept as short as possible to reduce energy consumption to a very minimum. On the other hand, extensive passive periods may reduce the accuracy and reliability of event detection. When a node may switch to a power saving mode highly depends on the application running. Therefore the ESL provides means that help to adjust the update rates of sensor readings. Thus, an event specification contains an <TIMEINTER-VAL> element to configure application-oriented execution constraints for each phenomenon. This element defines the event evaluation frequency as a time interval. Time intervals can be quantified by acceptable periods or exact time slots that must be adhered to.

The <CONSEQUENCE> element is the last mandatory component of an event specification. It links procedures to the event specification, which have to be executed upon phenomenon detection. These procedures are called event handlers. Event handlers are listed as <TRIGGERHANDLER> elements, containing the name of the event handler. Specifying several event handlers in a single event specification is allowed and all of them are executed in the sequence listed, when the respective phenomenon occurs. Since event handlers trigger available functions or processes at the sensor nodes, those must also be adapted by the language interpreter to the target platform and the respective Operating System (OS). For example, a general event handler such as *sendalert* could be mapped to a respective interrupt routine of the OS. This is automatically done by the event configuration system.

Determining the Region of Event

Besides the temporal resolution of the event detection, configuration of the expected spatial expansion of the phenomenon is necessary. Wireless sensor nodes can communicate up to approximately 300 meters but many phenomena usually appear only locally. For example in an environmental surveillance scenario, temperature changes usually appear widely, whereas the size of an emerging fire is relatively small but has to be detected as well. As we learned, a suitable collaboration region closely relates to the expected spatial expansion of the phenomenon. Hence, the ESL allows to describe this collaboration region. If sensor nodes may jointly share their resources for collaborative event detection, these nodes must know whether they share a certain collaboration region. The ESL configures this valid region within the <DIMENSION> element. The shape or topology of the collaboration region can be specified by one of the following elements: <CIRCLE>, <SQUARE>, <BALL>, <CUBE>, <HOPS>. According to their names, these elements enable to define 2-dimensional collaboration regions, i.e., <CIRCLE> and <SQUARE>, as well as 3-dimensional ones, i.e., <BALL> and <CUBE>. Rather dedicated to the topology of the WSN is the <HOPS> element defining the collaboration region as number of hops in a multi-hop sensor network. If the <DIMENSION> element is omitted, the 1-hop neighborhood is taken as the default collaboration region, which is determined by sending range. Collaboration regions are virtually spanned around each sensor node. Each sensor node is the centre of a collaboration region and can be part of other collaboration regions spanned by neighboring nodes as well, see Figure 4.

An Example Event Specification for Fire Detection Scenarios

Along the example of fire detection with a WSN that is stressed throughout this chapter, we use this section to exemplary introduce a complete event description, illustrating ESL. Besides other criteria, a fire can be detected by monitoring the ambient temperature, the emission of smoke or the existence of carbon monoxide. Traditional and widely used fire detectors set off a fire alarm if monitored smoke or carbon monoxide emissions exceed a given threshold. Also changes in temperature can be analyzed to indicate or even detect a fire. In spite of using well-engineered sensing devices these methods are still vulnerable to false alarms, e.g., triggered by smoking, burnt food or influences of various heat sources. Each detection method is suitable to detect fires indeed, but proper fusion of all systems enhances the reliability of detection and decreases the false alarm probabil-

Figure 4. Example deployment of nodes with circular collaboration regions configured by radius r. Whereas node 4 is isolated, node 1 shares its event region with node 2, node 2 may collaborate with 1 and 3 and 3 may evaluate events with node 2.

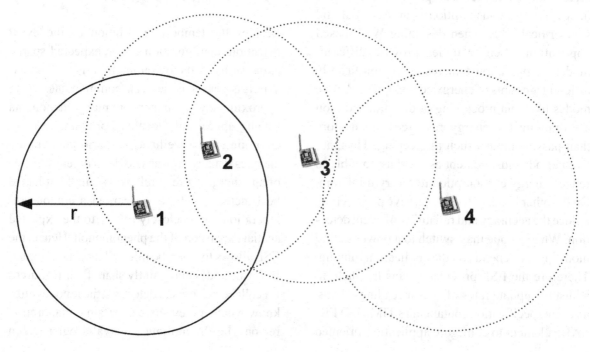

ity at the same time. It further enables to detect different kinds of fire that also reveal different physical properties, e.g., flaming and smoldering fires. Thus, a proper fire fighting system should apply temperature, smoke and carbon monoxide detectors simultaneously.

Listing 2 displays an event specification that can be used in fire detection scenarios. To decide about the existence of fire, each detection method usually determines a fixed threshold. This example proposes to apply 100 ppm (parts per million) as the threshold for carbon monoxide, 1.1 percent

Listing 2. Example of an event specification for fire detection scenarios.

```
<EVENT id="fire" version="1" priority="high" lease="6"
    reliableMode="yes">
    <SENSORDATA>
        <OR>
            <GREATEROREQUAL>
                <VARIABLE> carbon monoxide </VARIABLE>
                <CONSTANT unit="partsPerMillion">100</CONSTANT>
            </GREATEROREQUAL>
            <AND>
                <GREATER>
                    <VARIABLE> temperature </VARIABLE>
                    <CONSTANT unit="Kelvin">353</CONSTANT>
                </GREATER>
                <GREATEROREQUAL>
                    <VARIABLE> smoke </VARIABLE>
                    <CONSTANT unit="percentage">1.1</CONSTANT>
                </GREATEROREQUAL>
            </AND>
        </OR>
    </SENSORDATA>
    <CONSEQUENCE>
        <TRIGGERHANDLER> sendalert </TRIGGERHANDLER>
    </CONSEQUENCE>
    <EXECUTION>
        <TIMEINTERVAL relation="EqualTo">
            <CONSTANT unit="seconds">10</CONSTANT>
        </TIMEINTERVAL>
    </EXECUTION>
    <DIMENSION>
        <BALL relation="LessOrEqualTo">
            <CONSTANT unit="meters">2.5</CONSTANT>
        </BALL>
    </DIMENSION>
</EVENT>
```

as smoke limit and 353 Kelvin (80 centigrade) as the ambient temperature limit. Whereas the existence of carbon monoxide is a good stand-alone indicator for fire, temperature and smoke readings should be suitably combined to gain a higher false alarm resistance. Therefore, smoke and temperature thresholds are linked using a logical AND and are combined with the carbon monoxide threshold using a logical OR. Hence, an event *fire* is detected if either the carbon monoxide readings exceed 100 ppm OR both smoke AND temperature readings exceed their assigned thresholds. In case of having evaluated the phenomenon *fire* to exist, the sensor node triggers the *sendalert* event handler. A radius of 2.5 meters around the sensor nodes is assumed a reasonable collaboration region for distributed detection. Hence, the dimension element defines that region as a ball specifying a maximum radius of 2.5 meters.

Generation of Deployable Binary Event Specifications

Event specifications provide flexible and easy-to-use configuration means for using sensor networks beyond the scope of research, even for non-experts in the field such as medical employees adapting them for customized patient monitoring. However, XML is oversized for direct use on sensor nodes, which are subject to strict energy and memory constraints. To minimize the calculation effort on the sensor nodes as well as to minimize the amount of data to be transferred, event specifications are pre-parsed to generate smaller versions before in-network deployment. These compacted versions are called binary event specifications. Binary event specifications are applied for initial configuration as well as for updates, i.e., reconfiguration or deletion of configured event specifications. This section presents implementation details and the workflow of the event specification generator, which is depicted in Figure 5.

The event specification generator creates hardware-specific binary event specifications of universally valid event specifications. It is obvious, that general event specifications cannot be uniformly transferred to every sensor platform due to different hardware and software properties. To overcome these problems introduced by pervasiveness and heterogeneity, the event specification generator adapts variables, thresholds, handlers, phenomenon constraints etc. to the target sensor platform regarding expected hardware, sensing capabilities and the available OS. Afterwards, the elements in the adapted event specification are substituted by symbols and compressed into the final minimized binary event specification, which can then be used for configuration. All mentioned steps are fully-transparent to the user and automatically done by the event specification generator. That allows to keep the event definition process quite simple and intuitive by decoupling it from the configuration process.

The ESL event specification generator is written in Java to enable execution on different devices and platforms providing a Java Virtual Machine (JVM). In particular, we focus on mobile devices like laptops or smartphones. This provides the necessary mobility for envisioned applications in pervasive technologies. The integrated hardware abstraction layer interface enables to implement the mentioned adaptation to meet the requirements of target sensor platform. More precisely, this interface provides a couple of functions for harmonization of general ESL elements. These functions process the elements that need to be adapted to hard- and software specifics and return the customized variants. Hence, each sensor platform only needs to provide a suitable implementation of this interface to gain compatibility to the introduced event configuration system. That allows to easily create different hardware-specific binary event specifications for deployment on various platforms. To simplify matters, the following presents the generation of the binary event specification for the introduced

Figure 5. Architecture of the ESL event specification generator

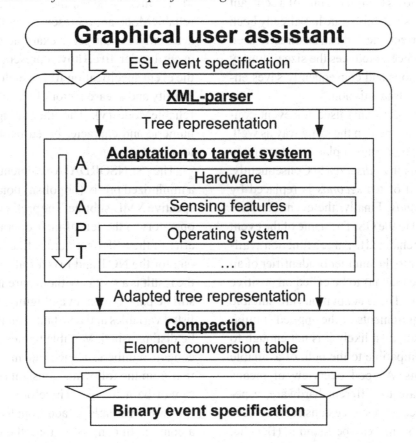

exemplary fire detection scenario, while using the simulator OMNeT++ with an upgrade for WSNs as the target platform. The generation of binary event specifications for other platforms consequently follows the same scheme but may of course require other customization.

Adaptation to Target Sensor Platform

Event specifications are first parsed into an in-memory representation of the XML-tree. The following describes the customization process for meeting the requirements of the target sensor platform. Therefore, the implementation of the hardware abstraction layer interface is used. First, constants and variables are adjusted. The names of variables, which identify sensing capabilities, are modified to internal identifiers as being used

on the sensor nodes. In the example scenario, the variables *carbon monoxide*, *temperature* and *smoke* are mapped into *CO*, *T* and *S* respectively. Besides different identifiers, assigned constants (thresholds) are converted into those matching the target platform, e.g., equal sensing capabilities may be measured by different sensors with varying physical units. For example, temperature values given in Kelvin are converted to centigrade or time data is converted from minutes to milliseconds if necessary. In the given scenario, the thresholds for temperature and smoke readings need to be aligned. Since the temperature readings in the simulations are measured in centigrade, the threshold of 353 Kelvin is converted to 80 centigrade. Similar to that, the threshold for smoke readings is changed from 1.1 percent to 11 per mille. As another important gain of this processing, it allows to omit the unit of a constant for deployment, since this value has already been scaled to the correct one and can be directly used as threshold. Hence, it reduces the size of binary event specifications and consequently saves energy required for transmission.

Certainly, the constants used for event constraints must be adapted in the same way as well. Here, the timers of the target platform demand to provide time data in *milliseconds*. Consequently, the time interval of ten *seconds* is replaced by 10000 *milliseconds*. Finally, the event handlers must be adapted to the OS. The name of the event handler is either changed to name a function available at the OS or to the number or identifier of an interrupt routine that has to be called on positive event evaluation. These adaptations are suitable to fulfill the requirements of the applied simulator. However, but most likely it is not enough to remain fully compatible to the bulk of available sensor platforms. A good overview of means adapting software to different hardware, especially with respect to resource constraint devices or embedded systems, can be found in (Beuche, 2004).Detailed customization requirements are expected to emerge from experiences with real deployments in future work.

Creation of Binary Event Specifications

After adaptation, all elements are successively transformed into minimized descriptions before being deployed as a binary event specification. A binary event specification consecutively lists all elements of the respective event specification. Keeping a given order allows to describe these elements by their content only. More precisely, each binary event specification lists the event header, followed by the sensor data element, the event handlers, the execution constraint and finally the dimension constraint in exactly that order.

In the shortened form, all parameters of the event header are associated to one string. Whereas lease and version numbers as well as the event id are directly taken, the attributes priority and reliableMode are represented by their first character only. For the given example, the compacted event header **fire.1h6y** represents version **1** of the event specification **fire**, which assigns a **h**igh priority and a lease factor of **6** while enabling the reliableMode (**y**). The alternating sequence of numeric and character-based parameters allows to omit delimiters.

The <SENSORDATA> element is converted to a minimized prefix (or polish) notation of the respective XML-subtree. The prefix notation places operators to the left of their operands. Since the arity of the ESL operators is fixed, which is here one for the NOT and two for all other elements, the result is a syntax without parentheses that can still be parsed without ambiguity. Consecutively listed variables and constants can in principle not be distinguished. Variable names are allowed to contain numbers. Hence, an implicit delimitation from the following constant (numbers only) cannot be achieved. Therefore, a constant that follows a variable is additionally separated by a comma. In contrast to that, the case of a variable following a constant is implicitly identified and allows omitting the comma, since variables have to begin with an alphabetic character while constants contain numbers only. To minimize the final size of binary event specifications, the tags of the ESL elements are represented by short symbols, see Table 2. These symbols are assigned via the hardware abstraction layer and may differ depending on the target platform. Additionally please note, usually the - or the Δ symbolize the algebraic difference operation. Herein, the # is used to symbolize the difference operation. Automatic distinction of the - symbol when being used for signed constants and differences as well unreasonably increases the parsing complexity. The Δ symbol is not used because it is not contained in the standard ASCII character set and may be not supported by each sensor platform. For the same reason, the use of symbols ≤ and ≥ is deprecated.

The character sequences <= and >= are used to describe the respective relations.

As the next part, the event handlers are added to the binary event specification, which are consecutively listed and separated by comma. Finally, the binary event specification is completed by adding the remaining elements containing the phenomenon constraints, which are the execution element and the dimension element. Phenomenon constraints consist of their short identifiers, followed by the symbolized relation attribute and one or two constants. These constraints are described in infix notation and are evaluated on the sensor nodes by string matching operations according to the following regular expression:

$$[A-Za-z]^+[<|>|=|<=|>=|<>]^{\{1\}}[0-9]^+([,]^{\{1\}}[0-9]^+)^{\{0,1\}}$$

Binary event specifications are transmitted as Byte-Streams to the sensor nodes whereby the base elements are separated by colons. Adherence to such strict layout reduces the size of binary event specifications compared to the event specification by an average factor greater than ten. For instance, that downscales the size of the introduced event specification for fire detection by a factor of 12

from 710 Bytes plus white-spaces down to 56 Bytes provided as binary event specification. Figure 6 displays the respective binary event specification.

Deployment on Sensor Nodes as Event Decision Tree (EDT)

This section presents how sensor nodes are autonomously configured according to binary event specifications. It describes the conversion of binary event specifications into their processable form as Event Decision Tree (EDT). The EDT enables every node to self-divide configuration queries according to its resources and to execute the complete event evaluation process. Unlike in other approaches, nodes are not only used as data sources for sensing and distributing raw data. In fact, every node can independently analyze and process its sensor readings and come to a final decision about the existence of a phenomenon. The EDT is a fully distributed concept that does not require special nodes for information-fusion and final evaluation. This is considered mandatory to prevent from SPoFs, which are naturally arising if only one or a few nodes are enabled to execute the complete detection and evaluation process. Such concept significantly reduces the energy

Table 2. Conversion table containing event specification elements and respective binary event specification elements. Unlisted elements of the event specification need not to be converted. These are implicitly represented by the fixed-order structure of the binary event specification.

Event specification	Binary event specification	Event specification	Binary event specification
<AND>	&	<PRODUCT>	*
<OR>	|	<QUOTIENT>	/
<NOT>	!	<MODULO>	%
<EQUAL>	=	<TIMEINTERVAL>	I
<GREATER>	>	<CIRCLE>	C
<LESS>	<	<SQUARE>	S
<GREATEROREQUAL>	>=	<BALL>	V
<LESSOREQUAL>	<=	<CUBE>	K
<SUM>	+	<HOPS>	H
<DIFFERENCE>	#		

Figure 6. Binary event specification of the introduced fire detection example. It contains all information necessary for configuring sensing devices according to the event specification. The numbers displayed on top of the binary event specification represent the respective offset addresses in the byte stream.

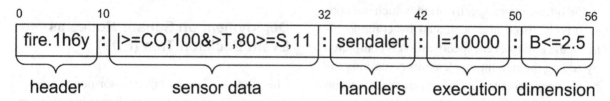

consumption in contrast to other approaches by omitting the distribution of sensed data at each detection interval.

Configuration and maintenance of EDTs is performed by the EDT-engine on each sensor node. This includes implementation features for generating and evaluating EDTs as well for partitioning complex events into less complex ones based on the sensing facilities of individual sensor nodes. It further introduces efficient means to detect nodes for collaboration, which may provide missing information to evaluate the complete EDT. Finally, simulation results of a prototype implementation applied to a failure scenario underline the robustness and the cost-efficiency of the presented approach.

On the sensor nodes, the EDT-engine, which is depicted in Figure 7, configures the sensor node with respect to each received binary event specification. First, the EDT generator processes the sensor data element. As a result, it generates the representation of the phenomenon to be sensed as an EDT. Depending on the sensing features and resources provided by the node, the EDT adaptation splits this EDT into local and remote parts. Local parts can be evaluated by the node itself, whereas remote parts have to be requested from external sources, e.g., from neighboring nodes. The EDT adaptation further configures application-related constraints as parameters of the EDT, i.e., collaboration regions, handlers, sensing intervals etc.

The EDT processing unit integrates the final EDT and maintains compliance with all parameters of the configured EDTs. The EDT processing unit consists of the EDT evaluation, an EDT scheduler and a Handler box. The EDT scheduler autonomously schedules all EDTs with respect to their configured evaluation intervals. This schedule is currently implemented by timers assigned to each EDT. On timer wakeup, the respective EDT is enqueued into a queue that holds all EDTs pending for execution. That guarantees evaluation of all EDTs, even if several of them are triggered simultaneously or with short lags. This queue is in principle a First In-First Out (FIFO) queue, but enqueued EDTs are secondary sorted with respect to their assigned priority. The priorities can be *low*, *normal* or *high*. EDTs with a *high* priority are ranked first, of course. Similarly the EDTs with a *low* priority are added to the end of the queue. Future implementations are supposed to use available schedulers of the underlying OS, such as an integrated Earliest Deadline First (EDF) scheduler, to provide a more precise and fair scheduling.

On dispatching an EDT into the EDT evaluation for execution, the sensing devices are triggered to deliver actual sensor readings required to decide about the existence of the described phenomenon. In case of a positive evaluation result, the Handler box is called to execute the respectively associated handler methods. The EDT evaluation also manages collaboration with other sensor nodes if necessary. Details about collaboration are given

Figure 7. Detailed architecture of the EDT-engine

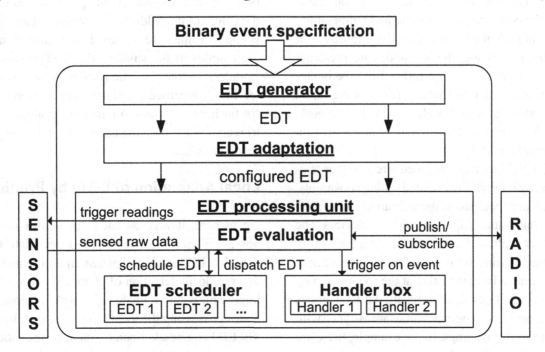

later in this section. Finally, the timer of the EDT is set up to the next evaluation interval and the EDT is returned to the EDT scheduler. In addition to the configured evaluation interval, EDTs are also triggered on demand by collaboration requests from other devices. In that case, evaluation of the EDT is executed as usual but consequently answers the request, too. After finishing an unscheduled evaluation, the corresponding timer is reset to a full detection interval. On the one hand, that assures a sufficient detection interval as required by the event specification. On the other hand, it simultaneously reduces the number of evaluation processes to a certain minimum to save energy resources.

Establishing Event Decision Tree

Binary event specifications are parsed at the sensor nodes to generate evaluable event configurations by establishing EDTs. These represent the phenomenon based on the sensor data element of the binary event specification. The EDT generator is based on a tiny Generating Finite State Machine (GFSM) with eight states. That enables to implement the EDT generator on almost every available sensor platform. In the simulator the implementation of the GFSM required only 25 lines of C/C++ code. The EDT generator transforms the prefix notation of the sensor data element into a congruent representation as an EDT. Leaf nodes identifying sensing capabilities or constant values according to the specification of thresholds provide the basis for EDTs. Leaf nodes are child nodes of relational or algebraic elements. Algebraic nodes define algebraic operations between its child nodes. On top of leaf nodes or algebraic nodes, relational nodes constitute the respective relation between its two children. These minimal trees of three nodes are primitive events. In complex events they become respective subtrees.

Logic nodes, representing the logic combinations of several primitive events, are generated as parent nodes on top of relational elements. In the fire detection example, the root node of the EDT represents a Boolean OR-relation between the thresholds regarding the carbon monoxide and the combination of smoke and temperature. The equivalent EDT is depicted in Figure 8. For further processing, the tree nodes are pre-order numbered during their creation from the binary event specification. That assures the same initial tree labeling on every device in the network, which is necessary for efficient exchange of event information later.

An EDT evaluation procedure is either triggered by internal EDT related timing constraints, which are specified in the execution element, or by collaboration requests from other devices. The EDT is evaluated automatically in a bottom-up manner starting from the leaf nodes in order to determine a Boolean value at the root node, i.e., the final EDT evaluation result. All EDT nodes representing sensing capabilities are assigned with actual sensor readings. In the example, these are the node *CO* for carbon monoxide numbered as 3, the node *T* for temperature numbered as 7 and the node *S* for smoke readings numbered as 10. Afterwards, the EDT is evaluated by execution

of the operations stated at the parent nodes with the values of its children as operands. As a result, Boolean values are assigned to relational and logic nodes. If the value of the EDT root node evaluates to true, i.e., the phenomenon was detected, all specified event handlers are triggered for further processing. A new EDT evaluation is triggered when the next assigned evaluation interval has elapsed.

Local Adaptation of EDTs by Pruning

Up to here, it was assumed that sensor nodes possess all sensing capabilities to evaluate the complete EDT itself. If that assumption cannot be assured, local detection of phenomena becomes impossible without collaboration with other sensor nodes possessing the locally missed capabilities. The EDT engine additionally enables sensor nodes to evaluate the EDT even if they provide only a subset or even no sensing capability. Such lack of capabilities could either be intended by design or due to failed sensing units. Hence, certain branches

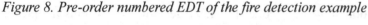

Figure 8. Pre-order numbered EDT of the fire detection example

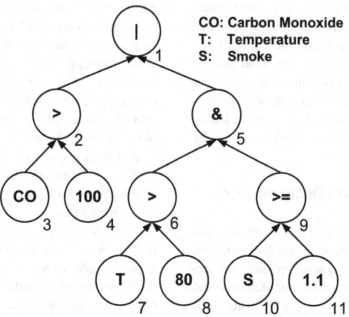

or subtrees of the EDT cannot be evaluated by the node itself. In that case, sensor nodes need to collaborate to exchange information about sensor readings or partial evaluation results.

The exchange of sensed raw data, which is done by most approaches, is very inefficient from two points of view. First, permanent exchange of sensor readings leads to a huge number of transmissions and hence, consumes much energy and reduces network performance. Second, transmitting raw sensor data requires to use rather large data packages, depending on the number of readings and their accuracy, i.e., the size of each value usually varies from two to four bytes. Since a conceptual main goal is to remain very energy efficient, we focus on minimizing the number of transmissions and the amount of data to be exchanged. Instead of exchanging raw sensor readings at each detection interval, sensor readings are locally processed first and only one bit is eventually submitted, which is the Boolean value of a particular EDT node. Other existing approaches that share information in a comparable style state the complete detection result only, i.e., the Boolean value of the root node. This concept focuses on efficiently sharing information about both, complete and partial EDT evaluation results.

In case of using EDT, the Boolean value of only one particular EDT node has to be transferred. Missing node values may be delivered by neighboring nodes that share the specified collaboration region. To prepare these data exchanges, every sensor node has to determine which EDT node information is missing at the local EDT. Therefore the following algorithm prunes the established EDT until it contains the minimum required EDT for local event processing:

1. Mark each leave as pruned that represents an unsupported sensing capability.
2. Search all nodes that possess at least one marked child excluding the root node. Since an EDT is a binary tree, every node possesses at most two child nodes. Hence, either one

or both child nodes are marked as pruned in that case.
   a. Mark node as pruned, if
      i.   It represents an algebraic operation or
      ii. The unmarked child represents a constant or
      iii. All child nodes are marked as pruned.
3. Repeat step 2 until no new nodes are marked. After that, all undecidable subtrees are marked.
4. Prune all marked nodes except for the root nodes of the marked subtrees.
5. Declare all left marked nodes as *undecidable*.

After pruning, the EDT may contain nodes, which are marked as *undecidable*. Respective Boolean node values must be obtained by other nodes in the collaboration region. Let us assume to use two different types of nodes (A and B) for the introduced fire detection example. Nodes of type A provide carbon monoxide and temperature sensors, whereas type B nodes provide sensing facilities for carbon monoxide and smoke. Hence, the initial EDTs generated at these nodes must be pruned with respect to the available sensing capabilities.

Accordingly, type A nodes cut the branch containing the smoke readings and type B nodes respectively cut the branch containing the temperature readings. That results in two different EDTs at the sensing devices, each containing one node marked as *undecidable*. Thus, type A nodes require information about tree node number 9, whereas type B nodes require information about tree node number 6. Both resulting EDTs are displayed in Figure 9. At regular evaluation, the EDT also checks the status of the sensing devices. If sensing devices fail during application the sensor node runs the pruning again to locally self-adapt the EDT to the current situation. In addition, sensing devices may fail transiently only. In that case, the sensing device becomes available again

Figure 9. Pruned EDTs for two different types of sensor nodes monitoring the introduced fire phenomenon. Nodes of type A provide sensing facilities for carbon monoxide and temperature whereas nodes of type B provide sensing facilities for carbon monoxide and smoke. Consequently, each type of node prunes a certain part of the EDT that cannot be evaluated locally. Resulting undecidable nodes are labeled with question mark. Hence, the Boolean values of these nodes must be obtained from other nodes in the specified collaboration region.

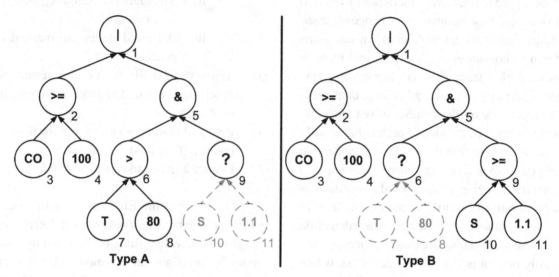

and hence, the EDT can be reconstructed into its original form by removing the *undecidable* marking from respective EDT nodes.

By pruning, the EDT may degenerate to a minimal tree consisting of only the root node with two *undecidable* children. Such an EDT enables sensor nodes that possess no suitable sensing capability for phenomena detection to serve as a bridge. These nodes are of interest if they are located between two or more nodes that possess the required sensing capabilities but cannot communicate directly or do not share the same collaboration region. The only prerequisite is that these nodes share the collaboration region with the bridge node. Figure 10 displays example deployments for both cases. Here sensor node 2 shares its collaboration region with the nodes 1 and 3 and hence, may perform the bridging functionality for these nodes. In Figure 10 (a), the nodes 1 and 3 do not share a collaboration region due to their distance. In Figure 10 (b), these nodes

share their regions indeed but cannot communicate directly due to an obstacle between them. In such a scenario, all participating nodes deliver their parts of EDT evaluation to the bridge node, which is eventually enabled to decide about the occurrence of the observed phenomenon. After having identified the *undecidable* parts for local detection on each sensor node, those have to efficiently share necessary information. A suitable collaboration scheme maintaining this data exchange is presented in the next section.

Collaborative Exchange of EDT-Node Values by Publish/Subscribe

To save energy resources, wireless sensor nodes should communicate if and only if it is absolutely necessary. A suitable collaboration mechanism in sensor networks must further self-adapt to changing network situations and consider application

Figure 10. Example deployments that may require node 2 to serve as a bridge for the nodes 1 and 3. In (a) the nodes 1 and 3 do not share an event region due to their distance. In (b) these nodes share their regions indeed, but cannot communicate directly due to an obstacle between them.

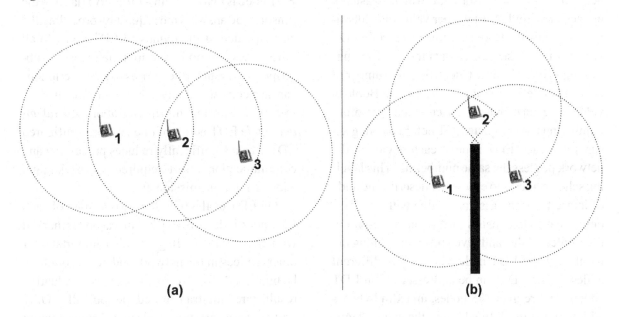

(a)   (b)

requirements. In particular, the following questions are of primary concern:

Is there a need to transmit some event information?

If yes, which node has to transmit what information?

Is there really a sensor node that receives the data?

Additionally, the amount of exchanged data ought to be kept as small as possible. This section presents an adaptive and easy-to-scale mechanism to efficiently share EDT evaluation results based on a publish/subscribe approach. A comprehensive comparison of other approaches using publish/subscribe is given in (Heinzelman, W. B., Murphy, A. L., Carvalho, H. S. & Perillo, M. A., 2004).

It is quite obvious that request-acknowledgement-based (ACK) communication schemes can be used for reliable collaboration. But they produce a huge amount of traffic and are therefore inefficient for sensor networks. In idealized scenarios,

the ACK-based data exchange requires at least two transmissions per detection interval and node, i.e., one request and one acknowledgement message. In usual application, such a request is spread as broadcast and hence, several nodes may answer to particular request. To simplify matters, this possibility is ignored but would of course further increase the required traffic for ACK-based data exchange. Hence, here we only consider the idealized-ACK data exchange requiring two messages per interval. The publish/subscribe approach maintains the exchange of EDT node values and reduces the traffic by submitting only changes of node values to achieve longer time intervals without any transmission. The focus is on reducing the package payload for application data as well as the number of transmissions. The simulation results presented in a later section show that the proposed publish/subscribe scheme outperforms idealized ACK-based variants.

Since every bit to be transmitted is expensive with regard to energy consumption, the amount of exchanged data has to be minimized. EDTs efficiently share local evaluation results using a few bytes only. In contrast to existing approaches that need to share raw sensor data, which is usually between two and four byte per value plus identifier, here only the Boolean value of a certain EDT node is of interest. Thus, a data transmission has to contain only the event identifier, the number of the respective EDT node and the current Boolean value assigned to that node. Remember, pre-order numbering the complete EDT before pruning assures that each EDT node at each device in the network possess the same numbering. This labeling scheme allows to efficiently describe the node of interest and the assigned value with one byte only. That byte consists of one bit representing the Boolean value and seven bits representing the number of the EDT node. Hence, 128 different nodes in one EDT can be addressed. If an EDT contains more than 128 nodes, an extra byte for addressing is used. In addition, the event identifier must be submitted given that a sensor node is enabled to configure several EDTs concurrently. If the event identifier is chosen to be a unique number less than 256, e.g., this number may be generated while preparing the binary event description, all necessary information can be transmitted by two bytes only. Hence, this scheme reduces the required data payload for collaborative exchange by at least 50 percent.

As mentioned, missing values of *undecidable* EDT nodes must be obtained by suitable other sources, e.g., neighboring nodes. Thus, the sensor node broadcasts a data interest (subscription) into the network to find suitable information suppliers. If the binary event specification defined a collaboration region, this subscription must also contain the location of the subscribing sensor node. On receiving a subscription, the sensor node compares the location data to determine whether both nodes share the collaboration region. Only if that holds true or if the request contains no location data, i.e., assuming the one-hop neighborhood collaboration region, the received subscription is of interest. The receiving sensor node searches its own respective EDT to determine whether it can provide the requested information. The requested EDT node is marked with a *toPublish* flag and the sensor node answers the request by providing the current value of the requested EDT node. In all other cases, the node discards the received subscription without further processing. Subscriptions can also consist of many concurrent data interests in case of requiring information about several *undecidable* EDT nodes of one or more configured EDTs. That significantly reduces processing and communication effort required for packaging, addressing, transmission etc.

On EDT evaluation, the current state of each EDT node is determined. Results at nodes marked with the *toPublish* flag are also important for other devices in the network and hence, ought to be published. To save resources these evaluation results are not transmitted periodically. Only first-time subscriptions and state changes require transmission of the current node state. If a device accepts a received subscription for the first time, it answers with the current node state to provide an initial value. Since a node state is of Boolean type, only state changes must be submitted to update the node state at the subscriber. If node states change rarely, the number of required publications is significantly reduced. Even in the worst case, i.e., the node state changes at each evaluation, this scheme requires the same overhead as usual methods where values are transmitted repeatedly at every evaluation period.

Using a publish/subscribe scheme is rather simple if reliable communication architectures and fixed network structures are provided, but WSNs are subject to unpredictable behavior caused by sudden changes in context, connectivity, working mode etc. That especially holds true if mobility of nodes is provided. To ensure a certain level of robustness and efficiency, some fundamentals have to be considered from respective points of view of subscribers and publishers. How does the subscribing node know, whether some other node received the subscription, accepted it or is still providing publications? On the other side, the publishing node requires to know whether there is still a subscriber awaiting information about EDT node values. These problems could indeed be solved by using a simple ACK-scheme for every transmission to inform the sender about the success. Unfortunately, pure ACK-based communication is inefficient for WSNs as mentioned. Furthermore, publish/subscribe is designed to achieve large periods without any transmission, which is not possible with ACK-based schemes.

Leasing of Publication Time

Due to assumed conditions in WSNs, the publish/subscribe scheme must adapt frequently to reach a certain level of robustness in phenomenon detection. Certainly, the overhead needed for adaptation must be kept as small as possible but still allow for balancing the adaptiveness with respect to the application. Accordingly, publications and subscriptions should either be removable or be valid for certain time periods only. The latter is much more suitable for WSNs where unforeseen changes leave no chance for appropriate responses or un-subscriptions. Therefore, an adaptive lease procedure limits the validity of publications and subscriptions. It allows to subscribe a data interest for a certain lease period only, after which the publish/subscribe relation has to be renewed. Such lease-based publish/subscribe requires significantly less transmissions than ACK-based variants and enables lease intervals assigned per phenomenon. Usage of lease-based approaches is also well known in other application areas, e.g., for labeling of references and objects in automatic garbage collection or for allocation of resources like the IP addresses from servers using the Dynamic Host Configuration Protocol (DHCP).

A lease-based subscription specifies a certain time interval determining the validity period of subscriptions during which associated publications have to be sent. This lease period is determined as the product of the phenomenon-associated lease factor and the EDT evaluation interval. Both factors are given by the binary event specification. The lease factor enables fine-tuned and customized lease intervals. It adapts the lease period to the monitored phenomenon and to expected conditions in the sensor network. For example, sensor networks, which are subject to permanently changing situations or node mobility, require a high adaptiveness. Those should apply short lease intervals. In contrast to that, sensor networks deployed at rather fixed network structures could make use of larger lease intervals to save energy and extend the overall network lifetime. If the lease factor is chosen to be one, i.e., the leasing time is one detection interval, this scheme converges to ACK-based approaches.

On receiving a matching subscription, the node determines the expiration date of the respective publication. The expiration date is assigned to the corresponding EDT node together with the *toPublish* flag. After initially publishing the current EDT node value, any further change is published as long as this flag is set. Consequently, the flag is automatically removed from the EDT node when the expiration date is reached, i.e., the lease has expired. Similar to the *toPublish* flag, the subscriber assigns an expiration date to the requested *undecidable* EDT node. Even if no publisher responds to the subscription, the node sends no new subscription before this expiration date has expired. That assures to renew the publish/subscribe relations with respect to the configured adaptation rate only. Other approaches usually try to subscribe at each detection interval again, which heavily drains the power resources.

To save more energy, new and renewed leases are distinguished. The initial respond of the publisher for renewals can be saved, since it is not necessary if no change has occurred. If earlier agreed leases are to be renewed only, the publisher does not respond with the initial node value but extends the lease period and continues providing state changes until the newly assigned expiration date is reached. In addition, publisher and subscriber renew the lease period automatically upon notification of a state change. When data is published during a valid lease, the expiration date of the *toPublish* flag is reset to the full lease period. Similarly, the subscribing node renews the expiration date of a current subscription when receiving a respective publication.

Figure 11 displays sequence charts of both lease extension cases as well as the ACK-based scheme for comparison. In the ACK-based variant, displayed in (a), the subscriber requests information at each detection interval, which is accordingly responded by the publishing node.

In contrast to that, (b) and (c) illustrate the lease allocation in case of no change (b) and change (c) in EDT node values while applying a lease factor of three. Both cases require to provide the current node value by an initial publication of course. In case of no change (b), the subscription is renewed by the subscriber after the lease has expired. If a change of the EDT node value occurs during a valid lease (c), the lease period is automatically extended on both sides via the publication message. In such simple scenario, the lease-based approach already saves more than 60 percent of the messages.

Figure 11. Sequence of information exchange between a single subscriber and a single publisher during four detection intervals i_n to i_{n+3}. (a) displays the performance of the ACK-based variant, which is constant regardless of the existence of events. (b) and (c) illustrate the lease allocation applying a lease factor of three, i.e., the subscription is valid for three evaluation intervals. In case of no change, see (b), the subscription is renewed by the subscriber whereas a change of the EDT node value allows to extend the lease on both sides via the publication message (c).

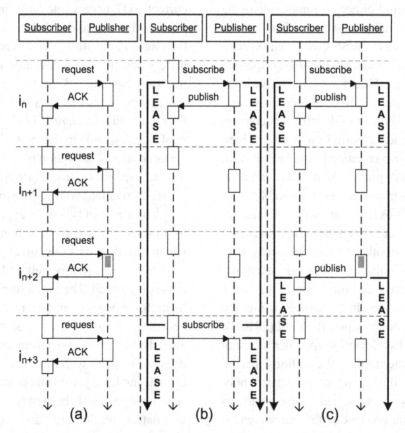

Since a lease can be automatically extended by publications without a respective acknowledgement message from the subscriber, there is a risk that the publisher side runs into a kind of infinite loop. In other words, after publishing the initial node value, the publisher may renew the lease and the *toPublish* flag again and again, while the subscriber disappeared in the meantime. To cope with that, an exceptional termination condition for publications was integrated. The publisher counts the number of automatic lease renewals and removes the *toPublish* flag, when the value of the counter equals the given lease factor. Hence, that exceptional condition forces the subscriber to renew the subscription again if it still requires information about the respective node value. Consequently, each subscription resets the counter at the publisher.

It is obvious that this communication scheme is well suited for low power applications such as environmental or structural health monitoring. Besides this high efficiency in power consumption, another main goal of this chapter is robustness of event detection, which consequently requires a stable and reliable communication scheme. Therefore the introduced approach can operate in a reliable mode as well. The reliable mode combines the advantages of the introduced publish/subscribe scheme with the reliability benefits provided by ACK-based communication. The reliable mode introduces retransmissions on the application level. Usually retransmissions in case of message loss can be assumed to be part of the Medium Access Control (MAC) layer. If retransmissions are not provided by the MAC protocol or if the link reliability of the underlying network is unknown, the publish/subscribe scheme can provide a similar feature on the application level.

The reliable mode is activated by setting the reliableMode attribute in the <EVENT> element of the event specification. The reliable mode applies the introduced lease-based publish/subscribe scheme, too, but enforces to explicitly acknowledge every transmitted data packet. If

the ACK-message fails while the reliable mode is enabled, the already renewed lease is removed immediately. A publication in response to an initial subscription is implicitly used as an ACK-message. This introduces a little overhead indeed, but still outperforms usual ACK-based variants. Figure 12 illustrates the performance of the reliable mode when applied to the same scenario as shown before in Figure 11. Similarly, it compares the behavior of the ACK-based variant (a) to the cases of no changes (b) and changes (c) of EDT node values in the publish/subscribe approach. Even here, the reliable mode still saves 50 percent of the required messages.

Finally, the reliable mode can be applied to a specific event specification and hence, allows customizing the used communication scheme for each configured EDT. In contrast to other approaches where the communication protocol is identical for all configured tasks, the EDT engine may execute both modes simultaneously depending on the configured EDTs. To summarize, it is a simple fact that the lease-based publish/subscribe provides a considerable benefit with respect to the number of required transmissions, even if the applied lease interval is rather short. This theory has been proven by simulations, which are presented in the next sections.

Side Effects of Collaboration

In spite of presented benefits of collaborative event detection, there exist some side effects that must be considered separately. Collaboration obviously includes distribution of partial evaluation results to subscribing nodes to enable these to evaluate their respective EDT. Certainly, that may essentially affect the final evaluation results at these sensor nodes. More precisely, the final EDT evaluation result at subscribing nodes may highly or directly depend on received (published) values. Hence, several subscriber nodes may always generate the same final evaluation result as their publisher. This is not of concern for usual detection, since

Figure 12. Sequence of information exchange for the same scenario as shown before in Figure 11 while applying the reliable mode for the lease-based publish/subscribe scheme in (b) and (c). (a) displays the performance of the ACK-based variant for comparison. Even with an enabled reliable mode, the lease-based approach requires 50 percent less messages.

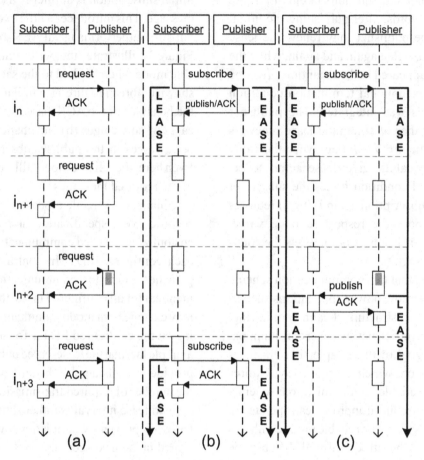

otherwise subscribing nodes may possibly not have the ability to generate a final evaluation result at all. In that case, local event detection would depend on the results of the publishing node in either way.

However, avoidance of fault propagation is of utmost importance in distributed systems like WSNs. In consequence of using the publish/subscribe collaboration scheme published faulty values could possibly propagate through the network from node to node. This happens when a value of an EDT node, which was formerly obtained through subscriptions, is published further. In the worst case, faulty values could be distributed to

all nodes in the entire network. Hence, stable or even reliable application becomes impossible. A simple condition circumvents this problem. The implementation of EDTs must not allow EDT nodes to assign values by subscriptions and to publish those values at the same time. In the presented implementation this is guaranteed by mutual exclusion of the *undecidable* and the *toPublish* flags. This assures that faulty values cannot propagate beyond the defined collaboration region of the publishing node.

Another side effect occurs if a subscriber has several publishers available at the same time. These may deliver different Boolean values for the same EDT node within a certain detection interval. Hence, the subscriber has to determine the correct value of that EDT node, or more precisely, the value that is most likely correct. To cope with that, the sensor node counts all *true* and *false* values per interval and finally decides on the majority. The respective counters at each EDT node are reset to zero after every evaluation run. In case of a tie situation, the last received value is taken.

Data security is a side condition that has not been considered so far but is an important issue for distributed application. This chapter does not focus on ensuring data security. But as it is essential with respect to reliability, especially when considering mission- and safety-critical applications, some means providing data security must at least be mentioned. Using wireless communication increases the risk of malicious attacks because the sensor network becomes accessible from outside. Whereas dozens of various attacks exist, the integrity of collaboration messages is of particular interest. The integrity and confidentiality of exchanged information can be assured by secure hashing and encryption techniques. These means can additionally be used on top of the presented event detection scheme, if necessary. Many different encryption methods are already available, but these quite differ in their strength and energy consumption depending on the algorithm and hardware used. Just as mentioned before, the associated overhead associated to security mechanisms is to be balanced between varying application requirements, too.

Performance Evaluation Methodology

To prove the concept, a prototype of the EDT was implemented in the discrete event simulator OMNeT++ (www.omnetpp.org) (Varga, 2002) with an extension for simulation of WSNs called Castalia (http://castalia.npc.nicta.com.au/) (Pham, Pediaditakis, & Boulis, 2007). The introduced fire detection scenario was applied to WSNs that are subject to failures in sensing devices. Based on that, application of the lease-based publish/subscribe approach is compared to the ACK-based variant. The simulation results are evaluated with regard to the detection accuracy and cost-efficiency of the introduced algorithms.

Application of Boolean event detection allows to generate compact snapshots of the system state containing the actual or respectively last detection results of all nodes, which are either *event* or *no event* respectively *1* or *0*. As a start, the first run simulated the correct behavior of the entire sensor network without any failures while snapshots from the system are frequently generated at every EDT evaluation interval. These snapshots represent the best case scenario and are used as the regular reference. In the following, all results and evaluations based on these snapshots are henceforth called *reference*. Consequently, such snapshots were taken in all other simulation runs at equal simulation time, too. Finally, the snapshots of equal simulation time are matched against the reference to determine whether the sensor nodes in the simulation runs gathered the correct detection result or not. The simulation results are not only compared to the reference scenario. Each failure scenario was also executed without improvement by collaboration to gather the usual local detection results of the sensor nodes. In the following, these runs are referred to as *standard*.

The simulation results are analyzed to determine the total detection accuracy and the number of required messages. The total detection accuracy states the number of correctly gathered positive and negative evaluation results per interval. Hence, a detection accuracy of 100% is given if all nodes within the phenomenon notify an event (positive result) while all other nodes do not register an event (negative result). As mentioned, the collaboration algorithms introduce a communication overhead represented by the total number of sent overhead messages. Additionally, the average number of required messages per node and interval is determined to directly compare the communication efficiency of all approaches.

Simulation Parameters and Deployment Patterns

According to the introduced event specification of the *fire* event, an EDT evaluation interval is ten seconds. The simulations ran three simulated hours, which is equivalent to 1080 EDT evaluation intervals in the fire detection scenario. In the following, the simulation time is given in discrete time steps, i.e., the EDT evaluation intervals. Finally, the simulation parameters regarding the wireless communication need to be identified. Wireless communication is subject to many restrictions resulting in an unreliable and sometimes nondeterministic performance. Many research projects already studied the parameters of link reliability, end to end delays, low power communication etc. These issues are indeed important, but were not considered in our simulations. These applied ideal conditions at the MAC layer and the wireless channel to generate deterministic results for comparison. Simulation results are taken from ten different random uniform node deployments using a field of 22.5×22.5 meters containing 100 wireless sensor nodes. The average results of all simulation runs on each of the ten deployments are determined. Each sensor node initially possesses all required sensing facilities, i.e., carbon monoxide, temperature and smoke detectors. Hence, all sensors are initially enabled to locally evaluate the complete EDT to gain local detection results.

For deterministic event generation, a simulated phenomenon is specified, which causes the actual sensor reading in a certain region. The simulated *fire* phenomenon had a circular dimension specifying high sensor readings in its centre, which decrease with the distance to the centre of the phenomenon. In particular, this phenomenon partitions the network into four areas. The region of the *fire* producing the highest sensor readings is defined as a circle around the centre point with a radius of 1.5 meters. In this area all sensor readings clearly exceed the defined thresholds. The area with radius between 1.5 and 3 meters specifies the immediate vicinity of the *fire* centre, where the sensor readings slightly exceed the thresholds and the phenomenon can still be recognized. The area with radius from 3 to 6 meters defines the outer expansion of the phenomenon. In this area the sensor readings are slightly below the thresholds. Finally, all nodes not located in one of these three areas of the phenomenon generate "usual" sensor readings that are clearly below the thresholds.

To trigger changes in sensor readings and node evaluation results, the centre of the *fire* phenomenon deterministically moves within the network boundaries at every minute or six EDT evaluation intervals respectively. In comparison to the spatial expansion covered by the entire sensor network the size of the phenomenon is rather small. Most sensor nodes will therefore generate negative evaluation results per interval whereas only a few nodes may possibly detect the phenomenon. This perfectly fits to the fire detection scenario where upcoming fires usually feature a small size. However, such moving behavior does not correspond to a fire in the real world. Nevertheless, the introduced fire detection scenario is a well descriptive vehicle to exemplify phenomenon definition and reliable phenomenon detection within a mission-critical context. The described phenomenon is used to generate deterministic sensor readings and simulation results. The case that sensor nodes may be damaged or destroyed by such phenomenon is also not considered in this scenario.

Failure Scenario: Permanently Failing Sensing Capabilities

Low cost production, decreasing energy supply and various environmental influences may not only lead to errors of measurement in sensor readings. These also cause sensing devices to fail transiently or to get even permanently lost. In that case, usual local event detection based on own sensor readings is limited or cannot further be provided. Of course, this results in decreased detection accuracy. Collaboration between sensor nodes exchanging missing information is a proper means to keep the functionality of the sensor network and its configured applications alive. In the context of EDTs, this requires to exchange values of EDT nodes. This section analyses the performance of event detection under random permanent failures of sensing devices. Therefore, the results of the standard detection are compared to the detection results in application of ACK-based and lease-based collaboration. Here the worst case failure scenario is simulated. Each available sensing capability, i.e., the temperature, the carbon monoxide and the smoke sensing devices, will eventually fail on each sensor node during the simulation run. Fortunately, such extreme failure scenario is far away from real deployments. However, it is necessary to test the collaboration schemes in worst case scenarios.

In such failure scenario, the total detection accuracy is the most important issue. Collaboration is not designed to explicitly enhance the mere detection of phenomena. It is rather designed to improve the robustness of the sensor network against failed sensing devices in the sensor nodes and to keep the applications running at all nodes. Therefore, collaboration schemes perform independent of the final detection results. A successive loss of all sensing features of each node in the entire WSN represents a complete operational breakdown for the application running on the sensor nodes. In the introduced fire detection scenario, the three sensing devices measuring carbon monoxide, temperature and smoke at each sensor node fail within the 1080 simulated time intervals. To slow down the decrease of detection performance in our simulation no more than one sensing device at one sensor node may fail per interval. The occurrence of failures is pseudo-randomly distributed. Of course, this requires to successively adapt (prune) the local EDT at each node when a sensing capability fails. It further triggers collaboration between neighboring nodes to gather detection results for substitution of locally missing information. When all sensing devices at a node failed, this is not equivalent to a crash. In that case, the respective EDT degenerated to a tree evaluating the children of the root node only. The sensor node then acts as a bridge node.

Table 3 presents a brief summary of the simulation results in case of permanently failing sensing capabilities. Unfortunately, the simulation environment was unable to finish the runs applying ACK-based collaboration. Due to the successively increasing number of necessary collaboration messages the process executing the ACK-based simulation has been killed by the simulation environment. For the affected runs we displayed the last known system state and marked it with an * in the table. This yet indicates that ACK-based collaboration becomes infeasible with a growing number of failures.

First, the results of all approaches, i.e., until the ACK-based simulation has been aborted, are evaluated. Comparing the average of correct detection results in the entire network, both collaboration schemes clearly improved the total detection accuracy. The ACK-based scheme performed slightly better than the lease-based one. This result was expected due to the fact that the ACK-based scheme always gathers the actual detection results at each interval. In contrast to that, the lease-based approach in average reflects changes slower depending on the leasing time, even if the lease is optimized to the expected behavior of the phenomenon. According to the simulated phenomenon, which moves every six intervals, the lease factor was also set to six. The lease-based publish/subscribe approach most likely will not outperform the ACK-based variant with regard to the detection accuracy. In fact, the goal of the lease-based detection is to provide a detection accuracy that closely meets the result of the ACK-based scheme, but with a significantly reduced message overhead.

Table 3. Comparison of applying lease-based publish/subscribe and ACK-based collaboration in case of permanently failing sensing capabilities. The lease-based approach performs best and enhances the standard detection by about 30%. Due to the successively increasing number of necessary collaboration messages in the ACK-based scheme, the simulation process has been killed by the simulation environment. For the affected runs the last known system state is represented and marked with an *.

Total detection accuracy in %			
Figure 13	Standard	Lease = 6	ACK
Uniform random deployment *	63.970	82.917	85.619
Uniform random deployment	59.765	77.968	-
Average number of collaboration messages per node and interval			
Figure 14	Lease = 6 (reliable)	Lease = 6	ACK
Uniform random deployment*	0.537	0.357	7.360
Uniform random deployment	0.525	0.356	-

The total detection accuracies of both collaboration approaches are compared to the standard detection in Figure 13. In case that 50% of the local detection results are lost in the standard detection, the lease-based and the ACK-based scheme still provide a detection accuracy of 82% and 85% respectively. If 70% of detection results are lost in the standard detection, i.e., only 30 nodes remain functional, the collaboration schemes still generate 67% (lease-based) and 70% (ACK-based) correct detection results. That is a temporarily detection improvement of 225% compared to the standard detection. The lease-based approach significantly outperforms the ACK-based variant in comparison of the number of collaboration messages, see the diagram in Figure 14. It requires only about one message within three detection intervals. The ACK-based scheme sent about 7.5 messages per node in average at each interval, which in total differs from the lease-based scheme by a factor of 20. This is obviously too much traffic to be simulated. It further limits the applicability of the ACK-based scheme with respect to the node density of the network and the amount of data that needs to be exchanged.

Only the lease-based approach and the standard detection have completed their simulation runs. The following compares the respective performances. Again, the lease-based approach enhances the total detection accuracy in the network by an average of 30% in the uniform random deployment. It further detected 82% of all existing phenomena, which represents a gain of 39% in comparison to the standard method. This significant increase is achieved by requiring a collaboration overhead of only 0.35 messages per node and interval. This is equivalent to the transmission of 35 messages in the entire network during one detection interval representing ten seconds in lifetime. Even using the reliable mode for lease-based collaboration, i.e., to explicitly confirm each published value, increased the overhead to 0.53 messages per interval only. The reliable publishing does not influence the detection accuracy. It merely triggers explicit acknowledgement messages for received publications.

An increasing number of unavailable sensing devices continuously decreases the performance of event detection of course. In contrast to the standard detection, both introduced collaboration schemes significantly extend the time of running the detection with high detection accuracy. Even if 50% of all sensor nodes cannot evaluate the EDTs with own sensor readings, both collaboration schemes still provide a total detection accuracy of at least 84%. As expected, the ACK-based

Figure 13. Comparison of detection results when applying lease-based and ACK-based collaboration in case of permanently failing sensing capabilities. The lease-based approach enhances the detection accuracy by more than 30%. The ACK-based scheme indicated similar or slightly better performance but has been aborted by the simulation environment due the huge number messages required. Moreover, even if only 50% of all nodes are able to generate local detection result in the standard scheme, both collaboration schemes still provide a detection accuracy that is higher than 80%.

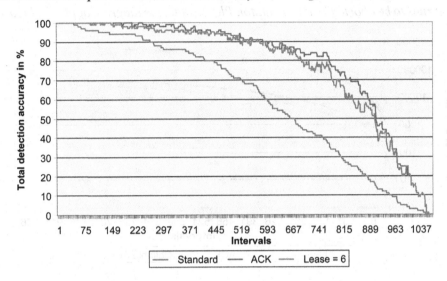

scheme performed slightly better than the lease-based scheme but required far more collaboration messages to achieve such results. The number of necessary messages differs by an average factor of 10 or higher. It is an unsolved question whether this overhead will also cause real applications to fail as it happened in the simulations. However, two remarks need to be emphasized. First, this failure scenario is (hopefully) rather unlikely to occur in real deployments. Second, applications running in such failure scenario possess a certain point in time where the detection accuracy falls below the required minimum in either way, regardless of detection enhancement. A sensor network that features too many failures should be renewed or not be relied to.

Lessons Learnt from Simulations

Presented simulation results strongly indicate a need for robust configuration means to enable reliable application, especially with regard to

the cost-efficiency of these means. Compared to the improved detection accuracy, the overhead associated with collaboration is worth to be spent in such scenario. Nevertheless, these methods need to be fine-tuned to achieve a sufficient cost-efficiency. The ESL provides means to customize parameters like the region and the leasing time for collaboration. The event detection concept based on ESL and EDT significantly improved available ACK-based collaboration with regard to cost-efficiency by introducing lease-based publish/subscribe. Of course, there are dozens of possible test deployments to further stress and analyze the performance of lease-based publish/subscribe under different conditions regarding varying phenomena, node density, node deployments, unreliable links etc. These are considered to be future work.

Presented simulation results only announce the advantages of autonomous configuration and phenomenon detection concept based on EDTs. We have simulated further failure scenarios at the

Figure 14. Comparison of required messages in the entire network in application of lease-based and ACK-based collaboration in case of permanently failing sensing capabilities. Despite the significantly enhanced detection performance, the lease-based approach only requires to transmit 0.35 messages per node and interval. Even using the reliable mode in lease-based collaboration, which does not influence the detection results, requires to transmit only about one message in two intervals. In contrast to that, the ACK-based approach required in average more than 7 messages per node and interval. This caused the simulation runs to be aborted by the simulator. Please note, the diagram applied a logarithmic scale.

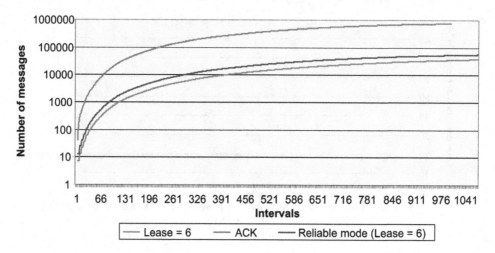

introduced deployments considering transiently failing devices and completely failing nodes, too. From these simulations we learned fundamental aspects about collaborative event detection. Collaboration can significantly enhance the robustness of a sensor network. It keeps on running its applications with high detection accuracy even in case of failed sensing devices. The presented ACK-based collaboration scheme provides the best detection accuracy since it refreshes the actual values of EDT-nodes after each interval. But simultaneously it requires a huge number of collaboration messages. It was shown that the cost-efficiency of the lease-based approach is very high and reduces the number of collaboration messages by a factor of 10 or higher. The lease-based publish/subscribe collaboration scheme can be configured to such extent that it is able to achieve detection accuracies that closely meet those of the ACK-based scheme by choosing a proper leasing time. This leasing time primarily depends on the expected properties and behavior of the phenomenon to be

sensed. The leasing time ideally is less or equal to the mean time of exposure to the monitored phenomenon. In the simulations, this was a leasing time of one minute (six intervals). In addition, changes that influence the event detection have to be considered, too. Such changes are caused by failed sensing devices and crashed or moved sensor nodes. By that, publisher nodes may disappear or become unable to publish further EDT-node values. Therefore, the estimated mean time to failure has to be regarded, too. For configuration of a proper leasing time, the user has to obey both of the following restrictions:

1. The maximum leasing time is less or equal to the mean time of exposure to the phenomenon to be sensed.
2. The maximum leasing time is less than the mean time to failure.

Of course, the lower bound of a leasing time is one EDT evaluation interval. In that case, the lease-based publish/subscribe approach converges to the ACK-based scheme. Finally, it is not clear whether ACK-based collaboration is generally executable on sensor networks with high node densities and high failure rates. In that case, the sensor network may be unable to manage the amount of traffic associated to this collaboration means. Even if this was possible, it significantly stresses the already scarce energy resources and reduces the throughput of the wireless network.

A sufficient performance further depends on the size of the applied collaboration region, which in turn highly depends on the density of nodes and on the expected size of the phenomenon to be sensed. A high density of nodes enables to downsize the collaboration region to such extent that a suitable average number of neighboring nodes is still available. The customizable collaboration region allows to fine-tune the collaboration process to a certain extent but the degree of freedom in this parameter is limited, too. If the collaboration region is chosen too small the sensor nodes may not share the respective collaboration regions and hence, other nodes may not be available for collaborative detection. In that case, the detection results converge down to those gathered by the standard detection without collaboration but require a message overhead for the subscriptions. In the presented node deployment, a collaboration region of 2.5 meters provided the best detection accuracy. Further simulation results indicated a proper average collaboration region to be smaller than the expansion of the phenomenon. Aiming at a proper ease of use for configuration of collaboration by non-professional users, these must be provided with restrictions indicating a proper size of the collaboration region. The user configuration assistant can help to ensure that the following principles apply:

1. The minimum size of the collaboration region is the mean distance between neighboring sensor nodes, which is determined by the density of the sensor network, and transmission technology.

2. The maximum size of the collaboration region is the estimated size of the phenomenon.

If one or both restrictions cannot be guaranteed, the application of collaboration should be omitted for cost-efficiency. In those cases, there would either be no other device in the collaboration region (collaboration region is smaller than minimum) or events are most possibly not notified because of sharing EDT node values with sensor nodes outside the phenomenon (collaboration region is larger than maximum). To summarize, customized collaboration offers proper means for WSNs to enhance the robustness of detection in event-based applications. However, the user is responsible for fine-tuning the collaboration region to achieve a sufficient performance. As we have already discussed, a user configuration assistant based on an experts system should be able to determine a proper size of the collaboration region automatically by asking simple questions about the phenomenon.

FUTURE RESEARCH DIRECTIONS

Future work should primarily focus on alternating test and improvement of convenient configuration means by participation of non-scientific test persons. WSNs should be designed to support all people in the world, who are predominantly not scientists. There is currently a lot of ongoing work in this research direction trying to visualize configuration properties for WSNs. The first step for ease of use could be to enable configuration of WSNs by graphical tools. Besides, means have to be found to create a kind of feedback system for announcement of WSNs, their features and properties and for reporting success of configuration. Configuration of a priori unknown WSNs requires establishment of request-response features to enable interactions between the sensor nodes and the configurations tools of users. Initially, the configuration tools require knowledge about the features and properties of the WSN to be configured. Therefore, the WSN should be enabled to describe the features it provides. Based on these feature descriptions, the configuration tools can even determine which kind of application or phenomenon could be executable at all. After specifying the application according to the features provided, the adapted application is submitted to the WSN. Finally, the most critical question is: "Is the submitted application working properly?" Means that can give a feedback about the reliability of configured applications could become one of the most significant advances in convenient sensor network design.

In view of automatic WSN configuration using the ESL and respective EDTs, those should be applied in real world scenarios like Ambient Assisted Living (AAL) or patient monitoring systems. This also stresses the designed support for mobility in this approach. The ESL allows to easily customize and configure a Body Area Network (BAN) to the needs of a patient, e.g., by configuring thresholds for blood pressure or body temperature. Enabling nurses or medical employees to easily configure a BAN for patient monitoring will be a big step towards an ease of use for WSN configuration. In AAL applications, like smart homes, the user may define personal interests as an event specification, which can be used to configure the local ambient sensor network around the user.

Some extensions of the ESL are possible and of interest for further research. The ESL may support other execution constraints to allow configuration of resource-oriented execution intervals, for example. This could be scaling of the EDT evaluation interval due to drained energy resources. In addition, the XML style of the ESL should allow to provide configuration means for WSNs by the use of web technologies and web services. This may further automate the configuration process and enable remote configuration via the Internet. The concept of EDT has to be enhanced to en-

able self-configuration of new nodes by sharing of EDTs during runtime. This may significantly improve the maintenance of a sensor network by allowing newly deployed nodes to populate with the EDTs from their neighboring nodes without having the binary event specification available. This allows to easily rebuilding the sensor network in areas where nodes have crashed or the node density has to be increased.

Furthermore, the robustness and performance of collaboration could also be extended. Sensor nodes could dynamically resize the applied collaboration region with respect to the local node density, the specified collaboration region and a determined preferred number of available publishers. For random distributions, the nodes in areas with low density may use the maximum configured collaboration region. In contrast to that, the nodes in areas with a high density may apply smaller collaboration regions, which still provide a sufficient number of potential publishers. The simulations indicated that the lease-based publish/subscribe approach may possibly hold EDT node values even if the respective publisher has failed during the leasing time. In the simulation scenarios, this caused false positive notification of events. Enabling neighboring nodes to recognize and signal failed devices to subscribing sensor nodes may possibly enhance the detection accuracy further.

CONCLUSION

The envisioned pervasiveness of WSNs faces two major problems. These are high fault probability and configuration complexity. First, an ease of use for task definition and configuration of WSNs is the key to make them widely accepted. Means that provide a high abstraction of WSNs are in demand. These must enable also non-professional users, which are usually short on experience of programming languages and sensor networks, to make use of WSNs. Second, pervasive WSNs consisting of large numbers of devices demand to use low cost sensor nodes with limited resources, which feature a high fault probability. WSNs are subject to sudden changes in operational conditions, varying deployments and hazardous environments that again increase the fault probability. Moreover, strict energy constraints on used devices require fault tolerant methods to achieve high cost-efficiency.

This chapter identified missing features for convenient high-level application design for WSN configuration. Therefore, we introduced a user-centric design flow of pervasive applications. It decouples the processes of application design and WSN configuration. Application design is advanced to a level that allows users to specify the "things-in-mind to be sensed" without regarding WSN properties. From our simulations we have learned how to deduce technical details like the collaboration region or the leasing time without explicitly asking the user for. Finally, the user is enabled to "configure" a WSN by answering straightforward questions about the phenomenon to be detected. Based on automatic generation of event specifications using the ESL, the EDTs allow to autonomously configure a WSN by submitting very compact binary event specifications. Reliable and robust execution of applications in pervasive WSNs further requires to cope with expected and unexpected heterogeneity and sudden failures. Therefore, we introduced objectives for reliable event-based applications in WSNs in terms of design criteria. These are *Robustness*, *Autonomy*, *Transparency*, *Energy efficiency* and *Convenience*. Existing solutions mostly provide *Robustness* and *Transparency* but disregard sufficient *Energy efficiency*, *Autonomy* and *Convenience*. It has further been shown that existing solutions lack of means to achieve an acceptable cost-efficiency.

Our introduced user-centric design and configuration of reliable event-based applications in WSNs can actually remedy these shortcomings. It tackles all design criteria and features cost-efficient robustness and a proper usability. So it combines a flexible Event Specification Language

with a self-adapting event-based detection scheme. The ESL provides ease of use for application programming allowing the user to ignore low-level details of the sensor network and to concentrate on a high abstraction level. Namely this is the phenomenon itself and its related constraints. To cope with the fault probability in WSNs, communication-efficient means for collaborative detection have been introduced and proven to be functional. In detail, the following contributions are made:

High abstraction for user-centric application design. The ESL hides low level details of WSNs to focus on pure phenomenon definition, which allows automatic configuration of event detection in WSNs. The ESL enables to combine sensing features defining the complex phenomena to be sensed. Further, it enhances an event specification by assignment of customized application requirements regarding the spatial and temporal expansion and parameters for collaboration. Fine-tuning of the collaboration procedure by determining a proper collaboration region and suitable time limits is supported by the ESL. Finally, the event specification generator transparently processes and adapts the user-defined "things to be detected" to the target sensor platform and its possible heterogeneity. Thereby, it generates deployable versions of these "things", called binary event specifications.

The ESL addresses the following design criteria: *Transparency*, *Energy efficiency*, *Convenience*.

A novel decentralized mechanism to autonomously set up event-based detection and in-network processing on sensor nodes, called EDT. Binary event specifications are deployed on the sensor nodes as EDTs, which are directly generated on the nodes by a tiny GFSM requiring eight states only. An EDT enables the sensor nodes to partition event specifications according to their own resources into local and remote parts by pruning. Local parts can be evaluated by the node itself, whereas values of remote parts must be requested from EDTs at other nodes. Sensor nodes are enabled to maintain several EDTs at the same time. Using EDTs, every node in the network can execute the complete evaluation process without a SPoF.

EDTs address the following design criteria: *Robustness, Autonomy, Transparency, Convenience Communication-efficient means to maintain EDTs in case of missing or failing sensing devices.* The EDTs are enabled to continue event-based detection with a high accuracy even in case of missing resources or failed sensing devices. For those cases, EDTs provide efficient collaborative event detection between neighboring nodes using a lease-based publish/subscribe approach. Appropriate on-node processing of sensed data allows to efficiently share values of EDT nodes by a few bytes only. The simulations clearly announced that the communication-efficiency of the lease-based approach is very high in contrast to the ACK-based variant. By choosing a proper leasing time, the lease-based approach closely meets the detection results of ACK-based collaboration but reduces the number of collaboration messages by a factor of at least 10. As learnt from simulations, the detection performance highly depends on the chosen leasing time as well as on the size of the collaboration region. Both parameters are customized in the event specification. To ease the configuration for non-professional users, the user assistant limits these parameters with respect to the configuration guidelines learnt from simulations.

The lease-based publish/subscribe approach addresses the following design criteria: *Robustness, Autonomy, Transparency, Energy efficiency, Convenience*

To summarize, this chapter presented and evaluated means that allow a user-centric design flow for pervasive applications. Besides straightforward definition means, it provides a robust and reliable concept for autonomous configuration of event-based applications in WSNs. Criteria for proper ease of use of application definition were deduced from the simulation results. These criteria support the configuration of an adequate collaboration region and leasing time by definition of lower and upper bounds. We expect these criteria to further ease the design of applications based on pervasive WSNs.

REFERENCES

Aboelaze, M., & Aloul, F. (2005). Current and future trends in sensor networks: A survey. In *Proceedings of the Second IFIP International Conference on Wireless and Optical Communications Networks WOCN 2005*, (pp. 551–555).

Akyildiz, I. F., Su, W., Sankarasubramaniam, Y., & Cayirci, E. (2002). Wireless sensor networks: A survey. *Computer Networks*, *38*, 393–422. doi:10.1016/S1389-1286(01)00302-4

Brouwers, N., Corke, P., & Langendoen, K. (2008). Darjeeling, a Java compatible virtual machine for microcontrollers. In *Companion '08: Proceedings of the ACM/IFIP/USENIX Middleware '08 Conference Companion*, (pp. 18–23). New York, NY: ACM.

Buonadonna, P., Gay, D., Hellerstein, J. M., Hong, W., & Madden, S. (2005). Task: Sensor network in a box. In *Proceedings of European Workshop on Sensor Networks*, (pp. 133–144). Istanbul, Turkey.

Cardei, M., Yang, S., & Wu, J. (2008). Algorithms for fault-tolerant topology in heterogeneous wireless sensor networks. *IEEE Transactions on Parallel and Distributed Systems*, *19*(3).

Heinzelman, W. B., Murphy, A. L., Carvalho, H. S., & Perillo, M. A. (2004). Middleware to support sensor network applications. *IEEE Network*, *18*, 6–14. doi:10.1109/MNET.2004.1265828

Kamiya, H., Mineno, H., Ishikawa, N., Osano, T., & Mizuno, T. (2008). *Composite event detection in heterogeneous sensor networks*. IEEE/IPSJ International Symposium on Applications and the Internet, (pp. 413–416).

Krasniewski, M., Varadharajan, P., Rabeler, B., Bagchi, S., & Hu, Y. (2005). Tibfit: Trust index based fault tolerance for arbitrary data faults in sensor networks. In *Proceedings of the International Conference on Dependable Systems and Networks DSN, 2005,* 672–681. doi:10.1109/DSN.2005.92

Krishnamachari, B., & Iyengar, S. (2004). Distributed Bayesian algorithms for fault-tolerant event region detection in wireless sensor networks. *IEEE Transactions on Computers, 53*(3), 241–250. doi:10.1109/TC.2004.1261832

Krishnamachari, B., & Iyengar, S. S. (2003). *Efficient and fault-tolerant feature extraction in sensor networks.* In 2nd Workshop on Information Processing in Sensor Networks, IPSN '03, Palo Alto, California.

Levis, P., Madden, S., Gay, D., Polastre, J., Szewczyk, R., & Whitehouse, K. … Culler, D. (2005). Tinyos: An operating system for sensor networks. In W. Weber, J. Rabaey & E. Aarts (Eds.), *Ambient intelligence.* Springer-Verlag.

Madden, S. R., Franklin, M. J., Hellerstein, J. M., & Hong, W. (2005). Tinydb: An acquisitional query processing system for sensor networks. *ACM Transactions on Database Systems, 30*(1), 122–173. doi:10.1145/1061318.1061322

Mainwaring, A., Culler, D., Polastre, J., Szewczyk, R., & Anderson, J. (2002). Wireless sensor networks for habitat monitoring. In *WSNA '02: Proceedings of the 1st ACM International Workshop on Wireless Sensor Networks and Applications* (pp. 88-97). NY, USA.

Pham, H. N., Pediaditakis, D., & Boulis, A. (2007). *From simulation to real deployments in WSN and back.* In IEEE International Symposium on a World of Wireless, Mobile and Multimedia Networks, WoWMoM 2007, (pp. 1 – 6).

Phani Kumar, A. V. U., Reddy, V. A. M., & Janakiram, D. (2005). Distributed collaboration for event detection in wireless sensor networks. In *MPAC '05: Proceedings of the 3rd International Workshop on Middleware for Pervasive and Ad-Hoc Computing,* (pp. 1–8). New York, NY: ACM.

Romer, K., & Mattern, F. (2004). Event-based systems for detecting real-world states with sensor networks: A critical analysis. In *Proceedings of 2004 Conference on Intelligent Sensors, Sensor Networks and Information Processing,* (pp. 389–395).

Schwiderski-Grosche, S. (2008). *Context-dependent event detection in sensor networks.* In 2nd Intl. Conf. on Distributed Event-Based Systems (DEBS'08), Rome, Italy.

Shih, K.-P., Wang, S.-S., Yang, P.-H., & Chang, C.-C. (2006). Collect: Collaborative event detection and tracking in wireless heterogeneous sensor networks. In *Proceedings of the 11th IEEE Symposium on Computers and Communications ISCC '06,* (pp. 935–940).

Simon, D., Cifuentes, C., Cleal, D., Daniels, J., & White, D. (2006). Java on the bare metal of wireless sensor devices: The squawk java virtual machine. In *VEE '06: Proceedings of the 2nd International Conference on Virtual Execution Environments,* (pp. 78–88). New York, NY: ACM.

Varga, A. (2002). Omnet++. Software tools for networking. *IEEE Network Interactive, 16*(4).

Vu, C., Beyah, R., & Li, Y. (2007). Composite event detection in wireless sensor networks. In *Proceedings of IEEE International Performance, Computing, and Communications Conference IPCCC, 2007,* 264–271. doi:10.1109/PCCC.2007.358903

Wada, H., Boonma, P., & Suzuki, J. (2007). A spacetime oriented macroprogramming paradigm for push-pull hybrid sensor networking. In *Proceedings of the 16th International Conference on Computer Communications and Networks ICCCN 2007,* (pp. 868–875).

Wang, T.-Y., Han, Y., Varshney, P., & Chen, P.-N. (2005). Distributed fault-tolerant classification in wireless sensor networks. *IEEE Journal on Selected Areas in Communications, 23*(4), 724–734. doi:10.1109/JSAC.2005.843541

Werner-Allen, G., Johnson, J., Ruiz, M., Lees, J., & Welsh, M. (2005, 31 January-2 February). Monitoring volcanic eruptions with a wireless sensor network. In *Proceedings of the Second European Workshop on Wireless Sensor Networks* (pp. 108-120).

Yao, Y., & Gehrke, J. (2002). The cougar approach to in-network query processing in sensor networks. *SIGMOD Record, 31*(3), 9–18. doi:10.1145/601858.601861

ADDITIONAL READING

Avizienis, A., Laprie, J.-C., & Randell, B. (2000). Fundamental concepts of dependability. In *3rd IEEE Information Survivability Workshop (ISW-2000)*.

Bahrepour, M., Meratnia, N., & Havinga, P. (2009). Sensor fusion-based event detection in wireless sensor networks. In *Proceedings of the Third International Workshop on Information Fusion and Dissemination in Wireless Sensor Networks (SensorFusion09)*, Toronto, Canada.

Beuche, D. (2004). *Composition and Construction of Embedded Software Families*. PhD thesis, Otto-von-Guericke-Universit" at Magdeburg.

Bohn, J., Coroama, V., Langheinrich, M., Mattern, F., & Rohs, M. (2004). Living in a world of smart everyday objects – social, economic, and ethical implications. *Journal of Human and Ecological Risk Assessment, 10*, 763–786. doi:10.1080/10807030490513793

Bonivento, A., Carloni, L. P., & Sangiovanni-Vincentelli, A. (2006). Platform-based design of wireless sensor networks for industrial applications. In *DATE '06: Proceedings of the conference on Design, automation and test in Europe*, pages 1103–1107, 3001 Leuven, Belgium, Belgium. European Design and Automation Association.

Castro, M., & Liskov, B. (2002). Practical byzantine fault tolerance and proactive recovery. [TOCS]. *ACM Transactions on Computer Systems, 20*(4), 398–461. doi:10.1145/571637.571640

Clouqueur, T., Saluja, K., & Ramanathan, P. (2004). Fault tolerance in collaborative sensor networks for target detection. *IEEE Transactions on Computers, 53*(3), 320–333. doi:10.1109/TC.2004.1261838

Haroun, I., Lambadaris, I., & Hafez, R. (2005). *Building wireless sensor networks*. Microwave & RF Magazine.

Kahn, J., Katz, R., & Pister, K. (2000). Emerging challenges: Mobile networking for smart dust. *Journal of Communication and Networks, 2*(3), 188–196.

Kahn, J. M., Katz, R. H., & Pister, K. S. J. (1999). Next century challenges: Mobile networking for "smart dust". In *International Conference on Mobile Computing and Networking (MOBICOM)*, pages 271–278.

Martincic, F., & Schwiebert, L. (2006). Distributed event detection in sensor networks. In *Proc. International Conference on Systems and Networks Communications ICSNC '06*.

Romer, K., & Mattern, F. (2004). The design space of wireless sensor networks. *IEEE Wireless Communications, 11*(6), 54–61. doi:10.1109/MWC.2004.1368897

Woodbridge, J., Nahapetian, A., Noshadi, H., & Sarrafzadeh, M. (2010). Hip: Health integration platform. In *First IEEE PerCom Workshop on Pervasive Healthcare*, Mannheim, Germany.

Chapter 8
A Methodology for UICC-Based Security Services in Pervasive Fixed Mobile Convergence Systems

Jaemin Park
Convergence WIBRO BU, KT (Korea Telecom), Republic of Korea

ABSTRACT

Nowadays, Fixed Mobile Convergence (FMC) is an emerging worldwide trend in the form of fixed and mobile telephony convergence. In this pervasive environment, security should be considered to be a more important factor than before because the security threats of heterogeneous infrastructures can happen simultaneously. Thus, UICC, the ideal and secure medium embedded on the mobile terminals, has been utilized to provide the security-sensitive services and the service security framework of the mobile terminals.

This chapter presents the fundamental and security characteristics of UICC and current practices of UICC-based security services (e.g. banking, stock, network authentication, etc.) in pervasive FMC systems. Moreover, we propose a novel UICC-based service security framework (USF), which implements the essential security functionalities used for FMC services, to provide the integrated security infrastructure and secure FMC services. The USF can be utilized to authenticate users, preserve privacy, and protect network infrastructures and business models of telephony companies.

INTRODUCTION

The FMC is a worldwide and clear trend in the form of fixed and mobile telephony convergence. The aim of the convergence between fixed and mobile telephony is to provide both services with a dual mode terminal. In this pervasive environment, the security should be considered as an important factor since the security threats of fixed and mobile networks and service infrastructures can be happened simultaneously. Most FMC services should necessitate personal sensitive

DOI: 10.4018/978-1-60960-735-7.ch008

information like ID/Password, certificates, bank accounts, credit card numbers, etc. Moreover, a single terminal can be used among different kinds of network and service infrastructures, which need an individual security protocol. Therefore, the integrated security infrastructure of the mobile terminal should be mandatory.

The trend of openness in the FMC environment can bring about more fatal security threats, for examples, leakage of private information, phishing, mobile viruses, etc. Accordingly, customers' interests in the security have been increased drastically to preserve their privacies and information. Telephony companies also would like to comply with customers' security requirements and protect their network infrastructures and business models against various threats.

Since the mobile terminals should be the endpoints of mobile services and storages of personal information, the security of terminals must be important for secure FMC services. However, due to the inevitable constraints of the mobile terminals such as lack of hardware-based crypto processor, insecure memories, etc., fully secure FMC services had seemed to be difficult.

Nowadays, UICC has been deemed to be the only solution to address the security issues of the mobile terminals due to the brilliant advances in technologies of the smartcards. Moreover, UICC is owned and controllable by mobile operators and is therefore more flexible than mobile terminals in providing security according to the security requirements of services and can be inserted in any terminal regardless of its base operating system.

In this chapter, we present methodologies for UICC-based security service in pervasive FMC systems. We briefly explain the fundamental and security characteristics of UICC and present current practices of UICC-based security services. Then, UICC-based Service Security Framework (USF) is proposed and its practices are explained. Finally, we describe the future research direction and conclude this chapter.

BACKGROUND

The UICC is the smartcard used in mobile terminals in GSM and UMTS networks. The UICC can guarantee the integrity and security of the personal data such as the phone number, messages, contact information (phonebook, e-mail, etc.) and so forth. SIM and USIM applications acting as the user authentication modules are stored in the UICC, respectively for GSM and UMTS networks. When the mobile terminals are starting to be activated, SIM and USIM applications begin to operate the authentication procedures with AuC (Authentication Center). For this, these applications and AuC should share the secret key for user authentication. These applications are the fundamental and most important among other applications in the UICC.

Several applications for UICC value added services can be stored in the memory such as EEPROM, flash, etc. of the UICC. Most of these applications can be pre- or post- loaded, installed and instantiated based on the GlobalPlatform, the UICC management platform for the issuers. These applications are usually implemented on top of the Java Card Platform, which provides the java card runtime environment, java virtual machine and APIs. The applications mostly facilitate the APIs to invoke the methods supported by Java Card Platform. The examples of these applications can be transportation, banking, stock, credit card, loyalty, etc. Most of these services are utilizing the security characteristics of UICC and further explained in the following chapters.

The applications installed on the UICC can be further categorized as the applets and the servlets. The applet is a simple Java card application without UI and communicates with the off-card entities via APDU ((Application Protocol Data Unit), which is the communication unit defined in ISO/IEC 7816-4. For the clarity, we'd like to explain more about the APDU. Two kinds of APDUs are existed: command APDUs and the response APDUs. A command APDU is sent by the off-card entity to the UICC and should contain a 5-byte header and from 0 to up to 255 bytes of data. A response APDU is sent by the UICC to the off-card entity after processing the specific task defined in the command APDU and should contain a mandatory 2-byte status word and from 0 to up to 256 bytes of data. The servlet is a web application which provides not only the processing of the requested operations but also the web-based UI which can be shown in the web browser in the off-card entity. The servlet on the UICC communicates with the off-card entities via HTTP and in the same way there are two kinds of HTTP:HTTP requests and HTTP responses. Currently, most UICC-based applications are developed as the form of applets.

In the view of hardware characteristics of UICC, the current UICC card usually consists of 16 or 32 bit CPU, CCP (Crypto Co-Processor), ROM, 5KB RAM, 256KB EEPROM and ISO 9600bps I/O circuits. This kind of UICC card had been already commercialized and widely utilized globally. These days, due to the brilliant enhancement of IC technologies, the UICC performance is evolving to the level of the mobile terminals. These UICC cards support 32-bit CPU and enhanced CCP to improve the cryptographic processing capabilities. It also utilizes tens kilobytes of RAM,

hundreds kilobytes of NOR flash and megabytes or gigabytes of NAND flash to enlarge the storage capacities. Due to the enlargement of capacity of UICC, the dimension of stored data in the UICC also increases drastically. To exchanges the large dimension of data, the high-speed interface such as 1.0 MBps IC-USB between UICC card and the phones is facilitated.

With a respect to the UICC-based security service, three memories, EEPROM, NOR flash and NAND flash should be carefully considered since the softwares for security services such as applet and servlet are installed in these areas. Therefore, lack of those memories yields the incapability of loading and installing more services. Figure 1 depicts the hardware architecture of two kinds of UICC mentioned above.

UICC-based security services such as the transport service, the debit card service, etc. usually require the contactless interface between the off-card entities where the UICC is inserted and the RF readers such as ATMs and so forth. For these contactless use cases, the NFC (Near Field Communication) technology is defined as the global standard. The characteristics of this contactless technology can be defined as the ETSI

Figure 1. The Hardware Architecture of UICCs

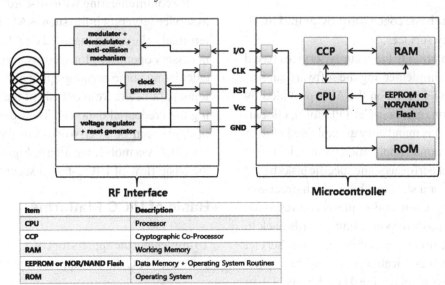

Item	Description
CPU	Processor
CCP	Cryptographic Co-Processor
RAM	Working Memory
EEPROM or NOR/NAND Flash	Data Memory + Operating System Routines
ROM	Operating System

specifications and there also exist the test speci-fication of this technology. Physically, only the contact 6 of the UICC is used to communicate with the NFC controller chip embedded in the mobile terminals. The logical communication protocols for the NFC technologies can be catego-rized as the SWP (Single Wire Protocol) and the HCI (Host Controller Interface). The SWP can be the physical and the data link layer protocol, which deal with the framing, the error manage-ment and flow control. Furthermore, the SWP supports the SHDLC (Simplified High Level Data Link Control), which a simplified version of ISO's High-level Data Link Control (HDLC ISO/IEC 13239) specification responsible for the error-free transmission of data between the UICC and the NFC controller chip on the mobile terminal. The HCI is a logical interface that enables contactless applications hosted on the UICC and supports the configuration where the one host is embedded in the UICC which is connected to the NFC control-ler chip. The HCI deals with the packet routing and message communications required for the NFC session initialization with the necessary configurations, the NFC transaction and so forth.

Basic of UICC-Based Security Services

We explain the basic concept to provide the UICC-based security services.

Mostly, to provide the security services based on the UICC, implementing the software such as applet or servlet based on the APIs provided by UICC platform (e.g. Java Card Platform, Global-Platform, etc.) is mandatory as explained earlier.

Applet is a small application without UI (User Interface) that performs some specific tasks based on the UICC or a state machine which processes only incoming command requests and responds by sending data or response status words back to the off-card entities via mobile terminal. Servlet is a small web application that performs some tasks and also displays the HTTP-based UI to

client (e.g. mobile terminals). The servlet can be implemented only in the SCWS-supported UICC, which means the small web server is embedded in the UICC. Therefore, UICC operates as a web server against to the mobile terminals which imple-ment HTTP-based client such as web browser.

Comparing between applet and servlet, cur-rently applet can be considered to be more secure and proper for UICC-based security services since the data communication between applet on UICC and mobile terminal is based on APDU format difficult to understand compared to the HTTP (servlet) and secured by SCP (Secure Channel Protocol) defined in GlobalPlatform, the standard for secure card management. However, in the case of servlet, it's practically difficult to support the HTTPS (HTTP over TLS/SSL) between servlet on UICC and mobile terminal even though the SCWS standard enforces to support it due to the shortage of RAM of UICC (even enhanced UICC).

Moreover, the UICC-based security services usually require the UICC to process some specific cryptography operations and store the necessary data securely, not to the UI. For these requirements, servlets may not be essential for the UICC-based security services.

Therefore, from now on, we only mentioned about the applet for UICC-based security services.

By communicating with off-card entities such as service servers or infra (such as ATM) via mobile terminals, the applet installed on UICC performs necessary operations for security services such as calculating some cryptographic algorithm about input parameters from outside of the UICC, stor-ing the credential data, etc. The operation result of applet can be inter-worked to the outside of the UICC via mobile terminals. Figure 2 presents the basic flow of UICC-based security services.

Basic of UICC Platforms

To implement the applets for UICC-based security services, UICC should support the platforms which

Figure 2. The Basic Flow of UICC-based Security Services

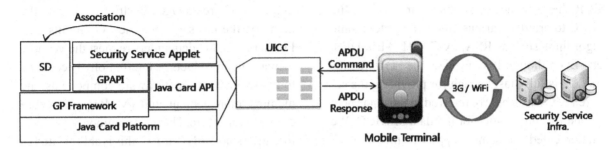

let the applet developers utilize the functionalities of UICCs, and manage the applets and UICCs.

The de-facto standard of UICC platforms are Java Card Platform for providing the functionalities to the applets and GlobalPlatform for securely managing the UICC and its installing applets.

Java Card Platform is a smart card operating system which includes Java Card Runtime Environment, Java Card Virtual Machine and APIs. This platform provides lots of useful APIs required to develop the applet for UICC-based security services such as cryptographic algorithms. Furthermore, this platform supports the code and context isolation for security as explained later. This feature acting as firewall among applets can prohibit applets from accessing the resources of other applets, except for the case when the applet implements the special interface named by SIO (Shareable Interface Object). Currently, version 2.2.x is widely utilized and version 3.0, which includes SCWS and other J2ME-level features, is planning to be commercialized in the near future.

GlobalPlatform is a secure, dynamic card and application management system that defines card components, command sets, transaction sequences and interfaces that are hardware-neutral, operating system neutral, vendor-neutral and application independent. This platform provides the method to manage the UICC and the installed software such as applet and servlet. Speaking of GlobalPlatform, SD (Security Domain) is a key component. SDs act as the on-card representatives of off-card authorities such as card issuer,

application providers, etc. ISD (Issuer Security Domain), on-card representative of card issuer (usually mobile operator in the case of UICC), is defined and installed onto the UICC, which can manage the SSDs (Supplementary Security Domain), on-card representative of application providers, with them actual UICC-based softwares interact. SDs support security services such as key handling, encryption, decryption, digital signature generation and verification for the applications. Each SD is established on behalf of a Card Issuer, an Application Provider or a Controlling Authority when these off-card entities require the use of keys that are completely isolated from each other.

Then, we'll briefly explain about the processes of managing the UICC applications. First of all, the systems of card issuer authenticate with the card using the key for ISD and then try to install the SSD for one specific application provider with the pre-shared key for that SSD. The UICC application developed by the application provider will be installed by the systems of card issuer and then the application and SSD are associated by the extradition process. Then, application provider utilizes the key for SSD to manage its own UICC application. If the UICC application does not necessitate the SSD for some business reasons, the installation of SSD can be omitted.

Security Characteristics of UICC

Speaking of the security features, the UICC is the ideal solution for the mobile services.

First, the UICC possesses the hardware-based CCP, the special-purpose hardware built in the UICC to provide various kinds of cryptographic algorithms such as RSA, ECC, DH, AES, DES, etc. Even though it's tiny size, the performance of CCP is fully fast enough for providing the secure FMC services. We referred to the data sheet of one IC chip vendor for the data of UICC. We implemented the sample applet to measure the performance of UICC for each cryptographic algorithm. The Table 1 depicts the result of our experiments. Each crypto algorithm is processed against one basic block. In the case of RSA key generation for 1024-bit and 2048-bit, experiments are performed 100 times and the results of them are averaged.

Second, the hardware of UICC supports the resistance to various side channel attacks such as timing attack, power monitoring attack (Simple Power Analysis, Differential Power Analysis), and so forth. Most of UICCs implement the technologies such as various sensors to detect the trials of side channel attacks, internal clock and variation of it to resist to the timing attack, etc.

Third, the UICC has the inherent features of the secure memory. All entities such as OS, serial interfaces, hardware-based firewall, etc. in the UICC are engaged in strictly securing the memory, the messages via the I/O circuits, etc. Furthermore, the demanders request the vendors to make their products be internationally certified to the security of the hardware components, the memory management unit (MMU), the secure crypto libraries, etc. The most commonly used certification standard is the CC, this is abbreviated as the Common Criteria for Information Technology Security Evaluation. The most of UICC products have been evaluated at more than EAL4+ level.

Fourth, most UICCs implement Java Card Platform to provide the various services based on itself. The basic principle of Java Card Platform includes the context isolation and code isolation, which means that the platform supports firewall among all softwares installed upon UICC. Thus, sharing the resource or information among applets is impossible in the UICC except for the Shareable Interface Object, specially defined in Java Card Platform for sharing information among applets. Any malicious applet or other softwares cannot access the information of which legitimate applets.

Fifth, UICC supports the secure remote administration methods by GlobalPlatform for issuers

Table 1. Cryptographic Performance of UICC

Cryptographic Algorithm	n-bit key (or block)	Performance
RSA key generation	1024	2.5 s
RSA key generation	2048	15 s
SHA-1 / SHA256 / MD5	-	1 ms / 2 ms / 1 ms
AES encrypt / decrypt	256	8 ms / 8 ms
SEED encrypt / decrypt	128	3 ms / 4 ms
DES encrypt / decrypt	64	3 ms / 3 ms
3DES encrypt / decrypt	128	4 ms / 3 ms
3DES encrypt / decrypt	192	5 ms / 4 ms
RSA CRT sign / verify	1024	199 ms / 8 ms
RSA non-CRT sing / verify	1024	277 ms / 9 ms
RSA CRT sign / verify	2048	1110 ms / 21 ms
RSA non-CRT sign / verify	2048	1925 ms / 21 ms

such as mobile operators. The GlobalPlatform defines the secure UICC management protocol between UICC and off-card entity such as mobile terminals, administration servers (SCMS – Smart Card Management System), etc. Currently, GlobalPlatform defines four SCPs depending on the applied security between UICC and the off-card entity ; SCP '01' (deprecated) – DES, SCP '02' – 3DES, SCP '10' – PKI and SCP '03' – AES

Related Works

Now, we present some related works about UICC-based security. Actually, there were lots of trials conducted by smart card vendors to utilize smart cards for security purposes. For example, DRM agents on smart cards and on-card key generation for PKI were developed and evaluated as the proof-of-concept; however, due to the resource-constraints of the former smart cards, it looked quite impossible to commercialize.

Yet, with improvement of hardware and software technologies of the smart cards, these vendors are now trying to make the trials be feasible. Tual, Couchard and Sourgen (2005) mention about the high-speed interface with devices and its possible use cases such as SIM-based DRM and conditional access in the field of the mobile pay TV or home networks. Handschuh and Trichina (2007) examine the security issues such as memory interactions, secure card personalization techniques, secure memory accesses of high-density cards, which have hundreds of megabytes of non volatile flash memory and high-speed interface (e.g. USB and MMC) with devices and other enhanced components. Trichina, Hyppönen and Hassinen (2007), Badra and Urien (2004), and Zheng, He, Wang and Tang (2005) introduce the security applications of the smart cards in the fields of DRM, PKI and TLS/SSL.

Till now, there has been several works about the security frameworks onto the mobile ter-minals. ESTI has been working on the USSM (UICC Security Service Module) as TS 102.266 since the release of stage 1 documents in 2006. The basic concept of this work is based on the GlobalPlatform to provide the security services such as PKI operations, storing security keys, data encryption/decryption, etc. to UICC applications via APIs. This work is in the progress of stage 2 and currently presents only the conceptualized architectures.

The mobile OS vendors usually implement the security functionalities and make them as APIs into their own products such as Android (Google), Windows Mobile (Microsoft), Symbian (Nokia), etc. These products usually provide only the fundamental crypto algorithms and some commonly used security protocols such as TLS/SSL, PKCS series, etc. To satisfy all the security requirements for the mobile operators, additional implementation should be accompanied to provide the secure services to the customers. Also, when the customers change their phones, all security implementations should be re-installed on their new phones or can be impossible to be installed again due to the differences in the type of OS, the version, the supported crypto algorithms, etc.

These days, TPM (Trusted Platform Module) has been introduced to enhance the security of mobile terminals. TPM usually refers to the name of specifications and the implementation of these specifications. This technology usually implements the primitive algorithms such as AES, SHA-1, RSA, etc. and the storages for the security keys. The TPM can be considered as the technology for chip such as the computer motherboards, the computer graphic boards, one component of the mobile terminals, etc. Since TPM only implements the fundamental crypto algorithms, additional implementations also should be completed in the upper layer of the mobile terminal such as the platform or application layer. The same obstacles to the mobile OS can be found in the case of TPM.

MAIN FOCUS OF THE CHAPTER

Issues, Controversies, Problems

As mentioned earlier, with the spread of pervasive FMC environments, the importance of security to provide the FMC services on mobile terminals is considered to be a crucial factor to mobile operators, service providers, etc. However, due to the inevitable constraints of mobile terminals, it's infeasible to meet all security requirements for FMC services.

Nowadays, UICC had been deemed to be the only solution to address the security issues of the mobile terminals due to the brilliant advances in technologies of the smartcards. Moreover, UICC has lots of benefits compared to the mobile terminals as discussed previously.

Currently, some security services are presented based on UICC such as debit card service, stock service, network authentication service, transport service and so forth. We further extend the possible practices of UICC in the field of secure pervasive FMC services by proposing a novel service security framework designed and developed for UICC.

We propose a novel approach to provide a secure service infrastructure in the side of mobile terminal, the UICC-based Service Security Framework (USF). We designed the USF as the core of personal security infrastructure for the FMC environments to provide the integrated personal security infrastructure and the security of the FMC services. The USF can be utilized to authenticate users, preserve the privacy and personal information, and protect the network infrastructures and business models of the telephony companies. The current version of USF supports the security functionalities such as PKI, DRM, TLS/SSL and Anti-Virus most likely utilized in the FMC services.

Current Practices of UICC-Based Security Services

In this section, we present the current practices of UICC-based security services already commercialized in the Republic of Korea.

Currently, UICC-based security services include the debit card service, credit card service, stock service, transport service and so forth. Most of these services utilize the UICC as the secure storage of personal information such as bank account number, stock account (ID/PW), etc. and calculator of crypto algorithms about stored data and incoming / outgoing data from off-card entities. For these UICC-based security services, the applets are developed using the Java Card Platform, and installed and issued securely by SCP defined in GlobalPlatform. UICC is also utilized to provide the network authentication service such as WiFi, WiBro and I-WLAN (Inter-networking WLAN) by facilitating the USIM and SIM applications for GSM and UMTS network authentication. We will describe two UICC-base security services in detail to explain more about currently available services.

UICC-Based Debit Card Service

UICC-based debit card service is to make the mobile terminal behave like debit card. The mobile terminal which possesses the UICC where the debit card applet is installed is operating as the debit card. Thus, customer can touch the mobile terminal on ATM via contactless interface such as ISO/IEC 14443 Type A technology based on NFC interface to deposit or withdraw the money from user's bank account. The information is protected by PIN, which is entered by user when the service is activated in the bank and transferring that to ATM with encryption using the symmetric key, whose master key is shared during the installation of the applet and session key is generated on demand.

For this, applet implements the functionalities to store the bank account number and PIN safely and perform security protocol between ATM for the safety of the information exchanges. Currently, in the Republic of Korea, this service has been commercialized since 2008. This service named by "UbiTouch" provided by KFTC (KOREA FINANCIAL TELECOMMUNICATIONS & CLEARINGS INSTITUTE) can also support to store the one hundred bank account information of multiple banks. Figure 3 depicts the conceptualized flow of UICC-based debit card service.

The service scenario is as follows: First, the user interacts with the ATM to enter the UICC-based debit card service mode where RF reader attached to the ATM can be activated. Then, the user touches his/her own mobile terminal to the RF reader of the ATM. The preferred bank account number configured by the mobile terminal previously is transferred to the ATM with encryption. The encrypted bank account number is recognized by the banking system and the user can perform the rest of his/her transactions such as deposit the money, withdraw the money, etc. In the middle of the transaction, there should be the user authentication by entering the PIN on the ATM.

UICC-Based Stock Service

UICC-based stock service is to store the sensitive user account information on the UICC securely. The information is encrypted and access to that information is protected by PIN, which is also entered by user when the service is activated in the stock office. When user wants to use the UICC-based stock service, he (she) can launch the application installed on the mobile terminals. Then, the application tries to access the PIN-protected stock account stored on the UICC by sending the specific APDUs. The application needs to display the input UI for acquiring the PIN from user. After user inputs the PIN and it is matched with the one stored in UICC, the stock account data can be utilized by the application to authenticate the user to the stock service servers and provide the stock services. Figure 4 depicts the conceptualized flow of UICC-based debit card service.

UICC-Based Network Authentication Service

UICC-based network authentication service is widely used in Republic of Korea, currently. The mechanisms implemented in the USIM applica-

Figure 3. The Conceptualized flow of UICC-based Debit Card Service

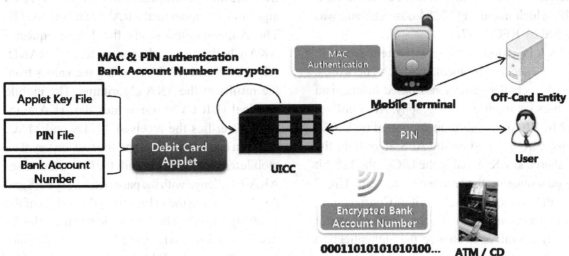

Figure 4. The Conceptualized flow of UICC-based Stock Service

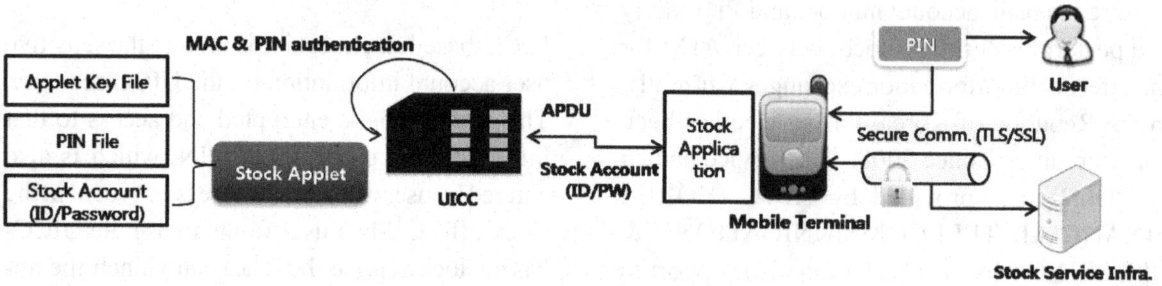

tion for 3G network authentication are reused to authenticate the users in the WiFi, WiBro and I-WLAN environments. The method to authenticate users using the USIM application is EAP-AKA defined in RFC4187, the abbreviation for Extensible Authentication Protocol Method for UMTS Authentication and Key Agreement. That is, the EAP-AKA is an Extensible Authentication Protocol (EAP) mechanism for authentication and session key distribution using the Universal Mobile Telecommunications System (UMTS) Subscriber Identity Module (USIM).

Then, we'd like to explain more detail about EAP and AKA, separately.

EAP is a kind of an authentication framework frequently used in the wireless networks and defines message formats to provide for the transport and usage of keying material and parameters generated by EAP methods. It is defined in RFC 3748, which made RFC 2284 obsolete, and was updated by RFC 5247.

AKA is a kind of a key agreement protocol, which is a security protocol, used in 3G networks. AKA is a challenge-response based mechanism that uses symmetric cryptography. AKA utilizes the MILENAGE algorithm supported by UICC, whose core is based on the AES algorithm, the pre-shared key K stored in the UICC, the 128-bit key guaranteeing the uniqueness for each UICC and OP (Operator Variant Algorithm Configuration Field) stored in the UICC, the input parameter used by operators to change the authentication algorithms in an operator-specific manner, to

compute the necessary values inside the UICC for user authentication.

With the features mentioned above, EAP-AKA provides the network authentication service using the secure UICC as follows: First, the Authenticator, usually AAA (Authentication, Authorization and Accounting) server, sends the EAP-Request / Identity message to the mobile terminal (UICC). Receiving this message, the mobile terminal sends the EAP-Response / Identity message by generating NAI (Network Access Identifier) from the IMSI (International Mobile Subscriber Identity) stored in the UICC or other values such as pseudonym ID and fast re-authentication ID when this mobile terminal had already finished the EAP-AKA procedure before. Then, the Authenticator retrieves the required security parameters to process the AKA against the received identity from the mobile terminal, and executes the AKA algorithms to generate the RAND and the AUTN. The Authenticator sends the EAP-Request / AKA-Challenge with the parameters AT_RAND, AT_AUTN and AT_MAC using the values from the results of the AKA algorithms. The mobile terminal (UICC) also executes the AKA algorithms, verifies the received AUTN and MAC, and then derives the RES and the session key. The mobile terminal (UICC) sends the EAP-Response / AKA-Challenge with the parameters AT_RES and AT_MAC using the values from the results of the AKA algorithms. The Authenticator then checks whether the given RES and MAC is correct or not and finally sends the EAP-Success or EAP-Failure

Figure 5. The Overall Architecture of UICC-based Service Security Framework (USF)

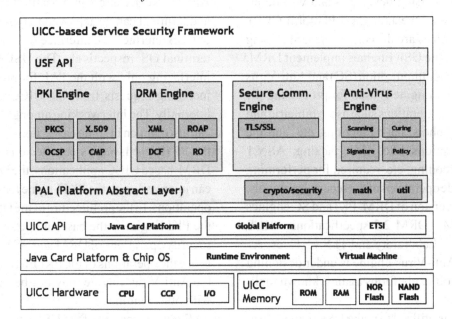

depending on the result of the verification. If the EAP-AKA procedures are successful, then the Authenticator and the mobile terminal (UICC) can communicate each other securely using the session key generated by the EAP-AKA.

Currently, the UICC-based network authentication service using the EAP-AKA is commercialized in the Republic of Korea for WiFi, WiBro and I-WLAN.

UICC-Based Service Security Framework

As explained earlier, the current UICCs are utilized as simple information storages and calculators of crypto algorithms. However, the current UICCs suffer from lack of memories utilized to load and install the applets and don't implement the PKI security functionalities such as RSA key generation, some digital signature algorithms and so forth, which can be utilized to extend the UICC usages even though those APIs are defined in the Java Card Platform standards due to the lack of memories.

Nowadays, the UICCs which include much more memories and enhanced performance are introduced to the world and ready to be commercialized in the near future. We would like to explain a novel methodology to provide a secure service infrastructure in the mobile terminal, the UICC-based Service Security Framework (USF) based on these enhanced UICCs.

We designed the USF as the core of security infrastructure for the FMC environments to provide the integrated security infrastructure and the security of the FMC services. The USF can be utilized to authenticate users, preserve privacy and personal information, and protect the network infrastructures and business models of the telephony companies. The current version of USF supports the security functionalities such as PKI, DRM, TLS/SSL and Anti-Virus most likely utilized in the FMC services.

We present the architecture of the USF. The overall architecture of the USF is depicted in Figure 5. The USF mainly consists of three components; USF APIs, USF Engines and PAL (stands for Platform Abstract Layer).

The USF is being developed and will be installed on top of the Java Card Platform (JCP). The USF Engines are the core of the USF. Using all JCP APIs, the USF Engines implement DRM, PKI, Secure Communication (SC) and Anti-Virus Engines. Each Engine is used for processing the cryptographic operations such as asymmetric and symmetric ciphers, hash functions, etc. and the related operations like XML parsing, ASN.1 encoding/decoding, etc. required for performing the client-side operations of the security protocols. The current version of DRM, PKI and SC engines supports OMA DRM 2.0 specifications, PKCS series of RSA Laboratory and TLS v1.1, respectively. The Anti-Virus Engine is under designing to protect mobile platforms against known malicious codes.

The PAL is utilized to make USF independent of the base platforms. This layer implements interfaces between USF and the base platform so as not to change the USF Engines even though the base platform is totally changed or updated. The cryptographic algorithms and the wrapper classes of primitives necessary for processing of the USF Engines but not supported in the base platform should be implemented in this layer. Due to this feature, even thought the USF is currently implemented on top of the JCP, it can be installed on other Java-based mobile platforms by changing the PAL accordingly.

The USF provides the developers with the USF APIs to implement UICC applications using the USF Engines. All interfaces and classes of the USF Engines are currently designed to be accessible from the UICC applications via the USF APIs. The mobile service applications usually can access the UICC via the interface APIs supported by terminal OS. Then, these applications can access applets and servlets developed based on the USF via these APIs for requests to and responses from the USF.

The USF Engines, the core of USF, can be accessible from mobile service applications via applets or servlets which implement using USF APIs. This external communication between UICC and terminal can be achieved via interfaces, ISO or USB interface and interface APIs supported by terminal OS, respectively. The USF Engines are interfacing only with the PAL for processing the incoming requests from the UICC applications internally. The interworking among USF Engines can also happen in some cases. For instance, when the RI (Right Issuer)'s certificate is verified for DRM-based UICC applications, the DRM Engine can interwork with the PKI Engine for PKI-related operations. In the architecture of the USF Engines, the PKI Engine is the base engine since all other security operations of DRM and SC Engines need to use the operations of the PKI Engine. However, the Anti-Virus Engine may not be interworking with other Engines.

For management of the USF, the interworking with USF Management Infrastructures (UMI), parts of FMC service infrastructures should be implemented to update virus signatures and manage certificates and DRM ROs (Right Objects) as depicted in Figure 6.

The USF Engines usually consist of a number of functional handlers, modules and parsers for the object oriented implementations and the ease of the management.

The PKI Engine provides the functionalities related to the certificates. The PKCS series operations, the generation and verification of the digital signatures, the management of the certificates and other PKI-related operations can be performed by this Engine. It mainly consists of ASN.1 handler, X.509 handler, CMP handler, OCSP handler and PKCS modules. By facilitating the handlers of ASN.1 and X.509, parsing of the certificate is performed. The PKCS modules are implemented to support the PKCS #1, #5, #8, #10 and #12. The CMP and OCSP handlers are related to processing of the protocols for communicating with the management servers. The role of the PKI Engine for these two protocols is to perform only the security-related operations. Therefore, the CMP handler is implemented to

Figure 6. Interworking among FMC terminal, USF-powered UICC and UMI

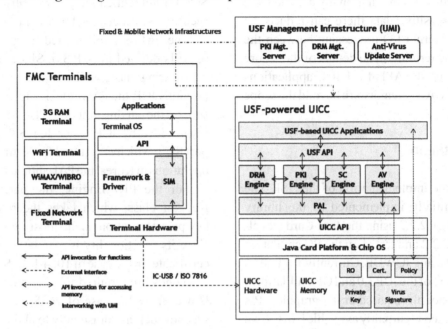

support the security operations for the certificate management defined in to generate, revoke and renew the digital certificates. The OCSP handler deals with the security operations for processing the OCSP messages.

The DRM Engine is implemented to process the security and other related operations. It mainly consists of XML parser, DCF (DRM Content Format) handler, RO handler and ROAP (Right Object Acquisition Protocol) handler. The XML parser and RO handler are used to parse and handle the RO, and DCF handler is used to encrypt and decrypt the DCF contents using the operation result of the RO handler. All other handlers are developed confirming to the OMA DRM 2.0 specifications.

The SC Engine includes the TLS/SSL feature. This engine provides the secure end-to-end communications between the UICC-inserted mobile terminals and the FMC service infrastructures. As UICC has no communication, this Engine only performs the cryptographic operations and handling of the incoming/outgoing messages of TLS/SSL.

The Anti-Virus Engine performs the scanning and curing of malicious codes such as viruses, Trojan horses, backdoors, etc. found in the files stored in the mobile terminals and UICCs. It mainly consists of the Depository of Signatures, the Depository of Policy, the Scanning module and the Curing module. Two modules are working together to find the malicious codes by comparing the contents of a file with a dictionary of virus signatures stored in the Depository of Signatures and to remove or heal them based on the Depository of Policy. To sustain two up-to-date depositories is an important factor for managing this Engine. For this, OTA (Over-The-Air), remote administration protocols in OMA SCWS (Smartcard Web Server) and user's action via the UI (User Interface) of the terminal application can be utilized. This Engine is currently in the step of designing.

The sensitive data for processing the operations of the USF Engines such as the chain of certificates, the private keys paired with certificates, the DRM ROs, etc. should be stored securely in the secure UICC memory for the strong security and the enhanced performance of the USF. The security of UICC memory is internationally certified and storing the sensitive data there can reduce the number of external I/O processing between the UICC and the terminal. The details of the secure file system and the APIs for UICC applications to access the UICC memory are beyond the scope of this chapter.

Implementation

We discuss the implementation of the USF. The USF was initially implemented as the library package of JCP 2.2.2 using the Java Card Development Kit 2.2.2 and tested on the PC emulation environment using JCWDE. Currently, the USF is installed on top of the JCP 3.0 and GlobalPlatform 2.2.1. Since not all required cryptographic APIs are implemented in currently available UICCs, we requested the vendors to support them.

The basic process to implement the library package is to implement the source codes consisting of several Java files and one build.xml file, build them using Apache Ant, and install it into the UICC.

We utilized the Eclipse IDE, SUN JDK 1.6.0, Java Card 3.0 libraries and the UICC vendor-specific tools for loading and installing USF into the UICC. Java Card 3.0 libraries are the kind of JAR file which contains all supported APIs defined in JCP 3.0. By including it in the Eclipse IDE, we can facilitate all the APIs supported by Java Card 3.0. After completing the USF implementation, we utilized the Apache Ant to build the USF source codes and build.xml file containing the invocation of the vendor-specific tool to convert the USF Jar files into the binary.

After this, we tried to install the USF binaries into the UICC by the vendor-specific tool to perform the authentication between the UICC and the development environment based on the GlobalPlatform. To install the software modules into the UICC, this authentication should be mandatory to manage the UICC securely. For this, GlobalPlatform specification defines the

SCP for authentication and establishment of the secure session between UICC and off-card entity.

The PAL is implemented to utilize the most of APIs defined in JCP 3.0. Since JCP 3.0 supports String class, which is not supported in the previous JCP, the PAL only needs to invoke it. To support the parsing function, TLV package should be provided by JCP. Since JCP 3.0 doesn't support RC2, which is required for certificate-related operations in Korea, the PAL should implement it.

For the PKI Engine, the performance of KeyPair class, which takes the role of public key pair generation, is the most important factor since its functionality is mandatory to issue the certificate. In the case of 1024-bit RSA key, about 2 seconds are required to generate the key pair. However, in the case of 2048-bit, the required seconds increase drastically to about 15 seconds. In the near future, for strong security, RSA key pair more than 1024-bit may be necessary. For this, hardware and software technologies for RSA key pair generation should be enhanced.

The high-speed interface such as IC-USB between UICC and terminal might be necessary for the USF depending on the applications. In the case of processing the DRM-protected multimedia files, the high-speed interface should be supported. However, for the certificate-related operations, the fundamental ISO interface may be enough for processing.

For the interoperability among different FMC service infrastructures, the DRM, PKI and SC Engines of the USF follow the global and de-facto standards. In the case of Anti-Virus Engine, all kinds of malicious codes found in the heterogeneous terminals have been considered to be targets to be scanned and cured since the USF-powered UICC can be inserted into any mobile terminal and communicate with any kind of network infrastructures.

The layered and object-oriented architectures of the USF can make it more powerful and flexible. According to the use cases of the USF and the available memory capacity of the UICC, the

USF Engines can be installed alternatively except for the PKI Engine, the base engine.

The USF can provide lots of benefits to the telephony companies, the customers and the application developers. The USF brings benefits to the telephony companies by supporting the integrated service security framework controlled and managed by themselves, providing their customers with the highly secure, efficient, durable and high-quality FMC services, reducing the time and cost for development and verification of the security logics and developing new business models and services in the FMC environments. The customers can enjoy the secure FMC services, ensure the security of personal information stored and managed in the terminals and preserve their own sensitive information and the security-related features without re-downloading them after changing the terminals. Finally, the developers can concentrate on developing the products without the consideration of security features.

Recently, we are developing the PKI feature of the USF for commercialization in 2011. We are currently developing the cryptographic token applets on the basis of the USF; instead of implementing full features of the USF, the PKI Engine and the part of the PAL for the PKI Engine are now being implemented as the form of the applet since the PKI feature is essential in Republic of Korea for the smart phone banking, stock and other finance services. To interface with the smart phone, the PKCS #11 library (Cryptographic Token Interface Standard) is also being implemented for the Google Android platform. The PKCS #11, the one of the PKCS series of RSA Laboratory, specifies an API called Cryptoki to devices which hold cryptographic information and perform cryptographic functions. With these implementation, the cryptographic token applet and the PKCS #11 library, the public certificates can be issued by the UICC and also be utilized for any purpose which requires the certificates such as banking, stock, user authentication and so forth.

Practices of USF in the Pervasive FMC

We describe the possible practices using the USF in the pervasive FMC environments.

Integrated Personal Authentication

All kinds of services usually start from the user authentications, which also provide the function of key agreement among participating entities. The Secure Channel Protocols also require the user authentications along with the key agreements, for example, TLS/SSL, PSK-TLS, IPSec, etc. Therefore, the user authentication is not only the start of the services but also the crucial and important factor of the security. Especially in the pervasive FMC environments, the integrated and strong user authentication should be inevitable since lots of the security threats are found in the fixed and mobile networks.

The USF can be facilitated as the integrated personal authentication in the pervasive FMC environments, as shown in Figure 7, since it embarks the PKI Engine. The mobile terminals loaded with the USF-powered UICC can be securely authenticated using the public or private certificates with all kinds of service infrastructures of banking, stock, payment, DRM, IPTV, VoIP, etc. The UICC applications based on the PKI Engine (and SC Engine in the case of the secure communications) for each service infrastructure can be installed on UICC to handle the user authentications.

Multimedia Contents Sharing

The customer, who pays for the multimedia contents via the mobile terminal, usually wants to access them in other devices such as personal computers, IPTV set-top box, etc. In the pervasive FMC environments, this kind of customer requirements can increase drastically. For this, somebody can try to copy the downloaded contents to other

Figure 7. The USF-based Integrated Personal Authentication in the Pervasive FMC Environments

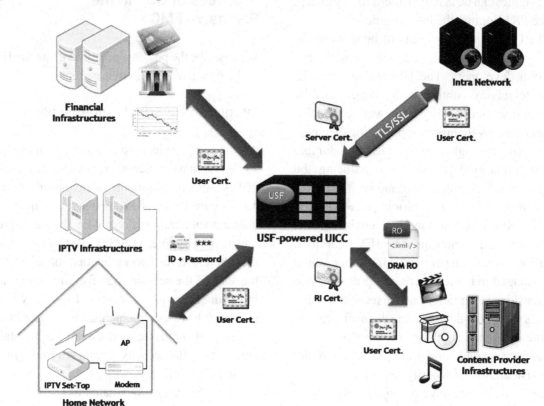

devices. Accordingly, the content provider may be afraid of illegal distribution of their products.

The USF can be the solution to address above issue since it supports the DRM Engine interworking with PKI Engine. Suppose that the customer buys content of one movie via the mobile terminal. When returning home or visiting friends' places, the customer may want to see this movie content with family or friends via the IPTV. The movie content should be protected by the DRM and be played by the mobile terminals where the USF-powered UICC is inserted so that illegal distributions can be blocked. If the customer would like to play that content in other devices, the corresponding DRM RO stored in UICC could be passed securely to the server in charge of verifying the ownership of the paid contents. For this secure communication, the SC Engine can be involved. After completion of the verification, the server will transfer same

content for IPTV with the combined RO to the IPTV set-top box. Then, the set-top box plays the movie content using the embedded DRM module. The example of the USF-based multimedia contents shared among heterogeneous devices is shown in Figure 8. This figure shows two possible scenarios of the USF-based multimedia contents shared among FMC devices.

Anti-Virus Solution

In the pervasive FMC environments, the terminal can be connected to various kinds of networks simultaneously. This means that the possibility that the terminal is infected by various malicious codes can increase drastically.

The USF supports the Anti-Virus Engine as shown in Figure 9, which scans and cures the malicious codes. The viruses which infect the files

Figure 8. The Example of the USF-based Multimedia Contents Sharing among FMC devices

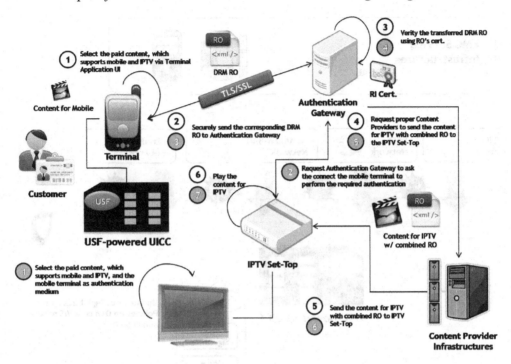

on the terminal itself can steal personal sensitive information in the terminal memory, disable the normal operations of the terminal and ruin the networks by unlimited communication requests such as SMS. The terminal can be the path for the viruses to invade the network devices even though they cannot attack the terminal. Therefore, the target viruses should be ones that can attack not only the information stored in the terminal but also the network devices in the FMC networks. Any file or any traffic can be transferred to the USF-powered UICC for the scanning and curing.

Finance Solution for Smart Phone

In the pervasive FMC environments, any terminal can be utilized as the device for finance services such as banking, stock, and so forth. Especially, the smart phone, which can be considered as the small computer supporting lots of features, can

be utilized as the FMC terminal for the finance services.

In Republic of Korea, the public certificates, the authenticity of it can be guaranteed by the government, should be utilized for the user authentication, the digital signature for each finance transaction and so forth. According to the guidelines for finance services of smart phones from the public organization in Republic of Korea, the smart phone should utilize the public certificates for the purpose mentioned earlier. The UICC supporting the USF can be utilized as the secure storage of the public certificates and also the cryptographic token for generating the digital signature using the public certificate stored in the UICC. Furthermore, the UICC can be facilitated for issuing the public certificates by supporting the RSA key generation and other required functionalities such as CMP, etc. With the help of the USF, the secure finance service environment for the smart phones can be achieved.

Figure 9. The USF-based Anti-Virus Solution in the Pervasive FMC Environments

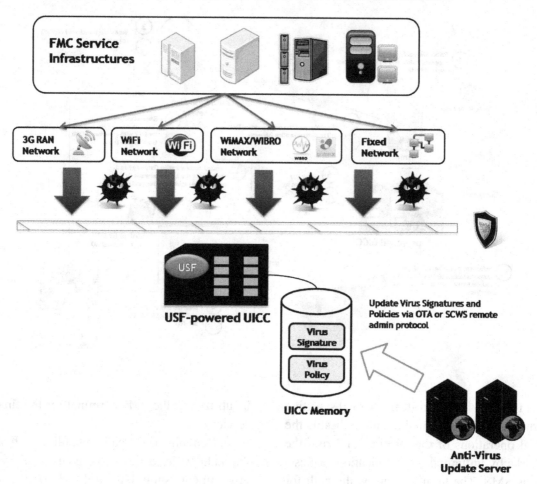

FUTURE RESEARCH DIRECTIONS

The current practices presented in this chapter require only the currently commercialized UICCs since they require only the simple cryptographic operations and small amount of memories. However, the USF necessitates the high-end UICC, which implements lots of cutting-edge technologies and in the near future, maybe within the year 2010, this kind of the UICC which can support the USF will be commercialized. Nevertheless, the UICC should be more advanced to support all functionalities of the USF fully; the DRM Engine may require more enhanced UICCs with respect to the hardware features such as the RAM for streaming the DRM contents or playing the DRM

contents in the low latency, the crypto co-process which supports more cryptographic algorithms for enhanced and efficient encryption and decryption and faster interface technology such as USB 2.0 Full Speed since more efficient DRM operations in the UICC might need more faster interface speed between the UICC and the mobile terminal.

Furthermore, the secure management system for UICC-based security services should be evolved further for completely secure UICC-based security services. For secure UICC management, the method to share the initial SSD key between the UICC issuer and the partners securely, the secure key management scheme for the SSD and more secure SCP should be enhanced and considered thoroughly.

Therefore, the hardware technologies and management system for UICC will have to undergo significant evolutions in order to provide the completely secure UICC-based services to the customers. Key areas of interest include developing the secure NAND flash embedded on UICC, IC-USB or further enhanced interface technologies between UICC and mobile terminal and faster on-card public key generation (such as 2048-bit RSA key pairs, etc.), and designing and developing the management systems for UICC and UICC-based security services (such as key management, remote admin for SCWS, etc.)

CONCLUSION

This chapter presents the basic and inherent security characteristics of the UICC and the current practices for the UICC-based security services such as banking (debit card software embedded on the UICC), stock (customer account stored on the UICC), network authentication (EAP-AKA based user authentication for WiFi, WiBro and I-WLAN) and so forth.

Moreover, we explained a novel and promising methodology of the UICC-based service security framework (USF) to provide the integrated security infrastructure and the security services in the pervasive FMC environments. The main role of the USF is to perform the cryptographic operations of the security protocols required for the FMC services in the client-side. The USF can support the DRM, PKI, SC and Anti-Virus functions as defined in de-factor and global standards for interoperability among different kinds of FMC service infrastructures. Using this methodology, the UICC-based HSM, the integrated personal authentication, the multimedia contents sharing, the anti-virus solution and the secure finance services for the smart phones can be provided in the pervasive FMC environments.

REFERENCES

Aboba, B., Blunk, L., Vollbrecht, J., Carlson, J., & Levkowetz, H. (Eds.). (2004). *Extensible authentication protocol (EAP) – RFC 3748*. Retrieved September 29, 2010, from http://www.ietf.org/ rfc/ rfc3748.txt

Aboba, B., Simon, D., & Eronen, P. (2008). Extensible authentication protocol (EAP) key management framework – RFC 5247. Retrieved September 29, 2010, from http://www.ietf.org/ rfc/ rfc5247.txt

Adams, C., & Farrell, S. Kause., & Mononen, T. (2005). *Internet X.509 public key infrastructure certificate management protocol (CMP) – RFC 4210*. Retrieved March 29, 2010, from http:// www.ietf.org/ rfc/ rfc4210.txt

Arkko, J., & Haverinen, H. (2006). *Extensible authentication protocol method for 3rd generation authentication and key agreement (EAP-AKA) – RFC 4187*. Retrieved September 29, 2010, from http://www.ietf.org/ rfc/ rfc4187.txt

Badra, M., & Urien, P. (2004). *Toward SSL integration in SIM smartcards* (pp. 889–893). IEEE WCNC.

Blunk, L., & Vollbrecht, J. (1998). *PPP extensible authentication protocol (EAP) – RFC 2284*. Retrieved September 29, 2010, from http://www. ietf.org/ rfc/ rfc2284.txt

Dierks, T., & Rescorla, E. (2006). *The transport layer security (TLS) protocol v1.1 – RFC 4346*. Retrieved March 29, 2010, from http://www.ietf. org/ rfc/ rfc4346.txt

ETSI. (2006). *Smartcards UICC security service module: Stage 1*. (ETSI TS 102 266 V7.1.0). Retrieved March 29, 2010, from http://pda.etsi. org/ pda/ queryform.asp

GlobalPlatform. (2006). GlobalPlatform card specification v2.2. Retrieved March 29, 2010, from http://www.globalplatform.org/ specificationscard.asp

Handschuh, H., & Paillier, P. (1998). *Smartcard crypto co-processors for public key cryptography.* International Conference on Smart Card Research and Applications (pp. 386-394). Springer-Verlag.

Handschuh, H., & Trichina, E. (2007). *High density smartcards: New security challenges and applications.* Securing Electronic Business Processes: Highlights of the Information Security Solutions Europe/SECURE 2007 Conference (pp. 251-259). Vieweg Wiesbaden.

Jaemin, P., Kyoungtae, K., & Minjeong, K. (2008). The Aegis: UICC-based security framework. *IEEE FGCN, 2008,* 264–269.

Jaemin, P., Yongki, M., & Minjeong, K. (2009). UICC-based service security framework for pervasive fixed mobile convergence. *Journal of Internet Technology, 10*(5), 505–512.

Laboratories, R. S. A. (n.d.). *Public key cryptography standards (PKCS) series.* Retrieved March 29, 2010, from http://www.rsa.com/ rsalabs/ node.asp?id=2124

Microsystems, S. U. N. (2006). *Java card platform specification* 2.2.2. Retrieved March, 2008, from http://java.sun.com/ javacard/ specs.html

Microsystems, S. U. N. (2010). *Java card platform specification* 3.01. Retrieved March 29, 2010, from http://java.sun.com/ javacard/ 3.0.1/ specs.jsp

Myers, M., Ankney, R., Malpani, A., Galperin, S., & Adams, C. (1999). *X.509 Internet public key infrastructure online certificate status protocol (OCSP) – RFC 2560.* Retrieved March 29, 2010, from http://www.ietf.org/ rfc/ rfc2560.txt

Open Mobile Alliance. (2008). *OMA digital rights management* V2.1. Retrieved March 29, 2010, from http://www.openmobilealliance.org/ Technical/ release_program/ drm_v2_1.aspx

Open Mobile Alliance. (2009). *OMA smartcard Web server* V1.1. Retrieved March 29, 2010, from http://www.openmobilealliance.org/ Technical/ release_program/ scws_v1_1.aspx

Patroklos, G. A., Raja, V., Hitesh, T., & Donal, O. (2004). *Performance analysis of cryptographic protocols on handheld devices.* 3rd IEEE International Symposium on Network Computing and Applications (pp. 169-174).

Rankl, W., & Effing, W. (2004). *Smart card handbook* (3rd ed.). Wiley.

Trichina, E., Hyppönen, K., & Hassinen, M. (2007). *SIM-enabled open mobile payment system based on nation-wide PKI.* Securing Electronic Processes: Highlights of the Information Security Solutions Europe/SECURE 2007 Conference (pp. 355-366). Vieweg Wiesbaden.

Tual, J. P., Couchard, A., & Sourgen, L. (2005). *USB full speed enabled smartcards for consumer electronics applications* (pp. 230–236). IEEE ISCE.

Yusuke, M., Patrick, S., Kris, T., & Ingrid, V. (2004). *Java cryptography on KVM and its performance and security optimization using HW/ SW co-design techniques.* International Conference on Compilers, Architectures and Synthesis of Embedded System (pp. 303-311). ACM Press.

Zheng, Y., He, D., Wang, H., & Tang, X. (2005). *Secure DRM scheme for future mobile networks based on trusted mobile platform* (pp. 1164–1167). IEEE WCNM.

KEY TERMS AND DEFINITIONS

Anti-Virus: It is usually a software which is used to prevent, detect, and remove malware, including computer and mobile terminal viruses, worms, and trojan horses. Such programs may also prevent and remove adware, spyware, and other forms of malware.

API: It is an abbreviation of Application Programming Interface, which is an interface implemented by a software program that enables it to interact with other software. Using API, the caller such as software or program source can invoke the methods supported by the OS, platform, framework and so forth. An API is implemented by applications, libraries, and operating systems to determine their vocabularies and calling conventions, and is used to access their services.

DRM: It is an abbreviation of Digital rights management, which is a generic term for access control technologies that can be used by hardware manufacturers, publishers, copyright holders and individuals to limit the usage of digital contents such as software, music, picture, wallpapers, etc. and devices. The term is used to describe any technology that inhibits uses of digital content not desired or intended by the content provider. It can also refer to restrictions associated with specific instances of digital works or devices.

FMC: Fixed-Mobile Convergence is an emerging trend in the form of fixed and mobile telephony convergence. With sing phone, fixed and mobile services can be provided such as Voice Call Continuity.

GlobalPlatform: It is a secure, dynamic card and application management platform. Card issuer and application providers can manage their own applications by using the security domain (SD). SD is an on-card representative of off-card entities and provides necessary security services for UICC applications.

I-WLAN: It is an abbreviation of Internetworking WLAN, which enable users to use the 3GPP-based services via WLAN environment.

The fundamental concept of this technology is that the mobile terminals that support I-WLAN first access the WiFi network and then try to use the tunneling based on the IKEv2 for IPSec ESP with PDG (Packet Data Gateway), which is the gateway to access the 3GPP-based service infrastructures. After completion of the I-WLAN connection, the mobile terminal can access the 3GPP-based service via non 3GPP network (WiFi) and all exchange data are protected using the IPSec ESP.

Java Card Platform: It is a smart card platform that allows Java-based application (applet or servlet) to be executed securely. This platform usually consists of Java Card Runtime Environment, Java Card Virtual Machine and various APIs which can be called by UICC-based applications.

NFC: It is an abbreviation of Near Field Communication which is a short-range high frequency wireless communication technology which enables the exchange of data between devices over about a 10 centimeter (around 4 inches) distance. The technology is a simple extension of the ISO/IEC 14443 proximity-card standard (proximity card, RFID) that combines the interface of a smartcard and a reader into a single device. An NFC device can communicate with both existing ISO/IEC 14443 smartcards and readers, as well as with other NFC devices, and is thereby compatible with existing contactless infrastructure already in use for public transportation and payment. NFC is primarily aimed at usage in mobile phones.

PKCS: It is an abbreviation of Public-Key Cryptography standards devised and published by RSA Security. These standards include RSA asymmetric key algorithm and other related technologies for PKI. PKCS #1 is the RSA Cryptography Standard [RFC 3447] which defines the mathematical properties and format of RSA public and private keys (ASN.1-encoded in cleartext), and the basic algorithms and encoding/padding schemes for performing RSA encryption, decryption, and producing and verifying signatures. PKCS #2 is withdrawn and PKCS #3 is the Diffie-Hellman Key Agreement Standard which is a cryptographic protocol that allows two parties that have no prior knowledge of each other to jointly establish a shared secret key over an insecure communications channel. PKCS #4 is withdrawn and PKCS #5 is the Password-based Encryption Standard [RFC 2898 and PBKDF2]. PKCS #6 is the Extended-Certificate Syntax Standard Defines extensions to the old v1 X.509 certificate specification. PKCS #7 is the Cryptographic Message Syntax Standard [RFC 2315] which is used to sign and/or encrypt messages under a PKI and also for certificate dissemination (for instance as a response to a PKCS #10 message). PKCS #8 is the Private-Key Information Syntax Standard [RFC 5208] which is used to carry private certificate keypairs (encrypted or unencrypted). PKCS #9 is the Selected Attribute Types which defines selected attribute types for use in PKCS #6 extended certificates, PKCS #7 digitally signed messages, PKCS #8 private-key information, and PKCS #10 certificate-signing requests. PKCS #10 is the Certification Request Standard [RFC 2986] which is the format of messages sent to a certification authority to request certification of a public key. PKCS #11 is the Cryptographic Token Interface (Cryptoki) which is an API defining a generic interface to cryptographic tokens. PKCS #12 is the Personal Information Exchange Syntax Standard which defines a file format commonly used to store private keys with accompanying public key certificates, protected with a password-based symmetric key. PKCS #13 is the Elliptic Curve Cryptography Standard and PKCS #14 is the Pseudo-random Number Generation. PKCS #15 is the Cryptographic Token Information Format Standard which defines a standard allowing users of cryptographic tokens to identify themselves to applications, independent of the application's Cryptoki implementation (PKCS #11) or other API.

PKI: It is an abbreviation of Public Key Infrastructure, which is a set of hardware such as servers, client devices like mobile terminals, PCs, etc., software, people, policies and procedures required to issue, manage, distribute, use, store and revoke the digital certificates. In cryptography, a PKI is an arrangement that binds public keys such as RSA, ECC, etc. with respective user identities by means of a certificate authority (CA). The user identity must be unique within each CA domain. The binding is established through the registration and issuance process, which, depending on the level of assurance the binding has, may be carried out by software at a CA, or under human supervision. The PKI role that assures this binding is called the Registration Authority (RA). For each user, the user identity, the public key, their binding, validity conditions and other attributes are made unforgetable in public key certificates issued by the CA.

TLS/SSL: Transport Layer Security (TLS) and its predecessor, Secure Sockets Layer (SSL), are cryptographic protocols that provide security for communications over networks. TLS and SSL encrypt the segments of network connections at the Application Layer to ensure secure end-to-end transit at the Transport Layer.

UICC: Universal Integrated Circuit Card is a smartcard inserted into UMTS mobile phones for user authentication to access UMTS networks and an ideal medium for various UICC-based security services with supporting of Java Card Platform and GlobalPlatform.

USF: UICC-based Service Security Framework is designed and developed for mobile operators to provide UICC-based security services such as PKI, DRM, TLS/SSL and Anti-Virus and so forth. This framework supports lots of security functionalities via API called by UICC-based applications such as applet and servlet.

Chapter 9
Community Computing:
Multi–Agent Based Computing Paradigm for Cooperative Pervasive System

Youna Jung
University of Pittsburgh, USA

Minsoo Kim
University of Pittsburgh, USA

ABSTRACT

Many huge and complex pervasive services can be provided by employing cooperation among smart objects like agents. To offer such services efficiently, community computing was proposed as a new computing paradigm, in which pervasive services are provided through cooperation among agents (Jung, 2006). To design a community computing system, we proposed two abstraction models distinguished by intelligence level of community; the simple model (Jung, 2006) and the static community situation based model. In addition, we introduced a development process based upon the Model-Driven Architecture (MDA) approach for fast and convenient implementation of community computing systems. In this chapter, our contribution is to organize previous work related to cooperation and then clearly present the position of community computing in comparison. In addition, we refine the proposed two models including all their intermediate models in the development process, such as CCM (Community Computing Model), CIM-PI (Platform Independent Community Computing Implementation Model), and CIM-PS (Platform Specific Community Computing Implementation Model). To help automatic transformation from CCM to source codes, we improve a development toolkit called CDTK (Community Computing Development Toolkit). By using CDTK, a community computing system can be implemented semi-systematically. Finally, to verify the feasibility of community computing, we present implementation results of two scenarios by using proposed two models and CDTK. Through the simulated results, we examine the possibility of community computing.

DOI: 10.4018/978-1-60960-735-7.ch009

INTRODUCTION

Since ubiquitous computing was articulated by Mark Weiser in 1991 (Weiser, 1991), many researchers have attempted to realize the potential for diverse pervasive services. As we surveyed existing research, we were able to find the unique characteristics of pervasive computing. First of all, a pervasive computing system is composed of highly heterogeneous computing elements (Weiser, 1991; Kindberg, 2002). As computing elements have mobility and their status changes frequently, the environment of a pervasive system is dynamically changing. In such a dynamic environment, predictable or unpredictable pervasive services are dynamically requested. Among all characteristics, what we concentrate on the most is that many pervasive services can be provided by cooperation among heterogeneous smart objects rather than by the ability of a single smart object. In order to design and develop a pervasive system having all such characteristics, we surveyed existing approaches, but they were not perfectly adequate to do it.

In the PICO Project, community computing was introduced as a framework for cooperation among agents in a pervasive environment (Kumar, 2003). However, in this approach, some room was left to develop the pervasive systems providing services by using cooperation among intelligent devices. Most of all, there is no well-defined formal model. The PICO Project and Active Space Project have introduced a similar view of pervasive services to our community computing, but they provide no concrete model to represent such pervasive systems. Accordingly, to design cooperation among agents, PICO needs an abstraction model to describe cooperation. In order to find an appropriate model, we surveyed quite a few models, especially focusing on multi-agent models. It should be noted, however, that there are some differences between multi-agent approaches and our approach for cooperative systems. Furthermore, detailed and strong concern about cooperation is lacking. As the required pervasive services are getting larger and more complex, cooperation among pervasive objects becomes increasingly important. Accordingly, it is necessary to raise concern about cooperation in a pervasive environment. For example, it can be the cooperation-based service providing scheme, the configuration of cooperative organizations, cooperative behaviors between pervasive objects, etc.

The ultimate objective of our work is to design and develop pervasive computing systems efficiently which provide services by using cooperation among objects that already exist within a given environment. Existing approaches, including multi-agent approaches and other pervasive system development approaches, are not adequate for our purpose. Therefore, in this chapter, we introduce community computing, a new approach to design and develop such a cooperative pervasive computing system. In order to meet our objective, we are employing the concept of community. In community computing, community is a high-level abstract concept for organizing, managing, operating, and repairing groups of computing elements in a pervasive environment. Using the community concept, we are able to meet all requirements of pervasive computing. First of all, community computing can adapt to changes in runtime by dynamic creation of a goal-driven community and dynamic binding of the roles in the community to actual objects. Secondly, community computing supports dynamic cooperation among objects through dynamic decisions about cooperative behavior and dynamic injection, a cooperation process into member objects. Also, we can guarantee proper separation of concerns in community computing. In the community computing models, group concerns are discriminated from concerns about individual objects. Finally, community computing supports the scalability of services by merging of communities or the scalability of systems by merging of societies. (See section 3 for the definition of society).

In this chapter, we define community computing and a community computing system. To design a community computing system, we introduce community computing models: namely, the simple community computing model and the static community situation based community computing model and distinguish them according to their intelligence level. In addition, as a means for systematic development, we present a development process. As the proposed development process is based on the MDA (Model-Driven Architecture) (OMG, 2003) software development approach, we also provide more detailed models that can be derived from the most high-level abstraction model. To verify all the community computing models and their development processes, we implement two systems based on CHILDCARE and COEX-Mall scenarios.

This chapter is organized into 8 sections including the present section. An outline of the contents of the remaining sections is as follows. Section 2 introduces community computing generally. For better understanding of community computing, we specify basic concepts of community computing, especially focusing on community. In addition, we describe the development steps from the highest-level abstraction model to an actual system. In section 3, we distinguish various community computing models according to the intelligence level required by problem domains and then introduce the simple community computing model as a first step. As an improved model, we also propose the static community situation based model. In section 4, we introduce the computational model for community computing, and in section 5, we show the implementation results of two small community computing systems: the CHILDCARE system and COEX-Mall system. In section 6, we provide some background and related works. Finally, we conclude this chapter by acknowledging contributions in section 7, and we provide a few suggestions as to the direction of future work in section 8.

COMMUNITY COMPUTING

Community computing is a computing paradigm where pervasive services are provided by cooperation among existing agents. It focuses on how to satisfy the requirements of a pervasive system by cooperation among predefined agents, while multi-agent based and distributed computing approaches focus on what agents or distributed systems are needed to meet the requirements. In community computing, the requirements of a community computing system are fulfilled by communities. A community consists of members, which cooperate with others in the community to achieve their common goals. In this section, we introduce basic terms of community computing. Among those concepts, we concentrate on community, and here we introduce the levels of communities and the life model of a community. For better understanding, we give you the overview of community computing shown in Figure 1.

Basic Terms of Community Computing

Before we look into community computing in detail, it is worthwhile to introduce the basic terms of community computing. In this subsection, we define the terms used in community computing as follows:

1. **Space:** A space is a dynamically connected and coordinated set of heterogeneous pervasive computing objects. Its boundary is flexible and extensible due to the mobile objects. A pervasive object, an agent in a space, is able to represent various kinds of software and hardware devices and human users.
2. **Community Computing System:** It is a sort of pervasive computing system providing pervasive services through communities.

Figure 1. The overview of community computing

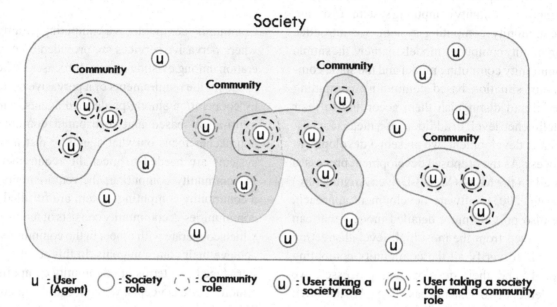

3. **Society:** It is a metaphor to abstract a community computing system and is constructed by members and communities.

4. **Community:** It is a metaphor to abstract a proactive organization that comprises members cooperating with others to achieve particular goals. A community has goals, necessary roles, and information about cooperation and role-member binding. A community is able to have more than one goal, and those goals are able to be issued in parallel. To abstract communities, we describe community types, and a community instance is dynamically created according to the associated community type in execution time.

5. **Role:** It is a well-defined position in a community with an associated set of expected behaviors (Ferber, 2003). A role represents a particular capability necessary to achieve a community's goals. The capability of a role is presented by attributes and actions of the role.

6. **Cooperation:** It is a cooperative interaction among members who take a particular role in a community.

7. **Member:** It is a metaphor to abstract a pervasive object belonging to a community computing system. In our community computing, the members are restricted to agents having their own context, capability, and intelligence. If necessary, a member is able to play a role within a community. Sometimes, it can take several roles in more than one community simultaneously.

8. **Role-member binding:** In order to create a community instance, we need to find the most proper members for each role. This process is called role-member binding.

Community

Community is the most essential concept in community computing. To help understand the community concept, we introduce the types of community and the life cycle. The pervasive services have different levels of difficulty. Some services need to be dynamically provided according to users' requests, while others, such as public security services, should be offered continuously. Besides, some urgent services have to be executed even though those services are unpredictable or not prepared. According to the difference of services' style, we distinguished levels of communities as follows: static, dynamic, and evolving community. According to the style of necessary services, we can decide the level of a community to create.

1. **Static community:** It is the simplest community. In this community, all members and their cooperation are predefined, so static communities are used to provide permanent services without replacing providers, such as a community of temperature sensors or a community of ambulances in a city.

2. **Dynamic community:** It dynamically decides its members and their cooperation, while its roles and goals are predefined like static communities. For example, a dynamic community which consists of nearby neighbors, policemen, and image sensors, can be used to help a community in finding a lost child. To find the child effectively, the closest member to the child should be selected in execution time and then cooperate with other members in the most efficient way possible.

3. **Evolving community:** It is capable of being built on demand. When a goal arises, the necessary roles and cooperation among roles are designed dynamically at request time and then operated. In urgent cases, an evolving community's services would be useful, since the evolving community can solve the emergent problems even though a system does not prepare such services at request time.

In our community computing, each community has a life cycle from initiation to termination. The community's life cycle has three stages from initiation to termination and one optional stage, deactivation.

1. **Initiation:** If a member involved in a society, called a society member, or community recognizes a community goal, it is able to request an initiation of a community instance from a society manager, an agent to oversee a whole society, (See section about computational models regarding society managers and community managers.) The society manager then creates a community manager, and the community manager performs member discovery based on members' condition. The community manager is able to decide the suitability of each member using the member-role binding condition described in the community type. After all members are selected, the community manager makes sure that all members are aware of their goal and cooperation process. If all members provide confirmation, an initiation stage is complete.

2. **Activation:** Most communities are activated as soon as they are initiated, which means that members start their cooperation process to achieve the community's goal. In the case of a static community, once a community is activated, it may be deactivated rather than terminated, because static communities typically need to exist all the time. If the deactivated community instance is reactivated, members restart or continue their cooperation according to previously established protocols.

3. **Deactivation (optional):** After a community instance is created, sometimes it is required that the cooperation process stops for a while. In this situation, the community instance is deactivated. When a community instance is deactivated, its community manager stores the information about an instance, including community members and the status of the

cooperation. When the instance is reactivated, the stored information is reused.

4. **Termination:** When the goal of a community instance is achieved or the community fails to achieve its goal, the instance is terminated.

MDA Based Development Process

In order to implement a community computing system systematically, we propose a development process based on the MDA (Model Driven Architecture) approach. Prior to explaining the development process in detail, it is worth to introduce MDA.

In 2001, OMG, the Object Management Group, proposed a software development approach entitled MDA (OMG, 2003). MDA is an approach to system development that increases the power of models in that area. It is model-driven because it provides methods for using models to direct the course of understanding, design, construction, deployment, operation, maintenance and modification. It attempts to establish the idea of separation of concern by separating the specification of the operation of a system from the details of how system uses its platform. To develop a software system, MDA specifies three models on different viewpoints: CIM, PIM, and PSM. A CIM, or computation independent model, focuses on the requirements and environments of a system. It is independent of how a system is implemented, and thus it does not specify detail of the structure of systems. A CIM is used to build a PIM, which is a platform independent model, and describes the system but does not specify details of use of its platform. A PIM is transformed into a PSM, which is the platform specific model, and specifies how that system makes use of the chosen platform. In the final development step, working from the PSM, the platform-specific source codes such as interface definitions, application code, makefiles, and configuration files are generated. Using the MDA approach, developers are able to expect portability, interoperability and reusability of models.

MDA proposes the process of building a high-level abstraction model should start by obtaining requirement analysis and then refining the model until the model directly represents the final system. In order to apply the MDA approach for developing a community computing system, we need several models that abstract a community computing system from different viewpoints. To develop a community computing system at first, a developer forms a CCM (Community Computing Model), the most high-level abstraction model. A CCM describes a community computing system in view of the community by showing how a community computing system satisfies its requirements with communities. The generated CCM is transformed to a CIM-PI (Platform Independent Community Computing Implementation Model). A CIM-PI considers implementation of a system without concern for specific platforms and describes a community computing system in more detail using the description of the member types. To describe implementation based on a specific platform, CIM-PI is converted to CIM-PS (Platform Specific Community Computing Implementation Model), which in turn specifies how a system is able to run in a particular platform. Using the model transformation process from a CCM to a CIM-PS, some portions of the source code are automatically generated, and then the remaining portions are manually filled by developers. This process makes development of community computing fast and systematic. Furthermore, developers are able to guarantee consistency throughout the entire development process by using a coherent metaphor, community.

COMMUNITY COMPUTING MODEL

The community computing model can be distinguished by the intelligence level of a community as shown in Table 1. It is not necessary for every community computing system to be highly intelligent, as some problems can be solved by a community computing system with low intelligence. In this chapter, we present two community computing models, the simple model and the static community situation based model, but additional models will be added in the future.

Simple Community Computing Model

The simple community computing model is the most static model and has no cooperation model. This model can support only static communities, and the cooperation processes of all communities are predefined. According to the MDA approach, each community computing model is represented as a family of models which have different abstraction levels: CCM in the highest abstraction level, CIM-PI in the intermediate level, and CIM-PS in the lowest abstraction level. Let's look into each model in detail.

CCM. CCM is the highest abstraction model of a community computing system. The objective of a CCM simple community computing model is to describe the requirements and boundaries of a system. In order to achieve these objectives, this model describes community types and a society

member. In the community type description, a designer specifies its necessary roles, goals, and cooperation protocols. The system's boundary is defined by all society members in a pervasive environment.

CIM-PI. The objective of the CIM-PI simple community computing model is to consider the implementation with existing pervasive objects in the space without the knowledge of specific platforms. In this model, the detailed description about community types and society is provided. In the community type description, mapping relationships of roles with member types and cooperative interactions among roles are also represented. The role-member mapping relationship defines which member types can take a community role. In addition, the cooperative interactions between the initiator role and the participant roles are described in the protocol description; the description of the protocol is based on Occam (Elizabeth, 1987). We used Occam constructs such as SEQ, PAR, ALT, IF and EXIT to represent communicative actions. The communicative actions, a unit of cooperation, should be matched with a member's own actions or primitive communication actions such as SEND and RECEIVE. In a protocol de-

Table 1. The comparison between community computing models

Community Computing Model	Simple model	Static community situation based model	Dynamic community situation based model	Autonomous community situation based model
Community Type	Static Community	Dynamic Community	Dynamic Community	Evolving Community
Role	O	O	O	O
Goal	O	O	O	O
Cooperation Model	X (Programmed)	Static community situation based Cooperation Model	Dynamic Community Situation based Cooperation Model	Autonomous Community Situation based Cooperation Model
		Certainty of community situations	Certainty of community situations	Uncertainty of community situations
		Certainty of members' tasks in a community situation	Uncertainty of members' tasks in a community situation	Uncertainty of members' tasks in a community situation
Necessary Tech. for Cooperation			Reasoning, Knowledge engineering, etc.	Reasoning, Knowledge engineering, Learning, Planning, etc.

scription, available message types are confined to those of FIPA (Foundation for Intelligent Physical Agents) (FIPA, 2000). In the Society description, object types in a physical space are modeled as member types. In the member type description, the hierarchy of member types is described using the *extends* keyword as well as attributes and actions which a member type has. For example, 'Streetlamp *extends* Electronic Appliance' would mean that the 'Streetlamp' member type is a child type of the 'Electronic Appliance' member type, and thus 'Streetlamp' type inherits all attributes and actions from 'Electronic Appliance' type.

An example CIM-PI based on the CHILD-CARE scenario (See Section 6: Implementation) is shown in Table 2. The 'Ghodam city' society has two communities, 'Home' and 'Childcare'. The 'Childcare' community consists of four roles: 'Child,' 'Family,' 'Neighbor,' and 'Observer,' and has a goal named 'take_a_child_home.' If the goal, 'take_a_child_home,' is detected, then an instance of 'Childcare' community is created by gathering suitable members for each role. The candidate member types who can take a role are presented in the description of role-member type mapping. For example, in the 'Childcare' community description, the 'Observer' role can be performed by three member types: 'Camcorder,' 'Camera,' and 'Streetlamp.' Among agents who are involved in those member types, we should choose proper members by using the cast description. Look at the 'Observer' role of 'Childcare' community for an instance. The members who will take the role of 'Observer' should satisfy two conditions as follows. Its monitoring service should be available, and it should be close to a missing child. In the role description, we are able to know the cardinality constraint of each role also. For the 'Observer' role, we can assign one member at the minimum and two members at the maximum.

CIM-PS. This model combines the simple community computing model CIM-PI with the details that specify how that system uses a particular platform. Actually, it is a bunch of source codes for a particular platform. Its cooperation portion can be derived from CIM-PI. In section 6, you can see the CHILDCARE community computing system implemented using the simple community computing model in the JADE platform.

Model Transformation. For developing a system, we perform model transformation from a high-level abstraction model to a low-level abstraction model representing the final implementation. According to the proposed development process, a model transformation process starts to build a CCM and then refines it until we obtain the source codes. The first step of the model transformation is that of turning a CCM into a CIM-PI. In the next step, a CIM-PI is converted to a CIM-PS using the specification of a particular platform. A CIM-PS is a collection of source codes that can realize members, communities, and a society. Finally, source codes are embedded into the existing smart objects in a space. After deployment, the coding objects become members in a community computing system, building up a Space.

Static Community Situation Based Community Computing Model

In a simple community computing model, cooperation among members is considered as a predefined procedure and described as a sort of pseudo program. To describe cooperation, a designer should decide which tasks of which members should be executed. However, in the case of a huge and complex cooperation model, it is not easy for a designer to lay out a whole cooperation procedure immediately. Besides, a cooperation model is necessary to design the cooperation intuitively among members in a community computing system. Therefore we propose the static community situation based model as an improved version. The major differences from the simple model are as follows:

Table 2. A CHILDCARE scenario based example of simple community computing model CIM-PI

```
Platform Independent Community Implementation Model{
  Community Home {
    Role Home_Stuff:1~100000 {
      Attribute: Address; Use;
      Cast: Use=residential; }
    Role Resident:1~20 {
      Attribute: Location;
      Address=home_stuff.address;
      Cast: Location=home_stuff.address;}
    Home_Stuff:Household_appliance; Resident:Human;
    Protocol announce_information_to_human_at_home {
      Communication of Initiator {
        SEND(MsgType="inform", ToWhom=Participant,
        InformedData); }
      Communication of Participant {
        IF(RECEIVE(MsgType="inform",FromWho="Initiator",
        informedData))
          Display_Info(InformedData);
        END IF } } }
  Community Childcare {
    Role Child:1 {
      Attribute: Safety_level={safe|warning|danger};
      Cast:Safety_level={warning|danger}; }
    Role Family:1~50 {
      Attribute: Relationship;
      Cast:Relationship={child.mother|child.father|child.sister|
      child.brother||child.grandmother|child.grandfather};
    Role Neighbor:1~20 {
      Attribute: Relationship;
      Cast: Relationship=child.neighbor; }
    Role Observer:1~2 {
      Attribute: Monitoring_Sevice={available|not_available};
      Location;
      Cast: Monitoring_Service=available;
        Location=child.location; }
```
```
  Child:Human,Smartbelt; Family:Human; Neighbor:Human;
  Observer:Camcorder,Camera,Streetlamp;
  Protocol take_a_child_home {
  communication of child {.....................}}
Society: Ghodamcity {
  Member Society_Member {
    Attribute: Location=ghodamcity;City_Address=ghodam;
    Safety_level={safe|warning|danger};
    Action: Wait_for_Msg(MsgType="inform", FromWho,
    InformedData); }
  Member Animate_Object extends Society_Member {
    Attribute: Species=string; Genus=string; Family=string; }
  Member Human extends Animate_Object {
    Attribute: Sex={male|female}; Age=(0~150);
    Relationship=string; Job=string;
    Action:Choose_the_nearest_family(Location,
    NearestFamily), Take_to(Who, Where);
    Request_for_picture(RequestWho=Observer.id,Location,
    RequestedPicture);Choose_the_nearest_person(Location
    ,NearestPerson);Choose_response(Choice1,
    Choice2,Choice); }
  Member Inanimate_Object extends Society_Member {
    Attribute: Status=string; }
  Member Electronic_Appliance extends Inanimate_Object {
    Attribute: Electronic_Power=string; Weight=integer;
    Height=integer; Usage={home|industry|research}; }
  Member Home_Appliance extends Electronic_Appliance {
    Attribute: Usage=home;Assigned_Room={livingroom|
    kitchen|bedroom|bath|reading};
    Actions: Display_Info(InformedData); }
  Member Streetlamp extends Electronic_Appliance {
    Attribute: Monitoring_Service={available|not_available};
    Lightening={yes|no};
    Actions: Send_picture(ToWhom, RequestedPicture);} } }
```

- Static community situation based model has its own cooperation model, the static community situation based cooperation model.
- It also has security policies such as society policy, community policy, and member policy, so that it solves conflicts in a community computing system.

To find an appropriate cooperation model for community computing, we surveyed existing cooperation models. In a number of previous works, cooperation is used, but in most cooperation models, cooperation is described as a predefined static program called a recipe, plan, or skill. The ways to realize cooperation have been introduced,

but the way to design cooperation itself was not discussed. Therefore, we arrived at a decision that a new cooperation model is needed for intuitive design of a community's cooperation. Before we describe our model in detail, please refer to the related works introduced in section 6.

Static Community Situation Based Cooperation Model

As a cooperation model for community computing, in this chapter, we propose the community situation based cooperation model. The idea is that cooperation is executed according to community situations. To provide dynamic pervasive services, context-awareness and/or situation-awareness are required as essential features of pervasive computing systems (Dey, 2001; Strang, 2004; Yau, 2006). In our community computing systems, we aim to guarantee dynamic community services by employing the community situation based cooperation model. In this cooperation model, when a community's situation changes, then tasks assigned to community members are changed accordingly. Therefore, tasks of members are decided depending on community situations. At this time, the final situation of a community should be the goal achievement situation or the community fail situation. Since the proposed cooperation model is based on the community situations, we define the community situation first.

In order to utilize community situations, we proposed the community situation model. In this model, a community situation is determined by situations of specific members. A member situation is decided by the member's contexts, which are determined by the attribute values of the member. In the present version of the community situation model, a community situation is represented as a logical association of attributes' values. However, the expression power of the community situation model can be improved, and the community situation based cooperation model can also be improved by following the advance in situation model. Using the proposed community situation model, we define the community situation based cooperation model that assumes the certainty of the community situation and the member's task in a certain community situation. Prior to defining the static community situation based cooperation model, let me introduce several assumptions of this model:

1. **Certainty of the community situations:** All community situations can be defined clearly, and all members in a community are aware of community situations.
2. **Certainty of tasks of each member in a given community situation:** Members in a community know their tasks to perform in a certain community situation.
3. **Ability of multiple task execution by a member:** In a community situation, each member can perform more than one task in sequential order.
4. **Situation transition that is independent of completion in a previous situation:** Although members' tasks are not completely finished in a previous community situation, a community situation can be changed into another situation.
5. **Cooperation should be ended:** Community situations can be dynamically changed but are capable of reaching a situation of community termination.

Based on these assumptions, cooperation is defined as a set of cooperation blocks. A cooperation block describes a piece of cooperation among roles in a certain community situation with the definition of a community situation and roles' tasks. The BNF definition of this cooperation

Table 3. BNF definition of the static community situation based cooperation model

```
<Static_Community_Situation_based_Cooperation_Model>
  ::= Community <Community_Type_Name> { <Community_Goals_Description> }
<Community_Type_Name>::=<Identifier>
<Community_Goals_Description>::= Goals <Goal_Description>¹⁺
<Goal_Description>::= <Goal_Name>(<Participant_Roles>) { <Community_Coopertion> }
<Goal_Name>::=<Identifier>, <Participant_Roles>::=<Role_Name>¹⁺, <Role_Name>::=<Identifier>
<Community_Cooperation>::=<Cooperation_Block>¹⁺
<Cooperation_Block>::=<Community_Situation_Name> => <Role_Task>¹⁺
<Role_Task>::=<Role_Name> : { <Role_Action_Name> {(<Parameter>⁰⁺)}ᵒᵖᵗ }¹⁺;
<Community_Situation_Name>::=<Identifier>,<Role_Name>::=<Identifier>
<Role_Action_Name>::=<Identifier>, <Parameter>::=<String>
```

model is shown in Table 3. A goal of a community is described by participant roles and cooperation blocks. Each cooperation block presents the cooperation among roles at a particular community situation. For an example of the cooperation model, see the cooperation part of the 'Find_Person' community in Table 4.

Conflict Resolution

When a member performs his own actions in a community situation, conflicts can occur. In the view of individual members, conflicts among a member's tasks can arise if the member is taking multiple community roles and necessary

Table 4. A COEX scenario example of static community situation based community computing model-CIM-PS

Society COEX_Mall {
 Community Type Description {
 Community Patrol_COEX{.....................}
 Community Find_Person{
   Role Patrol_Robot: 1 ~ 10 { .... }
  .... }
 Role-MemberType Mapping {
   Patrol_Robot:ARGUS; Guidian_of_Lost_Person:Human;
   Guide:Guide;Salesman:Human; }
 Goals Find_a_lost_person(Patrol_Robot,Guidian_of_Lost_
 Person, Guide, Resident) {
 FIND_PERSON_REQUEST=>
   Patrol_Robot:Read_Personal_Profile(); Broadcast_Info
   (∀Patrol_Robot and ∀Guide and ∀Resident, "Find a
   person", profile);
 FIND_PERSON=> Patrol_Robot:Find_Person(profile);
   Guide:Find_Person(profile); Salesman:
   Find_Person(profile);
 PERSON_FOUNDED=>
   Patrol_Robot and Guide and Salesman: Announce(
   ∀Patrol_Robot and ∀Guide and ∀Resident,
   "Person is founded", location); Guide_To(founded
   person, information office);;
 PERSON_NOT_FOUNDED=>
   Patrol_Robot and Guide and Resident:
   Announce("Person isn't founded", ∀Patrol_Robot);;
   Guide: Report_Police(" lost person", profile);;}
 Community Situation {
   FIND_PERSON_REQUEST={
    Patrol_Robot.TAKE_REQUEST_FIND_PERSON};
   FIND_PERSON={Patrol_Robot.FIND_PERSON};
   PERSON_FOUNDED={Patrol_Robot.PERSON_FOUNDED
    OR Guide.PERSON_FOUNDED OR Resident.
    PERSON_FOUNDED};
   PERSON_NOT_FOUNDED={Patrol_Robot.PERSON_NOT
    FOUNDED AND Guide.PERSON NOT_FOUNDED
    AND Resident.PERSON_ NOT_FOUNDED };}
 Community Creation {
 By Member: ARGUS.TAKE_REQUEST_FIND_PERSON; }
 Community Policy {
   Member Casting Policy {
    Patrol_Robot: distance-dependent; Salesman: distance-
    dependent; Guide: distance-dependent; }
   Sudden Secession of Member {
    Patrol _Robot: continue with a new;
    Salesman: continue with a new;
    Guidian_of_Lost_Person: initialize with a new;
    Guide: continue with a new; }
	Action Conflicts List={ **MEC**(Report_Police("lost person",
	 profile),Find_Person(profile)); }}
	 Ontology Patrol_COEX_Ontology;} } }
	 Member Type Description { ...
	 Member ARGUS *extends* Robot {
	   Attribute: MODEL=STRING;FIND_PERSON={YES|NO};
	   TAKE_REQUEST_FIND_PERSON={YES|NO};
	   PERSON_FOUNDED={YES|NO};
	   Action: Area_Assign(COEX_Mall, Patrol_Robot); END_Pa-
	 trol();
	   Patrol(COEX_Mall); Read_Personal_Profile();
	   Broadcast_Info(∀Patrol_Robot and ∀Guide and ∀Resident,
	   "Find a person", profile); Find_Person(profile);
	   Announce(∀Patrol_Robot and ∀Guide and ∀Resident,
	   "Person is founded", location); Guide_To(founded person,
	   information office); Announce("Person is not founded",
	   ∀Patrol_Robot);
	 Member Situation {
	 TAKE_REQUEST_FIND_PERSON:
	   TAKE_REQUEST_FIND_PERSON=YES;
	 FIND_PERSON:FIND_PERSON:
	   FIND_PERSON:FIND_PERSON=YES;
	 PERSON_FOUNDED:PERSON_FOUNDED:
	   PERSON_FOUNDED:PERSON_FOUNDED=YES;}
	 Member Configuration {
	 Vision_Sonsor_v3; Samsung_Location_Sensor_v1;}
	 Attribute Acquisition {
	 TAKE_REQUEST_FIND_PERSON:Vision_Sonsor_v3;}
	 Action Mapping {
	 Area_Assign(COEX_Mall, Patrol_Robot):Set_patrol_
	 range(location); Patrol(COEX_Mall):CyberCap(patrol);
	 END_Patrol_Service():CyberCap(patrolstop);
	 Read_Personal_Profile():Read_RFID(person_RFID);
	   Broadcast_Info(∀Patrol_Robot and ∀Guide and
	 ∀Resident, "Find a person", profile): BroadCast
	 (towhom, msg); Find_Person(profile):Search_Obj(Info);
	 Announce(∀Patrol_Robot and ∀Guide and
	 ∀Resident, "Person is founded", location):Notify
	 (towhom,msg);Guide_To(founded person, information
	 office):GuideServie(who,where);Announce("Person is
	 not founded", ∀Patrol_Robot):Notify(msg,towhom);}
	 Member Policy {
	   Exclusive Actions={
	    (Patrol(COEX_Mall),END_Patrol_Service()); } } } ...}
	 Society Policy {
	 Community Precedence { **High_Priority**: Find_Person;
	 Medium_Priority: Patrol_COEX,Sell_Product; **Low_Priority**:;}
	 Exclusive Community = { } } }

tasks to each community are conflicting, or if an executed task in a previous community situation is not finished but the member should perform a conflicting task according to the changed situation. In the view of a community, an action of a member can conflict with an action of others. No matter which kind of cases, conflicts should be resolved. To do this, we assumed that the tasks of a member in a certain community situation are executed sequentially by one thread, and thus we do not need to worry about conflicts on a thread. Conflicts arise when a member tries to execute conflicting actions of his own or when members try to execute conflicting actions simultaneously. To handle such conflicts, we classified conflicting actions into two types: mutually exclusive conflict type and time dependent conflict type. In the case of the mutually exclusive conflict type, if a conflict occurs, then one action among conflicting actions should be terminated. In case of the time dependent conflict type, one action among conflicting actions should be executed first, with execution of another action to follow. For handling conflicts in runtime, a community manager and each member have an action conflicts list about conflicts. In the list, the types of action conflicts are represented. At this time, conflicts between same actions can be included in the list. For example, assume that a member performs action a_2 in community situation S_1. After a few seconds, the situation is changed to S_2, although a_2 is not finished. After that, the situation would be changed again to S_3, and the member should perform a_2 again in situation S_3. However, a_2, which was executed in the previous situation S_1, would still be operating.

Static Community Situation Based Community Computing Model

Based on the static community situation based cooperation model, we develop the static community situation based computing model. The family of this model is as follows:

CCM. The major difference from simple community computing model CCM is shown in the cooperation description part. In the improved CCM, cooperation of a community is represented by community situations and descriptions about each role's tasks in a certain situation.

CIM-PI. Changes derived from the cooperation model are reflected in every part of CIM-PI. First of all, in the community type description, mapping information between roles and member types is added to represent which member types can play which role. Secondly, a detailed description of the cooperation is provided. In particular, tasks to be executed by a member are shaped as a sequence of members' actions, and community situations are also defined. Thirdly, conditions of community creation are described. Specifically, there are two ways to initiate a community instance: a member requires an initiation to a society manager, or a community manager requires an initiation as a part of cooperation. Finally, community policies are added to manage conflicts during the lifetime of a community instance. In the present version, there are three kinds of policies in the community policy description: member casting policy, member's secession policy, and action conflict's list. The member casting policy represents a rule about member selection such as distant dependent casting or response-time dependent casting. In the member secession policy, treatments for sudden secession of members are specified. For example, if a member disappears, then a cooperation process can be initialized with a new member, the cooperation can continue with a new member, or the cooperation can be terminated. In the member type description part, all member types are described, and the hierarchy of member types is also defined using *extends* keyword. In addition, member situations are specified as a logical association of attributes' values. Finally, member policies for each member are described. When a member performs tasks to play one or more roles, conflicts between tasks may happen. To resolve such conflicts, we define an action conflict list and represent it in member policy description. In the society description, additional society policies are described, and the precedence of communities and exclusive communities are defined. When a society manager takes more than one request for community instantiation, these policies are used to select requests to allow instantiations.

CIM-PS. In CIM-PS, the information about an attribute acquisition, action mapping, and member configuration is added. In the attribute acquisition part, we describe which values of each attribute are derived from where. The source of attribute values can be a kind of sensor or member's actions. In action mapping description, we describe how to realize actions of members. In cases where a system uses existing programmed objects, a developer should make a connection between actions in the model and programmed actions in an existing object. On the other hand, in cases where developers have to generate programs for member objects, developers are able to use action names in models to program a member. In the member configuration part, components of each member such as sensor drivers, operating systems,

and communication channels are described. An example based on COEX scenario (See Section 6: Implementation) is shown in Table 4.

Model Transformation. As the model transformation process of the simple model, we derive source codes from CCM to develop a community computing system. The specific transformation process for the static community situation based model is shown in Figure 2.

COMPUTATIONAL MODEL

To run a community computing system, we proposed a computational model as shown in Figure 3. According to the computational model, when a system starts to operate, only members exist in a society.

At the beginning of a community computing system, a society manager who manages the whole community computing system is generated. The society manager contains information about all the member and community types and protocols for society registration, community manager

Figure 2. Model transformation of the static community situation based community computing model

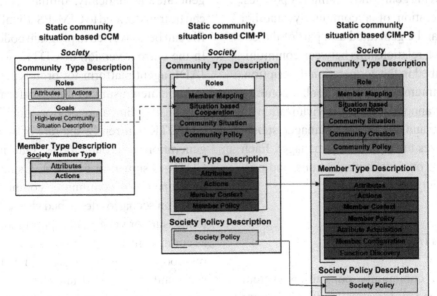

Figure 3. Computational model of a multi-agent based community computing system

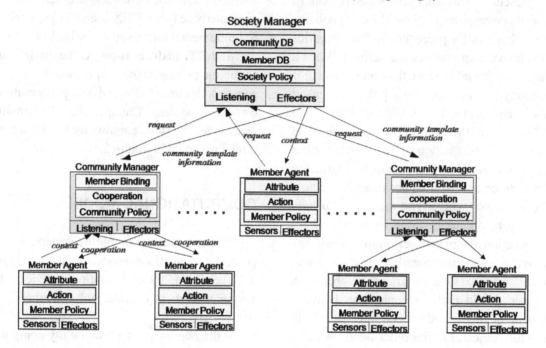

creation, and termination; every member should be registered with a society manager. When a member sets a particular goal, the society manager then generates a community manager to achieve the goal. A community manager has conditions to cast members, cooperation descriptions for achieving goals, and community policies. During cooperation of a community, another community can be generated as a part of the cooperation. Such relationships between communities are described in the cooperation description. After the community attains its goal, a community manager announces the disorganization to each member, and the society manager subsequently removes the community manager. Each member has its own attributes, actions, and protocols for society registration.

IMPLEMENTATION

To develop a community computing system conveniently and systematically, we implement a development tool called CDTK (Community Developing Tool-Kit). Using the CDTK, a developer can design a system as a CCM file and then transform the CCM file to its CIM-PI file using CDTK. At this time, the developer should fill the particular portion of CIM-PI which CDTK cannot generate automatically. Similarly, the CIM-PI file can be transformed to CIM-PS. Finally, a CIM-PS file can be converted to program codes by CDTK. In the current version of CDTK, we choose the JADE agent platform for prototypes. If we need to implement using another platform, we can do it by just adding a generation module or plug-in on CDTK. Currently, the rate of automatic code generation is around 60%. Our implemented CDTK is shown in Figure 4. Using CDTK, we developed two community computing systems based on scenarios described above. It is not easy to measure or verify a computing paradigm such as community computing. Accordingly, we made two cooperation scenarios, the CHILDCARE scenario and the COEX-Mall scenario, which show the necessity of immediate cooperation among

Figure 4. CDTK (Community Developing Tool-Kit)

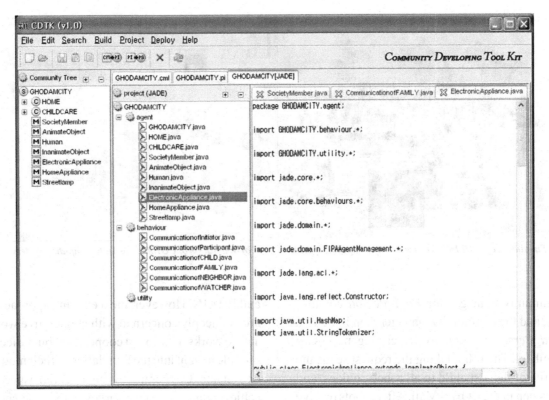

individuals. Then we implement two community computing systems based on those scenarios. By the simulation results of two systems, we show the feasibility and possibility of community computing as an emerging computing paradigm to provide urgent and complicated services by using cooperation.

CHILDCARE. In the CHILDCARE scenario, when a child goes out of home, a Smartbelt located on the child requests for a community instantiation to the society manager. Then, a community manager of the *CHILDCARE* community is created and organizes agent members for performing each role. For the safety of the child, the *CHILDCARE* community informs the situation of the child to the child's family, and the child's mother searches for the nearest person who can help the child to return home. Finally, when the child arrives home, the goal of the *CHILDCARE* community is achieved, and then the community

is disorganized. Simulation of the *CHILDCARE* community computing system is shown in Figure 5(a).

COEX. To examine the proposed static community situation based community computing model and the development process, we developed the *COEX* community computing system to offer *PATROL* and *FIND_PERSON* services at a COEX shopping mall. This scenario aims to find a lost child inside a huge building, COEX-Mall. When a robot is on patrol as a member of a *Patrol_COEX* community, the robot may be asked by a mother to find her lost child. The robot generates a *TAKE_REQUEST_FIND_ PERSON* member situation and then requests a creation of *Find_Person* community to a society manager (See Section 5: Computation Model for more information about a society manager and a community manager.) The society manager, who supervises the *COEX-Mall* community computing system, creates a

Figure 5. Simulation of CHILDCARE (a) and COEX (b) community computing system

a) Simulation of CHILDCARE community computing system   **b) Simulation of COEX community computing system**

community manager for *Find_Person* community, and the community manager then initiates a *Find_Person* community by casting necessary members. The robot taking the request sends the profile of the lost child to all robots, guides, and salesmen in the COEX-Mall. After robots receive the profile, they begin to search for the child while patrolling. At this time, each robot takes at least two roles, *Patrol_COEX* community and *Find_ Person* community. Simulation of the *COEX* community computing system is shown in Figure 5(b).

RELATED WORK

As mentioned above, our goal is to develop a cooperative pervasive system. In order to find a pathway and reach our goal, we surveyed existing development approaches for pervasive systems such as PICO or GAIA. There have been various approaches applied toward pervasive system development. Among those approaches, middleware approaches are used in several projects such as PICO and Active Space. Meanwhile, the multi-agent based approaches are also frequently used in several research projects such as Gaia, AALADIN

and BRAIN. However, most existing approaches are not deeply concerned with cooperative work. Those works mentioned cooperation but failed to provide insight into the foundation of their models or systems. Cooperation is an essential aspect to achieve our goal, so we surveyed existing cooperation approaches such as CSCW (Computer-Supported Cooperative Work) to fill the hole. In this section, we briefly introduce each previous work and declare our motivation.

Pervasive System Development Approaches

First of all, we introduce two middleware based approaches. Their objective is to offer an infrastructure to manage resources, sense context information, and assist in the development and execution of pervasive applications. In this section, we explore two major middleware approaches to offer pervasive services: Gaia and PICO.

- **Super Spaces (Al-Muhtadi, 2004):** In the Active Spaces Project (Roman, 2000), an experimental middleware infrastructure, called Gaia, was introduced to coordinate pervasive software objects and heterogeneous networked devices in a physical space. The major contribution was to present active spaces as a programmable environment instead of a collection of individual and disconnected heterogeneous devices. In 2004, an extended version, Super Space, was proposed to manage and orchestrate groups of Active Spaces. However, they did not suggest an abstraction model to conceptualize pervasive objects constructing the space or cooperative relationships between objects in their space.

- **PICO (Kumar, 2003; Sung, 2002):** PICO (Pervasive Information Community Organization) is a middleware framework for dynamically creating mission-oriented communities of autonomous pervasive software objects offering pervasive services. In several agent cooperation models, organization concepts have already been introduced (Jennings, 2003; Wooldridge, 2002), but PICO has applied this concept to pervasive domains. In this project, a community was defined as a pervasive object consisting of one or more agents working towards a common goal. In addition, they introduce community computing as a framework for collaboration among agents. Their fundamental concept satisfies requirements of pervasive computing, such as proactive real-time collaborations for automated and continuous services provided in a heterogeneous environment.

As the middleware-based infrastructure works, multi-agent based approaches are frequently used to develop pervasive systems, because agents' features such as flexible and autonomous problem solving behavior and the richness of interactions guarantee dynamic and intelligent services. Existing multi-agent approaches are interesting to study the way to seek out necessary agents to meet requirements of a pervasive system. When

requirements are given, they are concerned about the way to design and implement necessary agents to offer the required services. However, in the case of a pervasive system intending to provide services using existing agents, we can say that participant agents are already defined. Accordingly, in such a case, it is more important to consider how to meet the system requirements by existing agents rather than what agents are required. Furthermore, most multi-agent based development approaches do not deeply concentrate on cooperation. To achieve our goal, however, cooperation is the most important aspect, so we have to consider cooperation in more detail than others have. In this section, we briefly introduce previous works on multi-agent based pervasive systems development.

- **Gaia (Wooldridge, 2000; Jennings, 2003):** It introduced a methodology for analysis and design to develop a multi-agent system. In Gaia, a multi-agent system is regarded as a collection of computational organizations consisting of various interacting roles and allows an analyst to go systematically from requirement statements to a design through a process of developing increasingly detailed models of the system to be constructed.

- **AALADIN (Ferber, 1998):** It is a meta-model of a multi-agent system based on organizational concepts. It allows for describing any kind of organization using only the core concepts of groups, agents, and roles. In the extended version (Ferber, 2003), the model was improved into the AGR model (Agent/Group/Role model). In that model, the dynamic aspect was added by specifying the creation of a group, the entering and exiting mechanism of an agent within a group, and the role acquisition mechanism.

- **BRAIN (Cabri, 2003):** It is a framework for supporting the different phases of the development of interactions in multi-agent systems by modeling the interactions between agents based on the concept of roles and describing such roles using an XML-based notation, XRole. Authors implemented Rolesystem as an interaction infrastructure of BRAIN, but they did not concern themselves with cooperation.

Cooperative System Development Approaches

Cooperation has been a good way to solve a problem requiring diverse resource and capabilities and to perform a highly resource-consuming and time-consuming task (Wooldridge, 1999). The pervasive service is one of the domains having such problems, so cooperation has been used in some research. However, meanings and/or style of cooperation are slightly different between research studies. In this section, we inspect existing research studies and discriminate between them in terms of cooperation.

- **Team in Computer Supported Cooperative Work (CSCW):** The major objective of CSCW is to develop groupware that effectively performs a common task using information sharing among all users (Wilson, 1991; Borghoff, 2000). Typically, a group in CSCW is a small project-oriented team, and a team is defined as a set of predefined people. Members of a team are human, and their works are tightly coupled by sharing information about team membership as well as information about the skills and roles of the other members (Johansen, 1998). In the group protocol component, the ways in which team members cooperate and communicate with each other are described. Typical groupware of CSCW are video conferencing systems and joint document editing systems.

- **Group in Multi-agent System:** To provide services requiring complex interac-

tions, multi-agent systems are frequently developed (Wooldridge, 2000). To cooperate with other agents, an organization is constructed, and each role for performing a cooperative protocol is dynamically assigned to a member agent. The cooperation procedure is able to be predefined or dynamically determined depending on the agent's intelligence, but it has not been seriously studied.

- **Community in PICO:** PICO is a middleware framework for dynamically creating mission-oriented communities of pervasive objects. To describe structures of cooperating organizations, it employed the community concept. It is very similar to our community computing, but PICO leaves room for the life cycle of community, member specification, the way to assign software objects dynamically into actual objects, and the cooperation method.

- **Community Computing in Digital Tokyo Project:** The authors introduced community computing in 1998 in order to support the process of organizing diverse and amorphous people who are willing to share knowledge and experiences (Ishida, 1998). The objective of their work is to make a city-scale supporting system to assist a person's everyday life. In the Digital Tokyo project (Besselaar, 2002), a community is a digitalized representation of real human communities. All human members in a community share their preferences and knowledge and generate a consensus, and the community computing supports those processes.

- **Community Computing in Microsoft:** In 2005, Microsoft introduced its vision of community computing (Blau, 2005). It defines community computing as an emerging technological environment where devices sharing computing capacities of others and users' identities are widespread. It insisted that research about system engineering is required to manage massive connections among powerful devices in a community computing environment (Microsoft, 2005). Microsoft is systematically trying to support its community computing by developing various tools which enable people to interact with one another for gathering and exchanging services. In its research, a community is a sort of group of devices sharing one another's information and capacity to generate communication between people. It seems that it concentrates on systematic support to communities.

- **Community Computing in this chapter:** To design and develop a cooperative multi-agent system conveniently, we propose community computing as a new computing paradigm. Other research has not seriously concentrated on cooperation, so it did not provide a way to design and execute a cooperative group, such as a community and cooperation in that group, immediately. Towards this goal, in our community computing approach, we provide the abstraction models to design them intuitively and develop a community computing system quickly. Our community computing is more useful especially when a number of existing agents exist, and a developer needs to design cooperation among those agents and execute it immediately.

Existing Cooperation Models

To propose the static community situation based cooperation model which was described in section 3.2.1, we surveyed existing cooperation models for multi-agent systems. In this section, we briefly introduce some works as follows:

- **The cooperation model for ARCHON (Brazier, 1997):** In 1997, a refined formal cooperation model for ARCHON (Cockburn, 1996) was proposed. In this model, cooperation is represented as a recipe or a set of tasks. The generation of this recipe is an iterative process requiring interaction with other agents on their own schedules related to other projects. When a recipe is completed, it is sent to all participating agents, and the project commences. Once committed, each participating agent receives the final recipe and is committed to the relevant time interval in the recipe. The CM (Cooperation Management) is a component that is responsible for all tasks, commitments, and cooperation. Among the sub-components of CM, the PPC (Prepare Project Commitments) component decides a preferred set A of activities with which goal g can be accomplished and subsequently generates a dependency graph of the activities using the critical path method and domain knowledge. Using this dependency graph, PPC determines the participant agents and then sends a list of agents to the GMR (Generate and Modify project Recipe). The goal of a component GMR is to design a recipe R, where the recipe R is interactively designed by generating and sending the proposed recipe to agents interested in participation. A recipe R consists of a task A, willing participants capable of performing that task, a priority p, and a deadline T for that task. The participants accept, adapt, or reject the proposed recipe. In this model, however, the method used to make an agent cooperate with other members is specified, but how a recipe R itself is generated using a dependency-graph of activities is not specified. In addition, a means to describe cooperation among agents is not represented in that model.

- **AGDRSCOM (Hua, 2003):** It is an agent cooperation model in which member agents are able to adjust their own cooperative tasks according to the changes of environment and the feedback from other members. In AGDRSCOM, the idea of adaptive cooperation is introduced. In adaptive cooperation, the function structure of a cooperative member agent has skills, where a skill is represented with a five-element tuple: *Skill = <Activity, Pre-Processing, Programming, Action-Set, Post-Processing>*. In this representation, Activity is the basic action when a skill is executed. Pre-Processing is the processing of information required by a programming task prior to execution. Programming can be a rule set or state transfer figure and is referred to when the skill is executed. Action–Set is the possible action set, and Post-Processing is a result or post-processing of Programming. In this model, the function structure of the adaptation of cooperation was introduced, but the detailed method of adaptation was not proposed. In addition, cooperation was also represented as a programming element in the skill description.

- **Cooperation model of MAPFS (Perez, 2004):** MAPFS (MultiAgent Parallel File System) is a parallel file system integrated with a multi-agent system responsible for information retrieval. In the cooperation model of MAPFS, cooperation is achieved using shared plans, where plans contain precise instructions or actions for achieving such objectives. Thus, a cooperation process is also procedural and is described by actions and instructions.
- **IMCAC (Guo, 2006):** In 2006, Guo proposed hybrid cooperation using recipes, policies, and advertisements and implemented the idea of hybrid cooperation in IMCAC (Infrastructure for Managing and Controlling Agents' Cooperation). In this model, a policy is the obligations and restrictions that agents should meet, and advertisements are the records of interests of other agents. A recipe represents the funda-

mental cooperation process and is statically established according to the scheduling plan during the design of the application system. A recipe is defined by possible plans, plan steps, and sub-activities in these plan steps.

CONCLUSION

Our ultimate goal is to design and develop the multi-agent systems which provide complex and dynamic ubiquitous services through cooperation among existing agents. As mentioned above, existing research is not suitable for our goal. In this chapter, we therefore redefined community computing as a new computing paradigm in which services are provided by cooperation among given smart objects. In order to make the meaning of community computing concrete, we compared our work with other related work, proposed an overall concept, and defined terminology to help with understanding. In order to actualize community computing, we first proposed the community computing models and a development process. As an early version of the community computing model, we proposed a simple community computing model where a community has the necessary roles, goals, and code-like cooperation protocol. However, this model has no cooperation model and no conflict resolution scheme. Therefore, we proposed an improved model, the static community situation based community computing model. In this model, we employed the static community situation based cooperation model, which is a limited model that assumes certainty of the community situation and members' cooperative behavior. In addition, we also analyze conflicts in community computing systems and propose policies to resolve those conflicts. In order to examine feasibility of our community computing model and development process, we developed two small systems and presented the simulation results of several scenarios.

FUTURE RESEARCH DIRECTIONS

Despite our progress, our proposal suggests several avenues for future work.

1. **Improvement of the community situation based cooperation model and situation model:** The present version of the cooperation model is based on strict assumptions. To apply it to broad application areas, we need to develop more general models, or we can consider several variations for particular application domains.
2. **Improvement of the proposed conflict resolution scheme:** In this paper, we simply use a list which shows complicating actions or the priority of communities. However, it is not enough to prevent members' critical resources from unauthorized access or to protect members' privacy. Therefore, we need to be concerned about the security mechanism for community computing systems in detail.
3. **Various case studies:** To convince others of the effective value of community computing, it will be helpful to present various feasible case studies. The systems to protect people from natural disasters or terrorist attacks can be good examples. In addition, a system of emergency medical treatment will be an effective application domain.

REFERENCES

Al-Muhtadi, J., Chetan, S., Ranganathan, A., & Campbell, R. H. (2004, March). *Super spaces: A middleware for large-scale pervasive computing environments.* Paper presented at the IEEE International Workshop on Pervasive Computing and Communications (Perware '04), Orlando, Florida, USA.

Besselaar, P., Tanabe, M., & Ishida, T. (2002). Introduction: Digital cities research and open issues. [Springer-Verlag.]. *Lecture Notes in Computer Science, 2362,* 1–9. doi:10.1007/3-540-45636-8_1

Blau, J. (2005). Microsoft: Community computing is on the way. *InfoWorld Magazine.* Retrieved from http://www. infoworld.com/ article/ 05/ 11/ 22/ HNcommunitycomputing _1.html

Borghoff, U. M., & Schlichter, J. H. (Eds.). (2000). *Computer-supported cooperative work: Introduction to distributed applications.* Berlin/Heidelberg, Germany & New York, NY: Springer-Verlag.

Brazier, F. M. T., Jonker, C. M., & Treur, J. (1997). Formalization of a cooperation model based on joint intentions. In *Proceedings of the Third International Workshop on Agent Theories, Architectures and Languages* (ATAL'96), *Lecture Notes in Artificial Intelligence 1193* (pp. 141-155). Springer.

Cabri, G., Leonardi, L., & Zambonelli, F. (2003). A framework for flexible role-based interactions in multi-agent system. In *Proceedings of Conference on Cooperative Information Systems (CoopIS)* [Berlin, Germany: Springer.]. *Lecture Notes in Computer Science, 2888,* 145–161. doi:10.1007/978-3-540-39964-3_11

Cockburn, D., & Jennings, N. R. (Eds.). (1996). *ARCHON: A distributed artificial intelligence system for industrial applications* (pp. 319–344). Wiley. Foundation of Distributed Artificial Intelligence.

Dey, A. K. (2001). Understanding and using context. *Personal and Ubiquitous Computing -Special Issue on Situated Interaction and Ubiquitous Computing, 5*(1), 4-7.

Elizabeth, M., & Hull, C. (1987). Occam - A programming language for multiprocessor systems. *Computer Languages, 12*(1), 27–37. doi:10.1016/0096-0551(87)90010-5

Ferber, J., & Gutknecht, O. (1998). A meta-model for the analysis and design of organization in multi-agent systems. *In Proceedings of 3rd International Conference on Multi-agent Systems (ICMAS'98),* (pp. 128-135).

Ferber, J., Gutknecht, O., & Michel, F. (2003). From agents to organizations: An organizational view of multi-agent systems. *In Proceedings of AOSE 2003* [Springer Verlag.]. *Lecture Notes in Computer Science, 2935,* 214–230. doi:10.1007/978-3-540-24620-6_15

Guo, H., Gao, J., Zeng, Z., & Hu, B. (2006). Recipe, policy and self-organizing: A hybrid collaboration approach for agent-based cooperative design. In *Proceedings of the 10th International Conference on Computer Supported Cooperative Work in Design (CSDWD 2006),* (pp. 653-658). IEEE.

Hua, C., Gao, J., Su, J., & Chen, H. (2003). AG-DRSCOM: A complicated dynamic real-time strong cooperation system model. In *Proceedings of the Second International Conference on Machine Learning and Cybernetics: Vol.1* (pp. 318-323). IEEE.

Ishida, T. (Ed.). (1998). *Community computing and support systems. Lecture Notes in Computer Science* (*Vol. 1519*). Springer.

Johansen, R., Charles, J., Mittman, R., & Saffo, P. (Eds.). (1998). *Groupware: Computer support for business teams. New York, NY: Free Press.* London, UK: Collier Macmillan.

Jung, Y., Lee, J., & Kim, M. (2006, May). *Multi-agent based community computing system development with the model driven architecture.* Paper presented at the Fifth International Joint Conference on Autonomous Agents and Multiagent Systems, (pp. 1329-1331).

Kindberg, T., & Fox, A. (2002). System software for ubiquitous computing. *IEEE Pervasive Computing / IEEE Computer Society [and] IEEE Communications Society, 1*(1), 70–81. doi:10.1109/MPRV.2002.993146

Kumar, M., Shirazi, B., Das, S. K., Singhal, M., Sung, B., & Levine, D. (2003). Pervasive information communities organization: A middleware framework for pervasive computing. *IEEE Pervasive Computing / IEEE Computer Society [and] IEEE Communications Society,* (July-September): 72–79. doi:10.1109/MPRV.2003.1228529

Microsoft. (2005). *Community technologies research group.* Retrieved from http://research. microsoft.com/ community/

Object Management Group. (2003). *Technical guide to model driven architecture: The MDA guide* v1.0.1. Retrieved from http://www.omg. org / cgi-bin/ doc?omg/ 03-06-01

Perez, M. S., Sanchez, A., Robles, V., Pena, J. M., & Abawajy, J. (2004). Cooperation model of a multiagent parallel file system for clusters. In *Proceedings of IEEE International Symposium on Cluster Computing and the Grid* (pp. 595-601). IEEE computer Society.

Román, M., Hess, C., Cerqueira, R., Campbell, R. H., & Nahrstedt, K. (2002). Gaia: A middleware infrastructure to enable active spaces. *IEEE Pervasive Computing / IEEE Computer Society [and] IEEE Communications Society, 1,* 74–83. doi:10.1109/MPRV.2002.1158281

Strang, T., & Linnhoff-Popien, C. (2004). A context modeling survey. In *Proceedings of the 1st International Workshop on Advanced Context Modeling, Reasoning and Management at UbiComp2004.*

Sung, B., Shirazi, B., & Kumar, M. (2002). Pervasive community organization. In *Proceedings Eurasia 2002,* Tehran, November.

The Foundation of Intelligent Physical Agents (FIPA) Standard. (2000). *FIPA communicative act library specification.* Retrieved from http:// www.fipa.org/ specs/ fipa00037/

Weiser, M. (1991). The computer for the twenty-first century. *Scientific American, 265*(3), 94–104. doi:10.1038/scientificamerican0991-94

Wilson, P. (1991). *Computer supported cooperative work: An introduction.* Oxford, UK: Intellect Books.

Wooldridge, M. (2002). *An introduction to multiagent systems.* John Wiley & Sons.

Wooldridge, M., & Jennings, N. R. (1999). The cooperative problem-solving process. *Journal of Logic Computation, 9*(4), 563–592. doi:10.1093/logcom/9.4.563

Wooldridge, M., & Jennings, N. R. (2000). The Gaia methodology for agent-oriented analysis and design. *Journal of Autonomous Agents and Multi-Agent Systems, 3*, 285–312. doi:10.1023/A:1010071910869

Yau, S. S., & Liu, J. (2006). Hierarchical situation modeling and reasoning for pervasive computing. In *Proceedings of 3rd Workshop on Software Technologies for Future Embedded and the Second International Workshop on Collaborative Computing, Integration, and Assurance (SEUS-WCCIA '06)*, (pp. 5-10). IEEE Computer Society.

Zambonelli, F., Jennings, N. R., & Wooldredge, M. (2003). Developing multiagent systems: The Gaia methodology. *ACM Transactions on Software Engineering and Methodology, 12*(3), 317–370. doi:10.1145/958961.958963

Section 3
Clouds and Services

Chapter 10
How to Choose the Right Cloud

Stamatia Bibi
Aristotle University of Thessaloniki, Greece

Dimitrios Katsaros
University of Thessaly, Greece

Panayiotis Bozanis
University of Thessaly, Greece

ABSTRACT

Cloud computing is a recent trend in IT that moves computing and data away from desktop and portable PCs into large data centers, and outsources the "applications" (hardware and software) as services over the Internet. Cloud computing promises to increase the velocity with which applications are deployed, increase innovation, and lower costs, all while increasing business agility. But, is the migration to the Cloud the most profitable option for every business? This chapter presents a study of the basic parameters for estimating the potential infrastructure and software costs deriving from building and deploying applications on cloud and on-premise assets. Estimated user demand and desired quality attributes related to an application are also addressed in this chapter as they are aspects of the decision problem that also influence the choice between cloud and in-house solutions.

INTRODUCTION

Cloud computing is a recent trend in IT that enables the use of common business applications online using the providers' software and hardware resources and finally paying on-demand. This model opens a new horizon of opportunity for enterprises as it introduces new business models that allow customers to pay for the resources they effectively use instead of making upfront investments. This fact raises the question of whether such a technology reduces IT costs and the situations under which cost is actually a motive for migrating to cloud computing technologies.

As cloud computing services are maturing, they are becoming an attractive alternative to traditional in-house or on premise development. The variable costs calculated on scalable use of resources, the support of enterprise growth through on demand instant infrastructure provisioning and the shift of maintenance, administration and monitoring operations to third parties are among the compelling

DOI: 10.4018/978-1-60960-735-7.ch010

benefits of the cloud. Still a quantitative analysis of the relevant aspects of the potential IT problem is required before making a decision on the appropriate development and infrastructure model.

IT managers are recently faced with the problem of making a selection between cloud computing and on-premise development and deployment. Cloud computing option is attractive, especially if the quality delivered and the total cost is satisfying and the risks are reasonable. The real question for many IT departments is whether the cost of transition to an external computing cloud will be low enough to benefit from any medium-term savings (Armbrust et al., 2008), (Cloud Computing Congress, 2010). In order to be able to provide answers to the above question, a formal cost analysis of cloud and on-premise deployment should be performed in order to compare thoroughly the two alternatives.

A thorough analysis of the estimated costs and quality associated with the two alternatives will help an IT manager define the pros and cons of each solution. Such an analysis will point out which is the right combination of cloud and premise based assets and can indeed provide the optimal solution. As mentioned by Knight, (2009) the key is not choosing between the two solutions but being strategic about where to deploy various hardware and software components of a total solution.

Although there is a lot of research dedicated to cloud computing software engineering issues, economics and cost estimation drivers for adopting such a technology are not systematically addressed. This chapter presents basic parameters for estimating the potential benefits from Cloud computing and provides an estimation framework for determining if it is a technology that offers a long term profitable solution to IT business problems. Basic parameters for estimating the potential costs deriving from building and deploying applications on cloud and on premise assets are presented.

The assessment of cloud computing costs is more evident compared to the assessment of on

premises development and deployment. The cost of cloud computing services initially depends on the usage of three types of delivery models; namely, software-as-a-service, platform-as-a-service and infrastructure-as-a-service. The usage is counted and billed based on the committed resources per hour or the number of users per hour. As the cloud technology is relatively recent, measurement standards are not yet fully defined for each model. The usage metrics should be carefully selected in order to provision and receive effective services (Dikaiakos et al., 2009). The metrics that nowadays are frequently used are bandwidth, CPU, memory and applications usage, per hour. The target of this chapter is to discuss and suggest appropriate metrics that is/will be used for billing cloud computing services. These metrics will also be used to estimate the cost of an application moving or being developed over the cloud. Other important parameters that should be taken into account in order to evaluate cloud computing adoption is the business domain and objectives of the application considered, demand behaviour in the particular field and technical requirements (Klems et al., 2009). Of course this estimation would help in order to approximately predict the cost of cloud computing adoption, but still one should be able to estimate the costs of the alternative privately owned solution in order to compare them and make a justifiable choice.

Estimating the cost of software development and deployment based on on-premise assets is a more complex procedure. On–premises application development includes a variety of different costs associated with IT infrastructure and software development. Estimating in-house development and deployment of software is a difficult task, as there are different cost drivers related to personnel, product, process, hardware and operation expenses. Developing applications on privately owned IT infrastructure comprise, apart from software development and maintenance costs which remain the same in both cases, a series of cost drivers associated with physical attributes, performance factors and functional expenses (McRitsie et.al., 2008). Physical attributes, that may affect the in-source development, are related to the operating environment such as facility requirements, systems hardware and software costs and end users equipment. Performance attributes involve the technical non-functional requirements of the application relevant to the required reliability, transaction- rate, safety, accuracy. The non-functional requirements have an impact on the selected infrastructure. Finally the functional expenses of the company may involve years of operation, labor rates, size of the development and support team and replacement and upgrade policies.

These factors affect the total cost of an IT investment and may define the feasibility of a certain application development and the potential benefits of developing it in-sourcing or out-sourcing over the cloud.

This chapter is an overview of possible billing measures and metrics related to infrastructure and software either they are deployed in the cloud or in house. It is addressed to IT managers that face the dilemma of selecting to deploy applications on the cloud or on premise, to cloud providers that want to effectively bill their provisions and to Independent Service Vendors that want to offer to potential customers both of the two alternatives, clarifying long term benefits of each of the two. Specifically, in the sequel we pursue three main goals:

a. to analyze the different types of costs related to adopting cloud technologies and in house development. Our approach is based on the discussion of general cost categories that are taken into account by "cloud" providers and the traditional cost drivers considered in estimating in-source software and systems applications;

b. to provide an analytic comparison example for the deployment of a CRM system based on current economic status. The analysis is

based using commercial data from software development coming from the International Standards Benchmarking Group (ISBSG, 2010) and from (Yankee, 2005) report.

c. to define quality attributes and levels of demand behaviour that may affect the final choice. User demand is an indicator of the load of a system and the estimated traffic that greatly affects infrastructure costs. Desired quality attributes and the level these attributes are incorporated into on premise and on cloud solutions can also affect the final decision.

The rest of the chapter is organized as follows: The next Section provides an analysis of the background and the related work. Section entitled "Choose the right deployment model" describes cloud computing and traditional software and system costs and provides a three step procedure that will assist IT managers to understand the benefits of each solution. The two last sections discuss future work and conclude the Chapter.

BACKGROUND

There is fairly broad general interest on the benefits and drawbacks of moving or deploying an application to the cloud. Cost is recognized as an important factor that may motivate the transitioning of IT operations to cloud computing. Practitioners show an increased interest on the costs related to cloud computing however monetary cost- benefits are not yet fully recorded, assessed and analyzed by the scientific community.

Armbrust et. al. (2009) in their technical report, include a chapter devoted to cloud computing economics. Three issues are mentioned in (Armbrust et al., 2009) that should participate in cloud computing economic models. These issues are related to long-term cost benefits, hardware resource costs declines and resource utilization. A host service in the cloud should offer benefits over the long term. This means that one has to estimate the utilization over the cloud for a significant period of time. In these estimations the "pay as you go" billing system offered by cloud computing providers is evaluated in terms of elasticity measured in resource utilization. An IT manager will predict daily average and peak demand measured for example as the number of servers required and then he will be able to compare utility computing versus privately owned infrastructure. Also hardware expenditures should be taken into consideration into economic models. Hardware resource costs decline at variable rates a fact that may lead to unjustifiable expenditures compared to actual resource usage. Cloud computing can track changes to hardware costs and pass them through the client more cost effectively.

Klems et al. (2009) propose a framework for determining the benefits of cloud computing as an alternative to privately owned IT infrastructure. The model presented is based on the business scenario and the comparison of costs between the two alternatives. The business scenario is defined by the business domain and objectives, the demand behavior and the technical requirements. For example, the business domain defines whether an application will be used at a Business to Business level or Business to Client level, or for internal use. The business goals will point out particular benefits coming from web hosting in the cloud such as short time to market, reduced costs, and software licenses violations. Demand behavior also is an important factor that affects the performance of services and applications in the Web according to Kleims (2009). Demand behavior can be seasonal, temporary or caused by batch processing jobs.

Related studies that discuss the cost of familiar to cloud computing models like grid computing are (Kondol et. al., 2009) and (Optitz et al., 2008). Performance trade- offs and monetary costs of cloud computing compared to desktop grids are

analyzed in (Kondol et. al., 2009). The above comparison involves two relevant architectural platforms, cloud computing and volunteer computing, that present similar principles. Performance comparison is quantified in terms of execution, platform construction, application deployment and completion times. Cost comparison is performed in terms of technical requirements such as project resource usage. The costs of relevant aspects of cloud computing such as grid computing is addressed also in (Optitz et al., 2008). The study analyzes different types of costs and determines the total costs of a resource provider. Relevant cost for resource providers include hardware, business premises, software, personnel and data communication expenses.

Practitioners on the other hand seem to be bigot supporters of utility computing. Miller (2009) states that cloud computing is a type of web-based computing that allows easy and constant access to applications and data from all over the world through an internet connection and facilitates group collaboration. Though he mentions that cloud computing is not suitable for any case, stressing the advantages and disadvantages of cloud computing. Regarding costs he refers that cloud computing reduces hardware and software costs and increases the productivity of the employees as they have access to their files and applications from home as well. Among the disadvantages of cloud computing related to costs Miller (2009) mentions that cloud computing requires fast and instant internet connections. Also data confidentiality in the cloud is a subject under examination that may cause economic loss (McGowan, 2009). Knight (2009) argues that the dilemma between cloud computing and on-premise development is wrong and should be substituted by the question of which is the right combination of cloud and premise based assets. The combination of the two approaches can indeed exploit the best of both worlds.

CHOOSE THE RIGHT DEPLOYMENT MODEL

In this Section our goal is to clarify which services are offered by cloud computing and how they are related to on-premise software and system costs. We record and analyze thoroughly all relevant costs related to cloud deployment and in-house development and finally suggest a three step decision model that will support the decision of migrating or not to the clouds.

Cloud Utilities

The main purpose of Cloud Computing is to provide a platform to develop, test, deploy and maintain Web-scale applications and services. A formal definition of cloud computing is not found in literature but most resources refer to this term for anything that involves the delivery of hosted services over the Internet. These services are broadly divided into three categories (Dikaiakos et al., 2009), (Lenk et al., 2009): Software-as-a-Service (SaaS), Platform-as-a-Service (PaaS) and Infrastructure-as-a-Service (IaaS). Figure 1 depicts the services offered by the cloud.

A. Software as a Service

Software as a Service is a software distribution and usage model that is available via a network to the customers. Both horizontal and vertical market software are offered by SaaS. Typical examples of horizontal SaaS are subscription management software, mail servers, search engines and office suites. Examples of vertical SaaS are more specialized software such as Accounting software, Management Information systems and Customer Relationship Management systems.

SaaS software is leased through Service Level Agreements (SLAs). An SLA (SLA definition, 2010) is a contractual service commitment. An SLA is a document that describes the minimum performance criteria a provider promises to meet while delivering a service. It typically also sets out the remedial action and any penalties that will take effect if performance falls below the promised standard. It is an essential component of the legal contract between a service consumer and the provider. SaaS investment is typically limited to the subscription fee. This pricing model provides a predictable investment that follows a pay per usage billing scheme. Usually costs are calculated considering user licenses, customizations costs and end user support and training costs

Figure 1. Cloud services

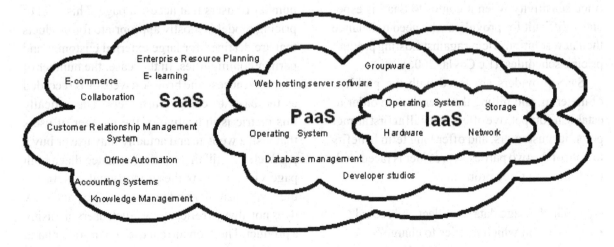

(CRM Landmark, 2009). The last three types of cost refer mostly to software for vertical needs. All these costs are determined in SLAs that define the pay-on-demand rates.

Defining the billing model of SaaS is a challenging task for potential customers, providers and Independent Software Vendors. Many Independent Software Vendors (ISVs) have developed their SaaS solutions offered in parallel with the corresponding commercial products. Among the challenges ISVs are confronted is the restructuring of pricing models. In order to establish attractive pay- as- you go subscription fees, the understanding of the differences in cost between software products and services is required. These differences need also to be clearly presented to candidate customers.

Major SaaS providers bid very low prices hoping that perpetual licensing will lead to upfront earnings. SaaS providers usually provide scalable types of licensing based on the number of users or on the number of applications accessible to the user. One pricing model may not be appropriate for all types of applications and software services. For example, eCommerce or supply-chain SaaS solutions could be priced based on the number of transactions or volume of data transmitted. Customer relationship management (CRM) or Salesforce Automation (SFA) solutions can be priced based on the number of accounts, prospects, or bookings they support. Determining customers' price-sensitivity when it comes to SaaS is especially difficult for providers who need to balance their new solution pricing against existing product pricing schedules. (Le Cayla, 2006).

SaaS providers are faced with the problem of metering and billing their services in order to establish competitive offers that will at first attract potential customers, and offer long term benefits to both of the two parties. A provider is faced with the following three problems:

- Which usage data to collect and record?
- Based on which metrics to charge?

- Should process and ratings be flexible per customer? Per contract?

Answering the first question we can say that the relevant data collected so far by providers generally falls into three categories, resource data, transactional data and workflow data.

Resource data most of the times describe the customers usage of the premises offered by the provider. Relevant data that can be recorded is the number of users, or connections to the application that can be 'per use' or per 'concurrent use'. The number of registered users of a product per month is an increasingly popular method of pricing SaaS. SalesForce, (2010) is a major SaaS provider that use among others this model for most of its offerings. This billing model has different prices for each level usage based on the number of users. The payment per user is appropriate for software that serves internal needs of the customers company. In that case the customer needs to isolate and record the number of employees that will actually utilize the SaaS software. The number of registered users is a good indicator of the value that a group derives from the product (Rothbart, 2009). Risks deriving from this method involve possible user's abandonment. The customer company needs to control, manage and remove users that do not regularly use the software.

Another way of pricing resource usage is based on per- user page view fees counted as the number of users that access a page. This kind of pricing model is mostly appropriate for products that are destined for large external customer and partner communities. In that case, the number of users that access and browse a website is recorded as the basis to charge customers. Theoretically this metric is indicative of the number of users that visit a website and actually may use or buy a product, but still there is no guarantee that a high page view presents the proportional benefits to the SaaS customer and its clients. The page view does not always reflect how much users are using a product. The "concurrent use" on the other hand can be an alternative metric in the cases of SaaS products that require concurrent user intensive functions. Examples of such SaaS products may be teleconferencing applications, discussion forums, calendars, or even information portals. Concurrent user is an industry standard term that refers to the total number of people (as measured by network connections), that are connected to a server or online service at any one point in time. The term "concurrent user" is analogous to "port" or "line" with respect to a telephone branch exchange (Nefsis, 2010). In general, the pricing based on number of users or user licences may be combined with additional fees for extra bandwidth and storage.

Transactional data refer to the interaction between a subscribed customer and the SaaS provider and usually are one –time fees based on the needs of the customer. For example, SaaS Optics (2010) define several types of transaction items within the subscription life cycle. In essence, these transaction items are the events that can occur with regard to a term agreement over time. Such transactions may involve *New Subscription, Upgrade, Downgrade, Adjustment, Renewal, Cancellation.* New Subscription service is a one time fee that can break down to license and professional services fees. License costs are related to the initial subscription to the SaaS service. Professional services fees may include consultancy, training, user support and several other customer needs that may occur. Upgrade, Downgrade or Adjustment are three services that can be offered to a single customer subscription that allow the customization of the application to the customers needs. The fees charged are based on the level, the costs and the time required for the incorporated changes. Renewal charges include the fees related to the continuation of the services to the customer while cancellation fees include penalties to the customer in case of cancelling the contract based on the time period of the notification.

Workflow data may involve usage metrics involving process oriented activities. Such metrics are relative to the specific SaaS application and are forced by the business goals. For example an E-commerce system may count the number of sales or invoices send, an Advertising & Marketing system may count the number of emails or forms received. The usage of a document management system is reflected by the number of documents download or uploaded. Workflow metrics are defined by the procedures and user tasks incorporated in the SaaS software and are indicators of the level of successful usage of a system. A high level of workflow metrics is associated with relevant economic benefits of the SaaS customer.

We mentioned possible data and metrics that can be used to bill SaaS based on the type of the application and the customer's needs. As with any variation of products available to market there should be differences in pricing taking into consideration the basic marketing mix: the four P's of product, price, promotion, and place (Lovelock, 2007). Depending on the potential customer the SaaS services might be different, the price might be different, the hosted place and the product might be different. Table 1 summarises the metrics that are currently used by SaaS providers to charge their services. Still the pricing models of SaaS are in their infancy at a lot of research is devoted to capturing the correct price model that will better reflect the usage and value of SaaS.

B. Platform as a Service

Platform as a Service (PaaS) includes the delivery of operating systems and associated desktop services over the Internet without download or installation. PaaS is an outgrowth of Software as a Service targeted to middleware distribution. Platform as a service is a development platform hosted to the cloud and accessed via a network. The functionality that PaaS offers involves at least the following: operating systems, developer

Table 1. SaaS billing metrics

Type of Metric	Metric	Explanation	Unit of measurement	Charges and current SaaS vendors
Resource metrics				
	Number of users	Internal enterprise employees	# of licences	Based on ranges of # licences www.salesforce.com www.salesboom.com
	Pay per user	External community users, potential customers	# of page views per month	Based on usage per search http://www.ppcsaas.com/ (for a Search Engine SaaS is the number of searches per month)
	Pay per concurrent user	Systems of high concurrence	# of concurrent users per month	Teleconferecing and knowledge sharing systems http://www.nefsis.com
	Number of user + additional bandwidth and storage	Low prices for small number of users because of additional bandwidth and storage charging	# of users + infrastructure charges	Based on ranges of # number of users + ranges of infrastructure usage
Trasactional metrics				
	New Subscription	Licence fees + Professional services	Standard subscription fee, training costs, consultancy costs, user support costs	Subjective monetary costs by SaaS provider
	Upgrade	Cost of upgrading current application	Based on the level of upgrade. (time, infrastructure, labour costs are counted)	Subjective monetary costs by SaaS provider
	Downgrade	Cost of downgrading current application	Based on the level of degrade	Subjective monetary costs by SaaS provider
	Adjustment	Cost of adjustment of current application	Based on the level of adjustment	Subjective monetary costs by SaaS provider
	Renewal	Cost of renewing SaaS agreement	Subjective monetary costs by SaaS provider	Subjective monetary costs by SaaS provider
	Cancellation	Penalty costs of cancelling a SaaS SLA		
Workflow metrics				
	Succesful business scenarios that show the benefit of the customer using a SaaS	Invoices (proofs of sales), Emails (proof of marketing and advertisment)	# business metric/ month	Measure business successful usage http://www.verticalresponse.com/ http://www.zoho.com/invoice/index.html

studios that include all necessary tools to build a web application, seamless deployment to hosted runtime environment and management and monitoring tools. PaaS offers the potential for general developers to build web applications without having any tools installed in their own space. PaaS applications are hosted to infrastructure offered as a service by cloud computing providers.

Therefore, the costs of PaaS are connected to the costs of Infrastructure as a Service and will be analytically addressed in the next section.

C. Infrastructure as a Service

Infrastructure as a Service is a provision model in which the customer outsources the equipment used to support operations, including storage, hardware, servers and networking components. In that case the provider is the owner of the hardware equipment and all relevant resources and expenses related to housing, constant operation and maintenance are his own responsibility. The client typically pays on a per-use basis. Infrastructure as a Service involves the physical storage space and processing capabilities that enable the use of SaaS and PaaS if wanted otherwise these services are used autonomously by the customer. Virtualization enables IaaS providers to offer almost unlimited instances of servers to customers and make cost-effective use of the hosting hardware.

IaaS can be exploited by enterprises that chase quick time to market. The customer enterprise can accelerate the development time required to build new versions of applications or environments without having to worry about ordering, waiting, paying and configuring new hardware equipment. The most popular use of IaaS is website hosting. Website hosting is a convenient way for enterprises to shift the relevant IT resources away from an internal infrastructure whose primary purpose is to run the business, not the website. In this case the availability and the monitoring of the website are in the concerns of the IaaS provider.

IaaS offers relatively simple infrastructure as it includes basic hardware and operating services. Customers select software servers with operating systems that match their needs and then they load up their own libraries, applications and data and finally configure them themselves. This process requires that the in-house personnel possess considerable IT skills. In the case that the customer enterprise personnel is relatively inexperienced IaaS may not be enough to cover the needs of the customer and can be combined with PaaS. IaaS is then enriched with platform services such as database management systems, web hosting server software, batch processing software and application development environments that are installed in the relevant infrastructure. PaaS and IaaS costs in that case are interrelated.

IaaS and PaaS are billed based on the services delivered to the customer. The billing model is produced considering the level of usage of hardware, application, storage and networking components. Hardware and application components are usually charged simultaneously. These costs most of the times are calculated as on-demand instances per hour. On-Demand instances refer to the number of servers used. The prices differ according to the operating systems and middleware applications loaded to the offered servers. The payment is then processed based on per use instances that are indicative of the compute capacity. Additional metrics that can be used derive from the technical attributes of the server such as the hard disk size of the server, the cpu and the memory capacity. The usage of the servers may also be charged measured in bandwidth or as a daily percentage usage, along with additional IP generation. Also full back ups of cloud servers may be charged separately. PaaS services that may be included in the prices involve databases, web servers, application development environments and servers and video encoding and streaming software.

Storage services are billed based on the hard disk demands, the data transfer and the requests. Initially the data storage is measured in terabytes committed in the hard disk. The price depends on the level of hard disk usage. Data transfer involves transferring the data into databases. Data transfer may be charged autonomously, or is included in data storage fees or may be for free based on the regions of transfer. Data requests involve operations such as copy, get, put, list and other requests regarding the data. Data requests involve inquiries in the data set.

Networking services involves the possibility of establishing a virtual private cloud (Amazon, VPC) that will be the bridge between a company's existing IT infrastructure and the cloud. A private cloud enables enterprises to connect their existing infrastructure to a set of isolated cloud compute resources via a Virtual Private Network (VPN) connection, and to extend their existing management capabilities such as security services, firewalls, and intrusion detection systems to include their cloud resources. The billing of such services is based on the number of VPN connections per hour and the data transferred.

The metrics used to bill IaaS and PaaS services are presented in Table 2.

Traditional Software and Systems Costs

This Section discusses the costs related to IT infrastructure and software development for an application based on on–premise assets. Companies that possess their own IT department have the dilemma of selecting between in-house

and hosted SaaS solutions will find very useful to predict software development costs, as these costs define all relevant on-going costs such as maintenance, training, upgrades and also costs related to infrastructure.

A. IT Infrastructure Costs

When estimating software development and maintenance costs, IT infrastructure costs should also be accounted. IT costs are non-negligible as usually they stand up to 60% of Total Ownership costs (Gray, 2003), (McRitsie, 2008). Unlike software development estimation, IT estimation is a simpler process as infrastructure and services are more tangible. The cost drivers that influence IT

Table 2. IaaS and PaaS billing metrics

Type of Metric	Metric	Explanation	Charges and current SaaS vendors
Hardware and application metrics			
	No Instances of servers	Number of servers.	The prices are based on the operating system and the software installed on the server. The pricing models depend on the provider and can be calculated based on the usage per hour or per month.
	CPU	Level of CPU usage	The CPU usage may is calculated in hours or cores.
	Bandwidth	Incoming, outgoing bandwidth	The gigabytes transferred from and to the cloud measured in gb/ per unit of time
	RAM	Megabytes, Gigabytes	RAM memory committed measured in MB or GB /per unit of time
Storage metrics			
	Data Storage	Hard disk storage, Terabytes	GB or TB/ per unit of time
	Data transfer	Amount of data transferred in different regions	GB or TB/ per unit of time
	Data requests	Copy, get, put, list	Number of requests per month
Networking services			
	No of VPN connections	Virtual Private Network that will bridge the cloud to private infrastructure	Number of VPN connections per hour
	Monitoring operations	Monitor the cloud computing resources, statistics	A charge based on the number of instances monitored per hour
	IP addresses	Additional public IP adresses	Number of IP addresses generated

costs as mentioned in (McRitsie, 2008), (Optitz, 2008) and (TechAmerica, 2008) can be operational attributes and business premises.

Operational attributes refer to hardware costs, software and system license fees. Hardware costs include new resources acquisition, replacement and maintenance of existing resources. Hardware acquisition costs depend on the infrastructure hardware list (servers) and the end user hardware list (laptops, CPU, printers). Hardware maintenance costs usually are estimated using measures that compute the Mean Time To Failure (MTTF) or Mean Time Between Failures (MTBF). Software, system and database license fees refer to operational software that will be installed in computer systems necessary for the operation of the new application. License costs are defined by the number of inbound and outbound workstations in which the new application will be installed. The number of users usually affects cost mainly through the number of software licenses needed and recruitment and training costs.

Several performance factors are associated with the non-functional requirements of an application that apart from the need to incorporate them in the software also rise the need for business premises. The average transaction rate, the storage needs, security issues and reliability factors require computational power and capacities. Computational power in low level is related to electricity costs. Other business premises that are necessary for IT development and are associated to total costs involve labor rates, outsourcing agreements and operational locations. Labor rates are related to the personnel expenses and training procedures. Outsourcing agreements may include hardware/software leasing or development. Different physical locations of the organization and different access points to the application are associated to rental or leasing expenses. Tables 3 and 4 summarize in-house infrastructure costs.

B. Software Costs

Software development costs are divided into four groups. Product, platform, process and personnel drivers are pointed out by literature (Boehm, 1981) as the most important aspects that determine software costs. Tables 5 to 8 summarize in-house software development cost drivers.

Product attributes related to a software project include descriptive variables and size indicators. The aggregation of variables of both categories is indicative of the complexity of the new projects and the expected difficulties that might rise. Descriptive variables provide information regarding the development type of the project, the application type (IT project type ERP, MIS, CRM or Web applications, etc.) and the user type of the application (professional, amateur, concurrent, ca-

Table 3. Operational Drivers

	Drivers
	Operational Drivers
New resources	Servers, Laptops, PCs
	Peripheral devices, CPU, memory
	WAN/LAN equipment
Maintenance and replacement costs	CPU
	Hard Disk
	Power supply
	CPU Cooler
License fees	Application Software (office applications, mail)
	System Software (Operating system)
	Database (Licences for end users)

Table 4. Business Premises

	Drivers
	Business Premises
Personnel Expenses	Labor Rates
	Training expenses
Electricity costs	Electricity consumption
Physical Locations	Rental expenses

Table 5. Product Drivers

	Drivers	
	Product Drivers	**Metric**
Type of project	Application Type	ERP, Telecommunications, Logistics, etc.
	Business Type	Medical, Public Sector, Transports, Media, etc.
	Development Type	New Development, Re-development, Enhancement
User type	Level of usage	Amateur, Professional, Casual
	Number of Users	1-50, 50-200, 200-1000, >1000
Size	Source Code Lines	Lines of Code (LOC)
	Function Points	Number of Function Points

sual. In order to estimate size attributes an initial assessment of functional requirements is necessary. From functional requirements we can provide a size estimate measured in function points (Albrecht, 1979) or in Lines of Code (Boehm, 1981). Accurate size estimation is a very important task as it is considered to directly affect the amount of effort required to complete a software project.

Non-functional requirements affect the values of platform drivers and can oppose certain con-straints or lead to conflicting interests. Examples of non-functional requirements are software reliability, database size, security issues, performance standards, usability issues and transaction rates. Other drivers that directly affect platform costs are incremented memory needs, increased storage facilities and maintenance of back up files. All the above parameters capture platform complexity of the software under development.

Process attributes refer to all project supplements that may be used and enable the development and delivery of quality software within cost and time limitations. Among these characteristics the use of CASE (Computer Aided Software Engineering), the utilization of methods, techniques and standards are the main aspects that define the level of support and observation of the development procedure. Productive development teams usually follow a well-defined and guided process. Proven best practices, methodologies and the selection of the appropriate lifecycle processes are aspects that a development team should rely on to complete a project. The success of a project, the time and cost required for its completion depends on the existence of a well-managed process.

Software costs are also dependant on personnel team attributes. Typical examples of this group

Table 6. Platform Drivers

Table Head	Drivers	
	Platform Drivers	**Metric**
Technical attributes	Distributed Databases	1-5 Scale that depicts the necessity of the attribute.
	On-line Processing	1-5 Scale
	Data communications	1-5 Scale
	Back-ups	1-5 Scale
	Memory constraints	1-5 Scale
	Use of new or immature technologies	1-5 Scale
Non-functional requirements	Reliability	1-5 Scale
	Performance	1-5 Scale
	Installation Ease	1-5 Scale
	Usability	1-5 Scale
	Security	1-5 Scale

Table 7. Process Drivers

	Drivers	
	Process Drivers	**Metric**
Use of Case Tools	Versioning tools	% of usage
	Analysis & Design Tools	% of usage
	Testing Tools	% of usage
Management Process	Use of lifecycle models	Yes or No
	Managed development Schedule	1-5 Scale
Methodologies	Existance of best practices	1-5 Scale
	Software Reuse	% of the total LOC

Table 8. Personnel Drivers

	Drivers	
	Personnel Drivers	**Metric**
Experience	Analysts cababilities	1-5 Scale
	Programmers experience	1-5 Scale
	Familiarity with the problem domain	1-5 Scale
Cultural issues	Reward mechanism	1-5 Scale
	Collaboration	1-5 Scale
	Cabable leadership	1-5 Scale

of cost drivers are the experience of the team, the analysts' capabilities, the familiarity with the programming language and the application. Recent studies also point out that cultural characteristics also determine software costs. Well structured teams that encourage communication allow knowledge exchange and support reward mechanisms are more productive compared to impersonal teams. The capabilities of the personnel and the motivation of the environment affect directly the productivity of a development team thus the total developments costs.

Estimating Cloud Computing Migration

IT managers are faced with the problem of selecting how and where to develop and deploy their applications. The requirements of an application will determine the choice between cloud computing and development on premises or even a combination of both (Armbrust, 2008). Each of the two different options presents advantages and disadvantages on various fields. The business goals and priorities of the application will determine the level of usage of cloud or premise assets. IT decision making often requires trading between

innovation and time-to-value advantages of cloud computing against performance and compliance advantages of development on-premise. For this reason we propose a three step procedure that will assist in decision making:

A. Assess software and infrastructure development costs.
B. Define quality characteristics.
C. Estimate user demand.

The issue of deciding whether to develop and deploy the applications in the cloud was also addressed in (Klems et al., 2009), but our three-step process is somewhat more generic as it includes detailed recording of relevant parameters.

A. Assess Software and Infrastructure Development Costs

This procedure involves costs assessment of the two alternative solutions. The previous sections will be useful to keep in mind all the relevant aspects of the problem. A five year total cost of ownership projection will be useful to determine long-term benefits of each solution.

We will discuss the deployment of Customer Relationship Management Systems; a common business application that is becoming popular on the cloud. We will focus on software development costs of such an application.

Customer Relationship Management (CRM) is an information industry term for methodologies, software, and Internet capabilities that help an enterprise manage customer relationships in an organized and efficient manner (Laudon & Laudon, 2009). CRM functionality may include product plans and offerings, customer notifications, design of special offers, e.t.c.

Development and cost data for CRM applications built in-house can be found in the International Standards and Benchmarking Group (ISBSG, 2010) data base. Based on data coming from ISBSG, CRM systems on the average require 1867 total effort hours for completion. Keeping in mind average US salaries (4141 US$), 1867 effort hours correspond to 233 workdays, 11,65 months and 48242$. Analyzing the projects that include development data we can see that 56% of the projects require development teams larger than 9 people. All CRM projects developed in-house followed a particular methodology while only 33% of projects that presented values for that field were supported by the use of CASE tools. Cost and development data for CRM applications developed in-house are presented in tables 9 and 10.

On the other hand CRM cloud applications with Zoho (Zoho, 2010) and Salesforce (Salesforce, 2010) leading providers charge based on the number of users and the number of applica-

tions accessed. The prices range from 12$ per month to 75$ per month, per user. Considering in that case 5 potential users that will use a sublist of the product features charged 50$ per month the annual costs are calculated to be 3000$.

In both cases analyzed previously costs associated to software development and usage are recorded. In order to calculate infrastructure, maintenance and deployment costs we consider certain assumptions made by the analysis presented in (Yankee, 2005). In Table 11 we present a five year cost analysis including infrastructure and software costs for in-house and hosted to the cloud solution for a CRM application; the costs presented are only indicative and they may vary from case to case.

We make the following assumptions (These assumptions and costs cannot be generalized in all possible deployment models but still provide an initial support to enterprises that want to calculate relevant costs):

- The number of end users of the CRM application is 10. This number was selected in order to simulate real world situation for a Small Medium Enterprise (SME). Keeping in mind that each employee serves from 50 to 100 clients we consider that the guest list of a SME is 500-1000 people.

- The functionalities of the CRM support Sales, Marketing and Relationship management.

Table 10. Development data statistics for on-premise CRM applications

Development data	Values and percentages
Development Team Size	> 9 people. (56%)
Use of CASE tools	Yes (33%)
Programming Languages	C, C#, Cobol, Visual basic and Oracle (65%)
Platform	PCs (39%), clients and servers (15%).
Database	Oracle (41,1%.

Table 9. Cost data statistics for on-premise CRM applications

Cost data	Average value
Effort (hours)	1867 h.
Size (function points)	181.5 fp
Cost (US $)	48242 $

- The price per user for the hosted solution is calculated based on the Professional support offer of Salesforce 65$ per user per month. (The prices of other providers present slight differences that do not distort the results).
- The number of in-house servers is considered to be three; data base server, application server and web server. Three- tier architecture is a popular model adopted by many similar applications, therefore selected in this study. In all of the servers the appropriate middleware is installed and the relevant costs should be considered. Considering that the middleware can be either open source software or commercial solutions, the total infrastructure costs can range from 9000$ (3000$ per server ma-

chine considering no costs for middleware) to 70000$ when using commercial middleware (for example Oracle database server (47500$) and Windows (400$) or other commercial products). An average price considered in the analysis is 30000$.

- Application support and maintenance costs in an on premise solution are calculated as 18% of the development costs. Professional Services are calculated as 75% of the development costs. For the next four years they are calculated as 25% of the development costs. Customization and integration costs for the first year are calculated as 75% of the development costs and for the next four years they are calculated as 10% of the development costs. The percentages used in

Table 11. 5 year cost analysis of hosted and on premise software deployment

	Cost Category	Cost driver	Year 1	Year 2	Year 3	Year 4	Year 5
Hosted	Infrastructure Costs		included	included	included	included	included
	Software Costs	Number of Users	7800$	7800$	7800$	7800$	7800$
		Professional Services	5850$	1950$	1950$	1950$	1950$
		Customization	5850$	780$	780$	780$	780$
TOTALS			19500$	10530$	10530$	10530$	10530$
On premise	Infrastructure costs	Hardware + middleware	30000$	1500$	1500$	1500$	1500$
		Network Infrastructure (including internet)	19000$	19000$	19000$	19000$	19000$
		Power, Electricity	12000$	12000$	12000$	12000$	12000$
		Floor Space	12000$	12000$	12000$	12000$	12000$
	Software Costs	Development costs	48242$	0	0	0	0 $
		Application support and maintenance	8683$	8683$	8683$	8683$	8683$
		Customization and Integration	36182$	4824$	4824$	4824$	4824$
		User Training	1500$	750$	750$	750$	750$
TOTALS			167607$	58757$	58757$	58757$	58757$
TCO Hosted							61620$
Tco On premise							402635$

the calculations are based on the analysis of the Yankee Group(Yankee, 2006).

- Hardware costs for the second to the fifth year are calculated as 5% of the costs of the first year.
- Training costs varies based on the number of users.

B. Define Quality Characteristics

Quality characteristics are closely associated to business goals and most of the times are defined as non-functional requirements. An initial assessment involves the definition of non functional requirements and their priority. Table 12 summarizes quality attributes and which of the two solutions best incorporates them.

Among the quality characteristics that are incorporated in cloud computing is improved performance. Computers in a cloud computing system boot and run faster because they have fewer programs and processes loaded into memory (Miller, 2009). Compatibility is another attribute that is supported by cloud computing. Documents created in a Web application can be read and processed without any special installation on the users PCs. Increased data reliability is also ensured as cloud is considered the ultimate backup. Interoperability and availability are two other quality characteristics of cloud computing. Interoperability and availability allow user to have access to the system any time, anywhere by any computer or network.

On premise software advantages involve data accessibility, ownership and safety. The biggest advantage of on-premise software is that businesses have complete control over their critical business data (MacGowan, 2006). This is also a

Table 12. Quality characteristics

Quality Attribute	Cloud vs On premise?
Reliability	Reliability is an indicator of the ability of system to perform its required functions. Cloud-based providers are usually better equipped to recover from a failure. Most providers guarantee their uptime and have built-in continuity systems to ensure continuity of the operations.
Availability	Cloud solutions offer instant and universal access to the data and the applications of the customer thorough an internet connection. On the other hand cloud computing is impossible if you can't connect to the Internet or you have low connection speed.
Flexibility & Customization	Customization and integration are considered to be better addressed in on premise solutions. With the software running on its premises, a business retains complete control over its entire hardware and software environment, including the flexibility to select the peripherals and third-party applications that best complement and support its processes (McGowan, 2006).
Data confidentiality	The biggest advantage of on-premise software is that businesses have complete control over their critical business data. This data is physically located on a business's premises and does not require the transmission and storage of data off-site. Owning the hardware and supporting systems provides a business with maximum control.
Back ups	Cloud-based solutions are generally considered to ensure a more secure backup of data and data recovery as data stored in the cloud are replicated across multiple machines. Still there are arguments in case of data loss in cloud you have no physical or local backup.
Interoperability	The ultimate cloud computing advantage is device independence (McGowan,). Existing applications and documents are visible even if local systems and devices alter.
Maintenance and upgrades	Maintenance and upgrade is an intensive and time consuming task especially for web applications where servers, storage, software, backup systems and network are in constant operation. In case of hosted applications this burden is transferred to the provider and usually agreed upon SLAs.
Usability	McGowan states that many web-based applications do not provide the same functionality and features compared to their desktop-based brethren. Users that are tight with existing desktop applications might find interesting the learning curve of the web based corresponding applications.

main benefit for data intensive applications that should support high volumes of transactions. Other advantage of the on-premise software is that it allows integration with existing software/hardware resources. Customization is one more quality characteristic of in–premise software.

CRM systems usually store, handle and process sensitive private data of customers that should not in any case leak to competitors. Therefore safety is an important non functional requirement. Other important features involve the back-up file storage, and online any-time, any where immediate access to the system. Usability is another important feature for such an application. A customer should be able to navigate through different functionalities and access the information he needs easily and quickly. Prioritizing non functional requirements is an indicator that will help managers take a decision regarding the development and deployment of a system.

C. Estimate User Demand

Estimating the expected demand of the application is also very important in order to assess costs. Expected demand is associated with the number of users. The number of users affects licensing costs and hardware costs. Licensing costs are considered for users that access the applications and make changes of any kind. On the other hand, for hardware as the number of users increases, the hardware must also be improved or performance becomes unacceptable. Centralized database models present reasonable costs for 5-10 users, but present exponential growth of costs as the number of users increases. Distributed models are a solution to such problems shifting costs to PCs. Administration fees are also affected by the number of users as normally one administrator is considered every 5-10 users.

While estimating the number of users according to (Klems et al., 2009), one should keep in mind four types of demand.

- Expected Demand: Seasonal demand. This type of demand is associated with consumers' interest in particular products only during a specific period within the calendar year. For example, Christmas ornaments and snow ski equipment are subject to seasonal demand.
- Expected demand: Temporary effect. Expected temporary demand may be caused due to offers, or low prices, or clearance period.
- Expected Demand: Batch processing. Batch processing demands involve computational intensive tasks that demand execution of a series of programs. Usually such batch processing procedures may be cost, time consuming or even unfeasible tasks when in house resources are considered.
- Unexpected Demand: Temporal Effect. The unexpected demand as mentioned by Klems et al, (2009) is similar to Expected temporary effect but the demand behavior cannot be predicted at all or only in short time in advance.

For the CRM system seasonal demand refers to sales and retails periods that usually present increased demand volume. In that case the number of in-house users may increase as the sales are increased. Temporary effect may refer to clearance period or possible relocation that are seldom events that may cause extra demands. Expected demands: Batch processing may involve for the CRM a period that massive advertisements are shifted. Finally, unexpected demands for the CRM may occur when a new product of the company becomes very popular unexpectedly.

FUTURE WORK

As future work we aim to evaluate the proposed model on real world applications deployment and compare the three alternatives (cloud, on–premise, a combination of the two) based on data coming from both in-house development and cloud hosting. In particular for the hybrid of the two worlds, we plan to elaborate on the cases where it is more profitable and derive appropriate "rules-of-thumb", since we argue that this model will be the one that will finally dominate the market.

In general, for companies it will be a big mind change to give up the convenience and comfort of local deployment, control, and operation to cloud computing vendors but the advantages of cost reduction, scalability, speed to market and high powered computing will allow them to return to their core business and differentiate themselves from their competitors. For the cloud computing vendor the key success factors will be to get the variable pricing right, ensure sustainability of the services provided, coordinate a smooth evolution of the services and that the quality of the services needs to be of a high value. Based on these, we understand that a broad horizon of research topics open up as described in the June 2009 issue of ACM SIGACT News magazine.

CONCLUSION

In this chapter we have taken a first step towards identifying all relevant costs of cloud computing and on-premises infrastructure and software. We proposed a three step decision model for evaluating the two alternatives. Software development and infrastructure costs, desired quality characteristics of the application and expected number of users are the main aspects that a software manager has to consider. The final choice may be the deployment of an application on the cloud, on business premises or by adopting a combination of the two aforementioned alternatives.

A thorough analysis of the costs of cloud computing solutions has been performed. All costs, metrics and measurements related to Software as a Service, Platform as a Service and Infrastructure as a Service has been recorded in order to help

potential providers and ISVs bill and provision their services and potential customers calculate their expenses. SaaS costs do not only include the subscription fee but the customization and other professional services fees as well. The subscription fee can be charged based on the number of users, on number of page views or based on metrics coming from business oriented goals. PaaS and IaaS costs are related to the infrastructure and middleware utilized. The level of data storage and transfer, networking, server and middleware utilization are some of the measurements used by providers to charge a customer.

On premise costs on the other hand are split into software development costs and infrastructure costs. Software development costs are related to product drivers, such as the type of the application, the process maturity, ability of the development team to follow standard procedures, platform drivers, related to non functional requirements of the applications and personnel capabilities drivers. Companies possessing their own IT department and have the dilemma of selecting between in-house and hosted SaaS solutions will find very useful to predict software development costs, as these costs define all relevant on-going costs such as maintenance, training, upgrades and also costs related to infrastructure. Infrastructure costs are split into operational costs such as hardware, maintenance and networking and business premises costs such as personnel, physical locations and electricity costs. Infrastructure costs are tangible assets and can be estimated more accurately compared to software costs.

The choice of selecting between in house development and cloud deployment is a dilemma that nowadays concerns an increasing number of companies. Cloud computing is a term covering a wide range of online services and seems an attractive proposition for small medium companies that seek to exploit IT services at lower costs, instant time to market and limited risk. As mentioned the initial investment remains to relatively low levels compared to on premise development, the total cost of ownership is reduced and maintenance burden is shifted to providers. On the other hand on premise supporters argue about security, systems' redundancy, functionality and data privacy as obstacles to cloud computing. Aspects that can point out the way to IT deployment are potential costs, user demand and desired quality attributes. User demand is an indicator of the load of a system and the estimated traffic that greatly affects infrastructure costs. A thorough five year cost analysis will enlighten potential long term cost benefits of both solutions. Desired quality attributes on the other hand and the level these attributes are incorporated into on premise and on cloud solutions can also affect the final decision.

Today, most organizations tend to adopt exclusively one of the two solutions limiting the possibilities that a combined solution can offer. An hybrid approach can provide the best of both worlds by allowing the customer organizations to maximize the benefits of both a hosted delivery model and those of the on-premise model. Such a model may exploit just IaaS combined with on premise software applications to avoid infrastructure costs. An alternative is to use SaaS on VPNs to minimize potential data privacy risks. Or even a company can use PaaS service to build each own applications and deploy them using IaaS or private infrastructure. Services offered by the cloud cover a wide variety of IT needs. A potential customer can find the optimal development and deployment solution keeping in mind all relevant aspects of his own specific IT problem and how these are incorporated in the two models.

Closing, as future work we aim to evaluate the proposed model on real world applications deployment and compare the three alternatives (cloud, on–premise, a combination of the two) based on data coming from both in-house development and cloud hosting. In particular for the hybrid of the two worlds, we plan to elaborate on the cases where it is more profitable and derive appropriate "rules-of-thumb", since we argue that this model will be the one that will finally dominate the market.

REFERENCES

Aggarwal, S. (2005). *TCO of on-demand applications is significantly better for SMBs and mid-market enterprises*. Yankees Group report. Retrieved March 10, 2010 from http://www. intente.net/pdfs/ Yankee_On_Demand_vs_On _Premises_TCO_1_.pdf?ID=13165

Albrecht, A. J. (1979). Measuring application development productivity. *Proceedings of the Joint SHARE, GUIDE, and IBM Application Development Symposium*, (pp. 83–92). Monterey, California, October 14–17, IBM Corporation.

Amazon Elastic Cloud. (2010). *Amazon platform as a service*. Retrieved March 10, 2010, from http://aws.amazon.com/ec2/

Armbrust, M., Fox, A., Griffith, R., Joseph, A. D., Katz, R. H., Konwinski, A., et al. (2008, February). *Above the clouds: A Berkeley view of cloud computing*. (Technical Report EECS-2009-28), University of California at Berkeley.

Boehm, B. (1981). *Software engineering economics*. Englewood Cliffs, NJ: Prentice-Hall.

Cloud Computing Congress. (2010). *Cloud computing China*. Retrieved March 10, 2010, from http://www.cloudcomputingchina.org/

Dikaiakos, M. D., Katsaros, D., Mehra, P., Pallis, G., & Vakali, A. (2009). Cloud computing: Distributed Internet computing for IT and scientific research. *IEEE Internet Computing*, *13*(5), 10–13. doi:10.1109/MIC.2009.103

Gray, J. (2003, March). *Distributed computing economics*. (Technical Report MSR-TR-2003-24), Microsoft Research.

International Software Benchmarking Group. (2010). *ISBSG dataset release 10*. Retrieved March 10, 2010, from http://www.isbsg.org

Klems, M., Nemis, J., & Tai, S. (2009). *Do clouds compute? A framework for estimating the value of cloud computing. Lecture Notes in Business Information Processing* (pp. 110–123). Springer-Verlag.

Knight, D. (2009). *Why cloud vs. premise is the wrong question*. Retrieved March 10, 2010, from http://blogs.cisco.com/collaboration /comments/ why_cloud_vs._premise _is_the_wrong_question/

Kondol, D., Bahman, J., Malecot, P., Cappello, F., & Anderson, D. (2009). Cost-benefit analysis of cloud computing versus desktop Grids. *Proceedings of the 18th International Heterogeneity in Computing Workshop*, May, 2009, Rome.

La Cayla. (2006). *A white paper for independent software vendors*. Retrieved March 10 2010, from http://www.opsource.net/

Landmark, C. R. M. (2009). *SaaS total cost of ownership*. Retrieved March 10, 2010, from http:// www.crmlandmark.com/ saasTCO.htm

Laudon, K., & Laudon, J. (2009). *Management Information Systems*. Pearson.

Lenk, A., Klems, M., Nimis, J., Tai, S., & Sandholm, T. (2009). What's inside the cloud? An architectural map of the cloud landscape. *Proceedings of the International Conference on Software Engineering (ICSE) Workshop on Software Engineering Challenges of Cloud Computing (CLOUD)*, (pp. 23-31).

Lovelock, C., & Wirtz, J. (2007). *Services marketing: People, technology, strategy* (6th ed.). New Jersey, USA: Pearson International - Pearson/ Prentice Hall.

MacGowan, G. (2006). Helping small businesses choose between on-demand and on-premise software. Retrieved March 10, 2010, from http:// www.computerworld.com /s/article/9002362/ Helping_small _businesses_choose_between_ On_demand_and_On_ premise_software

McRitchie, K., & Accelar, S. (2008). *A structured framework for estimating IT projects and IT support*. Joint Annual Conference ISPA/SCEA Society of Cost Estimating and Analysis.

Miller, M. (2009). *Cloud computing pros and cons for end users*. Retrieved March 10, 2010, from http://www.informit.com/articles/article. aspx?p=1324280

Nefsis. (2010). *Pricing model*. Retrieved March 10, 2010, from http://www.nefsis.com/Pricing / concurrent-user.html

Optitz, A., Konig, H., & Szamlewska, S. (2008). What does Grid computing cost? *Journal of Grid Computing, 6*(6), 385–397. doi:10.1007/s10723-008-9098-8

Rothboard, J. (2009). *Linking SaaS software pricing to value*. Retrieved March 10, 2010, from http:// www.readwriteweb.com/ enterprise/2009/01/ linking -saas-software-pricing-to-value.php

Saa, S. Optics. (2010). *SaaS optics deep dive*. Retrieved March 10, 2010, from http://www.saa-soptics.com/ saas_operations_operating_model/ saas_metrics_management_deep_dive/saas_metrics_management _deep_dive.html

Salesforce. (2010). *CRM SaaS*. Retrieved March 10, 2010, from http://www.salesforce.com/ plat-form/platform-edition/

SLA definition. (2009). *Definition of service level agreement*. Retrieved March 10 2010, from http:// looselycoupled.com/ glossary/SLA

TechAmerica. (2008). *Chapter 12, software cost estimating*. Retrieved March 10, 2010, http:// www.techamerica.org/

Zoho. (2010). *CRM SaaS*. Retrieved March 10, 2010, http://www.zoho.com/

ADDITIONAL READING

Barroso, L. A., & Holzle, U. (2009). *The Data-center as a Computer: An Introduction to the Design of Warehouse-scale Machines*. Synthesis Lectures on Computer Architecture, Morgan & Claypool Publishers.

Brantner, M., Florescu, D., Graf, D., Kossmann, D., & Kraska, T. (2008). Building a database on S3, *Proceedings of the ACM SIGMOD Conference on Management of Data*, pp. 251-263.

Buyya, R., Yeo, C. S., Venugopal, S., Broberg, J., & Brandic, I. (2009). Cloud computing and emerging IT platforms: Vision, hype, and reality for delivering computing as the 5th utility. *Future Generation Computer Systems*, *25*(6), 599–616. doi:10.1016/j.future.2008.12.001

Cohen, J. (2009). Graph twiddling in a MapReduce world. *IEEE Computational Science & Engineering*, (July/August): 29–41.

Foster, I., Zhao, Y., Raicu, I., & Lu, S. (2008). Cloud Computing and Grid Computing 360-Degree Compared, *Proceedings of the IEEE Grid Computing Environments Workshop (GCE)*.

Geng, L., Fu, D., Zhu, J., & Dasmalchi, G. (2009). Cloud computing: IT as a service. *IT Professional*, *11*(2), 10–13. doi:10.1109/MITP.2009.22

Grossman, R. L. (2009). The case for cloud computing. *IT Professional*, *11*(2), 23–27. doi:10.1109/MITP.2009.40

Kandukuri, B. R., Paturi, V. R., & Rakshit, A. (2009). Cloud security issues, *Proceedings of the IEEE International Conference on Services Computing (SCC)*, pp. 517-520.

Kaufman, L. M. (2009). *Data security in the world of cloud computing, IEEE Security & Privacy* (pp. 61–64). July/August.

Kaufman, L. M. (2009). Cloud computing and the common man, *IEEE Computer*, August, pp. 106-108.

Keahey, K., Tsugana, M., Matsunaga, A., & Fortes, J. A. B. (2009). Sky computing. *IEEE Internet Computing*, *13*(5), 14–22. doi:10.1109/MIC.2009.94

Lasica, J. D. (2009). *Identity in the Age of Cloud Computing: The next-generation Internet's impact on business, governance and social interaction*. The ASPEN Institute.

Lin, J., & Dyer, C. (2010). *Data-Intensive Text Processing with MapReduce*. Synthesis Lectures on Human Language Technologies, Morgan & Claypool Publishers.

Mather, T. Kumaraswamy, S. & Latif, S. (2009). *Cloud Security and Privacy: An Enterprise Perspective on Risks and Compliance*, O'Reilly Media.

Miller, M. (2008), *Cloud Computing: Web-Based Applications That Change the Way You Work and Collaborate Online*, Que, 1st Edition, Ohlman, B. & Eriksson, A. (2009). What networking of information can do for cloud computing, *Proceedings of the 18th IEEE International Workshops on Enabling Technologies: Infrastructures for Collaborative Enterprises*, pp. 78-83

Reese, G. (2009). *Cloud Application Architectures: Building Applications and Infrastructure in the Cloud*, O'Reily Media.

Rhoton, J. (2009). *Cloud Computing Explained: Implementation Handbook for Enterprises*. Recursive Press.

Sotomayor, B., Montero, R. S., Llorente, I. M., & Foster, I. (2009). Virtual infrastructure management in private and hybrid clouds. *IEEE Internet Computing, 13*(5), 14–22. doi:10.1109/MIC.2009.119

Stonebraker, M., Abadi, D., DeWitt, D., Madden, S., Paulson, E., Pavlo, A., & Rasin, A. (2010). MapReduce and parallel DBMSs: Friends or foes? *Communications of the ACM, 53*(1), 64–71. doi:10.1145/1629175.1629197

Storage Networking Industry Association and the Open Grid Forum (2009). *Cloud Storage for Cloud Computing*.

Thomas, D. (2008). Next Generation IT – Computing In the Cloud: Life after Jurassic OO Middleware. *Journal of Object Technology, 7*(1), 27–33. doi:10.5381/jot.2008.7.1.c3

Varia, J. (2008). *Cloud Architectures*, Amazon White Paper.

Voas, J., & Zhang, J. (2009). Cloud Computing: New Wine or Just a New Bottle? *IT Professional, 11*(2), 15–17. doi:10.1109/MITP.2009.23

Zehua Zhang, Z., & Zhang, X. (2009). Realization of open cloud computing federation based on mobile agent [ICIS]. *Proceedings of the IEEE International Conference on Intelligent Computing and Intelligent Systems, 3*, 642–646. doi:10.1109/ICICISYS.2009.5358085

Zhang, L.-J., & Zhou, Q. (2009). CCOA: Cloud computing open architecture, *Proceedings of the IEEE Conference on Web Services (ICWS)*, pp. 607-616.

KEY TERMS AND DEFINITIONS

IaaS: Infrastructure as a Service is a provision model in which the customer outsources the equipment used to support operations, including storage, hardware, servers and networking components.

Infrastructure Costs: Hardware, networking, and physical location costs

PaaS: Platform as a Service (PaaS) includes the delivery of operating systems and associated desktop services over the Internet without download or installation

SaaS: Software as a Service is a software distribution and usage model that is available via a network to the customers.

SLA: Service Level Agreements (SLA) is a contractual service commitment.

Software Development Costs: Development costs that are affected by the process, the product, the platform the personnel

TCO: Total Cost of Ownership, direct and indirect costs and benefits related to the purchase of any IT component

Chapter 11
Cloud as a Computer

Vishnu S. Pendyala
Santa Clara University, USA

JoAnne Holliday
Santa Clara University, USA

ABSTRACT

The evolution of the cloud as a computer is a very significant milestone in this golden era of computing that changed both the technology and the business model of computing. The cloud has the potential to give access to all possible resources on the Internet using minimal hardware in hand, such as a mobile device with Internet access. This chapter explores the various aspects of cloud computing and makes predictions as to the future directions for research in this area. Some of the issues facing the paradigm shift that cloud computing represents are discussed, and possible solutions presented.

INTRODUCTION

Imagine a computer that can grow or shrink exactly according to your needs, however huge or small they may be; one that can take on any form that you like it to take in terms of the Operating System, machine architectures and other needs; one which can be accessed from virtually anywhere there is network access. To top it all, you don't have to buy it – just pay for how much ever you use. Sounds interesting already? Cloud computing offers all this and much more.

Cloud computing essentially shifts capital expenditure to operational expenses much like we pay for utilities such as electricity and water. Quite a few startups in the Silicon Valley have setup their shops in the recent times without any infrastructure costs, benefiting from Cloud Computing, instead. The economies of scale that the cloud model helps to leverage are explained in this chapter. The business model that evolved as a result of the paradigm shift in computing is very appealing.

There are a number of technologies behind the cloud landscape. The cloud on the Internet is a gateway to a number of services such as Infrastructure (IaaS), Software (SaaS), Platform (PaaS),

DOI: 10.4018/978-1-60960-735-7.ch011

Communications (CaaS) and more recently (Lenk et al. 2009), Humans (HuaaS) and Personalization (Guo et al. 2009). The last service, Personalization is very important in the context of mobile users. A classification of the technologies behind the Everything as a Service (XaaS) paradigm helps understand the cloud better. It is interesting to explore the Cloud ecosystem and get insights into the services that Cloud offers, understanding the myriad technical terms used in the cloud parlance. The literature cited at the end of this chapter has abundant discussion on the tools and example of the services offered.

Cloud computing works best assuming that there are no significant constraints on the bandwidth. However, bandwidth is expensive and could be constrained, particularly since the distances could be huge. Therefore, ideally, there may be a need for writing applications that can adopt to bandwidth and other constraints as applicable in that context. Cloud computing often crosses country boundaries, calling for a need to evaluate and adapt to legal frameworks. Trust and privacy become extremely important in such contexts. In this chapter, we talk about these and other difficulties that Cloud Computing brings with it, explaining some of the challenges and discussing any opportunities that they could be translated into.

The changes happening in the web world are also helping the paradigm shift to Cloud Computing. To the user, the original web was read-only. Web 2.0 made it read-write: WWW became World Wide Wall, where anyone could write. Web 3.0 attempts to make it executable as well, making it the ubiquitous computer. Now that this ubiquitous computer is fully functional, what would be the next avatar of the web? How does the cloud landscape change with developments on the web front? This chapter answers these questions by pointing to future directions for research in this area. The authors predict that the ubiquitous computer will take the same route as the Von Neumann machine and improve drastically in performance

and scalability, driven by certain key aspects such as mobility and intelligence.

There is already a discussion on forming virtual cloudlets (Satyanarayanan et al. 2009) to address the issue of response times when using expensive applications on the mobile devices such as augmented reality. This chapter covers these exploratory ideas and present the authors' perspective on them.

BACKGROUND

We have been already using cloud computing whenever we use free e-mail or for that matter do a search on the Internet. Thanks to the levels of transparency that cloud computing provides, the user is unaware of the thousands of clusters working behind the scene for her when an Internet search is done. The same idea of thousands of clusters doing the job transparently is now borrowed into cloud computing. Solving tough problems that involve large data and massive computation has traditionally been a forte of major business houses, such as Google. In fact, most of the Cloud Computing techniques evolved from the technologies used by Google (Chang 2010) and others in this area. This is no longer true with the advent of Cloud Computing. Even startups can enter the fray with minimal investment. The traditional datacenter with thousands of machine clusters typical of the environment in these big companies has transformed into the cloud, open to wider access and use.

In a sense, Cloud Computing takes us back to the days when users "rented" computing time on Mainframes to get their jobs processed. Though there is a distinction between "renting" computing time and "utility computing" that the Cloud represents (Michael et al. 2009), for convenience, we use the term "rent" to mean either. Computing as a utility is not really new. What makes Cloud Computing really interesting now is the all-pervasive Internet and the networking bandwidth that did not exist in the olden days. A cloud can potentially include virtually everything that we can access over the Internet – hardware and software included. That is almost synonymous with infinite computing. Include in the equation, the proliferation of the inexpensive mobile devices that can access the Internet from virtually anywhere in the world, and we have a ubiquitous, infinite capacity cloud as a computer. Some authors (Durkee 2010) consider cloud computing as timesharing reborn. It is indeed true that cloud computing has similar impact as timesharing in the 1980s.

Business Model

Cloud Computing is based on Cost Associativity (Michael et al. 2009), which is the concept of paying the same price for 'N' units of computational power for 1 hour or 1 unit of computational power for 'N' hours. This allows the supply and demand of computing resources to be elastic. Economists will readily recognize what elasticity can do in the market. Price elasticity is a very important economic parameter of a product. The elasticity in Cloud Computing refers to the fact that users can vary their demand of the computing power and the cloud providers oblige their demand accordingly. Statistical multiplexing is used to handle the varying demands from clients, increasing throughput.

This commercially available elasticity of resources, without paying a huge premium is completely new to IT. Like other virtual computing schemes such as virtual memory, the virtualization in the cloud creates an illusion of unlimited computing power to the clients connecting to it. Virtualization can take the form of hardware or software virtualization. Hardware virtualization provides transparency with respect to the backend configuration of machine resources and enables plug-and-play mode of hardware resources. Software virtualization, on the other hand, refers to provisioning of software images of the needed software configuration in terms of Operating Systems and applications. Code can be assembled

and executed on these images. Clients can be rest assured that their capacity needs are automatically met, without budgeting for maximum capacity, as is typically done with datacenters. They can still pay for just what they used.

The greatest advantage of Cloud Computing is that anyone who can afford for operating expenses can jump start into a business by deploying their applications in the cloud, without having to invest in the capital intensive IT equipment. The Cloud Computing business model changes Capital Expense (CapEx) into Operational Expense (OpEx). Imagine businesses having to setup their own power generators to operate, as they used to do in early 1900s. Cloud Computing does the same thing to IT as the Power Utility companies did to electricity.

Cloud Ecosystem and Tools

Cloud Computing, as a technology is not completely new. It can be viewed as a descendant of a host of other technologies like Client-Server Computing, Software As A Service (SaaS), and Virtualization. Though the technologies existed, Cloud Computing is unique in bringing them all together. There are a number of XaaS (X as a Service) terms in the cloud computing paradigm today, but all stake holders agree that Cloud Computing can be broadly divided into 3 layers or service models: SaaS (Software as a Service), PaaS (Platform as a Service), and IaaS (Infrastructure as a Service). IaaS is the layer Saas provides ready-made applications to the end user that are developed and run on PaaS or can use IaaS directly. There are several other XaaS, as listed in the introduction, but we shall eschew them for better clarity, as the authors of (Michael et al. 2009) did.

The whole idea of XaaS is to harness the various resources available in the cloud. These resources can be raw hardware such as processors and storage, software such as development tools, application servers, and databases. Other resources can be applications such as word processors and other office productivity tools. The Cloud ecosystem involves vendors, partners and end-users of the Cloud Computing environment. Cloud partners provide value additions to what the vendors have to offer to the end-users. Some of the tools in each of the XaaS areas are summarized in Table 1. More details about the specific tools and their place in cloud computing can be obtained from sources listed in the additional reading section at the end of the chapter and from (Lenk et al. 2009).

The Cloud Computing ecosystem makes it suitable for use from thin clients such as mobile devices. As indicated in the section titled Future Directions, towards the end of this chapter, Mobility is bound to be a key driving factor for Cloud Computing. A good discussion of cloud comput-

Table 1. Service Models and Sample Tools Offered in Each Layer

SaaS	PaaS	IaaS
Google Docs, WebEx, Sales-force.com	Google App Engine, Microsoft Azure, Django, Coghead (acquired by SAP)	Amazon EC2, GoogleFS, Google BigTable

Figure 1. Cloud Layers

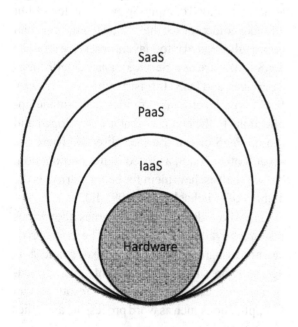

ing for mobile users is given in (Kumar and Lu 2010). Energy savings, according to the analysis alluded to in the article, depend on B (Bandwidth), C (Cycles of Computation), and D (Data to be transmitted). The Cloud Ecosystem helps with C and D, assuming that most of the data is already stored in the cloud and the mobile device only needs to pass a pointer to it for the computation to take place.

VIABILITY OF CLOUD AS A COMPUTER

In this section, we talk about the issues controversies, and problems facing Cloud Computing and discuss possible solutions. The very enabling factors for Cloud Computing can also become limiting factors, as we shall see below.

Economic Viability of the Business Model

It can be easily seen that buying computing power by the hour is more expensive over a long run than owning the same equipment for the same period of time. Otherwise, Cloud Providers will go out of business. What then, is the rationale behind the utility computing that the cloud stands for? Will the rationale suffice for the business model to be viable in the long run? After all, utility computing did exist a few decades ago, when computing power of the mainframes was rented by the hour. Affordable desktops and personal computers changed it all. The trend changed from centralized computing to distributed computing, owing to the drastic and non-uniform advances in technology. For instance, computer networking grew at a much faster pace than other hardware and software technologies until a few years ago. This non-uniform growth of the computing areas caused a shift in business models.

Though the trend is still for technologies to shrink costs, the shrinkage continues to be non-uniform. Hardware costs are reducing faster than computer networking costs. This can be seen as a threat to Cloud Computing, which is based on the premise that buyers cannot afford for the hardware costs but are willing to connect to the rented data-center to have their jobs done and get the results over the network. While the electronic costs are reducing, there is increasing focus on electrical and energy costs. In this day of price pressures and almost free resources on the internet, (Durkee 2010) presents an interesting argument as to why cloud computing can never be free. However, there are ways to meet the price pressures at least partly as the next paragraph indicates.

Solutions and Recommendations

We are optimizing the utilization of resources and using otherwise idle resources in cloud computing. So, there is not doubt that the overall cost benefit analysis will favor cloud computing. Still, energy costs cannot be ignored. Modern technologies are amazingly cheaper than the traditional ones. Following the trend is the data networks versus electrical networks tradeoff. It is much cheaper to transmit data (photons) on fiber optic cables than it is to transmit power currents (electrons) on copper cables. It is therefore cost-effective to locate the computing machinery at places where electric power is cheaper and utilize WANs to harness the computing power remotely. This trend is already in affect with quite a few companies locating their data centers in energy efficient locations. This is a clear direction that cloud computing should take in future as well.

Deployment Issues and Standardization

Cloud Computing is ideally suited for large applications requiring large scale parallel processing. However, virtualization that is a necessary ingredient of Cloud Computing limits the amount of parallelism (Michael et al. 2009) that the pro-

grammer can harness. Bugs cannot be easily tested in local environments, so may have to be tested and fixed in the cloud itself. There does not seem to be enough support or tools for debugging and development or even version control in the cloud. Storage and representation of large amounts of data is a significant problem. Currently, there are only a few providers of the cloud infrastructure, so discovery as a manual process is feasible. However, as the cloud providers grow in number and services offered, discovery will become an issue.

As Richard Stallman of the free software foundation fame feared (Michael et al. 2009), there is a risk of the clients getting captivated in the proprietary systems in the cloud, without much recourse. This fear is not unfounded. Customers participating in cloud computing can lose in several ways (Durkee 2010), if they are not careful. As of now, there do not seem to be many attempts at standardizing the cloud environment for portability. Not all applications yield to the map-reduce framework that is typically used for deploying applications in cloud. There is a need to come-up with other techniques to deploy such applications.

Solutions and Recommendations

Google's Bigtable (Chang 2010) is a popular solution to the problem of data storage and representation. The solution is designed to easily scale to thousands of machines handling petabytes of data. Parallel programming constructs must be made available to the programmers to allow massively parallel computing in the cloud. There is a scope of research in this area. Development and debugging environments should be provisioned in the cloud.

Standardization of the APIs and the cloud environment is key to portability, mobility, and wider usage of the cloud computing paradigm. Eucalyptus (Nurmi et al. 2009) is an attempt towards standardization. But there is a lot that needs to be done in this area. Standardization could also help in discovery of the services. As newer technologies such as semantic technologies evolve, there is hope for using them to aid in the discovery process.

FUTURE RESEARCH DIRECTIONS

There are a number of interesting developments lately in the area of cloud computing, that provide a peek into the future of this exciting technology. There is talk about "Sky Computing" where multiple clouds work as one (Fortes 2010) to harness applications and services spread across different clouds. Users can then mix and match what the various clouds have to offer them and use the Virtual Cloud.

In the authors' view, research drivers for the cloud can be represented by the following research vector tuple:

$$R = (M, I, A, R, T)$$

Where M = mobility, I = intelligence, A = Architecture, R = Robustness and Security, and T = Trust and Privacy

These aspects are further discussed below.

Mobility

Computation is increasingly becoming mobile with the proliferation of the relatively inexpensive and networked mobile devices. Mobile devices will continue to be the only computing devices accessible to populations in developing countries. The global market for mobile devices is bound to grow in leaps and bounds, as more and more echelons of the global society get added to the economic mainstream. The Ubiquitous Computer that the cloud represents, needs to scale to this need very quickly. Any paradigm shift in computing cannot afford to overlook mobility aspect to be successful.

As the demand for computationally intensive applications such as for providing augmented reality, on-the-fly decision making, and learning grows, there will be increasing demand on the cloud to provide real-time, scalable compute resources. Energy critical mobile devices will have to depend on Cloud Computing (Kumar and Lu 2010) for machine cycles. Computation offloading seems to be the way to go, to give mobile devices access to applications that can revolutionize quality of life. Response time is extremely critical for many such applications. There is already research to address this issue. Virtual cloudlets (Satyanarayanan et al. 2009) and Ad hoc cloud computing can be possible solutions to this issue.

Intelligence

There are multiple reasons for building intelligence in the cloud. The very idea of elasticity in the cloud requires Artificial Intelligence techniques to control computation. Machine Learning is needed to train the load balancing modules in the cloud to predict and handle demand elasticity. This is a crucial aspect to the elastic and dynamic nature of cloud computing. Probabilistic graphic models could possibly be applied to abstract load balancing and used for effective prediction. This will also improve resource utilization. Having a quantitative model of the cloud is quite important for the end customer (Durkee 2010), when signing the contracts. Artificial Intelligence techniques are expected to play a role in modeling the cloud behavior.

Applications themselves will need to demonstrate intelligence as the dependence on the web for many high end needs increases. Web 3.0 has already been a step in this direction. Combined with mobility and intelligence, cloud computing provides a promising platform for useful applications (Pendyala and Holliday 2010). Semantic technologies already provide for reasoning and deduction. This area needs to further consolidate and cover increasing needs for intelligence, such as reasoning, inferencing, and machine learning. There are presently significant holes in this area. Knowledge representation to facilitate efficient reasoning is one of them. The current techniques using triple stores seem simplistic for the needs and need to evolve further. Natural Language Processing, speech recognition and computer vision applications can significantly improve the quality of life. There is a need to construct frameworks for easy and rapid development and deployment of these applications in the cloud, just like there are for business processes.

Architecture

Computer Architecture evolved extensively at the rate given by Moore's law. The Ubiquitous Computer architecture that is in the cloud similarly needs to evolve substantially to meet the above demands. The concept of viewing the cloud as a computer is still in its infancy and there does seem to be plenty of scope for improving its architecture, just like there was scope for improving the early Von Neumann machine. Response time is a key driver for developments in Cloud Computing architecture. A radical idea would be to go a few levels down to see if a "machine language" can be evolved for faster computation in the cloud. Another possibility is to see if there are better caching mechanisms to speed-up computation in the cloud. The idea here is that so far, systems in a datacenter have evolved individually. There is scope for viewing the datacenter itself as a single computing resource and exploiting its architecture to make improvements.

Robustness and Security

As the Ubiquitous Computer that the cloud represents grows in power and scale, there will be increasing trends to misuse it or compromise its security. As the criticality of applications deployed in the cloud increases, the need for making the infrastructure robust also increases. The problem of fault tolerance has been sufficiently addressed in the past, so the newer techniques can build-up on them to scale-up to the cloud computing level. Similarly, security assumes paramount importance, as more and more applications and data move to the cloud. Cisco Systems, Inc. has unveiled a Collaboration Cloud architecture (Cisco 2010) where users are provided enterprise-level security and privacy based on a private network that can be used for scalable web-based collaboration. Security and performance issues that are typical of the Internet connectivity can be avoided using this architecture. The current solutions seem to be still inadequate to entirely secure the cloud, particular for smaller players who cannot afford a private network and there is plenty of scope for research here too.

Trust and Privacy

Trust is a crucial aspect to the success of Cloud Computing. Customers have to rely heavily on the cloud providers for the safety and integrity of their data and applications. As can be seen from (Durkee 2010), there are ways in which trust can be misused. This issue has to be probed further and solutions, more far reaching than what is described in (Durkee 2010) need to be arrived at. Related issue is privacy. As cloud computing potentially crosses international borders, privacy becomes a paramount issue. There is scope for techno-legal research in this area and the future cannot ignore this aspect.

CONCLUSION

In this chapter, we provided enough introduction and pointers to the area of cloud computing. There is plenty of jargon, hype, and reality buzzing around in the cloud computing arena. We tried to clarify some of the confusion and present a concrete picture of cloud computing aspects. A google search for "why cloud computing will fail" results in 51,400 hits. So, the threat to cloud computing cannot be ignored. We attempted to discuss the viability of cloud computing itself and some solutions and recommendations. There are several future directions that cloud computing can take. We provided a description of key aspects of cloud computing that the future will be focused on.

REFERENCES

Chang, F., Dean, J., Ghemawat, S., Hsieh, W. C., Wallach, D. A., & Burrows, M. ... Gruber, R. E. (2006). Bigtable: A distributed storage system for structured data. In *Proceedings of the 7th USENIX Symposium on Operating Systems Design and Implementation.* Seattle, WA: USENIX Association.

Cisco Systems, Inc. (2010). *Cisco collaboration cloud.* Retrieved September 26, 2010 from http://www.cisco.com/en/US/prod/ps10352/collaboration_cloud.html

Department of Energy, US Government. (2010). *Report to congress on server and data center energy efficiency.* Retrieved April 25, 2010, from http://www1.eere.energy.gov/ femp/pdfs/ epa_dc_report_congress.pdf

Durkee, D. (2010). Why cloud computing will never be free. *Communications of the ACM, 53*(5), 62–69. doi:10.1145/1735223.1735242

Fortes, J. A. B. (2010). Sky computing: When multiple clouds become one. *Cluster, Cloud and Grid Computing Conference (CCGrid)* (pp. 4, 17-20). IEEE Computer Society.

Guo, H., Chen, J., Wu, W., & Wang, W. (2009). Personalization as a service: The architecture and a case study. In *Proceedings of the First International Workshop on Cloud Data Management* (pp. 1-8). Hong Kong, China: ACM.

Kumar, K., & Lu, Y. (2010). Cloud computing for mobile users: Can offloading computation save energy? *IEEE Computer, 43*(4), 51–56.

Lenk, A., Klems, M., Nimis, J., Tai, S., & Sandholm, T. (2009). What's inside the cloud? An architectural map of the cloud landscape. In *Proceedings of the 2009 ICSE Workshop on Software Engineering Challenges of Cloud Computing* (pp. 23-31). Washington, DC: IEEE Computer Society.

Michael, A., et al. (2009). *Above the clouds: A Berkeley view of cloud computing.* (Technical Report No. UCB/EECS-2009-28). Retrieved on April 25, 2010, from http://www.eecs.berkeley.edu/ Pubs/TechRpts/2009/ EECS-2009-28.html

Nurmi, D., Wolski, R., Grzegorczyk, C., Obertelli, G., Soman, S., Youseff, L., & Zagorodnov, D. (2009). The Eucalyptus open-source cloud-computing system. In Cappello, F., Wang, C.-L., & Buyya, R. (Eds.), *CCGRID. IEEE Computer Society* (pp. 124–131).

Pendyala, V., & Shim, S. (2009). Web as the ubiquitous computer. *IEEE Computer, 42*(9), 90–92.

Pendyala, V. S., & Holliday, J. (2010). Performing intelligent mobile searches in the cloud using semantic technologies. In *Granular Computing GrC* (pp. 381–386). IEEE Computer Society.

Satyanarayanan, M., Bahl, P., Cáceres, R., & Davies, N. (2009). The case for VM-based cloudlets in mobile computing. *IEEE Pervasive Computing / IEEE Computer Society [and] IEEE Communications Society, 8*(4), 14–23. doi:10.1109/MPRV.2009.82

ADDITIONAL READING

AjayKumar. S., Nachiappan, C., Periyakaruppan, K., Boominathan, P. (2009) "Enhancing portable environment using cloud and grid," pp.728-732, 2009 *International Conference on Signal Processing Systems.*

Das, A., Reddy, R. Y., Wang, L., & Reddy, S. (2009). Information intelligence in Cloud Computing: how can Vijjana, a collaborative, self-organizing, domain centric knowledge network model help. *In Proceedings of the 5th Annual Workshop on Cyber Security and information intelligence Research: Cyber Security and information intelligence Challenges and Strategies.* Oak Ridge, Tennessee: ACM.

Kaufman, L. M. (2009). Data security in world of cloud computing. *IEEE Security and Privacy, 7*(4), 61–64. doi:10.1109/MSP.2009.87

Li, X., Li, Y., Liu, T., Qiu, J., & Wang, F. (2009). The method and tool of cost analysis for cloud computing, *In Proceedings of IEEE International Conference on Cloud Computing,* pp.93-100.

Lodi, G., Querzoni, L., Baldoni, R., Marchetti, M., Colajanni, M., Bortnikov, V., et al. (2009). Defending financial infrastructures through early warning systems: the intelligence cloud approach. *In Proceedings of the 5th Annual Workshop on Cyber Security and information intelligence Research: Cyber Security and information intelligence Challenges and Strategies.* Oak Ridge, Tennessee: ACM.

Mukherjee, K., & Sahoo, G. (2009). Mathematical model of cloud computing framework using fuzzy bee colony optimization technique, *In Proceedings of International Conference on Advances in Computing, Control, & Telecommunication Technologie.* pp.664-668.

Napper, J., & Bientinesi, P. (2009). Can cloud computing reach the top 500? *In Proceedings of the Combined Workshops on Unconventional High Performance Computing Workshop Plus Memory Access Workshop (*pp 17-20). Ischia, Italy: ACM.

Pallis, G. (2010). Cloud Computing: The new frontier of Internet computing. *Internet Computing, IEEE, 14*(5), 70–73. doi:10.1109/MIC.2010.113

Pearson, S. (2009). Taking account of privacy when designing Cloud Computing services. *pp* 44-52. *In Proceedings of ICSE Workshop on Software Engineering Challenges of Cloud Computing.* Washington, DC: IEEE Computer Society.

Rimal, B. P., Choi, E., & Lumb, I. (2009). "A taxonomy and survey of cloud computing systems," pp.44-51, *In Proceedings of Fifth International Joint Conference on INC, IMS and IDC.*

Sukhyun, S., Ryu, K. D., & Da Silva, D. (2009). Blue eyes: Scalable and reliable system management for cloud computing, *In Proceedings of IEEE International Symposium on Parallel & Distributed Processing,* pp.1-8.

US Government. (2010). Resources on energy efficiency in datacenters. Retrieved April 25, 2010 from http://search.nrel.gov/ query.html?qt=datacenter

Chapter 12
Principles, Methodology and Tools for Engineering Cloud Computing Systems

Luis M. Vaquero
Telefónica Investigación y Desarrollo, Spain

Clovis Chapman
University College London, UK

Luis Rodero-Merino
INRIA, France

Maik Lindner
SAP Research, UK

Juan Cáceres
Telefónica Investigación y Desarrollo, Spain

Fermín Galán
Telefónica Investigación y Desarrollo, Spain

ABSTRACT

Cloud computing has emerged as a paradigm to provide every networked resource as a service. The Cloud has also introduced a new way to control cloud services (mainly due to the illusion of infinite resources and its on-demand and pay-per-use nature). Here, we present this lifecycle and highlight recent research initiatives that serve as a support for appropriately engineering Cloud systems during the different stages of its lifecycle.

1. INTRODUCTION: CLOUD SYSTEM PRINCIPLES AND IMPLICATIONS FOR THE MARKET

Following a quite comprehensive and often cited definition, Clouds can be described as follows: "Clouds are a large pool of easily usable and accessible virtualized resources (such as hardware, development platforms and/or services). These resources can be dynamically reconfigured to adjust to a variable load (scale), allowing also for an optimum resource utilization. This pool of resources is typically exploited by a pay-per-use model in which guarantees are offered by the Infrastructure Provider by means of customized SLAs" (Vaquero et al. 2009).

Cloud Services can be divided into three major areas. Within these areas each service should fulfill the characteristics above. As many companies bundle their offers and put their own description behind them, the boundaries of provided services are not always sharp. Nevertheless, a general un-

DOI: 10.4018/978-1-60960-735-7.ch012

derstanding in the community has been established that these are the main areas of Cloud Computing services/product that are offered on the market (also see Figure 1):

- At its most basic level Infrastructure-as-a-Service (IaaS) delivers resources like pre-packaged sets of e.g. CPU and RAM. Virtualized system images can be uploaded to a cloud provider who provides placement and execution of these images on physical hardware within their data centers or within a federated cloud infrastructure.

- Platform-as-a-Service (PaaS) delivers virtualization and scaling of abstracted software packages above the level of the operating system. Packaged applications are usually uploaded to a cloud platform, or directly developed on the cloud platform itself.

- Software-as-a-Service (SaaS) is perhaps the most common of the 'as-a-Service' terms, and describes fully managed applications delivered as a service. Customers do not need to upload server images or software packages. Instead, they rent ac-

cess to the software which has been created and is maintained by the cloud provider.

The approach described here represents a lifecycle-based methodology that is illustrated with relevant examples from significant and most recent literature and research. A coherent methodology, which could support companies to embrace the Cloud, is still lacking. That has held back progress both on provider and on consumer side. The presented innovative approach, once applied, has the potential to create transparency for the promising IT paradigm of Cloud Computing. To strengthen the proposed approach we apply principles, present a methodology and showcase tools for engineering Cloud Computing systems.

While understanding the basic technical and business features of this new computing paradigm is essential, one has to see the complete picture and understand the implications for the provision of complex Cloud services including components such as networks, machines, infrastructures and software. Therefore, management of the complexity of consuming Cloud services needs to be understood as a supply chain. As an explicit definition for the Cloud Supply Chain (C-SC),

Figure 1. Cloud Supply Chain

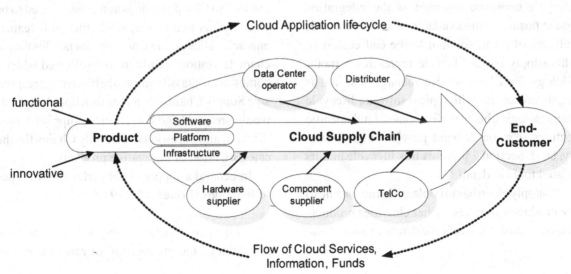

we propose the following definition: "A Cloud Supply Chain is two or more parties linked by the provision of Cloud Services, related information and funds" (based on Tsay, A. et al. 1998; Paulitsch, M. 2003).

On a strategic and operational level a Cloud Supply Chain Management (C-SCM) has to be established as part of companies' IT organizations as part of a whole life-cycle concept. A C-SCM represents the management of a network of interconnected businesses in the Cloud Computing area involved in the end-to-end provision of product and service packages required by end Cloud customers. In order to capture all these aspects we define it as followed: "Cloud Supply Chain Management (C-SCM) is the term used to describe the management of the provision of Cloud Services, information, and funds across the entire supply chain, from hardware suppliers to component to data center operators producers to distribution channels, and ultimately to the end-consumer". Based on (Johnson, M. & Pyke, D. 1999) Cachon and Fisher show that supply chain management is not only sharing of information that leads to cost improvements in a supply chain. But it is the management and restructuring of services, information, and funds based on a life-cycle approach (Cloud Application life-cycle) (Cachon, G. & Fisher, M. 2000) as shown in Figure 1. This lifecycle could be regarded as the integration and exposure of the available resources towards delivery of a full solution to the end customer. This supply-based lifecycle represents a methodology for Cloud service management and is highly coincident with typical software lifecycle methodologies, but including some Cloud-specific features (e.g. on-demand provisioning, elasticity, etc.). Section 2 presents this lifecycle and its related tools in detail.

A supply chain has to be classified according to the product it supplies. Fisher classifies products primarily on the basis of their demand patterns into two categories: products are either primarily functional or primarily innovative (Fisher, M. 1997).

Functional products satisfy basic needs that do not change much over time, have predictable and stable demand with low uncertainties and have long life cycles (typically more than 2 years). Due to their stability, functional products favor competition, which leads to low profit margins and, as a consequence of their properties, to low inventory costs, low product variety, low stockout costs, and low obsolescence (Lee, H. 2002; Fisher, M. 1997). Whereas innovative solutions are characterized by additional reasons for a customer in addition to basic needs that lead to purchase, unpredictable demand (that is high uncertainties, they are difficult to forecast and variable in demand and have short product lifecycles (typically 3 months to 1 year) (Lee, H. 2002).

In general, the products coming out of emerging (Information and Communication Technologies) ICT are to be classified as innovative products, but have certain characteristics of functional products as well. Cloud Services should fulfill basic needs of customers and favor competition due to their reproducibility. But they also show characteristics of innovative products as the demand is in general unpredictable (on-demand business model) and have due to adjustments to competitors and changing market requirements very short development circles. So Cloud Services as a product need to be classified as innovative, while they still feature characteristics of functional products. This mixed characterization is furthermore reflected when it comes to the classification of efficient vs. responsive Supply Chains. Whereas functional products would preferably go into efficient Supply Chains, the main aim of responsive Supply Chains fits the categorization of innovative products.

In general a supply chain performs two types of functions (Fisher, M. 1997):

- Physical function comprises the production of the product out of raw material or intermediate parts or components, and the transportation of all components to the right place.

- Market mediation function ensures that the variety of products reaching the market-place matches what customers want.

While for functional products the physical function dominates, the market mediation function is more important than the physical function for innovative products. (Paulitsch, M. 2003) Here again the mixed characteristics of the C-SC lead to a high importance of the physical function, as this is the core product of Cloud Services, but more so the need for a strong market mediation function arises from the modular design of these services.

The major aim of this chapter is to highlight the relevant stages of service production lifecycle and align them with some of the most relevant recent approaches applied to Cloud environments. The reader should note that the efforts here highlighted are not unique and a detailed comparison is not herein provided, although the referenced papers immediately lead to most relevant systems and provide readers with that comparison. Hereby, the various stages a service runs through during its lifetime have to be followed, monitored and finally managed. The following section will describe service lifecycle management in Cloud environment and will give detailed technical approaches on this core management functionality.

2. SERVICE LIFECYCLE MANAGEMENT IN CLOUD ENVIRONMENTS[1]

This section will deal with all the different stages a "cloudified" service goes through during its lifecycle. All the subsections should provide state of the art and challenges, showing current principles, methodology and tools.

2.1 Service Development, Deployment and Composition, Testing and Maintenance

The Cloud is a powerful tool for application developers. It frees them from the complexity of infrastructure management (provision and scaling of hardware resources and tools), and simplifies the access to the services that the application requires. These services can be provided out-of-the-box by the Cloud platform itself, or accessed remotely through well known interfaces and protocols.

Depending on the type of cloud, services have a different lifecycle. As mentioned above, Clouds are categorized in three groups. Thus, each service can have a different lifecycle, and no support is supplied by the cloud to enforce it. Likewise, SaaS clouds do not implement the concept of 'user service lifecycle', but for a different reason: users cannot run their own services on them, so it makes not sense to define a lifecycle for them. Thus, this section deals with services lifecycle in PaaS platforms, as they do define the different stages of users services, usually deployed as one or more components running in the PaaS container.

In Figure 2, we show a schematic view of Platform as a Service (PaaS) Clouds, which run the software components (modules) of the deployed services. A service can be composed by one or several of these components. This Figure further develops the PaaS elements shown in the "Cloud stack" presented in (Lenk et al. 2009). Please keep in mind that this Figure does not depict a standard architecture of PaaS clouds. It only shows the different 'functional units' that can be expected in typical PaaS platforms. Such architecture is strongly dependent on how the Cloud provider decides to implement the container, framework and functionalities (for control, monitoring, etc.) supplied.

The core element of the PaaS platform is the *Container*, which provides a runtime for the software components (modules) of the service. Also, the Cloud will offer *Cloud Services* that

Figure 2. Cloud Platform Elements

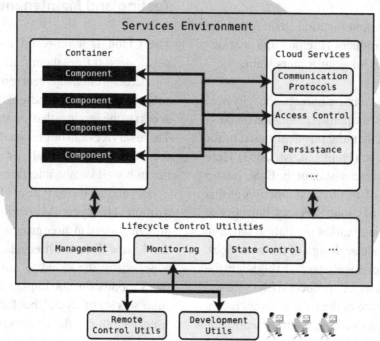

provide useful functionalities for components; and *Lifecycle Control Utilities* so service providers can handle their components lifecycle. Finally, developers can use a set of *Utils*, given by the PaaS provider, to control and develop their components. This section will discuss the nature and state of the art of these elements.

2.1.1 Components Container

The Container must host the components deployed by developers. The runtime environment must implement several features. We will focus on the support of a clear lifecycle and the provision of a secure environment.

Support for Components Lifecycle. Once deployed in the Container, a component will go through several stages during its lifecycle. The transition between states could be triggered by external events or by the component itself. Pre-

vious component systems have already defined their own lifecycles for the components they host. Figure 2 shows the lifecycle of components in two standard components system, J2EE (JSR244 2006) *Servlets* and OSGi (OSGi 2009). OSGi defines a more complete (although also more complex) lifecycle that takes into account activities such as the resolution of dependencies or the update of the software bundle. The contrast between the two *technologies depicted in Figure 3* clearly exposes the conflict that Cloud containers must address. On the one hand, simplicity is an important goal for developers, on the other hand a proper control of components required to take into account different circumstances during their lifecycle. In addition to clearly defining the possible events that trigger the transitions among states, the container must have means to communicate to the components about those events (e.g. through well defined interfaces). Finally, the platform must allow ser-

Figure 3. Lifecycle in Different Containers

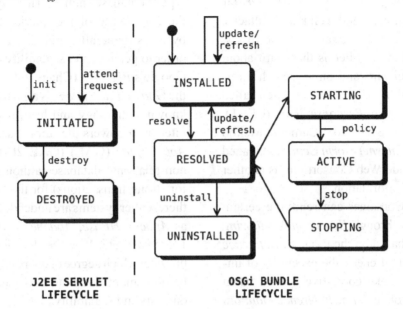

J2EE SERVLET LIFECYCLE

OSGi BUNDLE LIFECYCLE

vice deployers to control the lifecycle through the remote tools provided.

Security in Containers. Security (along with availability) is probably the most important feature that users expect from Clouds. The Container must provide a safe environment to run, protecting components from internal or external threats. Security is a very complex aspect, and it must be addressed with several measures at different parts of the Cloud platform.

First, the Container must provide full *isolation* (Herzog et al. 2005) of components from different application providers. For better resource usage, it is likely that the same container will host components from several different developers. This should be totally transparent to them, and no component shall be able to interfere with other components. This implies, for example, that the Container shall not allow components to use resources without restriction, to avoid potential starvation situations due to one or more (malicious or not) components exhausting or locking resources. Instead, the Container will have to implement fair resource sharing policies. As a result, the Container will need resource accounting mechanisms. Also,

the Container shall be able to withdraw access to resources to those components that exceed their quota (e.g. avoid memory exhaustion because of memory leaks from faulty components. Apart from resource control, the Container must also impose strict restrictions so components will not be able to interfere to other components or to the platform itself. Depending on the base platform used, this can be troublesome. For example, the Java platform provides Class Loaders to control what functionality some code can access to. However, this is not the only way for malicious users to attack some other components in the same environment, the are other well known problems such as the visibility of object references in static classes, possibility for malicious tenants to block other tenants through shared data structures (such as queues) or static synchronized methods.

Besides implementing secure multitenancy, the Container must block external attacks. It is reasonable to assume that many (if not all) services hosted in the Cloud will be accessed through Web interfaces. Thus, Cloud providers must focus on defensive mechanisms against Web-attacks. *Denial of Service, Distributed DoS, SQL Injection,*

255

Cross-Site Scripting, *Sybil* and *Buffer Overflow* are the most prominent and well known attacks. Also, the Cloud administrators must follow notification and alert bulletins that warn about new security incidents and threats. Such information is offered by several entities often called *Computer Emergency Response Team* (CERT), like for example the one from Carnegie Mellon University. The *Internet Storm Center*, managed by the World Wide Web Consortium, is another source of useful information.

Finally, the Container can reinforce certain security policies through *Execution Monitoring* (EM), which is based on the usage of *Reference Monitors* (RM) that check the execution of untrusted code and take corrective actions when some policy is broken. *Inline Reference Monitors* (IRM) are a type of RM injected in the code to be monitored. Containers could use *Aspect Oriented Programing* (AOP) techniques to transparently weave IRMs with the users' code to monitor it (Yi et al. 2004).

2.1.2 Cloud Services

Besides providing a runtime for components, the Cloud can supply several *Cloud Services* that implement useful functionality for components. Which functionality is provided, how to access it, the guarantees included (SLAs)... must be clearly specified, possibly in the form of service contracts. Here we will comment some fundamental services that we deem any Cloud platform should provide.

Persistence. Data storage services are needed by almost any application (save maybe stateless ones). Storage can be oriented to provide a simple repository for (typically big) chunks of data, or to make available a database system for the management of structured data.

Structured data has typically being managed through relational, SQL-compliant databases and Cloud systems like *Microsoft Azureus* do provide components with such solutions. However, Cloud systems have promoted the usage of a different type of database engines. These systems sacrifice the complexity of the queries that can be run by users (generally, joins are to be avoided) in order to get a greater scalability and availability. Google's *BigTable* (Chang 2008), built on top of the *Google File System*, is arguably the best well-known technology and has raised considerable interest. It powers the storage service of *Google App Engine* (GAE) (GAE 2010), providing a non-relational database (although with support for strong transactions) for the Servlets running there. Other systems are under development, such as *Apache HBase*, *Apache Cassandra*, *Project Voldemort*, etc. It is the decision of the Cloud provider which degree of query complexity should be implemented, taking into account the impact on costs and scalability.

Access Control. This is provided by the Cloud so components can know the identity of the callers of their clients. This identity is handled by the platform itself, which has its own user management system. For example, GAE Servlets can identify users by their Google account. It is Google who takes care of the login process.

It is up to the platform, however, to provide greater access control capabilities, for example to assign roles to users and define mappings of allowed actions/roles to be reinforced by the system. Also, this could be combined with *accounting* capabilities that allowed monitoring the amount of resources demanded to attend each user request. This kind of control granularity will be more demanded as the complexity of the applications deployed grows.

Communication Protocols. Due to security issues, it is likely that the Cloud platform will ban components from directly handling network connections. Instead, they will only be allowed to communicate through the set of APIs available in the Container. On the other hand, these APIs can be used to provide an easy way to use a wide range of protocols and communication models. For example, a communication service could be based on the deliverance of a distributed bus for message passing among components. Depending on the support of protocols for queue/message architectures (JMS, AMQP) and for integration with external entities (SOAP, REST) the same APIs could be used to communicate with other elements outside the platform. Beside message bus systems, the platform could also bring the possibility to use other protocols such as HTTP, SMTP, etc. In some cases, the platform could even allow components to use telephonic network services to send SMS, establish communication sessions with (or among) users through SIP, etc.

2.1.3 Lifecycle Control Utilities

These are quite standard utilities for developers to control their components remotely. The specific set of utilities will depend on the functionalities to be provided to developers. However, we can envision a minimum set of tools that platforms should be made available:

Component State Control. The platform must make available mechanisms so developers can not only deploy and remove components from the platform, but also to control transition about states (depending on the components lifecycle supported by the platform). For example, if the platform implemented an OSGi-like lifecycle, developers should be able to perform actions such as stopping components or to update its software.

Component Monitoring. The service developer or provider will need to be aware about the state and events of the components that form the service. Thus, the Cloud should made available different monitoring functionalities: 1) reports about platform-controlled metrics such as number of requests, resources consumed, etc. 2) notification and alarms, configured by the component administrator; 3) accounting (and possibly billing) info; 4) mechanisms to notify application specific metric values (subtasks processing times, for example) from components through the Container and the Monitoring system to the service provider.

Component Management. Some technologies, such as Java Management Extensions, allow developers to expose methods for the remote management of components. The functionality exposed and the parameters exposed will be service dependent, and so programmed by components developers. However, they should be made available only through the Cloud platform utilities.

The interfaces to use these utilities can differ, for example they could be accessed only through a web interface or they could be called also through protocols such as CORBA, Web Services, etc.

2.1.4 Developer Utilities

Finally, the Cloud provider can make available for developers different tools that enable the remote management of components through the Lifecycle Control Utilities. These tools can be *Development Utils*, oriented for developers to deploy/update service components, or *Remote Control Utils* for service administrators to monitor and manage those components. It is a requisite for these tools to implement secure communication mechanisms (SSH, PKI) to access the Cloud platform. Also, these tools could be integrated with IDE tools through the plugin mechanisms they usually implement.

Testing Development Utils. Depending on the Cloud platform capacities and characteristics, it could be possible to offer a testing environment that emulates the Cloud container and provides "toy" implementations of the Cloud Services (storage, etc.). Such environment is provided for example by GAE, and it is undoubtedly a very useful tool for developers. However it cannot provide information about its performance under high load situations, scalability, etc. Cloud platforms should allow developers to define and run high load tests on the platform itself with new experimental versions of the software without interfering with the actual service.

Versioning. Another functionality that should be available for the Cloud platform to be a mature environment is the possibility of storing different versions of the components code, for example to roll back to a previous version if some error is detected after the last component update.

2.2 Service Definition

Having their service defined, providers are ready to deploy their application service, i.e., a clear specification of the requirements of this service must be communicated to the underlying platform. This includes overall requirements such as the minimum hardware profile required by the different service components, in terms of CPU, memory and so on, alongside required application data such as a virtual disk, ISO image, or application code and libraries. This Section is unavoidably related with Section 2.4, since service definition includes mechanisms for controlling service scalability.

Most Cloud platforms, IaaS, PaaS, or SaaS, will provide means for a client to define service requirements and configuration data typically in the form of a deployment descriptor. This may be via a graphical user interface such as Amazon's Web Service Management console[2], or as a separate document with a clear specified syntax, semantic and structure. Upon deployment the provisioning framework binds the necessary infrastructure capabilities declared in the graphical user interface or descriptor to the application, in the form of hardware resources, such as CPU cores or memory (which is the usual case in IaaS clouds), or alternatively software dependencies (usually for PaaS).

IaaS users will describe upon submission their hardware and software requirements via a suitable interface or descriptor. Amazon's EC2[3] offers a Xen (Barham et al. 2003) based proprietary format called an Amazon Machine Image (AMI) for cloud applications. Pre-configured or custom built images can then be deployed on Amazon's cloud via their API or management interface, at which time the user defines the preferred hardware configuration in terms of CPU cores, memory

and storage, networking configuration, firewall, security, etc. Other commercial services such as GoGrid[4], Flexiscale[5] follow similar approaches to deploy cloud applications on their infrastructure, offering proprietary ways for packaging and configuring the cloud applications.

Similarly, Windows Azure[6], as a PaaS Cloud framework and provider, relies for example on service models. These enable services to be described as distributed entities: clients can specify the interfaces exposed by services, communication end points and channels, roles, whether web for front-end communication or worker for background processing, and various other configuration data which must be provided when hosting a service. In addition, similarly to IaaS platforms, because each role will run its own virtual machine instance, different hardware requirements may be allocated at different costs.

However, as cloud based offerings become increasingly popular, the complexity and scale of services deployed in the cloud means that additional degrees of flexibility and control over the provisioning process must be provided to the customer. Services may incorporate an increasingly wide range of components, data or application resources and dependencies and constraints may exist between these resources that must be clarified when deploying, migrating and resizing services in a cloud.

Service provider will also wish to describe how the service responds to load variations and faults. In order to minimize over provisioning and optimize the use of resources, there must exist means of specifying the adjustment of service capacity or configuration throughout the entire service lifetime according to application state and workload and communicating this information to the infrastructure provider.

These concerns highlight the fact that service definition cannot be solely focused on the initial deployment of fixed size application instances. There must exist an ability to for a client to describe the overall service architecture of applications hosted in clouds, the entire service lifecycle and the behavioral aspects of the service during such lifecycle, using a declarative language in the form of a service definition manifest.

2.2.1 Requirements for a Cloud Based Service Description Language

The requirements for a service definition language for cloud computing can be broadly broken down in a number of subsets described as follows. In order to illustrate some of the requirements, we will use a typical three tier web architecture to be deployed on an IaaS or PaaS clouds via Amazon EC2 or Azure. The application will consist of a single database, web server and a load balancer.

1. Service Architecture: We are concerned here with the overall structure of service deployed on a cloud and any capacity or capability requirements in terms of hardware or software dependencies. This may include for example the overall network topology and interconnections among services, specific hardware requirements of individual components (e.g. CPU, memory, etc.), which may vary according to the nature of the service.

2. Service Elasticity: When dealing with rapid changes in service context and load (e.g., due to sudden pike in the number of service users), timely adjustments may be necessary to meet service level obligations that cannot be met by human administrators. In such a case, it may be necessary to automate the process of requesting additional resources or releasing existing resources to minimize costs. In order to automate the scaling of applications to meet variations in workload the service provider must be able to describe the conditions within which this scaling takes place and the actions to follow should these conditions hold true. Referring to the web application example, it may be necessary to increase the number of web servers available

to meet demand, though the load balancer would continue to serve as a single point of entry.

3. Relevant KPI Description: Providing support for elasticity requires the state of the application to be exposed to the infrastructure in the form of monitorizable performance indicators. These KPIs (Key Performance Indicators) may be infrastructure level indicators such as current disk use, but application level performance indicators may prove necessary to maximize the optimization and response. We can consider in our example the number of simultaneous sessions that our web application will handle as a basis for scaling the application.

4. Constraint policies: The use of virtualization technologies introduces a degree of location transparency – users may not know where their services are running and loosely coupled services may be deployed across multiple physical and administrative domains. However, there may exist cases where users are in fact concerned with controlling the spread of their applications for administrative or technical reasons: legalities may mean that some data may not leave a particular country for example, or a provider may simply wish to minimize latency between components by ensuring that certain service components remain co-located. It must hence be possible to provide clear constraint policies on the distribution of services across sites. Constraints may also exist regarding the portability of the applications deployed on the cloud. The overall service may be tied to specific hardware or hypervisor technologies for example, and heterogeneous hosting environments must cater for such limitations. In addition we must also consider potential constraints when migrating services, and provide means of specifying the optimum conditions that have to be met to minimize disruption.

5. Component Startup and Shutdown dependencies: The inter-relationships between components may require some components to be made available before others and configuration data may be dependent on specific deployment instances. Similarly terminating applications may require specific undeployment dependencies to be taken into account. In our example we may wish to deploy the database before the web server.

6. Component customization: The service manifest or definition language should serve as a template for provisioning instances of particular components. Multiple instances of web servers for example may be created from a same basic template and virtual image and may require instance specific configuration data, such as dynamically allocated IP addresses. The manifest language must provide constructs to support the automatic generation of instance specific values.

7. Security and access policies: The manifest should provide means of specifying security policies. We may consider authenticating the actual submission of the description itself for deployment but must also take into account security requirements once the service has been deployed, such as the use of particular certificate files for using or managing the application service.

8. Quality of service requirements: When leasing third-party resources, failures of these resources to meet a particular level of performance may lead to financial losses for the service provider. The service provider can mitigate these risks through the establishment of Service Level Agreements (SLA). SLAs specify acceptable thresholds of performance and reliability as well as penalties, most likely in the form of financial compensation that will be incurred should the quality of service fall below acceptability. SLAs related to our example may deal with

access time, specific hardware provisioning, or elasticity response time.

Finally, we must also consider the openness and platform independent nature of the service definition language. If a service provider has prepared his application for use on Amazon EC2, shifting this to another provider such as GoGrid is not a straightforward endeavor. In order to facilitate the transition from one cloud provider to another, it is desirable for the manifest language to be specified in a standard way that is free of platform specific concerns. This provides an opportunity for scaling across multiple providers and generally avoids vendor lock-in.

2.2.2 Adapting Standards for the Cloud: The OVF Experience

We have examined a number of software architecture description languages, standards and existing commercial offerings in order to identify a suitable language for the definition of application services deployed on an open IaaS cloud. In particular we describe here the Open Virtualization Format (OVF), a DMTF standard backed by VMWare, Citrix and many other IT vendors (DMTF, 2010). We will cover here how the language can be adapted and extended in order to support cloud computing capabilities, focusing primarily on elasticity and service level objectives description.

OVF allows multiple virtual machines to be packaged as a single entity containing an OVF descriptor, along with any resources which may be referred to in the descriptor, such as virtual disk, ISO images, etc., and finally X.509 certificate files to ensure integrity and authenticity. It is the OVF descriptor that we will focus on here. It is an XML document composed of three main parts: a description of the files included in the overall architecture (disks, ISO images, etc.), meta-data for all virtual machines included, and a description of the different virtual machine systems. The description is structured into various "Sections", describing virtual disks, logical networks and hardware resource requirements of each virtual system. Virtual machines sharing common descriptive elements can be grouped in virtual system collections. Users may specify a virtual machine booting sequence and the deployment time configuration of virtual machine instances is supported through the definition of a communication protocol between host and guest (the target virtual machine) via the use of crafted CD/DVD images to be used as boot disks during the start-up process. A simplified example of this service definition language is shown in Figure 4.

There are a number of requirements however that OVF in itself does not meet. In particular it is focused solely on initial deployment of fixed

size services, and does not provide measures to handle potential changes in requirements over the lifetime of a service. It also does not handle potential migration across hosts, nor issues related to performance and service level quality. These are crucial requirements in clouds and such language abstractions must be introduced into the standard.

We have proposed a number of extensions to OVF to facilitate the deployment of OVF-described resources in Clouds (Galan et al. 2009). This includes attribute and section changes to incorporate support for service components dynamic IDs in elastics arrays, IP dynamic addresses and elasticity rules and bounds. We consider here two particularly important extensions, automated scal-

Figure 4. OVF-based Cloud Service Specification Example (simplified)

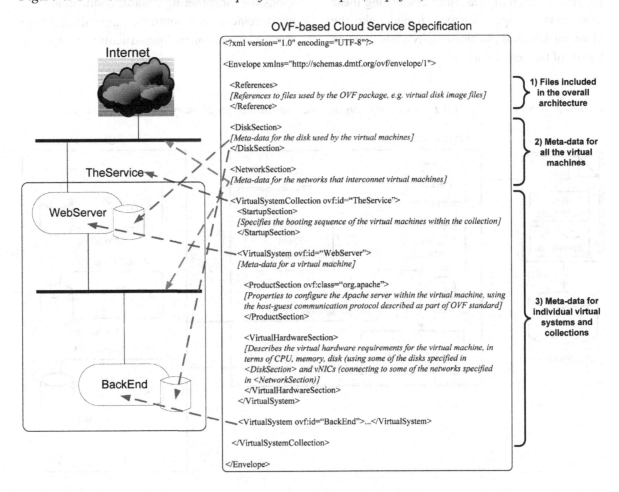

ing based on application level state, and service level objectives considerations.

Elasticity Specification

The automated scaling of service capacity to support potential variations in load and demand can be implemented in numerous ways. Application providers may implement such scaling at the application level, relying on an exposed interface of the cloud computing infrastructure to issue specific reconfiguration requests when appropriate. Alternatively, they may have a desire to keep the application design free of infrastructure specific operations and opt instead to delegate such concerns to the infrastructure itself. With a sufficient level of transparency at the application level for workload conditions to be identified, and through the specification of clear rules associating these conditions with specific actions to undertake, the cloud can handle dynamic capacity adjustment on behalf of the service provider.

It is the latter approach that we describe here. By providing a syntax and framework for the definition and support of elasticity rules, we can ensure the dynamic management of a wide range of services with little to no modification for execution on a cloud. With regards to the syntax, we can identify the two following subsets of the language that would be required to describe such elasticity: service providers must first be able to describe the application state as a collection of Key Performance Indicators (KPIs), and the means via which they are obtained in the manifest. These will then serve as a basis for the formulation of the rules themselves.

Alongside the syntactic requirements, a suitable monitoring framework must exist. A service provider is expected to expose parameters of interest through local Monitoring Agents, responsible for gathering suitable application level measurements and communicating these to the service management infrastructure via suitable

Figure 5. Overview of an OVF processing engine plus additional machinery for service provision

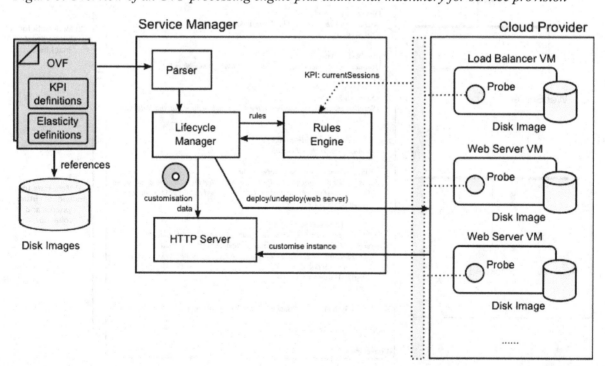

communication channels. This is illustrated in Figure 5.

In this example, the service manager is responsible for parsing an OVF document and extracting from it a set of appropriate scalability rules. All virtual machines launched in the Cloud will regularly output measurements of key performance indicators via the use of probes interconnected via an appropriate communication channel. Such information is passed to a rule engine, which will then trigger an appropriate management response, such as the deployment of new instances. In the example illustrated, the number of concurrent sessions handled by the load balancer is used as a basis to deploy new instances of web servers.

With respect to the rule syntax itself, we adopt a simple KPI based ratio system, illustrated in Box 1 (based on the OVF example previously shown in Figure 4).

In summary, we define a proportional relationship between the average value of a collection of KPI measurement obtained during a particular time frame and the number of instances of a particular component that should be deployed. This allows us for example to express that we should deploy additional web servers should the average number of sessions obtained during the last 10 minutes period (sampling with a frequency of 60 samples per period) is above 20 up to a maximum of 5.

While more complex specifications based on a rule-based syntax could be adopted, we found that the majority of cases that were tackled could be specified in this manner. As the KPI measurements are forwarded to the infrastructure by the application itself, the application level probes can implement more complex operations on performance indicators, such as aggregations of multiple values before passing this information to the infrastructure itself.

Service Level Objectives

While the potential of Cloud computing infrastructures is evidently great, there exists much risk in service providers outsourcing hardware provisioning in this manner. Indeed, if the resources leased fail, or do not meet the performance expectations of the service provider, this may result in considerable financial loss. In addition to the losses incurred from the inability to provide the service to the end-client, there may have also been costs involved in porting the service or applications to the leased infrastructure that cannot be recouped

Box 1.

```
<VirtualSystem ovf:id="WebServer" xmlns:rsrvr="http://schemas.telefonica.com/
claudia/ovf" rsrvr:min="1" rsrvr:max="5" rsrvr:initial="1">

...

<rsrvr:ElasticArraySection>
<Info>String</Info>
        <rsrvr:Rule>
                <rsrvr:KPIName>totalSessions</rsrvr:KPIName>
                <rsrvr:Window unit="minute">10</rsrvr:Window>
                <rsrvr:Frequency>60</rsrvr:Frequency>
                <rsrvr:Quota>20</rsrvr:Quota>
        </rsrvr:Rule>
</rsrvr:ElasticArraySection>
```

in such circumstances. These possibilities are likely to inhibit the adoption of Cloud computing, and means of mitigating these risks though clear contractual agreements between service and infrastructure provider must exist. These agreements should define the obligations of both parties regarding the level of service to be provided and the behavior deemed acceptable on both parts, and enable financial compensation to be sought should a party fail to meet these obligations.

We are primarily concerned here with agreements between service provider and Cloud infrastructure provider regarding the performance constraints of the physical resources allocated to an overall application service. As such, the SLA must define expected performance, reliability, and the conditions within which these can be guaranteed, in addition to the compensation to pay when the agreed objectives are not matched.

Most Cloud providers will describe some form of SLA. Amazon for example details a broad commitment of 99.95% uptime for all service instances and will provide some form of credit should the performance not be met[7]. Users can provide details by email regarding the observed failures including date and time.

However, when dealing with large scale services involving multiple components potentially distributed between several locations and administrative domains, such measures can be found to be insufficient. The process of gathering performance records and evaluating them against expected detailed quality of service requirements must be automated as much as possible. This requires service level objectives to be specified in a clear and unambiguous manner that can be evaluated at run time against observed performance measurements. In addition service providers may have several concerns beyond projected uptime. A failure to respond to elasticity requirements in a timely manner may lead to an inability to meet overall demand and generally the provider will be concerned with performance level objectives tied to application specific behavior, such as the

overall turn around time of individual service requests involving multiple components.

Several standards and frameworks exist for the definition, negotiation and monitoring of service level agreements. Many of these are tied to specific types of applications, but we may consider for example the WS-Agreement specification as an example of a highly extensible framework suited for such a purpose (OGF, 2006).

Generally an SLA description will require some form of service description, enabling us to pinpoint the specific characteristics of the service that the SLA is meant to protect, guarantee terms in the form of specific service level objectives, the conditions within which these apply and the perceived business value of these objectives. In addition, appropriate metrics used as a basis for the formulation of the service level objectives will have to be defined with respect to the application domain, and a monitoring environment. It must be possible to obtain and communicate the value of key performance indicators specified in the SLA via appropriate measurement probes.

An example of how SLAs may be monitored and generally integrated within the rest of a Cloud platform is illustrated in Figure 6. An SLA compliance monitor is responsible for parsing a set of guarantee terms and conditions from an SLA, such as a WS-Agreement based document. This can then evaluate dynamically compliance to these rules by matching measurements obtained from measurement probes at various levels of the infrastructure to specific metrics specified in the SLA. Conditional expressions can then be evaluated against the collection of measurement records obtained in specified time frames.

Identified violations can then be passed to suited components, such as an SLA protection engine, which would try to adjust allocations accordingly, or alternatively to a business information manager which will enact some penalty in the form of financial compensation or otherwise. Such penalties would be described in the SLA.

Figure 6. Sample SLA management system for Cloud service provision

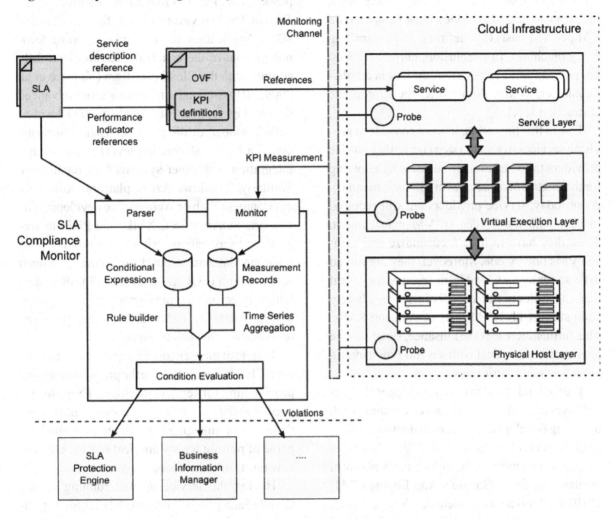

2.3 Service Provisioning

After developing and defining the service, the next stage will lead Cloud users to focus on the way service provisioning is done in current IaaS/PaaS/SaaS clouds and its APIs (relying on work done in the previous section).

IaaS Clouds allow for service providers to quickly arrange new computing infrastructure in a pay-as-you-go way. This way, virtual hardware resources can be dynamically provisioned according to their services' load. For instance, when the number of incoming requests grows, new Virtual Machines (VMs) need to be manually allocated to avoid a possible service outage and greatly decreasing the offered Quality of Service (QoS); upon requests shrinks the allocated VMs would then need to be released to avoid paying for unneeded elements.

However, available IaaS interfaces are usually too close to the infrastructure, forcing the SP to manage manually the VMs assigned to support the service. See for instance, the typically WSDL- or REST-based: Amazon's API, GoGrid's API, Sun's Cloud API or VMware's vCloud (Varia 2009, GoGrid 2010, Sun Cloud API, vCloud API 2010). The available APIs are way too low level for the abstraction required by service providers.

They are too close to the VM and, consequently, the provisioning of a service must be done on a VM per VM basis (i.e. defining and controlling every machine). In conclusion, current IaaS do not provide ways to describe services in a holistic manner, as they do not offer the appropriate abstraction level.

Due to this limitation, it is not possible to provision services in a single step (i.e. letting service providers to focus on their business by allowing for the treatment of services in a holistic manner). As of today, service providers are still required to deal with the burden of VM management. Thus, they have to install, customize and manage VMs one by one. Moreover, they are forced to do so for every Cloud infrastructure they want their machines to run at. XEN images are barely compatible with KVM ones or Amazon AMIs. This further increases the nuisance, since service providers need to deal with several provisioning procedures and intricacies.

PaaS Clouds tried to provide a higher abstraction layer to quickly deliver a service to the Cloud, by easing developers' lives and reducing services time to market (Vaquero et al. 2009; Chohan et al. 2009). The most paradigmatic PaaS platform available so far is Google's App Engine (GAE 2010). GAE offers a complete development stack that uses conventional technologies to build and host Web applications. GAE claims to free Web developers from system administration, which is a step forward as compared to IaaS Clouds in which developers still have to take care of some administration-related tasks. The user has to keep in mind that GAE is a Python or Java development environment easing creation (e.g. by including Persistence managers and other development facilities), packaging and porting of We applications only. Extensions for other type of applications are required that would imply having predefined "computing environments" to ease other type of applications development too. For instance, JBoss-Cloud is an example of such efforts to provide developers with all the advantages and power provided by GAE to Web applications[8]. JBoss-Cloud provides a pre-configured Cloud of JBoss Application Servers and supporting technologies out-of-the-box. However, in order to fully comply with the Cloud paradigm (Vaquero et al. 2009), JBoss-Cloud still misses more advanced developing support (higher abstraction level to help developers dealing with persistence, security, etc. at a higher abstraction level) and smoother integration with other systems (e.g. databases). Similarly, Windows Azure platform[9] offers an environment Web or Web-service developers (its supports SOAP, REST, XML, and PHP) to create Cloud applications. Although Azure provides relational database support for basing developed services on it (SQLAzure), this still fails to deal with very complex typical problems found when scaling databases (table distribution, partition, replication, redundancy, etc.)

In spite of these encouraging advances, today's PaaS Clouds do not alleviate the problem of service provisioning for service providers. They are still needed to define service components, packaging them and/or engaging specialized personnel capable of porting legacy applications (or creating new ones) into the Cloud.

Having the service up and running on the Cloud (SaaS provisioning model) avoided application providers' need to provision (services are already there). These players, aiming to expose "on the Cloud" services for end users, thus benefit from no administrative burden whatsoever. They do not have to deal with VM provision (like in IaaS Clouds), software development, packaging, patching, maintenance nor security. However, the SaaS paradigm is not new to the Cloud. Service-orientation and Application Server Providers already tried to deliver this vision (Foster et al. 2002; Erl 2005; Huhns and Singh, 2005). Some common issues that arise from avoiding on-demand provisioning have to do with service publishing, discovery, updates, etc. In order for these service-oriented systems to provide users with the illusion of infinite resources, automated scalability, etc. new elements are required to make these tasks more transparent and automatic for application providers.

Figure 7 shows a summary of the major features with regard to provisioning that the different Cloud layers expose. Every layer increases the offered abstraction level; unfortunately, none of them seems suitable enough for application providers to focus on their business only.

2.4 Service Scalability

Provisioning the service is just part of the whole picture. Controlling how the service (not just VMs) can automatically be scaled is also a very desirable feature to be asked for to current IaaS Cloud providers (Rodero-Merino et al., 2010; Cáceres et al., 2010). This section shows how current methods and tools are limited for the task of providing different degrees of scalability at the service level.

Cloud computing is, partially, but importantly about on-demand provision of resources (Cáceres et al., 2010). Thus, mechanisms to allow resources to grow or shrink in accordance with their utilization are required. Scalability is a gigantic task that needs to be tackled at the different abstraction levels provided by the Cloud paradigm (see Figure 8).

At the IaaS level, Amazon provides higher level services, such as Amazon's Cloud Watch and AutoScale (Varia, 2009) to automate the scaling process of Amazon-deployed VMs. Similarly, RightScale allows for VM replication according to queues or user-defined hardware and process load metrics (Rightscale 2010). However, scalability can only be defined in terms of the variables monitored in the server templates RightScale provides. In other words, service-level metrics, those really relevant for service providers, cannot be employed. Other relevant example is Microsoft's Azure, the number of instances for Azure is specified in an XML configuration file which has to be manually changed so that Azure's the fabric controller will automatically adjust the number of running instances. These very same

Figure 7. Elements offered for provisioning different components at common Cloud layers. IaaS offer VM provisioning interfaces; PaaS development interfaces for provisioning software bundles (often Web-based, e.g. servlets); SaaS offer elementary service management interfaces (e.g. interfaces for publishing, provisioning

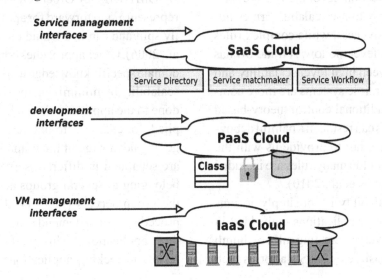

Figure 8. Summary of the scaling capabilities offered by the different Cloud layers

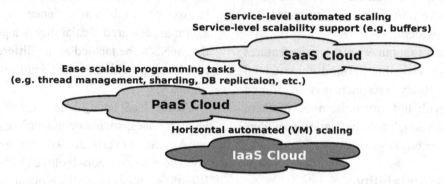

limitations are present in similar systems offering automatic scalability over Cloud platforms, such as Scalr, WeoCeo (Scalr, 2009; WeoCeo, 2009), etc.

The solutions above fail to provide automated tools for handling the lifecycle of whole services (rather than VM or service instances). To overcome this limitation, a new abstraction layer has been proposed that is closer to the lifecycle of services and allows for their automatic deployment and escalation depending on the service status (not only on the infrastructure) (Rodero-Merino et al., 2010). This approach was based on an expressive language to let users define scaling rules as logical expression containing service-level metrics. User customization degree of the rules scaling is based on and application–level metrics are hard to be delivered. Easy to use scalability rules imply lack of expressiveness, while complex rules put the abstraction level too low. A trade-off has to be reached between high level scalability and usability. Moreover, rule systems are more comprehensive than traditional control theory-based approaches, but this can result on a painful debugging process if rules fail to provide us with the expected behavior or too many rules are included in the system (Cáceres et al., 2010).

On-demand scalability is not simply accomplished by deploying applications embedded in VMs in the Cloud. Very interesting rules of thumb have been re-emphasized by PaaS platforms such

as Google's App Engine[10]. These rules consider minimizing paging through large datasets, avoiding datastore contention, etc. Less traditional mechanisms are also considered important for avoiding placing the customer of thread management or garbage-collection. It is the Cloud itself that should be in charge of providing such capabilities for programmers as a service (*à la* "networked libraries", i.e. PaaS).

For instance, scientific applications often require an accurate knowledge of the problem at hand in order to design the most appropriate parallelization strategy. The Cloud is an ideal environment for parallelizable applications. However, it is hard to write the code needed to do that with most programming languages. Attempts such as BOOM (Berkeley Orders Of Magnitude) project, represent a step forward for applications to be easily split and run in a Cloud environment (Loo et al., 2006). Other approaches consider application domain specific knowledge to increase application scalability by minimizing the changes need to be done to the application's code. This has been applied, for example, to online social networks by getting advantage of the graph structure. Groups are separated in different servers and the nodes belonging to several groups are replicated in all the group servers (Pujol et al., 2009). Current procedures often demand programmers to recode their applications. This platform-specific code results in locking applications to a determined

Cloud infrastructure or platform. Some attempts try to reduce this undesired code by hierarchically structuring servers to achieve scalability without significantly restructuring the program (Song et al, 2009). Other common technique is based on the usage of profiles. These profiles aim at capturing experts' knowledge for scaling applications without binding to specific Cloud infrastructure (Yang et al., 2009). Although some remarkable attempts have been made that try to add automatic scaling capabilities to service-based systems (see (Poggi et al., 2009) for example), these are often hard to develop, too dependent on the specific application, and hardly generalizable to be offered as a general-purposed service.

Being application domain or even application specific, these attempts fall close to the need to scale SaaS applications. Indeed, PaaS applications could be regarded as a special type of SaaS devoted to support service development. However, SaaS scaling is not just about having a scalable underlying (virtual) hardware or programming frameworks that help to increase application scalability.

Not all the applications are equally suited for the Cloud as a scalability-enabling environment. Although the Cloud is especially interesting for Web applications, transactional applications cannot be so easily ported to the Cloud. Web applications are usually stateless so, services can be migrated with minor effects on user-perceived performance. Also, if new service replicas need to be added (horizontal scaling), load balancers can reroute requests to any available service at any location. Transactional applications cannot be ported to the Cloud straightforwardly. They are inherently stateful and rollbacks and commits prevent easy service migration or database replication. Database replication and sharing are usually executed by expert administrators and is highly dependent on the specific data model, making it difficult for an automated scalability environment such as the Cloud. New transactional-like SaaS applications should rely on some basic program-

ming concepts that web applications have been using to achieve high performance or high availability in large-scale deployments (Barroso and Hölzle, 2009), not trying to emulate traditional transactional architectures (Cáceres et al., 2010).

Summing up, although IaaS Clouds have pushed scalability a step beyond by, defining automatic scalability actions based on custom service metrics is not fully supported (the degree of integration with underlying monitoring systems offered by most existent Cloud systems is to be further developed). Elements to help to select accurate utilization metrics are still to be defined towards effective on-demand scaling are still needed for public Clouds, in which it is difficult to extract relevant metrics from unknown and uncontrolled hypervisors or physical devices (e.g. network probes are difficult to locate). However, IaaS scalability is still too VM-level oriented, scaling decisions are made and executed on the basis of infrastructure metrics and the service provider is supposed to deal with these tasks manually. Full automation and application of scalability rules (or load profile–based models) to control services in a holistic manner are being produced on top of IaaS Clouds.

These scaling automation capabilities lay close to the aforementioned PaaS features. However, there is more to service lifecycle management than scaling the application horizontally (i.e., adding more VMs and load balancers). More elements helping to support scalable application design, development, parallelization, debugging, versioning, updating, etc. are still very much needed. SaaS application scalability is currently supported by exploiting traditional programming techniques to increase the scalability of services by minimizing its resource consumption.

SaaS delivery models imply a series of "hidden" requirements for the different players:

- for IaaS Cloud providers: these players will have to use underlying scalability mechanisms (such as VM replication, migration, etc.) so that the application providers or PaaS Cloud providers get IaaS automated scalability.

- for PaaS/SaaS Cloud providers: they will be requested to provide mechanisms for looking for, services, integrating services, sale developed services (i.e. an actual marketplace for services to be searched, sold and integrated) and mechanisms hiding the effects of an underlying VM migration or replication (e.g. buffers to queue requests while the new replica is being launched).

3. CONCLUSION

Starting off from a common understanding of Cloud Computing in the community, this paper motivated the idea of looking at Cloud Computing as a supply chain of not just a single provider, but hardware and component suppliers, data center operators and who provide the end-customer with Cloud services. This Cloud provisioning was defined as managing and coordinating the (partly) bi-directional movement of services, information and funds. For the defined supply chain the Cloud services were presented as products which need to be classified as innovative, and at the same time functional in their nature. Based on the idea of a Cloud supply chain the necessary management along the whole supply chain was defined and described. Followed by a technical deep dive it a potential technical approach for the management of user' components on a Cloud platform was illustrated.

For this, the paper depicted the main elements of a Cloud platform for third-party code execution: a components container, a set of Cloud services (such as persistence) and a set of utilities to control the

lifecycle of users' components. Regarding the container, we focused on the two main features to be considered, that were, 1) the support for the complete lifecycle of components and 2) security.

In fact security had received special attention, as it is arguably the most important feature in any Cloud system. Thus, we discussed the main threats that Cloud systems face due to both the execution of potentially malicious code, and the possibility of external attacks. When discussing Cloud services we had chosen those that we deem more important, as can be the most useful for developers deploying their components on the Cloud platform. These were persistence (service to store structured or unstructured data), access control (to govern on the developer's behalf who is performing a request on the component), and communication protocols (to allow the communication with external entities). Finally, we commented the utilities that Cloud platforms should provide developers with to support the control of the whole components lifecycle, including development, monitoring and testing.

In order to control the overall provisioning process of an application service by a Cloud, users must have means of describing their overall application structure and the requirements of the various components constituting the application. These requirements will relate to hardware and software needs at deployment time and at run-time, describe how to respond to changes in demand and the overall level of service that is expected from the Cloud platform. There may also raise additional concerns regarding the spread of the application, dependencies between components and run-time customization of component instances. We hence provided an overview of these requirements, identify the limitations of existing deployment description languages and illustrate how these may be incorporated into standards such as that provided by OVF.

Every layer increases the offered abstraction level, unfortunately, none of them seems suitable enough for application providers to focus on their business only. SaaS models, which may seem simpler for service providers, imply a series of tasks that call for further automation in order to make the Cloud vision come true.

IaaS scalability is essentially based on deploying new VMs and load balancing incoming requests. Although the automation mechanisms are still in their infancy a clear trend is observed in this way. SaaS (PaaS can be considered as a subset of SaaS services devoted to increase developing and maintenance procedures productivity) scalability currently relies on traditional programming methods to optimize resource usage without decreasing performance. New techniques are clearly required in order to optimize the scaling potential of all the currently available Cloud layers.

SaaS delivery models imply a series of requirements for the different stakeholders in the Cloud. PaaS and SaaS providers will rely on transparent and automated IaaS scaling mechanisms to offer their PaaS or SaaS features to programmers/service providers or application providers, respectively.

4. REFERENCES

Barham, P., Dragovic, B., Fraser, K., Hand, S., Harris, T., Ho, A., et al. Wareld, A. (2003). Xen and the art of virtualization. *Proceedings of the 19th ACM Symposium on Operating Systems Principles SOSP '03* (pp. 164-177). New York, NY: ACM.

Barroso, L. A., & Hölzle, U. (2009). *The datacenter as a computer: An introduction to the design of warehouse-scale machines: Synthesis lectures on computer architecture*. Morgan & Claypool Publishers.

Cáceres, J., Vaquero, L. M., Rodero-Merino, L., Polo, A., & Hierro, J. (in press). Service scalability over the cloud. In Fuhrt, B., & Escalante, A. (Eds.), *Handbook of cloud computing*. Springer.

Cachon, G., & Fisher, M. (2000). Supply chain inventory management and the value of shared information. *Management Science, 46*(8), 1032–1048. doi:10.1287/mnsc.46.8.1032.12029

Chang, F., Dean, J., Ghemawat, S., Hsies, W. C., Wallach, D. A., & Burrows, M. (2008). Bigtable: A distributed storage system for structured data. *ACM Transactions on Computer Systems, 26*(2), 1–26. doi:10.1145/1365815.1365816

Chohan, N., Bunch, C., Pang, S., Krintz, C., Mostafa, N., Soman, S., & Wolski, R. (2009). *AppScale design and implementation*. Retrieved from http://www.cs.ucsb.edu/ ~ckrintz/papers/appscale2009-02TR.pdf

DMTF. (2010). *Open virtualization format specification. (Specification DSP0243 v1.1.0)*. Distributed Management Task Force.

Erl, T. (2005). *Service-oriented architecture: Concepts, technology, and design*. Prentice Hall PTR.

Fisher, M. (1997). What is the right supply chain for your product? *Harvard Business Review, 75*(2), 105–116.

Foster, I., Kesselman, C., Nick, J. M., & Tuecke, S. (2002). Grid services for distributed system integration. *Computer, 35*(6), 37–46. doi:10.1109/MC.2002.1009167

Galán, F., Sampaio, A., Rodero-Merino, L., Loy, I., Gil, V., Vaquero, L. M., & Wusthoff, M. (2009). *Service specification in cloud environments based on extensions to open standards*. Fourth International Conference on COMmunication System softWAre and middlewaRE (COMSWARE 2009), Dublin, 2009.

GoGrid. (n.d.). *Website*. Retrieved from http://www.gogrid.com

Google. (n.d.). *Google's app engine*. Retrieved from http://code.google.com/ appengine/

Herzog, A., & Shahmeri, N. (2005). *Problems running untrusted services as Java threads. IFIP International Federation for Information Processing* (pp. 19–32). Springer.

Huhns, M. N., & Singh, M. P. (2005). Service-oriented computing: Key concepts and principles. *IEEE Internet Computing, 6*(4), 75–81. doi:10.1109/MIC.2005.21

Johnson, M., & Pyke, D. (1999). *Supply chain management.* Working Paper, The Tuck School of Business, Dartmouth College.

JSR244. (2006). *Java specification request 244: Java platform, enterprise edition 5.* Retrieved from http://jcp.org/en/jsr/detail?id=244

Lee, H. (2002). Aligning supply chain strategies with product uncertainties. *California Management Review, 44*(3), 105–119.

Lenk, A., Klems, M., Nimis, J., Tai, S., & Sandholm, T. (2009). What's inside the cloud? An architectural map of the cloud landscape. *Proceedings of the 2009 ICSE Workshop on Software Engineering Challenges of Cloud Computing* (pp. 1-5). IEEE Computer Society.

Loo, B. T., Condie, T., Garofalakis, M., Gay, D. A., Hellerstein, J. M., & Maniatis, P. … Stoica, I. (2006). *Declarative networking: Language, execution and optimization.* ACM SIGMOD 2006, (pp. 97–108).

OGF. (2006). *Web services agreement specification 2005/09.* Retrieved from http://www.ogf.org/ Public_Comment_Docs/ Documents/Oct-2005/ WS-AgreementSpecification Draft050920.pdf

OSGi. (2009). *OSGi service platform core specification,* v4. Retrieved from http://osgi.org/ Release4/HomePage

Paulitsch, M. (2003). *Dynamic coordination of supply chains.* PhD. Vienna University of Economics and Business Administration.

Poggi, N., Moreno, T., Berral, J. L., Gavaldà, R., & Torres, J. (2009). Self-adaptive utility-based Web session management. *Computer Networks, 53*(10), 1712–1721. doi:10.1016/j.comnet.2008.08.022

Pujol, J. M., Siganos, G., Erramilli, V., & Rodríguez, P. (2009). *Scaling online social networks without pains.* NetDB 2009. 5th International Workshop on Networking Meets Databases, co-located with SOSP 2009. Retrieved from http://www.rightscale.com

Rodero-Merino, L., Vaquero, L. M., Gil, V., Galán, F., Fontán, J., Montero, R. S., & Llorente, I. M. (in press). From infrastructure delivery to service management in clouds. [In Press]. *Future Generation Computer Systems.*

Scalr. (n.d.). *Website.* Retrieved from http://www.scalr.net

Song, S., Ryu, K. D., & Da Silva, D. (2009). *Blue eyes: Scalable and reliable system management for cloud computing IPDPS.* IEEE International Symposium on Parallel & Distributed Processing, (pp. 1-8).

Sun Cloud. (2009). *API.* Retrieved from http://kenai.com/projects/ suncloudapis/pages/Home

Tsay, A., Agrawal, N., & Nahmias, S. (1998). Modeling supply chain contracts: A review. In Tayur, S., Ganeshan, R., & Magazine, M. (Eds.), *Quantitative models for supply chain management* (pp. 299–336). Boston, MA: Kluwer Academic Publishers.

Vaquero, L. M., Rodero-Merino, L., Cáceres, J., & Lindner, M. A. (2009). Break in the clouds: Towards a cloud definition. *ACM Computer Communication Reviews, 39*(1), 50–55. doi:10.1145/1496091.1496100

Varia, J. (2008). *Amazon white paper on cloud architectures.* Retrieved from http://aws.typepad.com/aws/ 2008/07/white-paper-on.html

vCloud. (2009). *API programming guide.* VMWARE Inc.

WeoCeo. (2009). *Website.* Retrieved from http://weoceo.weogeo.com

Yang, J., Qiu, J., & Li, Y. (2009). *A profile-based approach to just-in-time scalability for cloud applications*. IEEE International Conference on Cloud Computing, (pp. 9-16).

Yi, G. S., Deng, Y., Yu, H., He, X., Beznosov, K., & Cooper, K. (2004). *Applying aspect-orientation in designing security systems: A case study*. International Conference of Software Engineering and Knowledge Engineering (SEKE), (pp. 360-365).

ENDNOTES

[1] This chapter will use several terms that given its ambiguity deserve some initial consideration: service provider: entity that places a given service in the cloud. The service may consist on several services or a single one offered or not to the end user. application provider: special type of service provider that either uses owned services or "packages" services offered in the Cloud to deliver a final application for end users. cloud provider: stakeholder offering some type of service in the Cloud.

[2] http://aws.amazon.com/console/

[3] http://aws.amazon.com/ec2/

[4] http://www.gogrid.com/

[5] http://www.flexiant.com/products/flexiscale/

[6] http://www.microsoft.com/windowsazure/windowsazure/

[7] http://aws.amazon.com/ec2-sla/

[8] See http://oddthesis.org/theses/jboss-cloud or http://java.dzone.com/articles/introduction-jboss-cloud

[9] http://www.microsoft.com/windowsazure/products/

[10] http://code.google.com/appengine/articles/scaling/overview.html

Chapter 13
QoS–Oriented Service Computing:
Bringing SOA Into Cloud Environment

Xiaoyu Yang
University of Southampton, UK

ABSTRACT

The idea of cloud computing aligns with new dimension emerging in service-oriented infrastructure where service provider does not own physical infrastructure but instead outsources to dedicated infrastructure providers. Cloud computing has now become a new computing paradigm as it can provide scalable IT infrastructure, QoS-assured services, and customizable computing environment. However, it still remains a challenging task to provide QoS assured services to serve customers with minimized cost, while also to guarantee the maximization of the business objectives (e.g. margin profit) to service provider and infrastructure provider within certain constraints. In order to address these issues, this chapter proposes a QoS-oriented service computing methodology, and discusses associated topics including service level agreement and associated reference architecture, green service, service metering and metrics, service monitoring, and on-demand resource provisioning. In the case study, we demonstrate how we employ QoS-oriented service computing in a multi-server, multi-user on-line game to facilitate the on-demand resource provisioning to maintain quality of service and quality of experience.

INTRODUCTION

Service computing is a multi-discipline domain that covers the science and technology of bridging the gap between Business Services and IT Services (Zhang et al., 2007). It aims to enable IT services and computing technology to carry out business services more efficiently and effectively. The supporting technology suite includes Web services and service-oriented architecture (SOA), and business process integration and management, etc. Although service computing

DOI: 10.4018/978-1-60960-735-7.ch013

is business-oriented, it has also been proved to be an effective approach that can be employed in e-Science to develop modern cyberinfrastructure to facilitate the scientific research and discovery.

More recently, the emergence of Cloud computing has brought new dimensions of applying IT and computing technologies to businesses and scientific research, which results in a new computing paradigm, where service provider dose not have to own any physical infrastructure but instead outsource to dedicated infrastructure providers. This computing paradigm can provide a scalable IT infrastructure, QoS-assured services and customizable computing environment. However, the current service computing technologies can not always meet the requirements of this computing paradigm, and there are several issues arose: (i) QoS-assured service delivery: while relationship between customer and service provider is inherently a "Customer – Service Provider" relationship, the service provider and infrastructure provider have also established a "Customer - Service Provider" relationship. As in this model the service provider faces both customer side and infrastructure provider side, the guarantee of the delivery of QoS-assured service becomes increasingly critical. (ii) Green service. How to provide QoS assured service to serve customers with minimized resource consumption cost and meet customer's satisfaction, while also to guarantee the maximization of the business objectives (e.g. margin profit) to service provider and infrastructure provider within certain constraints. (iii) Service discovery: One service can have several service providers with different service prices. Even the same service provider can provide a service with different Service Level Objectives (SLO) which incurs different cost. How customers can find appropriate services they want. (iv) Service metering, which plays a fundamental role in service computing as QoS-assured service and green service all require metered services to be delivered. This involves creating a generic metric model which can be used in different service occa-

sions. (v) On-demand resource provisioning. How to elastically provision resources on-demand?

Currently, service computing / service engineering mainly concerns about the service modeling, creation, deployment and service quality assessment during its lifecycle, known as Methodology of Service Engineering (MSE). For example, the discipline of service engineering, which was first proposed in the mid 90's in Germany and Israel (Bullinger, 2003; Mandelbaum, 1998), is concerned with the systematic development of services using suitable models, methods and tools. Service engineering promotes an integrated service by adopting technological methods and employing existing engineering know-how to maximize efficiency (Tomiyama, 2001; Bullinger et al., 2003). Product service co-design and service modeling claim that traditional engineering methods and tools in applied science can be borrowed for service design and development (Ganz et al., 2004). Service CAD argues that computer-based tools can be used to design services, just as CAD can be used to facilitate the design of products and simulation of their behaviors under various circumstances (Tomiyama, 2003). The driver for the emergence of New Service Development (NSD) is that the product development paradigm fails to address the unique characteristics inherent in services, such as customers as a participant in the service process, intangibility, and heterogeneity of customer demand (Fitzsimmons et al., 2000). Life cycle oriented service design (Aurich et al., 2004) argued that Life Cycle Engineering (LCE) (Jeswiet, 2003) can be adopted for the design of service.

However, these static service computing technologies mainly concern the modeling, creation and deployment of separate services. They can not well resolve issues occurring at the stage of service discovery, service outsourcing, and service usage. In order to address these issues in service computing, we proposed "QoS-oriented Service Computing" to accommodate needs for service computing in the context of Cloud environment.

In this chapter, we will discuss the following topics for QoS-oriented Service Computing, which includes Service Level Agreement (SLA), green service, service metering, service monitoring, QoS assured service, and on-demand resource provisioning. In a case study, we discuss how we employ QoS-oriented service computing in a multi-server, multi-user on-line game to facilitate the on-demand resource provisioning to guarantee the QoS-assured services.

BACKGROUND OF SERVICE COMPUTING AND CLOUD COMPUTING

This section reviews literatures related to service computing and Cloud computing. Especially, we provide a survey on relevant standards and specification languages which can be employed in presenting the SLA. We identified appropriate standards for SLA representation. The survey has also resulted in the formulation of reference architecture for SLA life cycle management.

Service-Oriented Architecture

A Service-Oriented Architecture (SOA) contains a collection of services which can communicate with each other. The communication can involve either data exchange or it could involve more services managing a specific activity. In this context, a service is a function that is well defined, self-contained, and does not depend on the context or state of other services. SOAs offer a variety of advantages over traditional distributed computing systems and for this reason they tend to replace the platforms upon which the business services are offered to the clients. They provide location independence for services, which means that services can run anywhere. The searching and connection to other service can be dynamic and follow a loosely coupled approach, which can thus enable the formulation of general purpose service

provision infrastructures interoperable with a broad set of technologies and business process. Other advantages of using SOAs include their ability to build composite applications by integrating Web services via workflow, which can automate the whole process without direct human interaction or control. SOA can also facilitate enabling a scalable infrastructure to meet the requirements of on-demand resource provisioning.

Standards and Specification Languages for SLA Representation

Web service has now been widely used in e-Science, service-oriented infrastructure, and various computing paradigms (e.g. Cloud computing, Grid computing, service computing), hence ensuring Quality of Service (QoS) is becoming increasingly important. Service Level Agreement (SLA) can be employed to serve as a bilateral contract that exists between a customer and a service provider to specify the user requirements, quality of service, responsibilities and obligations (http://www.gridipedia.eu). SLA can contain numerous service performance metrics with corresponding Service Level Objectives (SLO). It describes quality of service and other commitments by a service provider in exchange for financial commitments based on an agreed schedule of prices and payments (http://www.gria.org/about-gria/a-business-perspective).

It is critical that the electronic SLA can be presented in a certain specification language and this language should be extensible and standard-based, so that the SLA provisioning and management system can deal with SLA in a flexible manner. Although there were some articles (e.g. Dobson, 2004; Seidel et al., 2007) that reviewed the associated specification languages for QoS and SLA, the discussed specification languages are either out of data, or not complete.

The SLA life cycle typically includes associated service provider discovery, negotiation, conformance monitoring, enforcement, and end-of-life invoicing, etc. The SLA life cycle management requires a comprehensive SLA manager to provide a set of key functionalities such as negotiation of QoS terms, acquisition of usage data/QoS measurement, conformance check, and billing. Therefore it is essential to have a high level SLA reference architecture which can provide guidelines for SLA application / service development. Although various SLA managers have been developed in many research projects and industry applications, the generic SLA manger reference architecture with identified key components remains unclear.

Relevant SLA specification languages to be reviewed include: (i) QoS Markup Language (QML), (ii) Hierarchical QoS Markup Language (HQML), (iii) Web Service Level Agreement (WSLA), (iv) SLAng, (v) Web Service Management Language (WSML), (vi) Web Service Offering Language (WSOL), (vii) W3C WS-Policy (WSP), (viii) WS-Agreement, (ix) WSDM, and (x) WS-management.

QoS Markup Language

QoS Markup Language (QML) (Svend, 1998) was developed in 1998 by HP laboratory. It aims to define multi-category QoS specification for components in distributed object systems. QML is now out-of-date. It is mainly used for QoS terms specification and not appropriate for SLA specification.

HQML

The Hierarchical QoS Markup Language (HQML) (Gu et al., 2002) developed by University of Illinois in 2002, is an XML based language to enhance the distributed multimedia application over Web with QoS capabilities. HQML schema is simple. But it is more like a specification language for QoS management rather than a specification language for SLA. It is not closely tied up to the use of Web service. The proposed XML schema

(using xml DTD) mixes the QoS metrics and price terms together.

Web Service Level Agreement (WSLA)

The Web Service Level Agreement (WSLA) (Ludwig, 2003) is a specification language for service level agreement. It was proposed by IBM and version 1.0 was released in 2003. In WSLA, the structure of SLA can include: (i) Parties, (ii) Service definition, and (iii) Obligations (Ludwig, 2003).

- "Parties" define parties involved in the management of Web service such as customer, service provider, third parties, etc.
- "Service definition" describes: (i) definition of the service, (ii) SLA parameters, and (iii) the way SLA parameters are measured and computed. In service definition, a term service object is used to describe what Web service operations an SLA relates to.
- "Obligations" defines the service level that is guaranteed with respect to the SLA parameters, and promises to perform actions under particular conditions. It provides two kinds of guarantees: (i) Service Level Objective (SLO), and (ii) Action Guarantees. SLO expresses a commitment to maintain a particular state of the service in a given period, while Action Guarantees expresses a commitment to perform particular activity if a given precondition is met.

WSLA 1.0 is fully documented and publicly available. It has been widely used. WSLA 1.0 specification clearly defines the structure of SLA; especially it distinguishes the SLA parameter and metrics. It provides a framework for specifying and monitoring SLA for Web services. WSLA is also extensible. All these make WSLA promising as a QoS/SLA specification language. The identified problem is that the v1.0 was released in 2003, and it has not been officially supported since then.

SLAng: A Language for Defining Service Level Agreement

SLAng is SLA language developed by University of College London (UCL) under the TAPAS project (http://tapas.sourceforge.net/) (2002-2005). SLAng defines six different types of SLA, which are divided into Vertical SLAs and Horizontal SLAs (Lamanna et al., 2003). SLAng does not clearly describe the structure of SLA. The classification of vertical SLAs and horizontal SLAs is easy to confuse people. The TAPAS project finished in 2005, and the further development of SLAng cannot be guaranteed.

Web Service Management Language

Web Service Management Language (WSML) (Sahai et al., 2001) was developed in 2001 by HP Laboratories. It can be regarded as an extension of QoS Modeling Language (QML) (Svend et al., 1998) by allowing the definition of SLO, validity period and mathematical operation of measured data, etc. which were not supported in QML. However, WSML does not enable specification of management third parties. Further, WSML does not define the language for expressions to be evaluated. It is assumed that expressions will be written in some other mathematical languages, such as MathML. This means that the infrastructure for WSML constraints evaluation needs to support these mathematical languages.

Web Service Offering Language

Web Service Offering Language (WSOL) (Tosic et al., 2003) claims to be a language for the formal specification of various constraints, management statements, and classes of service for Web services. It was developed in 2003 by Carleton University, Canada. The motivation of development of WSOL is that the WSDL cannot support specification of various constraints, management statements, classes of service, SLAs and other contracts. The

development of WSOL has made much reference to WSLA and WSML discussed previously. One of the distinct features of WSOL is that it has defined external ontologies of QoS metrics and measurement units for the specification of QoS constraints. In the current implementation of WSOL, it is assumed that ontology of QoS metrics is a collection of names with information about appropriate data types and measurement units. Similarly, ontology of measurement units is a simple collection of names without any additional information.

Authors of WSOL have identified the drawbacks of WSDL and proposed such a solution attempting to address them. However, WSOL is not widely used and accepted. The W3C (http://www.w3.org/) recommended WS-Policy now becomes a standard to address these needs.

WS-Policy

WS-Policy is a W3C recommendation since September 2007. WS-Policy is a standard to describe the properties that characterize a Web service (http://www.w3.org/TR/ws-policy-primer/). By means of this specification, the functional description of a service can be tied to a set of assertions that describe how the Web service should work in terms of aspects like security, transactionability, and reliable messaging. WS-Policy document is in charge of composing assertions to identify how a Web service should work. These assertions can be used to express both functional aspects (e.g. constraints on exchanged data), and non-functional aspects (e.g. security, transactionability, and message reliability). WS-Policy language is an extensible language by design. The *Policy*, *ExactlyOne*, *All* and *wsp:PolicyReference* elements are extensible.

Although WS-Policy is recommended by W3C, it actually provides no advantage for QoS specification, other than it is a standard way of associating QoS-like descriptions with service (Dobson, 2004; Chaari et al., 2008). Also WS-

Policy does not support capabilities of negotiation, monitoring agreement compliance at runtime which SLA management needs. But WS-Policy is an extensible language and as one of W3C SOA standard stack, it has potential to be used for SLA representation.

WS-Agreement

WS-Agreements proposed by OGF (http://www.ogf.org/) is a popular standard to be aggregated into Web service architecture to support the management of non-functional requirements in Web service (Garcia et al., 2006). It is a protocol for establishing an agreement on the usage of services between a service provider and a consumer (http://www.ogf.org/documents/GFD.107.pdf).

WS-Agreement has more expressive power to describe service level objectives, which state the requirements and capabilities of each party on the availability of resources and service qualities. It has been widely used in Grid communities. Seidel et al. (Seidel et al. 2007) identified many research projects which employ WS-Agreement for SLA representation for resource management and scheduling.

Web Service Distributed Management

The Web Services Distributed Management (WSDM) (http://www.oasis-open.org/committees/tc_home.php?wg_abbrev=wsdm) standard published by OASIS (http://www.oasis-open.org/home/index.php) defines the methods, structure, and specification of a system for managing network resources (e.g. printers, routers, servers and services) and for managing Web service. WSDM contains two parts: (i) Management Using Web services (MUWS) and (ii) Management of Web services (MOWS) (http://www.oasis-open.org/committees/tc_home.php?wg_abbrev=wsdm).

However, as the aim of WSDM is about management using Web service and management of Web service, rather than focus on defining ca-

pabilities and requirements of service providers and customers. The support of defining metrics and measurement is limited. A domain-specific model or domain ontology needs to be defined when using WSDM in SLA. WSDM provides an event model which could be used for SLA monitoring, but it does not provide support for SLA negotiation.

Web Service Management (WS-Management)

Web Service for Management (WS-Management) (http://www.dmtf.org/standards/wsman), another SOA management protocol, is a specification for managing devices, computers, Web services and applications using Web service. It was proposed by Distributed Management Task Force (DMTF) (http://www.dmtf.org/home) and published in 2004 with support from IT companies such as AMD, Dell, Intel, Microsoft and Sun. DMTF is a standards organization that develops and maintains standards for systems management of IT environments in enterprises and the Internet.

WS-Management has some overlapping area with MUWS of WSDM but has addition on accessing resources. WS-Management can be regarded as sort of implementation of management model namely "Common Information Model" proposed by DMTF. Similar to WSDM, WS-Management aims at management of services, devices and applications, hence has same disadvantage as WSDM does. WS-management is not strong enough to be used in SLA. For example, it does not provide a negotiation model for SLA, not appropriate for defining agreement between customer and service provider.

Survey Findings

Research findings from the survey are summarised as follows:

1. The survey shows that WS-Agreement and WS-Policy can be two candidate standards to be

employed for SLA presentation. Especially, the WS-Agreement is widely used in many Grid computing projects. WS-Agreement not only provides a specification language for representing SLA, but also provides protocol for SLA negotiation and monitoring.

2. While there are many research projects which involve employing SLA for service and resource management, a comprehensive reference architecture which identifies key SLA components and illustrates how these components are engineered and interacted to provide a generic overview of SLA application / service has not been investigated in great depth. GRIA SLA Management Service (http://www.gria.org/) is usable, but the high level SLA architecture is still not quite clear. Web Service Level Agreement (WSLA) provides an SLA framework. It defines how basic metrics should be measured and how they are aggregated into composite metrics and SLA parameters. It also provides expression of the operations for monitoring and managing the service. However, WSLA was developed to provide an SLA specification language rather than SLA life cycle management. Although SLA has been used in many research projects, these projects are mainly concerned with one or two functional aspects of SLA (i.e. resource management and scheduling, negotiation) and do not provide a high-level view of the SLA manager.

3. It is recommended to incorporate domain ontology into the SLA to present semantic-rich policies and requirements. Semantics-enriched policies can facilitate more accurate SLA life cycle management than the syntactic approaches. Therefore, apart from the key SLA manager requirements identified in the survey, another requirement of the SLA manager is that it should be 'semantic-aware'.

Cloud Computing

Cloud computing has become a new computing paradigm as it can offer a scalable IT infrastructure, QoS-assured services and customizable

computing environment. Cloud computing can be illustrated from the following aspects:

SPI model - Cloud computing originates from the concept "Hardware as a Service" (HaaS), "Software as a Service" (SaaS). Cloud now advances from SaaS to "Platform as a Service" (PaaS) and "Infrastructure as a Service" (IaaS), known as SPI model. In Cloud computing, customers can avoid capital expenditure on hardware and software by renting the usage from service provider of third parties, rather than owning the physical infrastructure by themselves. The hardware and software are rendered to customers as IT services.

Scalability / elasticity - Klems and Gaw claim that automatic scale of infrastructure for load balancing is a key element in Cloud computing (Geelan, 2008). The delivered services can elastically / dynamically grow its capacity on an as-needed basis so that the quality of service can be guaranteed. "On-demand services are all Cloud computing based" (de HAAf, 2008).

"Pay-per-use" / "Pay-as-you-go" / "Utility computing" - There is also a vision that Cloud computing is more like a business revolution, rather than a technology evolution. Business model, or we call "pay-per-use", "pay-as-you-go", and 'utility computing' is another feature of Cloud computing (Kaplan and Cohen in Geelan, 2008; Watson et al., 2008; Buyya et al., 2009). The usage of the resource will be metered and service customers will pay bill to service provider for the actual resource usage.

Data centre - Another view of Cloud is that it is a powerful computer and the data centre is the basic unit of the infrastructure (McFedries, 2008). Data centre can offer huge amount of computing power and data storage. The capacity of the data centre can dynamically when handling a task. According to (Vaquero et al., 2009), this is associated with the concept "massive data scalability" proposed by (Hand, 2007).

Virtualisation - Cloud computing can also be regarded as a "virtualised hardware and software" (Gourlay and Sheynkman in Geelan, 2008). This perspective emphases the use of virtualisation technology in the Cloud computing. Virtualization technologies multiplex hardware and have made the flexible and scalable provision of resource as hardware and software on demand easier. Virtual machine techniques, such as VMware (http://www.vmware.com/) and Xen (http://www.xen.org/), offer virtualized IT-infrastructures on demand. Virtual network advances, such as VPN (Virtual Private Network), support users with a customized network environment to access Cloud resources.

Cloud service or Cloud Computing? – Apart from the above perspectives about the Cloud computing, we think it would be more accurate to call it "Cloud service", rather than using the term "Cloud computing", as eventually everything delivered by Cloud is presented as a Web service, e.g. storage service, computing service.

Currently many research and development work relating to Cloud computing focus on single provider Cloud within an administrative domain. This single provider Cloud has inherently problems of scalability and interoperability. For example, the single provider may not be able to provide infinite scalability. Also, this can result in an inability to scale through business partnerships across Clouds providers. Customer has to lock to a single Cloud vendor and no flexibility to choose Cloud vendors. More recently, "federated Cloud computing" is emerging. There is no global definition for federated Cloud computing but the aim of the federated Cloud computing is to federate disparate data centers, including those owned by separate organizations to enable a seemingly infinite service computing utility (Rochwerger et al., 2009). So far there is not much effort in research and development of federated Cloud computing. An EU FP7 funded project RESEVIOR (http://www.reservoir-fp7.eu/) is currently investigating this and proposed a RESEVIOR model and architecture for open federated Cloud computing (Rochwerger et al., 2009). In this RESEVIOR model the entity of "service providers" and "infrastructure providers" are clearly differentiated. The

"service providers" understand customer needs and offer associated services to address customer needs. But "service providers" do not own any computational resources by themselves; instead, they rent resources from "infrastructure providers" for service applications. The computational resources of each infrastructure provider (called "site" in RESEVOIR model) are partitioned by a virtualization layer into several Virtual Execution Environments (VEE). The federation of sites forms a RESEVOIR Cloud, where a service application will be deployed. The service application can be regarded as consisting of a set of software components working together to achieve a goal. Each component of such service applications executes in a certain VEE. These VEEs can be placed on the same or different VEE Hosts within the site, or even on different sites. The EU-funded Edutain@Grid project (http://www.edutaingrid.eu/) has also proposed a federated Cloud computing model with associated business infrastructure for real-time online interactive applications, where multiple independent infrastructure providers can cooperate seamlessly to provide scalable IT infrastructure and QoS-assured services. The distinct feature of Edutain federation Cloud computing model is that it lies in the concept of "code mobility". More about Edutain federated Cloud computing model can be found in the section "Case Study: QoS-oriented Service Computing in Edutain@Grid".

QOS-ORIENTED SERVICE COMPUITNG

The SPI model of Cloud computing determines that service is a fundamental construction unit. However, the traditional service computing usually focuses on the functional aspects of a service such as service modeling, service composition, etc. In order to accommodate the need for bringing SOA in Cloud computing, we proposed QoS-oriented service computing which aims to address the following major issues: (i) Service Level Agreement

(SLA) and associated reference architecture, (ii) green service, (iii) service metering and metrics, (iv) service monitoring, (v) service QoS assurance, and (vi) on-demand resource provisioning.

Service Level Agreement and Reference Architecture

Service Level Agreement (SLA) can be employed to serve as a bilateral contract that exists between a customer and a service provider to specify the user requirements, quality of service, responsibilities and obligations. SLA can contain numerous service performance metrics with corresponding Service Level Objectives (SLO). It describes quality of service and other commitments by a service provider in exchange for financial commitments based on an agreed schedule of prices and payments. A high-level and generic SLA reference architecture has been proposed based on the key requirements identified, as shown in Figure 1. One of the innovative features of the proposed reference architecture is the incorporation of domain ontology to allow the SLA manager semantic aware. The SLA manager contains the following key functional component modules, and each module is briefly discussed as follows:

Service Marketplace

Service marketplace provides a store for service providers to publish their services with price. Customer can search services not only by functionality but also QoS requirements. The service market place will return a list of EPRs of matching services with price. The returned list can be ranked by QoS requirements or price. The service marketplace can be implemented using standard-based technologies such as UDDI, ebXML, etc.

Negotiator

The negotiator component is responsible for SLA negotiation based on the SLA template. Once

customer/broker finds the appropriate service provider from Service Marketplace through SLA template, customer/broker makes a proposal to the service provider by modifying service level requirement terms. The service provider will then check the resources to make sure whether service level requirements can be guaranteed, and will accept or /reject the proposal. Once the SLA proposal is agreed by both parties, it becomes an SLA instance.

MetaScheduler

MetaScheduler can be used for resource metascheduling or resource access control. It involves the consideration of the current status of all available suitable computational resources and selecting the resource that is most suitable for the simulation in question. It accepts the agreed SLA instance as one of input, and returns a list of End Reference Points (ERP) of resources or returns none ERP. A list of ERPs returned or no ERP returned can be regarded as a kind of access control mechanism. For example, in the case that each job to be submitted has an SLA constraints, the metascheduler can return an ordered list of available computing resources on which the job can be carried out respecting SLA's constraints.

Runtime Monitor

It collects the resource usage information to monitor associated parameters related to service level objectives. This component usually interacts with a service-side / resource-side resource usage or QoS measurement component that is responsible for the acquisition of resource usage data and QoS measurement data. The monitoring protocol can be polling protocol, publish/subscribe, call-back, etc. *Runtime Monitor* contains the following functional sub-modules:

- Term Interpreter: mapping of high level application-specific business objectives

Figure 1. Generic SLA Reference Architecture. The reference architecture also depicts a working model of how various components interact through the associated workflow. The workflow starts with 0(a) where service/resource provider provides service/resources, and ends at 11 where a bill is sent to the customer

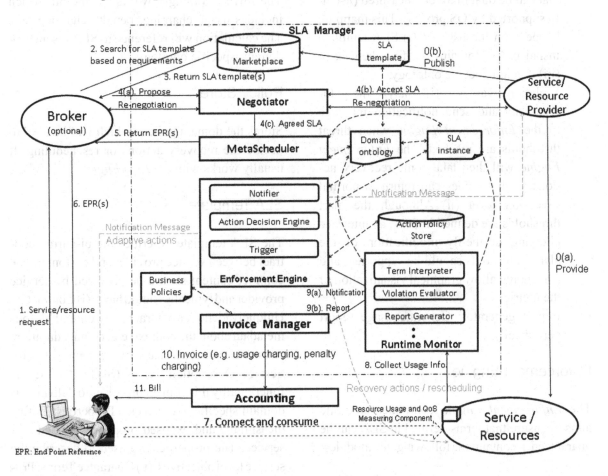

Figure 2. Service Marketplace where service providers can publish their services with prices. Customer can search the service by both functionality and QoS requirements

into low-level infrastructural parameters (such as CPU, bandwidth, memory usage) that can be quantitatively measured (usually supported by OS probes). This mapping happens on the basis of (i) SLA template instance, (ii) domain-specific schemas, or (iii) domain-specific ontology.

- Violation Evaluator: (i) Analyze the gathered data and send notification message to the *Enforcement Engine* when threat thresholds are reached. The *Enforcement Engine* will then take some recovery actions so that values can return to normal execution level (ii) Although the alert thresholds are defined in SLA, an interface allowing on-the-fly modification of the alarm thresholds should be supported, and (iii) should allow graphical visualization of the metrics.
- Report generator: Generate usage report periodically.

Enforcement Engine

The *Enforcement Engine* component module aims to ensure that terms defined in SLA can be guaranteed. It contains the following sub-modules:

- Notifier: Will send notification message to service provider or customer when violation event happens.
- Rule Engine: Based on the feature of the event, the *Rule Engine* will (i) retrieve relevant policy from the *Policy Store*, (ii) get parameters from SLA instance, or (iii) domain knowledge from the ontology, together to decide the recovery actions or rescheduling.
- Trigger: Responsible for taking recovery actions or rescheduling instructed by the *Rule Engine*. For example, to get a new service deployed, or get a new session created.

Invoice Manager

The *Invoice Manager* works out the bill which includes usage charging, penalty charging, etc. The calculation will reference to SLA instance or domain-specific ontology.

Policy Store

Stores the domain polices which will be used to decide the recovery actions or rescheduling. It usually works with the *Rule Engine*.

SLA Template

The SLA template describes the bi-partite contract between service provider and customer. The contract content should be provided by service provider and typically should have: (i) Contract Id: Uniquely identify a contract. (ii) Context: Various metadata about the context, e.g. contact duration, consumer name, service provider name, etc. (iii) Service Description Terms (SDT): Define the functionality this contact promises to deliver. It is domain specific. (iv) Service Properties: Define measurable and exposed properties related to a service. The properties are used to describe the service level objectives. (v) Guarantee Terms: Provide assurance on the service quality or resource availability offered by a service provider, and (vi) Business Terms: Usage charging or penalty. The survey has shown that WS-Agreement is an appropriate standard for the representation of the SLA template.

SLA Instance

Once terms and agreement of SLA have been agreed by both service provider and service consumer after negotiation, the SLA becomes an SLA instance. It serves as a signed contract between both parties.

Domain Ontology

It defines domain-specific knowledge so that the SLA manager can have a semantic understanding of a specific domain. This should be provided by service provider and usually works with SLA.

Green Service

Invoking a service involves the consumption of resources and may incur cost. Sustainable development advocates reduction of resource consumption, while delivering better and more widely available goods and services. Hence delivering "green service" has become increasingly important. Recent concerns regarding global climate change and the energy crisis have led to renewed interest in Green Computing. In order to address the issue, one of the aims of this proposed QoS-oriented service computing methodology is to investigate how we employ a variety of techniques and tools to model the performance of applications over a service-oriented infrastructure for the trade-off among QoS guarantees, cost, and margin profit to stakeholders in the value chain involving service customer, service provider and infrastructure provider.

The resource consumption of running an application can be subject to several factors: (i) application workload feature, (ii) user interaction, (iii) network features, and (vi) mean time to failure. We can use optimization technology to find a resource with associated configuration that can guarantee service's behavior within the constraints and can maximize an objective function. In EU-funded IRMOS project (http://www.irmosproject.eu/), the input parameters for the optimization function have been indentified as follows (Mitchell et al., 2009):

- Customer Requirements: The customer requirements will be recorded in the SLA. This will include key QoS performance indicators such as application / service completion time, mean time to failure, mean time for recovery (tolerated annoyance), application availability and associated cost. In some circumstances, the corresponding SLA values might differ from values initially requested by the customer because they may not reach.

- Customer Obligations: The customer need commit to certain behavior in order to receive the required QoS at a given cost. For example, the customer may simply be required to provide input data by a certain time or may need to agree more complex profiling such as using an application according to certain usage time distribution (mean usage rate for given time interval), workload volume distribution, workload complexity distribution. The customer obligations will ultimately be recorded as SLA terms. The process of deriving these constraints can be quite complex and will involve detailed knowledge to the customer behavior.

- Application and Resource Profiles: Application and resource profiles define a set of parameters for applications and resources that impact the key performance indicators. The technical characteristics of resource can include: specifications of CPU, volatile storage, persistent storage, operating system, system libraries; but could also include scores of the platform against a set of benchmark tests.

Application performance indicator predications can be carried out using a set of models describing aspects of the user, the resource and the application behavior, which are then combined to determine the behavior of the service as a whole. For example, in IRMOS project, it has identified that each service can have the following models (Addis et al., 2009):

- User Behavior Modeling: estimates customer behavior for a given service specifically dealing with interactivity and human aspects such the impact of attention, decision making and situational awareness. It should be noted that customer behavior (e.g. Kevin tends to submit large jobs and takes many short brakes!) is often the critical factor in accurately estimating resource requirements.

- Resource Behavior Modeling: estimates resource reliability probabilities including both in-house and third party resources obtained from infrastructure providers. These models use resource knowledge derived from both QoS reports from infrastructure providers and local Quality of Experience (QoE) measurements. The Application Provider may use QoE measurements to validate the QoS reported to it by the infrastructure provider.

- Un-interrupted Fault-free Application Behavior Modeling: estimates completion time probability from given customer requirements and obligations. A combination of techniques are used to determine completion time probabilities such as artificial neural networks, benchmarking, curve fitting, lookup tables, and discrete values based on actual knowledge

- Interactive Application Performance Estimation: estimates the key application performance indicators by combining information about the normal (uncorrupted) behavior of the application with information about exceptional circumstances that might occur, i.e. different failure probabilities and times for recovery. Finite State Automata (FSA) models are used to determine an applications reaction to both input and resourcing events.

Metric and Service Metering

Service metering is increasingly becoming an important issue as QoS-assured service, service monitoring and on-demand resource provisioning all depend on it. In order to meter the service usage, metrics must be defined to measure the service usage. The SLA manager should be able to retrieve usage information from functional services (e.g. job services), records the usage and optionally constrains and/or bills for the usage. Different functional services will need to report usage of different measurable quantities. For example, a job service will report usage of CPU but a data service will report usage of disc space. These measurable quantities, known as "metrics" are represented by URIs.

GRIA middleware (v5.3.1) (http://www.gria.org/) has a simple while practical service metering and monitoring component. The GRIA middleware provides a Service-Oriented Infrastructure (SOI) designed to support B2B collaborations through service provision across organisational boundaries in a secure, interoperable and flexible manner. In GRIA, the use of metrics is recorded in terms of "instantaneous" measurements and "cumulative" usage. The cumulative usage is the integration of the instantaneous measurements over time. For some metrics, data-transfer for example, the instantaneous measurement is best regarded as a rate (bytes per second) and the cumulative usage has no time dimension (bytes). For other metrics, such as CPU, the instantaneous measurement is just the quantity in use at the time (e.g. 3 CPUs) and it is the cumulative usage that has the time dimension, e.g. 180 CPU.seconds (Boniface et al., 2006). The GRIA SLA service can convert between the two, as shown in (http://www.gria.org/), e.g.:

- If a job runs on 1 CPU for 5 minutes then the SLA service will be notified that the instantaneous measurement of CPU usage went to 1 at the start and then to 0 five minutes later. The SLA service can infer that 300 CPU.seconds of CPU time have been used (1*5*60 = 300 CPU.seconds).

- If a service reported that it had used 120 units of a resource in a 1 minute period, the SLA service would infer that the average instantaneous measurement (rate of usage) had been 2 units/s.

Service Monitoring

Service monitoring involves providing the SLA manager with a document containing usage reports from each activity supported by the service. In principle, this can be an asynchronous message from the application service to the SLA manager. The GRIA middleware (v5.3.1) proposed to use the WS-BaseNotification specification (http://docs. oasis-open.org/wsn/wsn-ws_base_notification-1.3-spec-os.pdf) for implementing the service monitoring (http://www.gria.org/about-gria/relationship-to-standards. Access date: 22 Sept., 2010). It suggested that the full implementation would involve a lot of software development; hence we could let the SLA manager poll for usage information, using one specific WS-BaseNotification method. The agile software development approach can then be employed to extend the implementation of the support of push and brokered messaging iteratively and incrementally. Application services should support this by providing the message retrieval (GetMessages) request and response defined by the PullPoint interface in the WS-BaseNotification specification. The response to this request contains zero or more notification messages as defined by WS-BaseNotification, as shown in Figure 3.

Each NotificationMessage element should contain a usage report message from a single activity, and should give the activity's EPR as the ProducerReference. A single GetMessages response can contain several NotificationMessage elements, which mean the application service can generate messages from an activity at times of its choosing, and cache them until a GetMessages request is received. But the WS-BaseNotification requires that the producer should only send a message once to the recipient, so the application service will need keep track of which messages have been delivered. The notification message format is also defined by WS-BaseNotification, as shown in Figure 3.

QoS-Assured Service

Once the service is monitored, we can analyze the acquired QoS measurement data to guarantee the quality of the service. This involves the issue of capacity management, which concerns with resources being able to adapt themselves to meet the live requirements of service processes to ensure that the whole service provisioning will remain within performance compliance. This means the execution of trend analysis on historical

Figure 3. WS-Notification Specification Fragment

```
<wsnt:GetMessagesResponse>
 <wsnt:NotificationMessage />*
</wsnt:GetMessagesResponse>

<wsnt:NotificationMessage>
<wsnt:SubscriptionReference>wsa:EndpointReference</wsnt:SubscriptionReference>?
 <wsnt:Topic Dialect="xsd:anyURI">{any} *</wsnt:Topic>?
 <wsnt:ProducerReference>wsa:EndpointReference</wsnt:ProducerReference>?
 <wsnt:Message>{any}</wsnt:Message>
<wsnt:NotificationMessage>
```

monitoring data could predict the likely breach of contract in future. For example, if QoS data is showing a trend that the service is overloading (which might be due to growing data set sizes, or increasing numbers of concurrent users, or other factors) then at some point the service will no longer meet the criteria specified within the SLA. In order to ensure the compliance with agreed QoS constraints, the capacity management is charged to ensure that additional capacity is added in advance (additional CPUs, more memory, new database indexing) so that the trend lines are reset and the service will remain within the specified performance range. In other words, if the provisioning resource can not guarantee the QoS of a service, the resource should automatically scale. More will be discussed in next section "On-demand Resource Provisioning".

On-Demand Resource Provisioning

On-demand resource provisioning is one of key features of Cloud scalability. When the provisioning resource (as a service) cannot meet customer's quality of experience, the resource should automatically grow its capacity to meet the defined QoS requirements. This capacity growth is transparent to the users.

There are several approaches to address these needs. In this chapter we only introduce two EU funded research projects, namely Edutain@Grid project and IRMOS project, showing how they address the "capacity on demand" issues. The Edutain@Grid project (http://www.edutaingrid. eu/) has investigated the open federated Cloud computing initiative for on-demand resource provisioning. Edutain@Grid aims to develop a scalable QoS-enabled business Grid environment for multi-user Real-time Online Interactive Applications (ROIA) (Fahringer et al., 2007). ROIA application (e.g. on-line game) is characterized by the high rate of interaction between users, requiring very fast updates of information being passed from one computer to another (Fahringer et al., 2007). As

large numbers of users may participate in a single instance, and are typically able to join or leave at any time. Thus ROIA application has extremely dynamic distributed workloads, making it difficult to host them efficiently (Ploß et al., 2009). In this project, we developed a service-oriented infrastructure with enhanced security features to support a business model where multiple independent hosters can cooperate seamlessly to provide QoS assured ROIA service to customers, hence maximize the benefits.

In EU-funded IRMOS project (http://www. irmosproject.eu/), it introduced an Intelligent Service Oriented Network Infrastructure (INSONI) to address the on-demand resource provisioning (http://www.it-tude.com/isoni_whitepaper.html. Access date: 22 Sept., 2010). The ISONI is an infrastructure, consisting of a network of resources (e.g. CPU, storage, networking and software) managed and controlled by an ISONI middleware that allows resource sharing among multiple services. The general idea is to provide a service-oriented infrastructure for SOA components and services. A service is usually composed of several smaller and simpler services known as Service Components (SC). For SCs orchestrated into a complete service, a virtual machine will be provisioned, although it will still be possible to place several SCs in one virtual machine. ISONI ensures to provide the best resources for these SCs to be executed whatever these SCs are. Links between SCs will be provided as needed. There are three tasks involved in the ISONI. (i) To completely separate the management of all hardware resources distributed in a network from that of deployed services and their associated service components. Thus the actual status and distribution of resources are hidden from the service developer's view. (ii) To deploy and instantiate service on the ISONI. The ISONI will be able to accomplish this task automatically and autonomously, which is the main goal of the ISONI development. (iii) To monitor running services and their resource usage. This monitoring data will be available to the external, e.g. via web service interfaces.

The ISONI should be able to automatically deploy and instantiate the service. In order to facilitate this, ISONI introduces an abstract description of all the execution environment requirements of the service, including the description of the interconnections and their individual QoS demands, namely, Virtual Service Network (VSN). This VSN description needs to be delivered by the service developer. Each VSN maps to one or more Virtual Machine Unit (VMU). The VSN description is transferred to the ISONI with the request to instantiate the service. The ISONI then:

- Automatically and autonomously maps the highly abstracted resource request in form of the VSN description onto the network of real resources
- Deploys the components in tailored execution environments on suitable resources
- Interconnects them while observing QoS requirements

CASE STUDY: QOS-ORIENTED SERVICE COMPUITNG IN EDUTAIN@GRID

This case study demonstrates how QoS-oriented service computing is employed in Edutain@ Grid project to facilitate the on-demand resource provisioning.

Edutain@Grid: Cloud Computing Vision

When the Edutain project was sponsored there was no term called "Cloud computing". But the Edutain project inherently encompasses many concepts/ideas that Cloud computing is promoting (e.g. HaaS/SaaS, utility computing, on-demand resource provisioning), and many of which have been implemented and demonstrated for ROIA.

Currently ROIA-alike applications (e.g. on-line game) are hosted statically, which is independent from the actual user demand. This static hosting strategy can lead to significant over consumption of resources on average (and hence increased costs), yet may be unable to match peak demand on occasion, leading to customer dissatisfaction. On the other hand, Grid-based hosting has the potential to tackle these problems by allowing resources to be provisioned on-demand to match the dynamically changing user loads.

In order to accommodate these needs, the Edutain business model (as shown in Figure 4) introduces a concept, namely ROIA Coordinator to help realize the on-demand resource provisioning for ROIA application from the scalability and performance perspective. Coordinator can be regarded as an organization that plays a role of ROIA application service provider (e.g. online game). However, the Coordinator itself does not have any physical infrastructure for running ROIA, instead it outsources the ROIA hosting services to Hoster, which is an organization that dedicates to host core, usually computationally intensive processes that support a ROIA running environment. The Hoster plays a role of infrastructure provider. The Coordinator provides an integrated user frontend (e.g. portal) to make ROIA instances accessible to consumers. In order to get access to the ROIA instance, a customer need open an account with Coordinator to obtain a Security Assertions Markup Language (SAML) token, and then use this SAML token to get connection details of associated ROIA instances.

In this Coordinator-Hoster business model for ROIA applications, the ROIA hosting platform and ROIA application are delivered by Hosters as services to the Coordinator. The Coordinator has an account and a bipartite Service Level Agreement (SLA) with Hoster. The Hoster provides metered services to the Coordinator. When the hosting service finishes, the Hoster sends the bill to the Coordinator for the resource usage. This

Figure 4. ROIA application developer develops ROIA for Coordinator. Coordinator creates an account with Hoster, and outsources hosting ROIA applications service to Hosters. A service level agreement is established between a Coordinator and Hoster to ensure the quality of service. When a customer need access to a ROIA, he/she must register with Coordinator to get SAML token, and use this SAML token to get connection details of associated ROIA instance. The customer then uses this connection details to connect to the associated ROIA instance

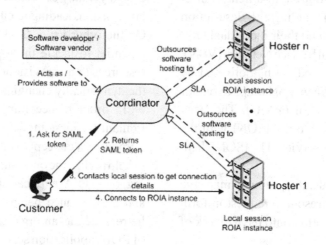

business model encompasses the concept of 'HaaS' and 'SaaS' which Cloud computing is promoting.

Load Balance: On-Demand Resource Provisioning

One of key benefits of introducing the Coordinator in Edutain business model is to facilitate the load balancing. A ROIA local session runs on a Hoster machine, and there are one or more zones that are attached to the local session. When a customer connects to a ROIA instance, the customer actually joins a particular zone. Coordinator can monitor the load of ROIA session running on a Hoster machine by periodically receiving the QoS measurement report. If the Coordinator predicts that one ROIA local session will become overload, a zone within that overloaded session will be migrated to an idle session. This zone migration process will occur transparently so that the ROIA application user will not feel that their connections have been migrated to another session.

The "zone migration" mechanism results in the ROIA process load has partially moved to another ROIA session. This actually means the capacity of running ROIA instance has dynamically grown on an on-demand basis. It enables ROIA applications to adapt themselves during runtime to meet an increased/decreased user demand and maintain QoS at a certain level defined in SLA by on-demand resource provisioning.

Test Scenario

We will use an on-line game called, Hunter, as a ROIA example (as shown in Figure 5). The Hunter game was developed by Edutain project partner Darkworks (http://www.darkworks.com/). It is a game of "search and capture". Players will basically have to find monsters disseminated around the map and capture them. During the capture phase, players will be fighting with other teams of players to make sure that they won't capture monsters. One of the major features of the Hunter game is the scalability, which means that if a given

Figure 5. Hunter game, where if a given number of player reaches maximum limit, the capacity will extend seamlessly for the player to fit with that number. The QoS-oriented service computing is employed and the scalability is realized by on-demand resource provisioning via zone migration

number of players reaches the maximum limit, the map will extend seamlessly for the player to fit with that number. This scalability means that the game can potentially host hundreds of players on the same map, along with providing players with a brand new experience online.

This scalability feature is realised through the on-demand resource provisioning via zone migration. A test case scenario is described as follows, as shown in Figure 6: As currently the widely used architecture for online games is the multi-client and multi-server mode of the client/server architecture (Bartle et al., 2003; Cai et al., 2002; Rosedale et al., 2003), where it consists of a set of servers that are concurrently accessed by a number of users that dynamically interact with each other within a game session, we deploy the Hunter game on two Hosters, namely, '*hoster1*'

and '*hoster2*'. Each Hoster is an individual infrastructure provider which delivers a platform presented as a collection of Web services required for running Hunter (e.g. Mgt. Layer, HMI), QoS assurance (e.g. SLA), and invoicing mission (e.g. Trade account service). Therefore each Hoster can be regarded as a single Cloud provider and they together formulate a service-oriented infrastructure of federated Cloud computing for on-demand resource provisioning. We also have a global session service running at the Coordinator side, which creates one global session '*gSession1*'. Two local sessions '*local session 1*' and '*local session 2*' are created at each Hoster and participate the global session '*gSession1*'. A '*zone0*' is created and attached to '*local session 1*'.

There are 5 authorized customers participated to '*zone0*' to start the use of ROIA application

Figure 6. Test case scenario, where (i) two local sessions are created at Hoster 1 and Hoster 2 (ii) Zone 0 is created and attached to local session 1,(iii) Game players are connected to Zone 0, and (iv)Zone 0 is migrated from Hoster 1 to Hoster 2. Each Hoster can be regarded as a single Cloud provider, and they together formulate a service-oriented infrastructure of federated Cloud computing for on-demand resource provisioning

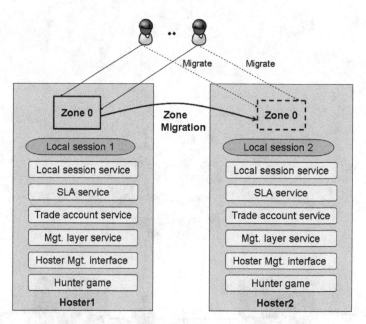

(i.e. Hunter). Six metrics, namely, (i) RTFRickDuration,(ii) AveragePacketLossTCP, (iii)RTFThroughputIn, (vi) RTFThroughOut, (v) AveragePacketLatency, and (vi) ClientConnectionCount are defined in the SLA. Once the Hunter game is in use, its usage is monitored and QoS measurement data of these metrics are reported back. The Coordinator then monitors the SLA conformance of the local session through Coordinator SLA monitoring service.

Assume some QoS measurement data (e.g. RTFThroughputIn, RTFThroughputOut) for '*local session 1*' at '*hoster1*' is predicted to exceed the thresholds defined in SLA, '*zone0*' can then be migrated to the idle '*local session 2*' at '*hoster2*' either manually or atomically. After the migration, the number of clients connected to '*local session 1*' (i.e. ClientConnectionCount) drops to zero, hence measurement data of metric RTFThroughputIn and RTFThroughOut are all zero. This is reflected in

the Figure 7 that the running total of QoS measurement data of RTFThroughputIn and RTFThroughOut remain unchanged. Now if we migrate back '*zone0*' from '*local session 2*' to '*local session 1*', the running total of QoS measurement data of RTFThroughputIn and RTFThroughOut start going up again, as shown in Figure 7. This whole migration process is transparent to the customers, whose quality of experience of playing the Hunter game will not be impacted.

DISCUSSIONS AND FUTURE RESEARCH DIRECTIONS

There is no doubt that security is paramount in SLA manager. The reference architecture proposed mainly concerns with the functional requirements of the SLA manager, and the security model is not included. The security model within SLA manager

Figure 7. On-demand resource provisioning through zone migration. If 'zone0' containing 5 players is migrated to the idle local session, the workload then falls down to 0 and the running total of the measurement data of RTFThroughputIn and RTFThroughOut remain unchanged. If 'zone0' is migrated back to original local session, the running total of measurement data of RTFThroughputIn and RTFThroughOut start increasing again

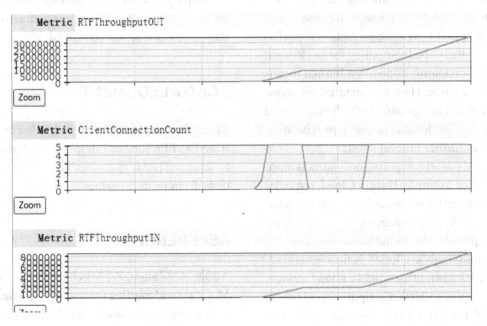

can be complex as it involves an infrastructure spanning multiple autonomous administrative domains of service providers. The SLA manager security model and associated policies can have specific architecture depending on the granularity of the domain system security requirements, which goes beyond the scope of this paper.

The reference architecture is proposed based on the requirements identified from SLA related research projects. It aims to provide an insight into a comprehensive SLA manager, and to present a working model of SLA manager starting from service provider publishing the service to billing the service consumer at the end-of-life SLA. It integrates most of the functional aspects during the SLA life cycle. However, some of components /sub-modules are not mandatory and may not be needed subject to the specific requirements. Informed by the research findings from the survey, the reference architecture also supports the incorporation of domain ontology to facilitate the semantic-aware SLA manager.

The proposed reference architecture recommends using OGF standard WS-Agreement for SLA representation. WS-Agreement has been widely used in Grid /e-Science communities. It is an extensible language and leaves open space for defining domain specific terms. This means the defined domain-specific ontology can be 'embedded' into the WS-Agreement based specification.

A generic SLA manager software framework can be developed based on the proposed reference architecture, to provide prefabricated software building blocks that developers can use, extend, or customize for specific SLA life cycle management solutions.

At the time of writing this chapter, the workshop "*The future of Cloud Computing*" held in January, 2010, (http://cordis.europa.eu/fp7/ict/ ssai/events-20100126-cloud-computing_en.html) has identified that the scalability and elasticity of Cloud computing are currently the major issues. This chapter discusses two approaches to facilitate on-demand resource provisioning, that is, the open federated Cloud computing through zone migration and ISONI. Although the case study has demonstrated how zone migration model is used in federated Cloud computing for on-demand resource provisioning, zone has a limited meaning in on-line game. How to generalize this zone migration model in the context of federated Cloud computing for on-demand resource provisioning still requires further investigation.

Federated Cloud computing now attracts more attentions. For example, Hybrid Cloud, a special kind of federated Cloud, where enterprise or organization provides and manages some resources in-house (i.e. private Cloud) and has others provided externally (e.g. public Cloud), is now emerging. An organization might use a public Cloud service, such as Amazon's Elastic Compute Cloud (EC2) for general computing but store customer data within its own data center. As large enterprises / organizations often already have substantial investments in the infrastructure required to provide resources in-house, they would prefer to keep sensitive data under their own control to ensure security. We can imagine that this hybrid Cloud has potential to be widely used. The QoS-oriented service computing proposed in this chapter and federated Cloud computing model investigated in Edutian project can have implications in building this hybrid cloud.

CONCLUSION

In order to meet the service requirements in Cloud computing, we proposed the "QoS-oriented service computing", which can be regarded as an extension of service computing discipline. Major research topics of the "QoS-oriented service computing" include service level agreement, green service, service metering and metrics, service

monitoring, and on-demand resource provisioning. We proposed an SLA reference architecture and discussed some research issues of the associated topics. In the case study, we demonstrate how we employ QoS-oriented service computing in a multi-server, multi-user on-line game to facilitate the on-demand resource provisioning.

ACKOWLEDGMENT

The author would like to acknowledge the support from EU FP6 funded Edutain@Grid project, EU FP7 funded IRMOS project, GRIA, and contributions from project partners.

REFERENCES

Addis, A., Zlatev, Z., Mitchell, B., & Boniface, M. (2009). *Modelling interactive real-time applications on service oriented infrastructures*. 2009 NEM Summit – Towards Future Media Internet, September 28-30, 2009, St Malo, France.

Bartle, R. (2003). *Designing virtual worlds*. New Riders Games.

Boniface, M., Philips, S., & Surridge, M. (2006). *Grid-based business partnerships using service level agreements*. Cracow Grid Workshop, 2006.

Bullinger, H., Fahnrich, K. P., & Meiren, T. (2003). Service engineering-methodical development of new service products. *International Journal of Production Economics, 85*, 275–287. doi:10.1016/S0925-5273(03)00116-6

Buyya, R., Yeo, C. S., & Venugopal, S. (2009). Cloud computing and emerging IT platforms: Vision, hype, and reality for delivering computing as the 5th utility. *Future Generation Computer Systems, 25*(6), 599–616. doi:10.1016/j.future.2008.12.001

Cai, W., Xavier, P., Turner, S. J., & Lee, B. S. (2002). *A scalable architecture for supporting interactive games on the Internet.* In *PADS'02* (pp. 60–67). Washington, DC: IEEE.

Chaari, S., Badr, Y., & Biennier, F. (2008). *Enhancing Web service selection by QoS-based ontology and WS-policy.* SAC'08, Fortaleza, Brazil.

de Haaf, B. (2008, August 8). Cloud computing – The jargon is back! *Cloud Computing Journal.* Retrieved from http://cloudcomputing.sys-con.com /node/613070

Dobson, G. (2004). *Quality of service in service-oriented architecture.* Retrieved from http://digs.sourceforge.net /papers/qos.pdf

Fahringer, T., Anthes, C., Arragon, A., Lipaj, A., Müller-Iden, J., & Rawlings, C. J. … Surridge, M. (2007). The Edutain@Grid Project. In D. J. Veit & J. Altmann (Eds.), *GECON 2007. LNCS, 4685,* (pp. 182–187). Heidelberg, Germany: Springer.

Fitzsimmons, J. A., & Fitzsimmons, M. J. (2000). *New service development: Creating memorable experiences.* Thousand Oaks, CA: Sage Publications, Inc.

Ganz, W., & Meiren, T. (2004). Co-design of products and services. *Proceedings of SusProNet Conference on Product Service Systems: Practical Value,* (pp. 21-22). 3-4 June 2004, Brussels, Belgium.

Garcia, D., & Toledo, M. (2006). *Semantic-enriched QoS policies for Web service interactions.* Web Media '06, Natal, Brazil.

Geelan, J. (2008). *Twenty-one experts define cloud computing.* Retrieved from http://cloudcomputing.sys-con.com /node/612375?page=0,1

Gu, X., Nahrstedt, K., Yuan, W., Wichadakul, D., & Xu, D. (2002). An XML-based quality of service enabling language for the Web. *Journal of Visual Language and Computing, Special Issue on Multimedia Language for the Web, 13*(1).

Hand, E. (2007). Head in the clouds. *Nature, 449*(963).

Jeswiet, J. (2003). A definition of life cycle engineering. *Proceeding of 36th CIRP International Seminar on Manufacturing Systems,* (pp. 17-20). June 03 – 05, 2003, Saarland University, Saarbrücken, Germany.

Lamanna, D. D., Skene, J., & Emmerich, W. (2003). SLAng: A language for defining service level agreements. *Proceedings of the Ninth IEEE Workshop on Future Trends of Distributed Computing Systems* (FTDCS'03).

Ludwig, H., Keller, A., Dan, A., King, R., & Frank, R. (2003). A service level agreement language for dynamic electronic services. *Electronic Commerce Research,* 43–49. doi:10.1023/A:1021525310424

Mandelbaum, A. (1998). *Service engineering: Modelling, analysis and inference of stochastic service networks.* Haifa, Israel: Faculty of Industrial Engineering and Management Technion.

McFedries, P. (2008). The cloud is the computer. *IEEE Spectrum Online.* Retrieved from http://www.spectrum.ieee.org/ aug08/6490

Mitchell, B., Zlatev, Z., Addis, M., Neple, T., Konstanteli, K., & Kousiouris, G. … Oliveros, R. (2009). *Interactive realtime multimedia applications on service oriented infrastructures.* Retrieved on September 22, 2010, from http://eprints.ecs.soton.ac.uk/ 17403/1/IRMOS_WP5_D5_1_1_IT_Innovation_v1_0.pdf

Ploß, A., Glinka, F., & Gorlatch, S. (2009). A case study on using RTF for developing multi-player online games. *Lecture Notes in Computer Science, 5415,* 390–400. doi:10.1007/978-3-642-00955-6_44

Ploß, A., Glinka, F., & Gorlatch, S. (2009). A case study on using RTF for developing multi-player online games. *Lecture Notes in Computer Science, Springer, 5415,* 390–400. doi:10.1007/978-3-642-00955-6_44

Rochwerger, B., Breitgand, D., Levy, E., Galis, A., Nagin, K., & Llorente, I. M. (2009). The RESEVOIR model and architecture for open federated cloud computing. *IBM Journal of Research and Development, 53*(4). doi:10.1147/JRD.2009.5429058

Rosedale, P., & Ondrejka, C. (2003). *Enabling player created online worlds with grid computing and streaming.* Retrieved on September 22, 2010, from http://www.gamasutra.com/resource_guide/20030916/rosedale_pfv.htm

Sahai, A., Durant, A., & Machiraju, V. (2001). *Towards automated SLA management for Web services.* (Research Report HPL-2001-310 R.1), Hewlett-Packard Laboratories Palo Alto. Retrieved from http://www.hpl.hp.com/techreports/2001/HPL-2001-310R1.pdf

Seidel, J., Waldrich, O., & Ziegler, W. (2007). *Using SLA for resource management and scheduling – A survey.* CoreGRID technical report, 2007. Retrieved on November 5, 2008, from http://www.coregrid.net/mambo/images/stories/TechnicalReports/tr-0096.pdf

Svend, F., & Jari, K. (1998). *QML: A language for quality of service specification.* Retrieved from http://www.hpl.hp.com/techreports/98/HPL-98-10.html

Tomiyama, T. (2003). Service CAD. *Proceedings of 1st SusProNet Conference*, Amsterdam, 5-6 June, 2003.

Tomiyama, T., Medland, A. J., & Vergeest, J. S. M. (2000). *Knowledge intensive engineering towards sustainable products with high knowledge and service contents.* TMCE 2000, Third International Symposium on Tools and Methods of Competitive Engineering, (pp. 55-67). April 18-20. Delft, The Netherlands: Delft University Press.

Tosic, V., Pagurek, B., & Patel, K. (2003). *WSOL – A language for the formal specification of various constraints and classes of service for Web services.* The International Conference On Web Services, ICWS'03.

Vaquero, L. M., Rodero-Merino, L., Caceres, J., & Lindner, M. (2009). A break in the clouds: Towards a cloud definition. *ACM SIGCOMM Computer Communication Review, 39*(1), 50–55. doi:10.1145/1496091.1496100

Watson, P., Lord, P., Gibson, F., Periorellis, P., & Pitsilis, G. (2008). Cloud computing for e-science with CARMEN. *Proceedings of IBERGRID Conference* (pp. 1-5). 2008, Porto (Portugal). May 12–14.

Zhang, L., Zhang, J., & Cai, H. (2007). *Services computing: Core enabling technology of the modern services industry.* Springer.

Compilation of References

Aboba, B., Blunk, L., Vollbrecht, J., Carlson, J., & Levkowetz, H. (Eds.). (2004). *Extensible authentication protocol (EAP) – RFC 3748*. Retrieved September 29, 2010, from http://www.ietf.org/ rfc/ rfc3748.txt

Aboba, B., Simon, D., & Eronen, P. (2008). Extensible authentication protocol (EAP) key management framework – RFC 5247. Retrieved September 29, 2010, from http://www.ietf.org/ rfc/ rfc5247.txt

Aboelaze, M., & Aloul, F. (2005). Current and future trends in sensor networks: A survey. In *Proceedings of the Second IFIP International Conference on Wireless and Optical Communications Networks WOCN 2005*, (pp. 551–555).

Achilleos, A., Yang, K., & Georgalas, N. (2010). Context modelling and a context-aware framework for pervasive service creation: A model-driven approach. *Pervasive and Mobile Computing*, *6*, 281–296. doi:10.1016/j.pmcj.2009.07.014

Adam, S., & Doerr, J. (2008). *The role of service abstraction and service variability and its impact on requirement engineering for service-oriented systems*. Annual IEEE International Computer Software and Applications Conference.

Adams, C., & Farrell, S. Kause., & Mononen, T. (2005). *Internet X.509 public key infrastructure certificate management protocol (CMP) – RFC 4210*. Retrieved March 29, 2010, from http://www.ietf.org/ rfc/ rfc4210.txt

Addis, A., Zlatev, Z., Mitchell, B., & Boniface, M. (2009). *Modelling interactive real-time applications on service oriented infrastructures*. 2009 NEM Summit – Towards Future Media Internet, September 28-30, 2009, St Malo, France.

Adjie-Winoto, W., Schwartz, E., Balakrishnan, H., & Lilley, J. (1999, December). *The design and implementation of an intentional naming system*. Paper presented at the 17th ACM Symposium on Operating Systems Principles (SOSP '99), Kiawah Island, SC.

Aggarwal, S. (2005). *TCO of on-demand applications is significantly better for SMBs and mid-market enterprises*. Yankees Group report. Retrieved March 10, 2010 from http://www.intente.net/pdfs/ Yankee_On_Demand_vs_On_Premises_TCO_1_.pdf?ID=13165

Aichi Steel Corporation. (2009). MI sensor. In *The general catalogue*.

Akyildiz, I. F., Su, W., Sankarasubramaniam, Y., & Cayirci, E. (2002). Wireless sensor networks: A survey. *Computer Networks*, *38*, 393–422. doi:10.1016/S1389-1286(01)00302-4

Albrecht, A. J. (1979). Measuring application development productivity. *Proceedings of the Joint SHARE, GUIDE, and IBM Application Development Symposium*, (pp. 83–92). Monterey, California, October 14–17, IBM Corporation.

Alkkiomäki, V., & Smolander, K. (2007). *Integration use cases – An applied UML technique for modeling functional requirements in service oriented architecture*. Paper presented at the Requirements Engineering: Foundation for Software Quality, 13th International Working Conference, REFSQ 2007, Trondheim, Norway.

Al-Muhtadi, J., Chetan, S., Ranganathan, A., & Campbell, R. H. (2004, March). *Super spaces: A middleware for large-scale pervasive computing environments*. Paper presented at the IEEE International Workshop on Pervasive Computing and Communications (Perware '04), Orlando, Florida, USA.

Amazon Elastic Cloud. (2010). *Amazon platform as a service*. Retrieved March 10, 2010, from http://aws.amazon.com/ec2/

Apple Computer Inc. (2003). Rendezvous website Retrieved May, 2003, from http://developer.apple.com/macosx/rendezvous/

Arkko, J., & Haverinen, H. (2006). *Extensible authentication protocol method for 3rd generation authentication and key agreement (EAP-AKA) – RFC 4187*. Retrieved September 29, 2010, from http://www.ietf.org/ rfc/rfc4187.txt

Armbrust, M., Fox, A., Griffith, R., Joseph, A. D., Katz, R. H., Konwinski, A., et al. (2008, February). *Above the clouds: A Berkeley view of cloud computing*. (Technical Report EECS-2009-28), University of California at Berkeley.

Arsanjani, A., Ghosh, S., Allam, A., Abdollah, T., Ganapathy, S., & Holley, K. (2008). SOMA: A method for developing service-oriented solutions. *IBM Systems Journal*, *47*(3), 377–396. doi:10.1147/sj.473.0377

Arsanjani, A. (2005). *Toward a pattern language for service-oriented architecture and integration, part 1: Build a service eco-system*. Retrieved January 19, 2010, from http://www.ibm.com/developerworks/webservices/library/ws-soa-soi/

Aurnhammer, M., Hanappe, P., & Steels, L. (2006). *Integrating collaborative tagging and emergent semantics for image retrieval*. WWW Collaborative Web Tagging Workshop, 2006.

Badra, M., & Urien, P. (2004). *Toward SSL integration in SIM smartcards* (pp. 889–893). IEEE WCNC.

Balazinska, M., Balakrishnan, H., & Karger, D. (2002, August). *INS/Twine: A scalable peer-to-peer architecture for intentional resource discovery*. Paper presented at the Pervasive 2002 - International Conference on Pervasive Computing, Zurich, Switzerland.

Baldauf, M., Dustdar, S., & Rosenberg, F. (2007). A survey on context-aware systems. *International Journal Ad Hoc and Ubiquitous Computing*, *2*(4).

Bartle, R. (2003). *Designing virtual worlds*. New Riders Games.

Benslimane, D., Dustdar, S., & Sheth, A. P. (2008). Services mashups: The new generation of Web applications. *IEEE Internet Computing*, *12*(5), 13–15. doi:10.1109/MIC.2008.110

Berners-Lee, T., Hendler, J., & Lassila, O. (2001). The Semantic Web. *Scientific American*, *284*(5), 34–43. doi:10.1038/scientificamerican0501-34

Besselaar, P., Tanabe, M., & Ishida, T. (2002). Introduction: Digital cities research and open issues. [Springer-Verlag.]. *Lecture Notes in Computer Science*, *2362*, 1–9. doi:10.1007/3-540-45636-8_1

Bettini, C., Brdiczka, O., Henricksen, K., Indulska, J., Niclas, D., Ranganathan, A., & Riboni, D. (2010). A survey of context modelling and reasoning techniques. *Pervasive and Mobile Computing*, *6*, 161–180. doi:10.1016/j.pmcj.2009.06.002

Bieberstein, N., Bose, S., Fiammante, M., Jones, K., & Shah, R. (2006). *Service-oriented architecture compass: Business value, planning and enterprise roadmap*. Upper Saddle River, NJ: IBM Press.

Blau, J. (2005). Microsoft: Community computing is on the way. *InfoWorld Magazine*. Retrieved from http://www.infoworld.com/ article/ 05/ 11/ 22/ HNcommunitycomputing _1.html

Bluetooth, S. I. G. (2001). *Specification of the Bluetooth system -- Core* (version 1.1). Retrieved from http://www.bluetooth.org/docs /Bluetooth_V11_Core_22Feb01.pdf

Blunk, L., & Vollbrecht, J. (1998). *PPP extensible authentication protocol (EAP) – RFC 2284*. Retrieved September 29, 2010, from http://www.ietf.org/ rfc/ rfc2284.txt

Boehm, B. (1981). *Software engineering economics*. Englewood Cliffs, NJ: Prentice-Hall.

Boniface, M., Philips, S., & Surridge, M. (2006). *Grid-based business partnerships using service level agreements*. Cracow Grid Workshop, 2006.

Borghoff, U. M., & Schlichter, J. H. (Eds.). (2000). *Computer-supported cooperative work: Introduction to distributed applications*. Berlin/Heidelberg, Germany & New York, NY: Springer-Verlag.

Brazier, F. M. T., Jonker, C. M., & Treur, J. (1997). Formalization of a cooperation model based on joint intentions. In *Proceedings of the Third International Workshop on Agent Theories, Architectures and Languages* (ATAL'96), *Lecture Notes in Artificial Intelligence 1193* (pp. 141-155). Springer.

Brouwers, N., Corke, P., & Langendoen, K. (2008). Darjeeling, a Java compatible virtual machine for microcontrollers. In *Companion '08: Proceedings of the ACM/IFIP/USENIX Middleware '08 Conference Companion*, (pp. 18–23). New York, NY: ACM.

Bullinger, H., Fahnrich, K. P., & Meiren, T. (2003). Service engineering-methodical development of new service products. *International Journal of Production Economics, 85*, 275–287. doi:10.1016/S0925-5273(03)00116-6

Buonadonna, P., Gay, D., Hellerstein, J. M., Hong, W., & Madden, S. (2005). Task: Sensor network in a box. In *Proceedings of European Workshop on Sensor Networks*, (pp. 133–144). Istanbul, Turkey.

Burgess, L. (2008). *Swirl. Notes on Swirl.* CMU.

Buschmann, F., Meunier, R., Rohnert, H., Sommerlad, P., & Stal, M. (1996). *Pattern-oriented software architecture: A system of patterns.* West Sussex, UK: John Wiley & Sons Ltd.

Bussler, C. (2001). The role of B2B protocols in inter-enterprise process execution. In *Proceedings of the Second International Conference on Technologies for E-Services* (pp. 16-29). Berlin / Heidelberg, Germany: Springer.

Buyya, R., Yeo, C. S., & Venugopal, S. (2009). Cloud computing and emerging IT platforms: Vision, hype, and reality for delivering computing as the 5th utility. *Future Generation Computer Systems, 25*(6), 599–616. doi:10.1016/j.future.2008.12.001

C4ISR Interoperability Working Group. (1998). *Levels of Information Systems interoperability* (LISI). Technical report, US Department of Defence, Washington, DC.

Cabri, G., Leonardi, L., & Zambonelli, F. (2003). A framework for flexible role-based interactions in multi-agent system. In *Proceedings of Conference on Cooperative Information Systems (CoopIS)* [Berlin, Germany: Springer.]. *Lecture Notes in Computer Science, 2888*, 145–161. doi:10.1007/978-3-540-39964-3_11

Cai, W., Xavier, P., Turner, S. J., & Lee, B. S. (2002). *A scalable architecture for supporting interactive games on the Internet.* In *PADS'02* (pp. 60–67). Washington, DC: IEEE.

Cardei, M., Yang, S., & Wu, J. (2008). Algorithms for fault-tolerant topology in heterogeneous wireless sensor networks. *IEEE Transactions on Parallel and Distributed Systems, 19*(3).

Chaari, S., Badr, Y., & Biennier, F. (2008). *Enhancing Web service selection by QoS-based ontology and WS-policy.* SAC'08, Fortaleza, Brazil.

Chakraborty, A. (2000). *A distributed architecture for mobile, location-dependent applications.* Master's thesis, Massachusetts Institute of Technology, Cambridge, MA.

Chang, F., Dean, J., Ghemawat, S., Hsieh, W. C., Wallach, D. A., & Burrows, M. ... Gruber, R. E. (2006). Bigtable: A distributed storage system for structured data. In *Proceedings of the 7th USENIX Symposium on Operating Systems Design and Implementation.* Seattle, WA: USENIX Association.

Chen, H., Finin, T., & Joshi, A. (2005). *The SOUPA ontology for pervasive computing. Whitestein Series in Software Agent Technologies.* Springer.

Chen, H., Finin, T., Joshi, A., Kagal, L., Perich, F., & Chakraborty, D. (2004). Intelligent agents meet the Semantic Web in smart spaces. *IEEE Internet Computing, 8*(6), 69–79. doi:10.1109/MIC.2004.66

Chen, H., Finin, T., & Joshi, A. (2004). An ontology for context-aware pervasive computing environments. *The Knowledge Engineering Review, 18*(3), 197–207. doi:10.1017/S0269888904000025

Cherbakov, L., Galambos, G., Harishankar, R., Kalyana, S., & Rackham, G. (2005). Impact of service orientation at the business level. *IBM Systems Journal, 44*(4), 653–668. doi:10.1147/sj.444.0653

Cheshire, S. (2002). *Discovering named instances of abstract services using DNS: Apple Computer.*

Chirita, P., Costache, S., Handschuh, S., & Nejdl, W. (2007). *PTAG: Large scale automatic generation of personalized annotation TAGs for the Web.* WWW 2007.

Cisco Systems, Inc. (2010). *Cisco collaboration cloud.* Retrieved September 26, 2010 from http://www.cisco.com/en/US/ prod/ps10352/ collaboration_cloud.html

Cloud Computing Congress. (2010). *Cloud computing China.* Retrieved March 10, 2010, from http://www.cloudcomputingchina.org/

Cockburn, D., & Jennings, N. R. (Eds.). (1996). *ARCHON: A distributed artificial intelligence system for industrial applications* (pp. 319–344). Wiley. Foundation of Distributed Artificial Intelligence.

Czarnecki, K., Hwan, C., & Kalleberg, K. T. (2006). Feature models are views on ontologies. In *Proceedings of the 10th International on Software Product Line Conference* (vol. 1). IEEE Computer Society.

Czerwinski, S., Zhao, B. Y., Hodes, T., Joseph, A., & Katz, R. (1999). *An architecture for a secure service discovery service.* Paper presented at the Fifth Annual International Conference on Mobile Computing and Networks (MobiCom '99), Seattle, WA.

Dabrowski, C., Mills, K., & Elder, J. (2002, July 2002). *Understanding consistency maintenance in service discovery architectures during communication failure.* Paper presented at the 4th International Workshop on Active Middleware Services, Edinburgh, UK.

Dan, A., Johnson, R., & Arsanjani, A. (2007). *Information as a service: Modeling and realization.* Paper presented at the International Workshop on Systems Development in SOA Environments, Washington, DC.

de Haaf, B. (2008, August 8). Cloud computing – The jargon is back! *Cloud Computing Journal.* Retrieved from http://cloudcomputing.sys-con.com /node/613070

Department of Energy, US Government. (2010). *Report to congress on server and data center energy efficiency.* Retrieved April 25, 2010, from http://www1.eere.energy.gov/ femp/pdfs/ epa_dc_report_congress.pdf

Dey, A. K. (2001). Understanding and using context. *Personal and Ubiquitous Computing, 5*(1), 4–7. doi:10.1007/s007790170019

Dey, A. K., & Abowd, G. D. (1999). *Towards a better understanding of context and context-awareness.* (Technical Report GIT-GVU-99-22), Georgia Institute of Technology, College of Computing.

Dierks, T., & Rescorla, E. (2006). *The transport layer security (TLS) protocol v1.1 – RFC 4346.* Retrieved March 29, 2010, from http://www.ietf.org/ rfc/ rfc4346.txt

Dikaiakos, M. D., Katsaros, D., Mehra, P., Pallis, G., & Vakali, A. (2009). Cloud computing: Distributed Internet computing for IT and scientific research. *IEEE Internet Computing, 13*(5), 10–13. doi:10.1109/MIC.2009.103

Dobson, G. (2004). *Quality of service in service-oriented architecture.* Retrieved from http://digs.sourceforge.net /papers/qos.pdf

DOLCE. (2010). *Laboratory for applied ontology.* Retrieved March 8, 2010, from http://www.loa-cnr.it/

DuraSpace Organization. (2009). *DuraCloud overview 2009.*

Durkee, D. (2010). Why cloud computing will never be free. *Communications of the ACM, 53*(5), 62–69. doi:10.1145/1735223.1735242

Edgington, T., Choi, B., Henson, K., Raghu, T., & Vinze, A. (2004). Adopting ontology to facilitate knowledge sharing. *Communications of the ACM, 47*(11), 85–90. doi:10.1145/1029496.1029499

Elizabeth, M., & Hull, C. (1987). Occam - A programming language for multiprocessor systems. *Computer Languages, 12*(1), 27–37. doi:10.1016/0096-0551(87)90010-5

Ellison, C. (2002). Home network security. *Intel Technology Journal, 6*(4), 37–48.

Endrei, M., Ang, J., Arsanjani, A., Chua, S., Comte, P., & Krogdahl, P. (2004). *Patterns: Service-oriented architecture and Web services.* IBM Press.

ETSI. (2006). *Smartcards UICC security service module: Stage 1.* (ETSI TS 102 266 V7.1.0). Retrieved March 29, 2010, from http://pda.etsi.org/ pda/ queryform.asp

Fahringer, T., Anthes, C., Arragon, A., Lipaj, A., Müller-Iden, J., & Rawlings, C. J. … Surridge, M. (2007). The Edutain@Grid Project. In D. J. Veit & J. Altmann (Eds.), *GECON 2007. LNCS, 4685,* (pp. 182–187). Heidelberg, Germany: Springer.

Ferber, J., Gutknecht, O., & Michel, F. (2003). From agents to organizations: An organizational view of multi-agent systems. *In Proceedings of AOSE 2003* [Springer Verlag.]. *Lecture Notes in Computer Science, 2935*, 214–230. doi:10.1007/978-3-540-24620-6_15

Ferber, J., & Gutknecht, O. (1998). A meta-model for the analysis and design of organization in multi-agent systems. *In Proceedings of 3rd International Conference on Multi-agent Systems (ICMAS'98)*, (pp. 128-135).

Fitzsimmons, J. A., & Fitzsimmons, M. J. (2000). *New service development: Creating memorable experiences.* Thousand Oaks, CA: Sage Publications, Inc.

Flick, U. (1998). *An introduction to qualitative research.* London, UK: Sage.

Fortes, J. A. B. (2010). Sky computing: When multiple clouds become one. *Cluster, Cloud and Grid Computing Conference (CCGrid)* (pp. 4, 17-20). IEEE Computer Society.

Franchi, A., Di Stefano, L., & Salmon Cinotti, T. (2010). *Mobile visual search using smart-M3.* In IEEE Symposium on Computers and Communications, (pp. 1065-1070).

Galal, G. H., & Paul, R. J. (1999). A qualitative scenario approach to managing evolving requirements. *Requirements Engineering, 4*(2), 92–102. doi:10.1007/s007660050016

Ganz, W., & Meiren, T. (2004). Co-design of products and services. *Proceedings of SusProNet Conference on Product Service Systems: Practical Value*, (pp. 21-22). 3-4 June 2004, Brussels, Belgium.

Garcia, D., & Toledo, M. (2006). *Semantic-enriched QoS policies for Web service interactions.* Web Media '06, Natal, Brazil.

Garcia-Macias, J. A., & Torres, D. A. (2005). *Service discovery in mobile ad-hoc networks: Better at the network layer?* Paper presented at the 2005 International Conference on Parallel Processing Workshops (ICPPW'05).

Geelan, J. (2008). *Twenty-one experts define cloud computing.* Retrieved from http://cloudcomputing.sys-con.com /node/612375?page=0,1

GlobalPlatform. (2006). GlobalPlatform card specification v2.2. Retrieved March 29, 2010, from http://www.globalplatform.org/ specificationscard.asp

Grassi, V., & Sindico, A. (2007). *Towards model driven design of service-based context-aware applications.* International Workshop on Engineering of Software Services for Pervasive Environments in conjunction with the 6th ESEC/FSE joint meeting - ESSPE '07, (pp. 69-74). New York, NY: ACM Press.

Gray, J. (2003, March). *Distributed computing economics.* (Technical Report MSR-TR-2003-24), Microsoft Research.

Gribble, S. D., Welsh, M., Behren, R. v., Brewer, E. A., Culler, D., Borisov, N., et al. (2001). The ninja architecture for robust Internet-scale systems and services. *IEEE Computer Networks, 35*(4).

Gu, T., Pung, H., & Zhang, D. Q. (2005). A service-oriented middleware for building context-aware services. *Journal of Network and Computer Applications, 28*(1), 1–18. doi:10.1016/j.jnca.2004.06.002

Gu, T., Wang, X. H., Pung, H. K., & Zhang, D. Q. (2004). *An ontology-based context model in intelligent environments.* In Communication Networks and Distributed Systems Modeling and Simulation Conference, San Diego, CA, USA.

Gu, X., Nahrstedt, K., Yuan, W., Wichadakul, D., & Xu, D. (2002). An XML-based quality of service enabling language for the Web. *Journal of Visual Language and Computing, Special Issue on Multimedia Language for the Web, 13*(1).

Guédria, W., Naudet, Y., & Chen, D. (2008). Interoperability maturity models – Survey and comparison. In R. Meersman, Z. Tari, & P. Herrero (Eds.), *OTM 2008 Workshop, LNCS 5333*, (pp. 273-282), Berlin / Heidelberg, Germany Springer-Verlag.

Guo, H., Chen, J., Wu, W., & Wang, W. (2009). Personalization as a service: The architecture and a case study. In *Proceedings of the First International Workshop on Cloud Data Management* (pp. 1-8). Hong Kong, China: ACM.

Guo, H., Gao, J., Zeng, Z., & Hu, B. (2006). Recipe, policy and self-organizing: A hybrid collaboration approach for agent-based cooperative design. In *Proceedings of the 10th International Conference on Computer Supported Cooperative Work in Design (CSDWD 2006)*, (pp. 653-658). IEEE.

Guttman, E., Perkins, C., & Kempf, J. (1999). *Service templates and service: Schemes: Sun Microsystems.*

Guttman, E., Perkins, C., Veizades, J., & Day, M. (1999). *Service location protocol*, version 2.

Hadim, S., & Mohamed, N. (2006). *Middleware for wireless sensor networks: A survey.* In the 1st International Conference on Communication System Software and Middleware, (pp. 1-7).

Hand, E. (2007). Head in the clouds. *Nature, 449*(963).

Handschuh, H., & Paillier, P. (1998). *Smartcard crypto co-processors for public key cryptography.* International Conference on Smart Card Research and Applications (pp. 386-394). Springer-Verlag.

Handschuh, H., & Trichina, E. (2007). *High density smartcards: New security challenges and applications.* Securing Electronic Business Processes: Highlights of the Information Security Solutions Europe/SECURE 2007 Conference (pp. 251-259). Vieweg Wiesbaden.

Harikumar, A. K., Lee, R., Hae Sool, Y., Haeng-Kon, K., & Byeongdo, K. (2005). *A model for application integration using Web services.* Paper presented at the Computer and Information Science, 2005. Fourth Annual ACIS International Conference.

Heinzelman, W. B., Murphy, A. L., Carvalho, H. S., & Perillo, M. A. (2004). Middleware to support sensor network applications. *IEEE Network, 18*, 6–14. doi:10.1109/MNET.2004.1265828

Henricksen, K., & Indulska, J. (2004). A software engineering framework for context-aware pervasive computing. In S. Das & M. Kumar, *Proceedings of the Second Annual Conference on Pervasive Computing and Communications* (pp. 77-86). Los Alamitos, CA: The IEEE Computer Society.

Hua, C., Gao, J., Su, J., & Chen, H. (2003). AGDRSCOM: A complicated dynamic real-time strong cooperation system model. In *Proceedings of the Second International Conference on Machine Learning and Cybernetics: Vol. 1* (pp. 318-323). IEEE.

Hunter, J., Khan, I., & Gerber, A. (2008). *Harvana: Harvesting community tags to enrich collection metadata.* Joint Conference on Digital Libraries 2008, (pp. 147-156).

International Software Benchmarking Group. (2010). *ISBSG dataset release 10.* Retrieved March 10, 2010, from http://www.isbsg.org

Ishida, T. (Ed.). (1998). *Community computing and support systems. Lecture Notes in Computer Science (Vol. 1519).* Springer.

Issarny, V., Caporuscio, M., & Georgantas, N. (2007). *A perspective on the future of middleware-based software engineering.* In Future of Software Engineering, (pp. 244-258).

Jaemin, P., Kyoungtae, K., & Minjeong, K. (2008). The Aegis: UICC-based security framework. *IEEE FGCN, 2008*, 264–269.

Jaemin, P., Yongki, M., & Minjeong, K. (2009). UICC-based service security framework for pervasive fixed mobile convergence. *Journal of Internet Technology, 10*(5), 505–512.

Jaroucheh, Z., Liu, X., & Smith, S. (February 2010). CANDEL: Product line based dynamic context management for pervasive applications. In *International Conference on Complex, Intelligent and Software Intensive Systems (ARES/CISIS 2010)* (pp. 209-216). Krakow, Poland: IEEE Computer Society.

Jaroucheh, Z., Liu, X., & Smith, S. (July 2010). *Apto: A MDD-based generic framework for context-aware deeply adaptive service-based processes.* In 8th IEEE International Conference on Web Services (ICWS2010). Florida: IEEE Computer Society.

Jarvenpaa, S. L., & Stoddard, D. B. (1998). Business process redesign: Radical and evolutionary change. *Journal of Business Research, 41*(1), 15–27. doi:10.1016/S0148-2963(97)00008-8

Jeswiet, J. (2003). A definition of life cycle engineering. *Proceeding of 36th CIRP International Seminar on Manufacturing Systems*, (pp. 17-20). June 03 – 05, 2003, Saarland University, Saarbrücken, Germany.

Johansen, R., Charles, J., Mittman, R., & Saffo, P. (Eds.). (1998). *Groupware: Computer support for business teams. New York, NY: Free Press.* London, UK: Collier Macmillan.

Johnson, R. K. (2002, November). Institutional repositories: Partnering with faculty to enhance scholarly communication. *D-Lib Magazine, 8*(11).

Jung, Y., Lee, J., & Kim, M. (2006, May). *Multi-agent based community computing system development with the model driven architecture*. Paper presented at the Fifth International Joint Conference on Autonomous Agents and Multiagent Systems, (pp. 1329-1331).

Kamiya, H., Mineno, H., Ishikawa, N., Osano, T., & Mizuno, T. (2008). *Composite event detection in heterogeneous sensor networks*. IEEE/IPSJ International Symposium on Applications and the Internet, (pp. 413–416).

Kang, K., Cohen, S., Hess, J., Novak, W., & Peterson, A. (1990). *Feature-oriented domain analysis (FODA) feasibility study*. Pittsburgh, PA: Carnegie Mellon University Software Engineering Institute.

Kantorovitch, J., & Niemelä, E. (2008). Service description ontologies. In Khosrow-Pour, M. (Ed.), *Encyclopedia of Information Science and Technology* (2nd ed., Vol. VII, pp. 3445–3451). Hershey, PA: Information Science Reference. doi:10.4018/978-1-60566-026-4.ch547

Kapitsaki, G., Prezerakos, G., Tselikas, N., & Venieris, I. (2009). Context-aware service engineering: A survey. *Journal of Systems and Software, 82*, 1885–1297. doi:10.1016/j.jss.2009.02.026

Kassab, M., Ormandjieva, O., & Daneva, M. (2009). *An ontology based approach to non-functional requirements conceptualization*. In the 4th International Conference on Software Engineering Advances, (pp. 299- 307), IEEE Computer Science.

Katasonov, A., & Palviainen, M. (2010). *Towards ontology-driven development of applications for smart environments*. In International Workshop on the Web of Things, IEEE Intl. Conf. on Pervasive Computing and Communications, (pp. 696-701).

Kindberg, T., & Fox, A. (2002). System software for ubiquitous computing. *IEEE Pervasive Computing / IEEE Computer Society [and] IEEE Communications Society*, (January-March): 70–81. doi:10.1109/MPRV.2002.993146

Klein, M., Konig-Ries, B., & Obreiter, P. (2003). *Service rings – A semantic overlay for service discovery in ad hoc networks*. Paper presented at the 14th International Workshop on Database and Expert Systems Applications (DEXA'03).

Klems, M., Nemis, J., & Tai, S. (2009). *Do clouds compute? A framework for estimating the value of cloud computing. Lecture Notes in Business Information Processing* (pp. 110–123). Springer-Verlag.

Knight, D. (2009). *Why cloud vs. premise is the wrong question*. Retrieved March 10, 2010, from http://blogs.cisco.com/collaboration /comments/why_cloud_vs._premise _is_the_wrong_question/

Kondol, D., Bahman, J., Malecot, P., Cappello, F., & Anderson, D. (2009). Cost-benefit analysis of cloud computing versus desktop Grids. *Proceedings of the 18th International Heterogeneity in Computing Workshop*, May, 2009, Rome.

Koning, M., Sun, C., Sinnema, M., & Avgeriou, P. (2009). VxBPEL: Supporting variability for Web services in BPEL. *Information and Software Technology, 51*(2), 258–269. doi:10.1016/j.infsof.2007.12.002

Kozat, U. C., & Tassiulas, L. (2004). Service discovery in mobile ad hoc networks: An overall perspective on architectural choices and network layer support issues. *Ad Hoc Networks, 2*(1), 23–44. doi:10.1016/S1570-8705(03)00044-1

Krasniewski, M., Varadharajan, P., Rabeler, B., Bagchi, S., & Hu, Y. (2005). Tibfit: Trust index based fault tolerance for arbitrary data faults in sensor networks. In. *Proceedings of the International Conference on Dependable Systems and Networks DSN, 2005*, 672–681. doi:10.1109/DSN.2005.92

Krishnamachari, B., & Iyengar, S. (2004). Distributed Bayesian algorithms for fault-tolerant event region detection in wireless sensor networks. *IEEE Transactions on Computers, 53*(3), 241–250. doi:10.1109/TC.2004.1261832

Krishnamachari, B., & Iyengar, S. S. (2003). *Efficient and fault-tolerant feature extraction in sensor networks*. In 2nd Workshop on Information Processing in Sensor Networks, IPSN '03, Palo Alto, California.

Kumar, M., Shirazi, B., Das, S. K., Singhal, M., Sung, B., & Levine, D. (2003). Pervasive information communities organization: A middleware framework for pervasive computing. *IEEE Pervasive Computing / IEEE Computer Society [and] IEEE Communications Society*, (July-September): 72–79. doi:10.1109/MPRV.2003.1228529

Kumar, K., & Lu, Y. (2010). Cloud computing for mobile users: Can offloading computation save energy? *IEEE Computer*, *43*(4), 51–56.

La Cayla. (2006). *A white paper for independent software vendors*. Retrieved March 10 2010, from http://www.opsource.net/

Laboratories, R. S. A. (n.d.). *Public key cryptography standards (PKCS) series*. Retrieved March 29, 2010, from http://www.rsa.com/ rsalabs/ node.asp?id=2124

Lagoze, C., Payette, S., Shin, E., & Wilper, C. (2006). Fedora: An architecture for complex objects and their relationships. *International Journal on Digital Libraries*, *6*(2), 124–138. doi:10.1007/s00799-005-0130-3

Lamanna, D. D., Skene, J., & Emmerich, W. (2003). SLAng: A language for defining service level agreements. *Proceedings of the Ninth IEEE Workshop on Future Trends of Distributed Computing Systems* (FTDCS'03).

Landmark, C. R. M. (2009). *SaaS total cost of ownership*. Retrieved March 10, 2010, from http://www.crmlandmark.com/ saasTCO.htm

Larson, R. (2009). Education: Our most important service sector. *The Service Science*, *1*(4), i–iii.

Lassila, O. (2007). *Programming Semantic Web applications: A synthesis of knowledge representation and semi-structured data*. PhD thesis, Helsinki University of Technology, November, 2007.

Lassila, O. (2008). *Semantic Web programming using PIGLET – Programmer's guide to the PIGLET Semantic Web toolkit*. Nokia Research Center 2008.

Laudon, K., & Laudon, J. (2009). *Management Information Systems*. Pearson.

Lenk, A., Klems, M., Nimis, J., Tai, S., & Sandholm, T. (2009). What's inside the cloud? An architectural map of the cloud landscape. *Proceedings of the International Conference on Software Engineering (ICSE) Workshop on Software Engineering Challenges of Cloud Computing (CLOUD)*, (pp. 23-31).

Lenk, A., Klems, M., Nimis, J., Tai, S., & Sandholm, T. (2009). What's inside the cloud? An architectural map of the cloud landscape. In *Proceedings of the 2009 ICSE Workshop on Software Engineering Challenges of Cloud Computing* (pp. 23-31). Washington, DC: IEEE Computer Society.

Levis, P., Madden, S., Gay, D., Polastre, J., Szewczyk, R., & Whitehouse, K. ... Culler, D. (2005). Tinyos: An operating system for sensor networks. In W. Weber, J. Rabaey & E. Aarts (Eds.), *Ambient intelligence*. Springer-Verlag.

Lifton, J., Seetharam, D., Broxton, M., & Paradiso, J. (2002). *Pushpin computing system overview: A platform for distributed, embedded, ubiquitous sensor networks*. London, UK: Springer-Verlag.

Lo, A., & Yu, E. (2008). From business models to service-oriented design: A reference catalog approach. In *Proceedings of the 26th International Conference on Conceptual Modeling - ER 2007* (Vol. 4801, pp. 87-101). Berlin / Heidelberg, Germany: Springer.

Lovelock, C., & Wirtz, J. (2007). *Services marketing: People, technology, strategy* (6th ed.). New Jersey, USA: Pearson International - Pearson/Prentice Hall.

Ludwig, H., Keller, A., Dan, A., King, R., & Frank, R. (2003). A service level agreement language for dynamic electronic services. *Electronic Commerce Research*, 43–49. doi:10.1023/A:1021525310424

Luukkala, V., Binnema, D.-J., Börzsei, M., Corongiu, A., & Hyttinen, P. (2010). *Experiences in implementing a cross-domain use case by combining semantic and service level platforms*. In IEEE Symposium on Computers and Communications, (pp. 1071-1076).

MacGowan, G. (2006). Helping small businesses choose between on-demand and on-premise software. Retrieved March 10, 2010, from http://www.computerworld.com/s/article/9002362/Helping_small_businesses_choose_between_On_demand_and_On_premise_software

Madden, S. R., Franklin, M. J., Hellerstein, J. M., & Hong, W. (2005). Tinydb: An acquisitional query processing system for sensor networks. *ACM Transactions on Database Systems*, *30*(1), 122–173. doi:10.1145/1061318.1061322

Mainwaring, A., Culler, D., Polastre, J., Szewczyk, R., & Anderson, J. (2002). Wireless sensor networks for habitat monitoring. In *WSNA '02: Proceedings of the 1st ACM International Workshop on Wireless Sensor Networks and Applications* (pp. 88-97). NY, USA.

Man, J., Yang, A., & Sun, X. (2005). Shared ontology for pervasive computing. *Lecture Notes in Computer Science*, *3818*, 64–78. doi:10.1007/11596370_7

Mandelbaum, A. (1998). *Service engineering: Modelling, analysis and inference of stochastic service networks*. Haifa, Israel: Faculty of Industrial Engineering and Management Technion.

Manzaroli, D., Roffia, L., Salmon Cinotti, T., Azzoni, P., Ovaska, E., Nannini, C., & Matarozzi, S. (2010). *Smart-M3 and OSGi: The interoperability platform*. In IEEE Symposium on Computers and Communications, (pp. 1053-1058).

Markines, B., Cattuto, C., Menczer, F., Benz, D., Hotho, A., & Stumme, G. (2009). Evaluating similarity measures for emergent semantics of social tagging. *WWW*, *2009*, 641–650. doi:10.1145/1526709.1526796

Marlow, C., Naaman, M., Boyd, D., & Davis, M. (2006). HT06, tagging paper, taxonomy, Flickr, academic article, ToRead. *Proceedings of the Seventeenth Conference on Hypertext and Hypermedia*, 2006, (pp. 31-40).

McFedries, P. (2008). The cloud is the computer. *IEEE Spectrum Online*. Retrieved from http://www.spectrum.ieee.org/ aug08/6490

McRitchie, K., & Accelar, S. (2008). *A structured framework for estimating IT projects and IT support*. Joint Annual Conference ISPA/SCEA Society of Cost Estimating and Analysis.

Meier, R., Harrington, A., Beckmann, K., & Cahill, V. (2009). A framework for incremental construction of real global smart space applications. *Pervasive and Mobile Computing*, *5*, 350–368. doi:10.1016/j.pmcj.2008.11.001

Mennie, D., & Pagurek, B. (2000, June 12, 2000). *An architecture to support dynamic composition of service components*. Paper presented at the 5th International Workshop on Component-Oriented Programming, WCOP 2000, Cannes, France.

Michael, A., et al. (2009). *Above the clouds: A Berkeley view of cloud computing*. (Technical Report No. UCB/EECS-2009-28). Retrieved on April 25, 2010, from http://www.eecs.berkeley.edu/ Pubs/TechRpts/2009/ EECS-2009-28.html

Microsoft. (2005). *Community technologies research group*. Retrieved from http://research.microsoft.com/community/

Microsystems, S. U. N. (2006). *Java card platform specification 2.2.2*. Retrieved March, 2008, from http://java.sun.com/ javacard/ specs.html

Microsystems, S. U. N. (2010). *Java card platform specification 3.01*. Retrieved March 29, 2010, from http://java.sun.com/ javacard/ 3.0.1/ specs.jsp

Mietzner, R., & Leymann, F. (2008). *Generation of BPEL customization processes for SaaS applications from variability descriptors*. 2008 IEEE International Conference on Services Computing, (pp. 359-366).

Miller, B. A., Nixon, T., Tai, C., & Wood, M. D. (2001). Home networking with universal plug and play. *IEEE Communications Magazine*, (December): 104–109. doi:10.1109/35.968819

Miller, M. (2009). *Cloud computing pros and cons for end users*. Retrieved March 10, 2010, from http://www.informit.com/articles/article.aspx?p=1324280

Mitchell, B., Zlatev, Z., Addis, M., Neple, T., Konstanteli, K., & Kousiouris, G. … Oliveros, R. (2009). *Interactive realtime multimedia applications on service oriented infrastructures*. Retrieved on September 22, 2010, from http://eprints.ecs.soton.ac.uk/ 17403/1/IRMOS_WP5_D5_1_1_IT_Innovation_v1_0.pdf

Moon, M., Hong, M., & Yeom, K. (2008). *Two-level variability analysis for business process with reusability and extensibility*. 32nd Annual IEEE International Computer Software and Applications, COMPSAC '08. Turku, Finland.

Muller, R., Greiner, U., & Rahm, E. (2004). AW: A workflow system supporting rule-based workflow adaptation. *Data & Knowledge Engineering, 51*(2), 223–256. doi:10.1016/j.datak.2004.03.010

Myers, M., Ankney, R., Malpani, A., Galperin, S., & Adams, C. (1999). *X.509 Internet public key infrastructure online certificate status protocol (OCSP) – RFC 2560.* Retrieved March 29, 2010, from http://www.ietf.org/rfc/rfc2560.txt

Nedos, A., Singh, K., & Clarke, S. (2005). *Service*: Distributed service advertisement for multi-service, multi-hop MANET environments.* Paper presented at the 7th IFIP International Conference on Mobile and Wirelss Communication Networks Marrakech, Morocco.

Nefsis. (2010). *Pricing model.* Retrieved March 10, 2010, from http://www.nefsis.com/Pricing /concurrent-user.html

Nidd, M. (2001). Service discovery in DEAPspace. *IEEE Personal Communications,* (August), 39-45.

Noel Yuhanna, M. G. (2008). *The Forrester wave: Information-as-a-service Q1 2008.* Retrieved February 16, 2010, from http://www.forrester.com/rb/Research/wave%26trade%3B_information-as-a-service%2C_q1_2008/q/id/43199/t/2

Northrop, L. (2002). SEI's software product line tenets. *IEEE Software, 19*(4), 32–40. doi:10.1109/MS.2002.1020285

Nurmi, D., Wolski, R., Grzegorczyk, C., Obertelli, G., Soman, S., Youseff, L., & Zagorodnov, D. (2009). The Eucalyptus open-source cloud-computing system. In Cappello, F., Wang, C.-L., & Buyya, R. (Eds.), *CCGRID. IEEE Computer Society* (pp. 124–131).

Object Management Group. (2003). *Technical guide to model driven architecture: The MDA guide* v1.0.1. Retrieved from http://www.omg.org / cgi-bin/ doc?omg/03-06-01

Open Mobile Alliance. (2008). *OMA digital rights management* V2.1. Retrieved March 29, 2010, from http://www.openmobilealliance.org/ Technical/ release_program/ drm_v2_1.aspx

Open Mobile Alliance. (2009). *OMA smartcard Web server* V1.1. Retrieved March 29, 2010, from http://www.openmobilealliance.org/ Technical/ release_program/ scws_v1_1.aspx

Optitz, A., Konig, H., & Szamlewska, S. (2008). What does Grid computing cost? *Journal of Grid Computing, 6*(6), 385–397. doi:10.1007/s10723-008-9098-8

Ovaska, E., Evesti, A., Henttonen, K., Palviainen, M., & Aho, P. (2010). Knowledge based quality-driven architecture design and evaluation. *Information and Software Technology, 52*(6), 577–601. doi:10.1016/j.infsof.2009.11.008

Pantsar-Syväniemi, S., Simula, K., & Ovaska, E. (2010). *Context-awareness in smart spaces.* In IEEE Symposium on Computers and Communications, (pp. 1023-1028).

Papazoglou, M. P., & Dubray, J.-J. (2004). *A survey of Web service technologies.* Retrieved February 16, 2010, from http://eprints.biblio.unitn.it/archive/00000586/

Papazoglou, M. P., Traverso, P., Dustdar, S., Leymann, F., & Kramer, B. J. (2006). Service-oriented computing: A research roadmap. In F. Cubera, B. J. Krämer & M. P. Papazoglou (Eds.), *Service oriented computing (SOC)* (vol. 05462). Internationales Begegnungs- und Forschungszentrum für Informatik (IBFI).

Patroklos, G. A., Raja, V., Hitesh, T., & Donal, O. (2004). *Performance analysis of cryptographic protocols on handheld devices.* 3rd IEEE International Symposium on Network Computing and Applications (pp. 169-174).

Pendyala, V., & Shim, S. (2009). Web as the ubiquitous computer. *IEEE Computer, 42*(9), 90–92.

Pendyala, V. S., & Holliday, J. (2010). Performing intelligent mobile searches in the cloud using semantic technologies. In *Granular Computing GrC* (pp. 381–386). IEEE Computer Society.

Perez, M. S., Sanchez, A., Robles, V., Pena, J. M., & Abawajy, J. (2004). Cooperation model of a multiagent parallel file system for clusters. In *Proceedings of IEEE International Symposium on Cluster Computing and the Grid* (pp. 595-601). IEEE computer Society.

Peristeras, V., & Tarabanis, K. (2006). The connection, communication, consolidation, collaboration interoperability framework (C4IF) for Information Systems interoperability. *IBIS – Interoperability in Business Information Systems, 1*(1), 61-72.

Pham, H. N., Pediaditakis, D., & Boulis, A. (2007). *From simulation to real deployments in WSN and back.* In IEEE International Symposium on a World of Wireless, Mobile and Multimedia Networks, WoWMoM 2007, (pp. 1 – 6).

Phani Kumar, A. V. U., Reddy, V. A. M., & Janakiram, D. (2005). Distributed collaboration for event detection in wireless sensor networks. In *MPAC '05: Proceedings of the 3rd International Workshop on Middleware for Pervasive and Ad-Hoc Computing,* (pp. 1–8). New York, NY: ACM.

Ploß, A., Glinka, F., & Gorlatch, S. (2009). A case study on using RTF for developing multi-player online games. *Lecture Notes in Computer Science, 5415,* 390–400. doi:10.1007/978-3-642-00955-6_44

Ploß, A., Glinka, F., & Gorlatch, S. (2009). A case study on using RTF for developing multi-player online games. *Lecture Notes in Computer Science, Springer, 5415,* 390–400. doi:10.1007/978-3-642-00955-6_44

Preuveneers, D., & Berbers, Y. (2008). Internet of things: A context-awareness perspective. In Yan, L. (Eds.), *The Internet of things: From RFID to the next generation pervasive networked systems* (pp. 287–307). CRC Press. doi:10.1201/9781420052824.ch13

Raman, R., Livny, M., & Solomon, M. (1998, July 28-31). *Matchmaking: Distributed resource management for high throughput computing.* Paper presented at the Seventh IEEE International Symposium on High Performance Distributed Computing, Chicago, IL.

Ramollari, E., Dranidis, D., & Simons, A. J. H. (2007). *A survey of service oriented development methodologies.* Paper presented at the 2nd European Young Researchers Workshop on Service Oriented Computing, Leicester, UK.

Rankl, W., & Effing, W. (2004). *Smart card handbook* (3rd ed.). Wiley.

Ratsimor, O., Chakraborty, D., Joshi, A., & Finin, T. (2002). *Allia: Alliance-based service discovery for ad-hoc environments.* Paper presented at the 2nd International Workshop on Mobile Commerce Atlanta, Georgia, USA.

Reichert, M., Rechtenbach, S., Hallerbach, A., & Bauer, T. (2009). *Extending a business process modeling tool with process configuration facilities: The Provop Demonstrator.* In BPM'09 Demonstration Track, Business Process Management Conference (vol. 1). Ulm, Germany.

Robson, C. (2002). *Real world research* (2nd ed.). Oxford, UK: Blackwell Publishing.

Rochwerger, B., Breitgand, D., Levy, E., Galis, A., Nagin, K., & Llorente, I. M. (2009). The RESEVOIR model and architecture for open federated cloud computing. *IBM Journal of Research and Development, 53*(4). doi:10.1147/JRD.2009.5429058

Román, M., Hess, C., Cerqueira, R., Campbell, R. H., & Nahrstedt, K. (2002). Gaia: A middleware infrastructure to enable active spaces. *IEEE Pervasive Computing / IEEE Computer Society [and] IEEE Communications Society, 1,* 74–83. doi:10.1109/MPRV.2002.1158281

Romer, K., & Mattern, F. (2004). Event-based systems for detecting real-world states with sensor networks: A critical analysis. In *Proceedings of 2004 Conference on Intelligent Sensors, Sensor Networks and Information Processing,* (pp. 389–395).

Rosedale, P., & Ondrejka, C. (2003). *Enabling player created online worlds with grid computing and streaming.* Retrieved on September 22, 2010, from http://www.gamasutra.com/ resource_guide/20030916/ rosedale_pfv.htm

Rothboard, J. (2009). *Linking SaaS software pricing to value.* Retrieved March 10, 2010, from http://www.readwriteweb.com/ enterprise/2009/01/linking -saas-software-pricing-to-value.php

Saa, S. Optics. (2010). *SaaS optics deep dive.* Retrieved March 10, 2010, from http://www.saasoptics.com/ saas_operations_operating_model/ saas_metrics_management_deep_dive/saas_metrics_management_deep_dive.html

Sadiq, S., Orlowska, M., & Sadiq, W. (2005). *The role of messaging in collaborative business processes.* Paper presented at the IRMA International Conference, San Diego, USA.

Sahai, A., Durant, A., & Machiraju, V. (2001). *Towards automated SLA management for Web services.* (Research Report HPL-2001-310 R.1), Hewlett-Packard Laboratories Palo Alto. Retrieved from http://www.hpl.hp.com/techreports/2001/ HPL-2001-310R1.pdf

Salesforce. (2010). *CRM SaaS.* Retrieved March 10, 2010, from http://www.salesforce.com/ platform/platform-edition/

Salutation Consortium. (1999). *Salutation architecture specification* (Version 2.0c).

Santhanam, G., Ryu, S., Yu, B., Afshar, A., & Shenoy, K. (2006). A high-performance brain–computer interface. *Nature, 442*(13). doi:.doi:10.1038/nature04968

Sarker, S., & Lee, A. S. (1999). IT-enabled organizational transformation: A case study of BPR failure at TELECO. *The Journal of Strategic Information Systems, 8*(1), 83–103. doi:10.1016/S0963-8687(99)00015-3

Satyanarayanan, M., Bahl, P., Cáceres, R., & Davies, N. (2009). The case for VM-based cloudlets in mobile computing. *IEEE Pervasive Computing/ IEEE Computer Society [and] IEEE Communications Society, 8*(4), 14–23. doi:10.1109/MPRV.2009.82

SCA. (2009). *Specification*, final version 1.0. Retrieved from http://www.osoa.org/display/Main/Service+Component+Architecture+Specifications

Schwiderski-Grosche, S. (2008). *Context-dependent event detection in sensor networks.* In 2nd Intl. Conf. on Distributed Event-Based Systems (DEBS'08), Rome, Italy.

Scrum. (2009). *What is Scrum?* Retrieved March 8, 2010, from http://www.scrumalliance.org/learn_about_scrum

Seidel, J., Waldrich, O., & Ziegler, W. (2007). *Using SLA for resource management and scheduling – A survey.* CoreGRID technical report, 2007. Retrieved on November 5, 2008, from http://www.coregrid.net/ mambo/images/ stories/ TechnicalReports/tr-0096.pdf

Sen, S., Vig, J., & Riedl, J. (2009). Tagommenders: Connecting users to items through tags. *WWW, 2009,* 671–680. doi:10.1145/1526709.1526800

Sheng, Q. Z., Pohlenz, S., Yu, J., Wong, H. S., Ngu, A. H., Maamar, Z., et al. (2009). *ContextServ: A platform for rapid and flexible development of context-aware Web services.* 2009 IEEE 31st International Conference on Software Engineering (pp. 619-622).

Shih, K.-P., Wang, S.-S., Yang, P.-H., & Chang, C.-C. (2006). Collect: Collaborative event detection and tracking in wireless heterogeneous sensor networks. In *Proceedings of the 11th IEEE Symposium on Computers and Communications ISCC '06*, (pp. 935–940).

Simon, D., Cifuentes, C., Cleal, D., Daniels, J., & White, D. (2006). Java on the bare metal of wireless sensor devices: The squawk java virtual machine. In *VEE '06: Proceedings of the 2nd International Conference on Virtual Execution Environments*, (pp. 78–88). New York, NY: ACM.

SLA definition. (2009). *Definition of service level agreement.* Retrieved March 10 2010, from http://loosely-coupled.com/ glossary/SLA

Smith, M. (2002). DSpace: An institutional repository from the MIT libraries and Hewlett Packard laboratories. *ECDL, 2002,* 213–226.

Sofia. (2010). *Smart objects for intelligent applications.* Retrieved March 8, 2010, from http://www.sofia-project.eu/

Song, Y., Zhuang, Z. M., Li, H. J., Zhao, Q. K., Li, J., Lee, W., & Giles, C. L. (2008). Real-time automatic tag recommendation. *SIGIR, 2008,* 515–522. doi:10.1145/1390334.1390423

Soylu, A., De Causmaecker, P., & Desmet, P. (2009). Context and adaptivity in pervasive computing environments: Links with software engineering and ontological engineering. *Journal of Software, 4*(9), 992–1013. doi:10.4304/jsw.4.9.992-1013

SPICE. (2010). *Spice mobile ontology.* Retrieved March 8, 2010, from http://ontology.ist-spice.org/index.html

Steen, M. v., Hauck, F. J., Homburg, P., & Tanenbaum, A. S. (1998). Locating objects in wide-area systems. *IEEE Communications Magazine*, (January): 104–109. doi:10.1109/35.649334

Strang, T., & Linnhoff-Popien, C. (2004). A context modeling survey. In *Proceedings of the 1st International Workshop on Advanced Context Modeling, Reasoning and Management at UbiComp2004.*

Strauss, A. L., & Corbin, J. M. (1998). *Basics of qualitative research: Techniques and procedures for developing grounded theory* (2nd ed.). Thousand Oaks, CA: Sage Publications Inc.

Sugiyama, S. (2008). Fundamental behaviour in communication method. In *Proceedings of IEEE/INFORMS International Conference on Service Operations and Logistics, and Informatics*. Beijing, China.

Sugiyama, S. (2008). Ubiquitous framework in service science. In *Proceedings of The 2008 Logic and Science of Service (The New Wealth and Wellbeing of Nations)*, Hawaii, US.

Sugiyama, S. (2009). Feature extraction in system. In *Proceedings of INFORMS International Conference on Service Science*. Hong Kong, China.

Sugiyama, S. (2010). Business plan oriented service in service science. In *Proceedings of INFORMS Service Science Conference*. Taipei, Taiwan.

Sugiyama, S., & Tharumarajah, A. (2007). Fundamental behavior of holonic system. *The International Journal of Services Operations and Informatics, 2*(4). INDERSCIENCE.

Sun Microsystems. (2001). *Jini™ technology core platform specification* (version 1.2). Sun Microsystem. Retrieved from http://wwws.sun.com/ software/jini/specs/

Sung, B., Shirazi, B., & Kumar, M. (2002). Pervasive community organization. In *Proceedings Eurasia 2002*, Tehran, November.

Svend, F., & Jari, K. (1998). *QML: A language for quality of service specification*. Retrieved from http://www.hpl. hp.com/ techreports/98/ HPL-98-10.html

TechAmerica. (2008). *Chapter 12, software cost estimating*. Retrieved March 10, 2010, http://www.techamerica. org/

The Foundation of Intelligent Physical Agents (FIPA) Standard. (2000). *FIPA communicative act library specification*. Retrieved from http://www.fipa.org/ specs/ fipa00037/

Tolk, A., Diallo, S. Y., Turnitsa, C. D., & Winters, L. S. (2006). Composable M&S Web services for netcentric applications. *Journal for Defense Modeling and Simulation, 3*(1), 27–44. doi:10.1177/875647930600300104

Tolk, A., Turnitsa, C., & Diallo, S. (2008). Implied ontological representation within the levels of conceptual interoperability model. [IOP Press.]. *Intelligent Decision Technologies, 2*, 3–19.

Tolk, A., & Muguira, J. A. (2003). The levels of conceptual interoperability model. In *Proceedings of the Simulation Interoperability Workshop*, (p. 10).

Tomiyama, T. (2003). Service CAD. *Proceedings of 1st SusProNet Conference*, Amsterdam, 5-6 June, 2003.

Tomiyama, T., Medland, A. J., & Vergeest, J. S. M. (2000). *Knowledge intensive engineering towards sustainable products with high knowledge and service contents*. TMCE 2000, Third International Symposium on Tools and Methods of Competitive Engineering, (pp. 55-67). April 18-20. Delft, The Netherlands: Delft University Press.

Toninelli, A., Pantsar-Syväniemi, S., Bellavista, P., & Ovaska, E. (2009). *Supporting context awareness in smart environments: A scalable approach to information interoperability*. In International Workshop on Middleware for Pervasive Mobile and Embedded Computing, Article No: 5, ACM, IFIP, USENIX.

Tosic, V., Pagurek, B., & Patel, K. (2003). *WSOL – A language for the formal specification of various constraints and classes of service for Web services*. The International Conference On Web Services, ICWS'03.

Trichina, E., Hyppönen, K., & Hassinen, M. (2007). *SIM-enabled open mobile payment system based on nation-wide PKI*. Securing Electronic Processes: Highlights of the Information Security Solutions Europe/SECURE 2007 Conference (pp. 355-366). Vieweg Wiesbaden.

Tual, J. P., Couchard, A., & Sourgen, L. (2005). *USB full speed enabled smartcards for consumer electronics applications* (pp. 230–236). IEEE ISCE.

Van Nuffel, D. (2007). *Towards a service-oriented methodology: Business-driven guidelines for service identification*. In On the Move to Meaningful Internet Systems 2007: OTM 2007 Workshops (pp. 294-303).

Vaquero, L. M., Rodero-Merino, L., Caceres, J., & Lindner, M. (2009). A break in the clouds: Towards a cloud definition. *ACM SIGCOMM Computer Communication Review, 39*(1), 50–55. doi:10.1145/1496091.1496100

Vaquero, L. M., Rodero-Merino, L., Caceres, J., & Lindner, M. (2009). A break in the clouds: Towards a cloud definition. *ACM SIGCOMM Computer Communication Review, 39*(1), 50–55. doi:10.1145/1496091.1496100

Varga, A. (2002). Omnet++. Software tools for networking. *IEEE Network Interactive, 16*(4).

Varshavsky, A., Reid, B., & Lara, E. d. (2005). *A cross-layer approach to service discovery and selection in MANETs*. Paper presented at the 2nd International Conference on Mobile Ad-Hoc and Sensor Systems (MASS), Washington, DC.

Viera, V., Brézillon, P., Salgado, A. C., & Tedesco, P. (2008). A context-oriented model for domain-independent context management. *Revue d'Intelligence Artificielle, 22*(5), 609–627. doi:10.3166/ria.22.609-627

Vu, C., Beyah, R., & Li, Y. (2007). Composite event detection in wireless sensor networks. In. *Proceedings of IEEE International Performance, Computing, and Communications Conference IPCCC, 2007*, 264–271. doi:10.1109/PCCC.2007.358903

Wada, H., Boonma, P., & Suzuki, J. (2007). A spacetime oriented macroprogramming paradigm for push-pull hybrid sensor networking. In *Proceedings of the 16th International Conference on Computer Communications and Networks ICCCN 2007*, (pp. 868–875).

Walker, D. M. (2006). *White paper - Overview architecture for enterprise data warehouses*. Retrieved February 16, 2010, from http://www.datamgmt.com/index.php?module=documents&JAS_DocumentManager_op=downloadFile&JAS_File_id=29

Wang, X., Dong, J. S., Chin, C., Hettiarachchi, R. S., & Dhang, Z. (2004). Semantic space: An infrastructure for smart spaces. *IEEE Pervasive Computing / IEEE Computer Society [and] IEEE Communications Society, 3*(3), 32–39. doi:10.1109/MPRV.2004.1321026

Wang, T.-Y., Han, Y., Varshney, P., & Chen, P.-N. (2005). Distributed fault-tolerant classification in wireless sensor networks. *IEEE Journal on Selected Areas in Communications, 23*(4), 724–734. doi:10.1109/JSAC.2005.843541

Wang, H. H., Li, Y. F., Sun, J., Zhang, H., & Pan, J. (2007). Verifying feature models using OWL. In *Web Semantics: Science, Services and Agents on the World Wide Web, 5*(5), 117-129.

Watson, H. J., Goodhue, D. L., & Wixom, B. H. (2002). The benefits of data warehousing: Why some organizations realize exceptional payoffs. *Information & Management, 39*(6), 491–502. doi:10.1016/S0378-7206(01)00120-3

Watson, P., Lord, P., Gibson, F., Periorellis, P., & Pitsilis, G. (2008). Cloud computing for e-science with CARMEN. *Proceedings of IBERGRID Conference* (pp. 1-5). 2008, Porto (Portugal). May 12–14.

Weiser, M. (1993). Some computer science issues in ubiquitous computing. *Communications of the ACM, 36*(7), 75–85. doi:10.1145/159544.159617

Weiser, M. (1991). The computer for the 21st century. *Scientific American, 265*(3), 66–75. doi:10.1038/scientificamerican0991-94

Werner-Allen, G., Johnson, J., Ruiz, M., Lees, J., & Welsh, M. (2005, 31 January-2 February). Monitoring volcanic eruptions with a wireless sensor network. In *Proceedings of the Second European Workshop on Wireless Sensor Networks* (pp. 108-120).

Wikipedia. (2010). *Institutional repository*. Retrieved from http://en.wikipedia.org/wiki/Institutional_repository

Wilson, P. (1991). *Computer supported cooperative work: An introduction*. Oxford, UK: Intellect Books.

Winograd, T. (2001). Architectures for context. *Human-Computer Interaction, 16*(2), 401–419. doi:10.1207/S15327051HCI16234_18

Wooldridge, M. (2002). *An introduction to multiagent systems*. John Wiley & Sons.

Wooldridge, M., & Jennings, N. R. (1999). The cooperative problem-solving process. *Journal of Logic Computation, 9*(4), 563–592. doi:10.1093/logcom/9.4.563

Wooldridge, M., & Jennings, N. R. (2000). The Gaia methodology for agent-oriented analysis and design. *Journal of Autonomous Agents and Multi-Agent Systems*, *3*, 285–312. doi:10.1023/A:1010071910869

Yao, Y., & Gehrke, J. (2002). The cougar approach to in-network query processing in sensor networks. *SIGMOD Record*, *31*(3), 9–18. doi:10.1145/601858.601861

Yau, S. S., & Liu, J. (2006). Hierarchical situation modeling and reasoning for pervasive computing. In *Proceedings of 3rd Workshop on Software Technologies for Future Embedded and the Second International Workshop on Collaborative Computing, Integration, and Assurance (SEUS-WCCIA'06)*, (pp. 5-10). IEEE Computer Society.

Yusuke, M., Patrick, S., Kris, T., & Ingrid, V. (2004). *Java cryptography on KVM and its performance and security optimization using HW/SW co-design techniques*. International Conference on Compilers, Architectures and Synthesis of Embedded System (pp. 303-311). ACM Press.

Zachman, J. A. (1987). A framework for Information Systems architecture. *IBM Systems Journal*, *26*(3), 276–292. doi:10.1147/sj.263.0276

Zambonelli, F., Jennings, N. R., & Wooldredge, M. (2003). Developing multiagent systems: The Gaia methodology. *ACM Transactions on Software Engineering and Methodology*, *12*(3), 317–370. doi:10.1145/958961.958963

Zdun, U., Hentrich, C., & Dustdar, S. (2007). Modeling process-driven and service-oriented architectures using patterns and pattern primitives. [TWEB]. *ACM Transactions on the Web*, *1*(3), 14. doi:10.1145/1281480.1281484

Zhang, L., Zhang, J., & Cai, H. (2007). *Services computing: Core enabling technology of the modern services industry*. Springer.

Zheng, Y., He, D., Wang, H., & Tang, X. (2005). *Secure DRM scheme for future mobile networks based on trusted mobile platform* (pp. 1164–1167). IEEE WCNM.

Zhou, J. (2005). *Knowledge dichotomy and semantic knowledge management*. In 1st IFIP WG 12.5 Working Conference on Industrial Applications of Semantic Web, Jyväskylä, Finland.

Zhu, F., Mutka, M., & Ni, L. (2005). Facilitating secure ad hoc service discovery in public environments. *Journal of Systems and Software*, *76*(1), 45–54. doi:10.1016/j.jss.2004.07.014

Zhu, F., Mutka, M., & Ni, L. (2006). A private, secure and user-centric information exposure model for service discovery protocols. *IEEE Transactions on Mobile Computing*, *5*(4), 418–429. doi:10.1109/TMC.2006.1599409

Zhu, F., Zhu, W., Mutka, M., & Ni, L. (2007). Private and secure service discovery via progressive and probabilistic exposure. *IEEE Transactions on Parallel and Distributed Systems*, *18*(11), 1565–1577. doi:10.1109/TPDS.2007.1075

Zhu, F., Mutka, M., & Ni, L. (2003, March 23-26, 2003). *Splendor: A secure, private, and location-aware service discovery protocol supporting mobile services*. Paper presented at the 1st IEEE Annual Conference on Pervasive Computing and Communications, Fort Worth, Texas.

Zimmermann, O., Schlimm, N., Waller, G., & Pestel, M. (2005). *Analysis and design techniques for service-oriented development and integration*. Paper presented at the INFORMATIK 2005 - Informatik LIVE! Bonn.

Zoho. (2010). *CRM SaaS*. Retrieved March 10, 2010, http://www.zoho.com/

About the Contributors

Xiaodong Liu received his PhD in Computer Science from De Montfort University, UK. He is a reader and the director of Centre for Information & Software Systems, in the School of Computing, Edinburgh Napier University, UK. As an active researcher, his current research focuses on Context-aware adaptive services, service evolution, mobile clouds, pervasive computing, software reuse, and component-based software engineering. Dr. Liu has led 6 externally funded projects, and published over 50 papers in established international journals and conferences and 2 book chapters. He is the inventor of 1 patent registered in UK, USA and at International Level. He has been the chair, co-chair or PC member of a number of IEEE and IASTED international conferences. He is the editorial board member of 3 international journals and editor of 2 research books. He is a member of IEEE Computer Society and British Computer Society.

Yang Li holds BSc, MSc, and PhD degrees in Computer Science, and is a Principal Researcher at British Telecom. He made original contributions to service science & systems, resulting in the granting of world patents, widely cited papers, two live BT systems, and a number of internal and external awards. He has more than 100 citations by Google Scholar and is the founding chair of an IEEE workshop series. Yang was included in Marquis Who's Who in the World, 28th Edition.

* * *

Ville Alkkiomäki, M.Sc., is currently working as an Enterprise Architect for Itella Corporation, where he is responsible for enterprise architecture governance and development. Alkkiomäki has over ten years of experience in the field of system integration, large scale system architecture, and related technologies. Originally starting out as a software developer in an EDI software vendor, his career is characterized by varying architect roles, including chief architect of an in-house system integration center, chief infrastructure architect and the current position as an enterprise architect. Additionally, his postgraduate studies in Lappeenranta University of Technology focused on service elicitation methods.

Stamatia Bibi is a contracted Lecturer at the University of Thessaly and University of Western Macedonia. Her research interests include software process models, estimation of software development cost and quality, cloud computing, and open source software. Bibi has a PhD in informatics from Aristotle University of Thessaloniki.

Panayiotis Bozanis is currently an Assistant Professor at the University of Thessaly, Greece. His publications comprise several journal and conference papers, and four books in Greek about data structures and algorithms. He is an EATCS member.

Lowry Burgess, having been educated at the Pennsylvania Academy of the Fine Arts, the University of Pennsylvania, and at the Instituto Allende in San Miguel Mexico, is an internationally renowned artist and educator who created the first official art payload taken into outer space by NASA in 1989 among his many Space Art works. He founded and administrated many departments, programs, and institutions during his 45 years as an educator in the arts. For 27 years he has been a Fellow, Senior Consultant, and Advisor at the Center for Advanced Visual Studies at MIT.

Juan Cáceres is Research Programme Manager on Cloud Computing at Telefónica Labs. He holds an Msc. in Computer Science and a Research Msc. in Distributed Systems (Universidad Politécnica de Madrid). Juan is coordinating the research agenda on infrastructure and platform as a service clouds, and supervising the EU-Funded projects RESERVOIR, IRMOS, VISION, StratusLab, and 4Caast. Juan's areas of interest include architecture of distributed systems, cloud computing and design & development of complex software (networking, multi-threading, high-performance computing).

Clovis Chapman received a BSc in Computer Science from King's College London in 1998, followed by an M.S.c in Data Communication and Distributed Systems and PhD in Computer Science from University College London. As a Research Fellow in University College London, he was involved in establishing a UK wide Grid infrastructure for molecular simulation in the context of the eMinerals project and worked alongside IBM research, Telefonica, and other institutions on the definition and implementation of a cloud infrastructure for the provisioning Web-based IT services in the context of the RESERVOIR FP7 European project. His research interests are in the area of large scale distributed computing, focusing specifically on Grid and cloud computing technologies. He has authored over 20 papers in the domain and has acted as a consultant for startups looking to rapidly scale their Web based service offerings.

Tullio Salmon Cinotti is Associate Professor of Computer Architecture and Logic Design at the Faculty of Engineering of the University of Bologna. He has a long standing experience in research and education on embedded systems. For many years he has been coordinating research teams in large projects on ambient intelligence and user interaction, in application domains ranging from cultural heritage to health monitoring. His current focus is on ambient information interoperability and on architectures to open innovation in cross-domain multi-actor smart space based applications. He is serving the research community by regularly contributing to workgroups of the European Platform on Embedded Systems.

Quansong Deng is currently a Master's student majoring in Computer Software and Theory in Web and Software R&D Center, Research Institute of Information Technology, Tsinghua University. He received his BS degree of Computer Science and Technology in Tsinghua University in 2008. He's interested in analysis and study in the areas of massive digital resource management and service, data mining in Web environment and content aggregation technologies.

Fermin Galan holds an M.Sc degree in Telecommunications and a Ph.D in Telematics from Universidad Politécnica de Madrid in 2002 and 2010 respectively. Since 2001, he has participated in several EU and Spanish research projects and involved in standardization activities at DMTF as Telefónica delegate. He has authored more than 40 papers in international conferences and journals. His current research interests include configuration management, networking testbeds, virtualization technologies, and cloud computing.

JoAnne Holliday is an Associate Professor at Santa Clara University. She received her B.A. from the University of California at Berkeley and her M.S. degree from Northeastern University. She got the PhD degree from the University of California at Santa Barbara. She has been on the faculty of the Santa Clara University Computer Engineering department since September 2000. Her research interests include distributed systems, mobile computing, wireless networks, and replicated databases.

Zakwan Jaroucheh received the B.Sc. (Honors) degree in Computer Science from Higher Institute for Applied Sciences and Technology (HIAST), Syria. He worked as a research engineer in the Information Technology Department in HIAST. He received the MSc. degree in Business Information Systems from ESIGELEC, France. His Master's research work was conducted at R&D Center of Océ Print Logic Technologies, Paris. He is currently working toward the Ph.D. degree with the School of Computing in Edinburgh Napier University. His research interests include ubiquitous and pervasive computing, context-aware systems, and service-based systems. He has published in several well-known international conferences.

Youna Jung received the PhD degree from Ajou University in 2007. She is currently a postdoctoral researcher in LERSAIS at the University of Pittsburgh. Her research interests include situation-aware computing, cooperative computing, community computing, security of intelligent systems, and security of cooperative systems.

Dimitrios Katsaros is a Lecturer at the University of Thessaly, Greece. His research interests include distributed systems, such as the Web and Internet, cloud computing, wireless ad hoc, and wireless sensor networks. Katsaros has a PhD in informatics from Aristotle University of Thessaloniki.

Minsoo Kim received the Master's and PhD degree from Ajou University where his research activities involved the developing the technique for situation-aware computing. His research interests include context-awareness, access control, Semantic Web, and multi-agent systems. He is a visiting researcher in LERSAIS at the University of Pittsburgh and now developing a situation-based access control model and security systems.

Peter Langendörfer holds a diploma and a doctorate degree in computer science. Since 2000 he is with the IHP in Frankfurt (Oder). There, he is team leader of the wireless sensor network group. He has published more than 80 refereed technical articles and filed seven patents in the security/privacy area. His research interests include wireless communication and especially privacy and security issues.

Maik Lindner works as a researcher and business development manager for SAP Research in the United Kingdom. In his function as a researcher, Maik is currently the SAP team lead of the European Union FP7 funded project RESERVOIR. For this he deals with aspects of large-scale enterprise software on on-demand IT resources including the importance of standardization for this. In his role as a business development manager, he builds an interface between SAP internal development groups and researchers for future ICT systems and architectures. Maik holds a PhD from University of Muenster (Germany), in Information and Controlling Systems with a focus on Business Intelligence. The cores of Maik's research are business aspects and business/market models for emerging technologies such as cloud/Grid computing.

Michael Maaser received his MSc in computer sciences in 2004 and his PhD in 2010 at the Brandenburg University of Technology Cottbus. During his research he was active in the area of privacy protection in location and context aware systems. Currently he is active in wireless sensor networks for tele-medical applications. Throughout his research career he has 20 reviewed publications in international conferences and journals and contributed to three book chapters.

Matt W. Mutka received the B.S. degree in electrical engineering from the University of Missouri-Rolla, the M.S. degree in electrical engineering from Stanford University, and the Ph.D. degree in Computer Sciences from the University of Wisconsin-Madison. He is on the faculty of the Department of Computer Science and Engineering at Michigan State University, where he is currently Professor and Chairperson. He has been a visiting scholar at the University of Helsinki, Finland, and a member of technical staff at Bell Laboratories in Denver, Colorado. His current research interests include mobile computing, wireless networking, and multimedia networking.

Lionel M. Ni is Chair Professor in the Department of Computer Science and Engineering at the Hong Kong University of Science and Technology (HKUST). He also serves as the Special Assistant to the President of HKUST and Director of the HKUST China Ministry of Education/Microsoft Research Asia IT Key Lab. A fellow of IEEE, Dr. Ni has chaired over 30 professional conferences and has received 6 awards for authoring outstanding papers.

Steffen Ortmann received his diploma in computer science in 2007 and his PhD by scholarship in 2010 from the Brandenburg University of Technology Cottbus. Since 2005 he is active in the sensor network research group of IHP in Frankfurt (Oder). He has published 15 refereed technical articles in conferences and journals and one book chapter about reliability, privacy, and efficient data processing in wireless sensor networks and ubiquitous environments. His current research focuses on wireless sensor networks for tele-medical innovations.

Eila Ovaska obtained the MSc degree in 1995 and the PhD degree in 2000 from the University of Oulu. Before graduation she worked fifteen years as a software engineer, from 1995 as a senior research scientist and from 1999 to 2002 as the group manager of the Software Architectures Group at VTT. Since 2001 she has been working as a Professor at VTT and since 2002 also as an adjunct professor of software architectures and components at the University of Oulu. She has acted as a reviewer for several scientific journals and conferences. She is a member of the IEEE.

Jaemin Park received the BS and MS degrees in Computer Science from Handong Global University, South Korea, in 2004, and from Korea Advanced Institute of Science and Technology (KAIST), South Korea, in 2006, respectively. He is currently an Assistant Manager in the Device R&D Center of the Korea Telecom (KT), South Korea. His current research interests include Security in UICC, NFC, RFID, I-WLAN, and FMC environments.

Vishnu Pendyala holds BE, MBA, and MS degrees from Indian and U.S. universities. He is currently pursuing his PhD in Computer Engineering at Santa Clara University. He presented papers in international conferences and reviewed technical papers for professional journals and conferences, including the annual IEEE International Conference on E-Commerce from 2003 - 2007. Vishnu received the Ramanujam memorial gold medal at State Math Olympiad and has been a successful leader during his undergrad years. He also played an active role in Computer Society of India and was the Program Secretary for its annual convention, which was attended by over 1500 delegates. Recently, Marquis Who's Who has selected Vishnu's biography for inclusion in Who's Who in Science and Engineering 2011-2012 (11th Edition). Vishnu spends his fast vanishing spare time volunteering and has been a judge at school science fairs for the past few years.

Luis Rodero-Merino is a researcher at the GRAAL group, part of the French INRIA's Laboratoire de l'Informatique du Parallélisme. He has a Master Degree in Computing from the Universidad de Valladolid, Spain. After working as an engineer at the Research and Development branch of Ericsson Spain, he obtained a PhD in Computing from the Universidad Rey Juan Carlos, Madrid, Spain, where he also worked as a teaching assistant. Later he joined Telefónica Research and Development as researcher, working in the field of cloud computing. In January 2010 he joined GRAAL, where he is working in the same research area.

Sally Smith is the Head of School of Computing at Edinburgh Napier University. She studied an MA (Hons) in Mathematics at Aberdeen University, Scotland and an MSc in Computer Science at City University, London. She has worked in the telecommunications and aerospace industries in the UK and Europe. She is a Teaching Fellow and her research and teaching interests combine mobile and pervasive computing with pedagogical research.

Kari Smolander is Professor of Software Engineering in the Department of Information Technology, Lappeenranta University of Technology, Finland. He has a PhD (2003) in Computer Science from Lappeenranta University of Technology and a Licentiate (1993) and Master (1988) degree from University of Jyväskylä, Finland. In addition to his long teaching experience, he has worked several years in industry and in 1990s he was the main architect in the development of MetaEdit CASE tool. He has more than 80 refereed research papers in international journals and conferences. His current research interests include architectural aspects of systems development and organizational view of software development.

Shigeki Sugiyama has been working on various fields from Industrial Engineering, Control, AI, Neural Networking, Virtual Reality, E-learning, Embedded Technology, Computer, to Consciousness Studies for more than 30 years and have published more than 70 papers. I also put much attention on Service Science, especially on a network behavior in a scalable situation. And I have touched upon setting up a science park project about the matters of IT during 1994 – 1999 and I have done some cooperative research works with Universities in US and in Europe about IT.

Yigang Sun is the director of the Information and Network department of the National Library of China, the deputy director of the Modern Technology Research Institution of the National Library of China, member of the expert working group on the Digital Library Project of China, the standing director of the Network Security Committee of the Internet Society of China, member of the Internet Application and Information Service Committee of China Institute of Communication, the deputy director of the Digital Library Construction Professional Committee of Library Association of China, editorial board member of the Journal of National Library of China. He has leaded several national key projects, and published over 10 research papers. His research interests include digital library, computer applications, et cetera.

Alessandra Toninelli is currently a post-doctoral fellow at INRIA within the ARLES research group. She received her PhD in Computer Science Engineering from the University of Bologna in 2008. Her recent research is focused on middleware to support the development of mobile social applications, but her background also includes context-aware applications, semantic technologies, semantic-based middleware, policy specification and management, and security for pervasive and mobile environments. She has authored several peer-reviewed publications, and actively contributes to the research community by taking part to conferences and workshops organization, participating in program committees and regularly undertaking review activities for research funding agencies, international journals, and conferences.

Luis Vaquero holds a BSc inElectronics, MSc. in Telematics and Pharmacology and Ph.D. in Medicine (Universidad Complutense de Madrid) and Computer Science (Universidad de Valladolid). After his Ph.D. he worked for several American Universities and then joined Telefónica Labs as a researcher. He is now patent manager in the cloud computing area and Assistant Professor at Universidad Rey Juan Carlos (Madrid, Spain, EU). His research interests are in the area of large scale distributed computing, focusing specifically on Grid and cloud computing technologies and its interdisciplinary use in different application domains.

Michael Whitney holds a PhD from Southern Illinois University Carbondale (SIUC) in Educational Administration and is currently a PhD student in the College of Computing and Informatics at the University of North Carolina Charlotte (UNCC). He has served as faculty as networking and security professor at SIUC, has developed a Human Computer Interaction expertise with adaptive technologies and accessible design and is currently focused on community based participatory sensing applications and methodologies.

Chunxiao Xing is the Director of Web and Software Technology R&D Center(WeST), Research Institute of Information Technology, Tsinghua University. Dr. Xing received his PhD from Department of Automatic Control, Northwestern Polytechnical University. From 1999 to 2001, he worked as a postdoctoral researcher in Tsinghua University. His research interests include digital library, digital government, digital entertainment, and personalized service.

Xiaoyu Yang is currently with the University of Southampton, UK. He is also a Senior Member of Wolfson College, University of Cambridge, UK. He was a post-doctoral Research Associate in the Earth Sciences Department, University of Cambridge, and an affiliated Software Engineer in Cambridge e-Science Center. His technical interests include Systems Engineering, e-Science, Grid / cloud computing, SOA, distributed system, and product lifecycle information management. He has got both MSc and PhD degrees from Faculty of Computing Science and Engineering, De Montfort University, UK.

Yong Zhang is an Associate Professor and deputy director of Web and Software R&D Center, Research Institute of Information Technology, Tsinghua University. He received his BSc degree in Computer Science and Technology in 1997, and PhD degree in Computer Software and Theory in 2002 from the CS department of Tsinghua University. From 2002 to 2005, he did his Postdoctoral studies at Cambridge University, UK. His research interests include massive digital resource management and service, personalized recommendation system, and high-volume transaction processing.

Feng Zhu received the B.S. degree in computer science from East China Normal University, the M.S. degree in computer science and engineering from Michigan State University, the M.S. degree in statistics from Michigan State University, and the Ph.D. degree from Michigan State University. He is an Assistant Professor at The University of Alabama in Huntsville. He was a program manager at Microsoft and a software engineer at Intel. His current research interests include pervasive computing, security for pervasive computing, computer networks, and distributed systems.

Wei Zhu received the Ph.D. degree in computer science and engineering from Michigan State University in 2006, the M.S. degree in statistics from Michigan State University in 2004, the M.S. degree in computer science and engineering from Michigan State University in 2001, and the B.S. degree in computer science from East China Normal University in 1994. Her research interests include human-computer interaction, computer graphics, augmented reality, and multimedia systems. She was a software design engineer at Microsoft Corporation. She is currently a software consultant at Intergraph Corporation.

Index